The Shape Of Religious Instruction

A SOCIAL SCIENCE APPROACH

**JAMES
MICHAEL
LEE**

RELIGIOUS EDUCATION PRESS INC.
MISHAWAKA, IND.

Library of Congress Catalog Card Number: 74-29823

ISBN 0-89135-000-4—Hardcover
ISBN 0-89135-002-0—Paperback

2 3 4 5 6 7 8 9 10

Religious Education Press Inc.
Box 364
Mishawaka, Indiana 46544

*Religious Education Press publishes books and educational materials
exclusively in religious education and in areas closely related to religious education. It is committed to enhancing and professionalizing
religious education through the publication of significant scholarly
and popular works.*

To James Lee, III,
my father

OTHER BOOKS WRITTEN OR EDITED
BY JAMES MICHAEL LEE

The Flow of Religious Instruction

The Shape of Religious Instruction

Forward Together: A Training Program for Religious
Educators

Toward a Future for Religious Education

The Purpose of Catholic Schooling

Seminary Education in a Time of Change

Catholic Education in the Western World

Readings in Guidance and Counseling

Guidance and Counseling in Schools

Principles and Methods of Secondary Education

CONTENTS

PREFACE

"O wie ist alles fern
und lange vergangen.
Ich glaube, der Stern,
von welchem ich Glanz empfange,
ist seit Jahrtausenden tot."

      — Ranier Maria Rilke[1]

Though I had been developing ideas and material for this book during the past several years, it was not until one day late in August, 1969, that I actually began to write it. The day was warm and sunny, the time midafternoon. I was sitting on a park bench in the Lehen *viertel* of Salzburg. Immediately in front of me the swift waters of the Salzach River were rushing by. Upriver, on my right, I could see the *Festung Hohensalzburg* majestically and almost mysteriously crowning the top of the lofty rock-mountain Mönchsberg. Downriver, on my left, the green sweep of meadow led my eye to the church of *Maria-Plain*, long a favorite pilgrimage spot. As I began to outline the book on a yellow legal-size pad, my mind and eyes frequently wandered upriver to the *Festung Hohensalzburg* and downriver to *Maria-Plain*. The eleventh-century fortress of Hohensalzburg bestowed on the city a power and a grandeur which were close to being awe-inspiring. For its part the seventeenth-century church of *Maria-Plain* gave to the setting an air of grace and tranquility. Fortress and church, at opposite poles of my angle of vision, represented the two great realities of the past. But as I sat on the park bench, I reflected on how in their 1969 architectural actuality both fortress and church were largely decorative ornaments to enhance the *Stimmung* of the beautiful city of Salzburg. So too the symbolic reality of the fortress and the church more often than not functions only as a decorative element in the life of modern man. The real here-and-now life no longer is lived in or governed by fortress or church. Real life lay in the river in front of me, rushing swiftly by so that each bit of water with which I came in contact was fresh and new and now. Real life lay also in the apartment houses behind me where people laughed and wept, ate and slept, quarreled and were reconciled, promised eternal love and betrayed the beloved in a *grosse Verrat*. Possibly it was the eagerness typical of an author who hopes his book will break fresh ground; in any case, I was almost irresistibly drawn to compare the theological approach to religious instruction to the fortress and the church: awe-inspiring, canonized by history, but not fundamentally effective in the lives of individuals except as ornaments and conversation pieces. It was the vitality and newness and nowness of the flowing river and the here-and-now existential concerns of the people in the apartments which seemed to me to be representative of the social-science approach which I was to advocate in the book I was just then beginning.

The purpose of this book is to lay the foundations for a social-science approach to religious instruction. Of course I have written other pieces on this approach, but typically these were short overviews which did not permit amplification.[2] The master's and doctoral programs in the social-science approach to religious instruction at the University of Notre Dame in Indiana have received national attention, but here again a professional academic program is by nature an activity internal to a university rather than a comprehensive external presentation of an approach. It is the intent of this book — which is the first of a three-volume series — to provide the theoretico-practical basis which hopefully will be nutritive of a fundamental redirection in the enterprise of religious instruction.

The central point of this book is that religious instruction is a mode of social science rather than a form of theology. This theme represents a radical departure from most, if not all, of the theorizing on religious instruction done by Catholics down through the centuries. Simply stated, the social-science approach regards religious instruction as basically a mode of the teaching-learning process rather than an outgrowth of theology. By this I mean that the central task of religious instruction becomes the conscious and deliberative facilitation of specified behavioral goals. Theology quite obviously plays a necessary and indispensable role in religious instruction. However, it is theology which is being inserted into the social-science approach, not vice versa. In other words, theology operates according to its nature and as such functions within the broad parameters of the teaching-learning dynamic, much as confirmation works within the broad parameters of the confirmand's physiopsychological personality structure.

The adoption of the social-science approach would have profound and far-reaching consequences for virtually every aspect of the religious instruction enterprise. The entire teacher-training program would have to be basically revamped to stress the development of facilitation skills in the teacher. The selection and functioning of administrators of religious education programs would be drastically altered to emphasize the deliberative use of idiographic leadership[3] forms. The whole process of curriculum building would be essentially changed in the direction of empirical validation along a wide range of axes.

The social-science approach represents more than a basic direction for religious instruction. Fundamentally this approach is a worldview, a way in which a person meets, interprets, and integrates reality. This accounts for the ignorance, misunderstanding, aversion, and even hostility which a number of theologically-oriented religious educators have shown toward the Notre Dame social-science approach. Religion teachers, administrators, and curriculum builders typically have been products of a lifelong educational process which provided them almost exclusively with a philosophico-theological world view. This is particularly true of those religious educators who attended seminaries, novitiates, or church-related schools. For these individuals the social-science approach to reality is understandably strange and foreign. Indeed, I have found that it takes from six to nine months for most of our beginning graduate students in the Notre Dame graduate program in religious instruction to meet and greet reality from a social-science perspective. Yet religious instruction is a work of teaching, not of theologizing; in other words, religious instruction is a process whereby learning is facilitated. Such a process is properly the work of social science, not of theology, as I shall discuss throughout this volume.

Much of the terminology and concepts I employ in the book are drawn from social science. For the benefit of those readers who might not be thoroughly familiar with these concepts, I have endeavored to explain or illustrate them as appropriate. In some instances, however, I trust the reader will take it upon himself to learn the meanings. By "reaching" for terms and concepts from time to time, the reader hopefully will be brought to a high level of understanding and involvement. It seems to me that any attempt to write a basic book on the social-science approach to religious instruction must utilize social-science concepts and terminology, or it will fail in its goal of adequately introducing the reader to this approach.

I have endeavored to write this book in a free-flowing literary style. The only exceptions to this are Chapters One, Five, and Six which are written in a tight, compact fashion somewhat reminiscent of a textbook. This was unavoidable, since each of these chapters represents a broad sweep of the fundamentals of education, namely theology and social science. By writing these chapters in a tight, concise manner, I was able to include much more information than would otherwise have been possible.

I am firmly convinced that if religious education is to succeed in the decades ahead, it must be an ecumenical affair in the fullest sense of the word. Therefore I have aimed to make this book as widely ecumenical as possible. To this end I have utilized as broad a scope of Protestant and Catholic contributions to religious education as possible. Unfortunately most of the books on religious education written by Catholics utilize Catholic religious educational theorists almost exclusively; Protestant writers exhibit the same tendency with respect to Protestant theorists. By abandoning this procedure, I hope to inaugurate a trend toward a truly ecumenical approach to religious education at every level, theoretical and practical.

A word about my use of the scriptures is in order. The validity of my use of the scriptures is not at all dependent upon an interpretation of them which is literal or allegorical, Bultmannian or Barthian, *historisch* or *geschichtlich*. I am taking the scriptures I cite at their face values as stories, with no reference as to whether these stories are pure myths, allegorical wrappings of a basic truth, or the literal truth itself. In other words, the scriptural stories or sentences precisely *qua* stories and sentences have pedagogical import; in this context, the scriptural or doctrinal exegesis of the story is not relevant.

No author is an island. This book could not have been written without the encouragement and generous help of my friends, colleagues, and students. Neil G. McCluskey, himself burdened with the press of the many duties involved in presiding over the crucial first year of Notre Dame's Institute for Studies in Education, always was on hand at the right moment to offer some penetrating insight or touch of sparkling wit. Carl Pfeifer and his genial associate,

Janaan Manternach, in animated discussions in widely scattered restaurants around the nation, gave me several helpful considerations drawn from their own considerable experience in religious education. Robert O'Gorman made several key comments which helped me clarify certain sections of the book. Harold Burgess, Mary Fallon, Reneta Glass, and Eugene Hemrick read parts of the manuscript and supplied significant suggestions. The well-oiled team of Kay Coleman and Nancy Wesolowski structured many office situations which made both the note-gathering and the writing much more efficient than would otherwise have been the case. Morton Trippe Kelsey's careful and scholarly critique of the manuscript, particularly from the Protestant viewpoint, broadened the book's ecumenical base. I am grateful also to Norine "Mary" Dugan, the program's velveteen rabbit, for the warm personal encouragement she gave me at every stage, particularly during the final days. John van der Beek, the happy Hollander in Flanders field, offered me stylistic advice which altered the course of the book, and also a steady flow of good conversation and Dutch cigars which made the long months of writing more bearable. Incalculable is my debt, as always, to Pobdwm, who worked on every stage of the manuscript with her usual high standards of excellence. But most of all, I would like to thank my father, James Lee III, whose inspiration and presence I deeply felt so often during each phase of writing. A man whose far range of intellect was matched only by the enormity of his heart, he set for me an example of humanness and Christ-likeness which I am coming to appreciate more and more with the passing of the years. This book is for him.

Notre Dame, Indiana   *James Michael Lee*
July 4, 1970

FOOTNOTES

1. Ranier Maria Rilke, "Klage," in Ranier Maria Rilke, *Selected Poems*, edited by C. F. MacIntyre (Berkeley, California: University of California Press, 1962), p. 34.
2. See, for example, James Michael Lee, "The *Teaching* of Religion," in James Michael Lee and Patrick C. Rooney, editors, *Toward a Future for Religious Education* (Dayton, Ohio: Pflaum, 1970), pp. 55-92.
3. See, for example, Jacob W. Getzels, "Administration as a Social Process," in Andrew W. Halpin, editor, *Administrative Theory in Education* (Chicago: Midwest Administrative Center, 1958), pp. 150-165.

CHAPTER ONE

PROLOGOMENON

". . . I was afraid of myself,
I was fleeing from myself.
I was seeking Brahman, Atman,
I wished to destroy myself,
to get away from myself, in

order to find in the unknown
innermost, the nucleus of all
things, Atman, Life, the Divine,
the Absolute. But by doing so,
I lost myself on the way."

— Hermann Hesse[1]

To Catholics it is commonly called "catechetics." Protestants typically refer to it as "Christian education." Sometimes Catholics and Protestants alike refer to it as "religious education." As a matter of fact, the term "religious education" is more accurate than either "catechetics" or "Christian education." I shall indicate in Chapter Two that "catechetics" is a technical term properly reserved for the second stage of the kerygma-catechesis-didascalia cycle of religious education employed in the apostolic period of the Church. The expression "Christian education" suggests a certain triumphalism, as if religious education has to bear the label "Christian" to be considered valid. I think the term "religious education" is more suitable and more correct than either "catechetics" or "Christian education."

Yet even the term "religious education" needs clarification. Education is a comprehensive term encompassing many kinds of related activities. In this short Prologomenon, I shall distinguish between the broad category of "education" and the more significant kinds of processes and activities which are contained within this category.

Education is the broad process whereby a person learns something. Therefore a person is always in the process of being educated at every moment of his waking life, and in a panoply of situations. Learning to walk, or to play the piano, watching a baseball game on television, strolling along the beach, developing facility in speaking a foreign language, falling in love — these are all part of a person's education. In other words, all of one's experiences are in one sense educational, since whatever a person experiences somehow modifies his behavior.

The terms "education" and "schooling" should not be taken synonymously as there is a significant difference between them.[2] *Schooling* is a system of complex, planned, organized, systematic, purposive, deliberative, and interrelated learning experiences which in concert bring about desired behavioral changes in the person. Sometimes referred to as "formal education," schooling represents the institutionalizing of education in order to sharpen, to enhance, and to codify the broad sweep that is the educational process. School experiences differ most significantly from other life experiences which are also educational in that school experiences represent a deliberately structured and consciously planned set of expanding and reinforcing experiences which are intended to have a more powerful effect than do ordinary life experiences in changing the individual's behavior in a given direction.[3] As Benjamin Bloom put it, school (and classroom) experiences have a special character, as contrasted with other kinds of life experiences which are educational, in that school experiences are selected and planned with a view to their impact upon the individual's learning.[4] Education in a school or classroom setting is, therefore, as John Dewey says: "a fostering, a nurturing, a cultivating process. All of these words mean that it implies attention to the conditions of growth."[5]

This distinction between education and schooling suggests that the two are not coequal or coextensive, as some religious educators and ecclesiastical officials seem to believe. Thus it is *possible* for a person to have had a fine religious education without ever having attended a formal religion class in school. The raison d'être of the church-sponsored school is that its unique learning-oriented environment makes it more *probable* that an individual, at certain levels of his development, will receive a religious education superior to that which occurs in a nonschool religious education situation. The relevant empirical research suggests that superior religious learning in school-age children tends to be produced by a simultaneous combination of church-sponsored school and religiously-oriented nonschool (for example, family) learning environments, as contrasted to the level and quality of religious learning produced by either the church-sponsored school or the religiously-oriented nonschool environments taken alone.[6] In other words, while

participation in religion-school classes tends to be normally promotive of religious education, such participation is not necessary to
acquire a religious education.

Instruction is the process by and through which learning is caused
in an individual in one way or another.[7] Instruction, then, is
identical with teaching. Instruction is typically carried out in some
sort of formal program such as in a school, although this is not
always the case. Therefore, instruction is not synonymous with
schooling. Instruction is a prime means of making the educational
process as efficient as possible in terms of promoting learning more
rapidly, of helping to effect the retention of learned behaviors for a
longer period of time, and of facilitating the translation of learned
behaviors into the permanent personal lifestyle of the student. The
word "instruction" is derived from the Latin *instruere*: "to set up,"
"to put together," "to build into," "to arrange." Thus instruction
can be seen as the arrangement of those situations and conditions
which will most effectively facilitate desired learning outcomes in an
individual. Instruction, therefore, is not a pejorative term to be used
in disparaging contradistinction to the more fulsome term education;
rather, it is a technical term used in pedagogical parlance to indicate
a specific type of educational activity.[8]

Guidance is the process by which an individual is aided in
fulfilling his human potential, in negotiating the tasks of his
individual development, and in solving his special personal problems.
Like instruction, it constitutes a special phase of the overall
educational process. Guidance is more than an activity; it is also an
orientation, a point of view.[9]

Counseling is the relationship between two or more persons in
which one of them attempts to assist the other(s) in so organizing
himself (themselves) as to attain a particular form of happiness,
adjustment to a life situation, or, in short, self-actualization.
Individual counseling is a one-to-one relationship, while group
counseling represents a one-to-many relationship. Counseling is the
most important activity in the hierarchy of guidance services. In the
second half of the twentieth century, religious guidance and
counseling developed its own distinctive and scientific modus
operandi, and freed itself from the centuries-old rationale and
techniques of spiritual direction and religious advisement.

As its title indicates, this book centers on religious instruction
rather than on religious education, or religious guidance, or religious
counseling. In other words, this book will be focused on the
teaching-learning dimension of religious education.

FOOTNOTES

1. Hermann Hesse, *Siddhartha*, translated by Hilda Rosner (New York: New Directions, 1951), p. 31.
2. For a further development of this point, see James Michael Lee, *The Purpose of Catholic Schooling* (Washington, D.C., and Dayton, Ohio: National Catholic Educational Association and Pflaum, 1968), especially pp. 6-10.
3. See James Michael Lee, "The *Teaching* of Religion," in James Michael Lee and Patrick C. Rooney, editors, *Toward a Future for Religious Education* (Dayton, Ohio: Pflaum, 1970), pp. 55-92.
4. Benjamin S. Bloom, "Testing Cognitive Ability and Achievement," in N. L. Gage, editor, *Handbook of Research on Teaching* (Chicago: Rand-McNally, 1963), p. 387.
5. John Dewey, *Democracy and Education* (New York: Macmillan, 1916), p. 12. Italics deleted.
6. See, for example, Andrew M. Greeley and Peter H. Rossi, *The Education of Catholic Americans* (Chicago: Aldine, 1966); Ronald L. Johnstone, *The Effectiveness of Lutheran Elementary and Secondary Schools as Agencies of Christian Education* (St. Louis: Concordia, 1966).
7. The initial inspiration for this definition sprang from that which Thomas Aquinas gives of teaching. See his *De Veritate*, q. XI, a. 1, obj. 1. Aquinas uses the word "knowledge," whereas I prefer "learning" which is broader and more nearly total in scope.
8. Persons who utilize the term "instruction" as a pejorative contrast to the term "education" are typically untrained in pedagogy. In the field of religious education, these persons — such as Iris V. Cully and Pius XII, to cite one Protestant and one Catholic example — are typically trained in theology and not in education, hence they function as theologians rather than as educationists. See Iris V. Cully, "Christian Education: Instruction or Nurture," in *Religious Education*, LXII, May-June, 1967, pp. 255-261; and Pius XII, "El especialismo amor," in *The Pope Speaks*, I, First Quarter, 1954, p. 21.
9. See James Michael Lee and Nathaniel J. Pallone, *Guidance and Counseling in Schools: Foundations and Processes* (New York: McGraw-Hill, 1966), pp. 63-126.

CHAPTER TWO

THE FOCUS

*"You are the way and
the wayfarer."*

— Kahlil Gibran[1]

INTRODUCTION

Of all the activities of the church, surely the enterprise of religious instruction ranks among the most important and the most significant. Indeed, even the core acts of sacrament and liturgy are in one sense kinds of religious instruction. Consequently it might be well to consider the focus of religious instruction.

Yet a moment's reflection will surely indicate that the nature and work of religious instruction are so rich, so multifaceted, and so variegated that any attempt to spell out their focus would be to encapsulate them in some sort of abstract form, thereby emasculating them. Therefore I think it is much closer to the mark to indicate certain focal points of religious instruction. In this way religious instruction will be seen as retaining its attributes of vitality and immediacy. Concentrating on specific operational focal points will serve to show how this vitality and immediacy are targeted and directed so as to make religious instruction both distinct and alive in the world's galaxy of activities.

FOCAL POINTS OF RELIGIOUS INSTRUCTION

Christian Living

Christian living is at once the means toward and the goal of religious instruction and indeed of all of religious education. The term "Christian living" means that the sum total of an individual's personality structure is integrated into and acts in accord with behavior we can call Christian. In the concrete, Christian living is the confluence of the thoughts, emotions, desires, and overt actions of a person to form an integrated behavioral pattern and lifestyle. Christian living is "living unto God," to use Horace Bushnell's felicitous phrase.[2] Christian living does not exclude human living but rather encompasses all of human living to which in its very fiber is admixed — I do not say "added onto" — the superabundance of divine being.

Christian living, or simply lived religion, is broader than faith (believing) or than charity (acting). Christian living subsumes both faith and charity, and indeed all the natural and supernatural virtues, and inserts them in an exquisitely appropriate manner into the self-system of the individual, into his behavior pattern, into his concrete here-and-now lifestyle. Christian living consists in our participation in the life of Jesus.[3] And this life of Jesus is not merely faith or not only charity, but the full, ongoing total actualization-in-person of all virtues. Since to live Christianly is to participate in the life of Jesus, he who lives Christianly is already experiencing salvation and is truly tasting the communion of saints.

Surveying and synthesizing the relevant research, Charles Glock has identified five dimensions of religiosity which, when all together incarnated as a unit at the human existential level, comprise lived religion: (1) the ideological dimension, that is, religious belief; (2) the ritualistic dimension, that is religious practice; (3) the experiential dimension, that is religious feeling; (4) the intellectual dimension, that is, religious knowledge; and (5) the consequential dimension, that is religious effects.[4] Religious living, then, is the person's actualizing of all five dimensions in concert. No one dimension, taken in itself, constitutes religious living. I mention this because while there is much lip service being given to such slogans as "modern religious instruction aims not at mere knowledge but lived religion,"[5] nonetheless both the writings of many specialists in religious education and the actual classroom practices of most religion teachers seem to stress primarily, if not at times exclusively, the intellectual component of religion. But to exalt religious knowledge by making it the axis and indeed the goal *in praxis* is to make an idol of only one dimension of religiosity. In so doing, the amalgam or lived synthesis of the totality of all five dimensions is thrown out of balance, and Christian living is emasculated and rendered unlivable for any person who is fully functioning in the natural-supernatural order. Christianity, as Herman Hendrickx reminds us, is not primarily a doctrine but a life;[6] consequently religious instruction must be ever rooted in the whole man, in all his dimensionalities. The modern age is an era steeped in rationalism, first through the still strong (though often denied) residual current of Cartesianism, Kantianism, and Hegelianism, and then in the very core and outpourings of our technical civilization. For the rationalist — be he philosopher or technocrat — knowledge is power; knowledge is at once the interpreter and the measure of life. But in André Brien's words, rationalism is something which disrupts man's internal unity.[7] It is against this rape of life by the rationalistic intellectuals, by the academics, and by the technocrats that the modern youth are rebelling. In their search for wholeness and authenticity, modern young people are affirming with all their being that fulsome and total living, not simply knowledge or understanding, is "where it's at."

In what even today remains as Marcel van Caster's most significant contribution to the field of religious education, the Belgian theologian identifies three ascending levels of individual development through which the person undergoing religious education successively passes. The first stage, that of instruction, has knowledge and understanding as its prime learning outcomes. These outcomes, because they are cognitive, share in all the defects of the cognitive domain of human existence. Thus, while the learner can know and understand doctrine about God, he can never be said to know God or understand God. The second developmental stage, that of formation, has values, attitudes, and feelings as its prime learning outcomes. At this level the learner is assisted to reconstruct his values, his attitudes, and his feelings along Christian lines, and through this stage the learner is helped to tap those crucial features of his self-system so often left untouched and undeveloped by the typical school or classroom. In this formation stage the learner is helped to become more a Christian precisely by increasing his openness not only to the gift which God has freely bestowed upon him, but also to external activities in congruence with the divine life within him. The third developmental stage, that of initiation, has interpersonal communion as its prime learning outcome. This interpersonal communion connotes the passage of the learner from the sector of the purely individual life to the lush green uplands of intersubjectivity both with his fellowmen and with God himself.[8] Through this interpersonal participatory life, the Christian lives fully the ongoing revelational experience which is divine life in the world.

In short, the stage of instruction pertains to doctrine, the stage of formation to morality, and the stage of initiation to sacrament. From another aspect, the stage of instruction represents the objective level, the stage of formation indicates the subjective level, and the stage of initiation signifies the intersubjective level.

Charles Glock's five dimensions of religiosity and Marcel van Caster's three stages of religious instruction[9] are complementary in that they describe two different but mutually-supporting axes of religious instruction. The five dimensions identified by Glock have as their axis the scope, range, and breadth of the outcomes of religious instruction. The three stages enunciated by van Caster, on the other hand, have as their axis the developmental and sequential stages of learning taking place during the process of experiencing religious instruction. Of interest is that both the five breadth dimensions and the three developmental stages highlight the basic point that religious knowledge, while an essential ingredient and outcome of religious instruction, nonetheless ranks at the lowest level of importance as contrasted to the other ingredients and outcomes of religious instruction.

The emphasis on the total cluster of religious behaviors, rather than simply on doctrinal knowledge and understanding, throws into bold relief my contention that it is Christian living, rather than any one of its components singly, that is at once the means and the goal of religious instruction. Indeed, this approach is in consonance with the religious instructional activities of the first era of the Christian Church. At that time religious instruction encompassed the total range of Christian behaviors; the catechumen not only had to pass an examination on the fundamental points of Christian doctrine, but more importantly, during a three-year probationary period had to manifest in his daily living the entire range and depth of behaviors identified as Christian.[10]

Experiencing

A person learns something most effectively when he has direct contact with it in its real form. This is the conclusion of virtually every empirical study done on the learning process.[11]

The further removed a vicarious learning experience is from the real and the original, the more distorted and the more ineffective will be the outcome resulting from this experience. Thus field trips and other experiences that simulate as closely as possible the original firsthand experience are superior, in terms of learning outcomes, to words or other highly abstract symbolic representations. Indeed, because words are among the most symbolic kind of realities to be learned, they are among the least effective ways of promoting desired learning outcomes. Yet strangely — indeed pathetically — religion teaching utilizes words as much as, and indeed possibly more than, any other area of the person's life-curriculum. Small wonder that religion is so far removed and so unreal to the child, the youth, and even the adult. Words and verbalizations become so deeply intertwined and psychologically identified with religion and Christian living that the teacher and parent have legitimate grounds to wonder whether the person's religious reactions to various aspects in the world or to events in his life correspond to primary experience or to a secondary reflexion due to religious verbal conditioning.[12]

If knowledge and understanding cannot be very effectively facilitated through the use of words, a fortiori religious feelings, religious attitudes, religious values, and religious practices are even more difficult to facilitate through words. A learner cannot adequately grasp a religious feeling or a religious attitude which is being verbally described to him until he has first experienced this feeling or attitude within himself through his own personal firsthand experience.[13]

The second-handedness of experience in the typical religion class is one clue to its mediocrity.

Personal, firsthand experience is of pivotal importance in the learning of religion because religion itself is an experience, and indeed a way of experiencing life. The more experiential religion is, the more living it is in the person. It has always struck me that the moments of the most profound mystical experiences in the lives of the great Christian mystics were the moments in which these persons *were* their experience. Hence to become one's experience fully and deeply is for any person the moment at which religion and self are fused and bonded together in the white heat of totally lived experience.

Like learning, experiencing is fundamentally an active process rather than a passive mode of endurance. Experience is not something simply received, merely undergone. Instead, experience consists in the mutuality, the dynamic relationship, the processing between the self and those points in his milieu with which he is in contact at the time. Sometimes the initiative in activity belongs to the milieu, stimulating or blocking his own endeavors. At other times it is the milieu which is affected and changed by the person. The experience itself lies not simply in the outcome produced on the milieu or in the individual, but even more importantly in the dynamic interconnection between the person and the milieu. If in the act of experiencing, the person has become in a certain restricted sense his milieu and his milieu has become he, it is because the dynamic interconnecting process which is experience has caused a kind of flowing, open-channeled unity between person and milieu.

Despite the great effectiveness of personal experience in the facilitation of learning, it is regrettable to note how frequently religion teachers wish to get finished as quickly as possible with the personal experience parts of the lessons, so that they can get to what they believe to be the heart of the lesson, namely the intellectual part. Religion teachers not infrequently regard the personal experience part of the lesson as at best an entry vehicle to what they consider the core of the lesson, or at worst a waste of time. These teachers have failed to grasp the irreplaceable educative richness of primary experience. Indeed primary experience, when properly used, results in the most meaningful kind of learning. The heart of any effective lesson is that it offers the individual primary experience in a situation so structured as to induce desired learning outcomes. The old and new testaments show quite clearly that in educating religious life in his people, God typically placed the learner(s) in an experiential situation. When verbal or intellectual elements were included, the scriptures clearly show that they were imbedded in a more generalized concrete experiential situation. In the scriptures, words typically reinforced and elaborated on the meaning of experience, rather than vice versa as is the case in so many religion classes.

Thus far in this section I have been stressing the necessity of firsthand experience in religious instruction, and also the fact that truly educational experiencing is an active process rather than simply a passive process of letting the world pour into oneself. But experience as such is not sufficient to produce desired learning outcomes. It is the *quality* of the experience which represents a necessary dimension of a truly educative experience. The terms of religious instruction, the educative level or quality of an experience, are ascertained by the effect which that experience has on the learner's Christian living here-and-now, and also by the degree of influence which the experience has upon the learner's later Christian living and experiencing. In John Dewey's words, "the central problem of an education based upon experience is to select the kind of present experiences that live fruitfully and creatively in subsequent experiences."[14] Experience should both be, and lead to, greater depth in one's own Christian life.

Paul Vieth reminds us that it is erroneous to suppose that the learner all by himself can create the most educationally fruitful kind of Christian living, or even the conditions for that living, totally out of his own unguided experiencing.[15] It is the task of the teacher to so structure the learning situation that the learner is provided with that pedagogical guidance so necessary to bring him to higher and deeper levels of Christian living. However, this learning situation, to be of optimal educational quality, must perforce itself be an experiential environment. The more primary are the experiences in the learning environment, the more probable it is that the learner will acquire the desired learning outcomes. The teacher's task thus becomes one of reorganizing and structuring experiences, in cooperation with the learners. What I am suggesting is that the teachers should not attempt to replace primary experiences with words or verbalizations.

One of the most significant concepts in modern Catholic theology is that experience is revelatory, is divine revelation. I will amplify the modern notion of revelation in Chapter Eight. At this juncture I would merely note that revelation is presently conceived by contemporary Catholic theologians to be not simply the deposit of faith left to us in the bible, but also to be God contacting man in every moment in experience. Revelation, then, is also ongoing, present, flesh-and-blood experiencing. If all experience is revelational, then the task of the religion class is to be that kind of deliberatively structured learning environment in which revelation is heightened both in itself and in the conscious awareness of the learner. It is not restricting the freedom of God to suggest that the religion lesson can heighten revelation; surely revelation, like any other living reality, can blossom more freely when radicated in a situation whose conditions are promotive of optimal growth. The religion class aims at facilitating contact with God as he reveals himself in experience; it is this contact, when acted upon by the learner, which constitutes Christian living. The task of the religion class is to so structure and recast the learner's experience that God's ongoing revelation is consciously, meaningfully, and affectively incorporated into the person's self-system and behavioral patterns of action.

This kind of ongoing divine revelation of which I have been speaking means that the religion class is an environment whose conditions are so shaped by the teacher that a personal living encounter between the learner and Jesus is facilitated. A person can encounter Jesus in any one of three ways, either singly or in combination. He can encounter his own self and the Jesus dwelling in his own self. He can encounter other persons and the Jesus abiding in those other persons. Finally, he can encounter Jesus as Jesus is in Himself. Religious instruction is the deliberative planning of that environment in which the learning Christian encounters Jesus as He contacts him in one or more of these three ways.

By its very nature, encounter can come only through experience. The deeper and the more primary the experience, the deeper and more meaningful the encounter. Encounter must be had directly in experience — it cannot be mediated by a teacher.[16] The religion class represents that distinctive learning environment which is so deliberatively structured that experience forms its axis and its medium. This notion of encounter as promotive of learning and self-actualization is not only a conclusion of empirical educational research, but also an important construct of theological science. The strong personalist vein in the current theology of grace, theology of sacrament, and theology of man all have their practical flow into the reservoir of encounter.[17] Indeed Josef Goldbrunner, following Kierkegaard, affirms that man becomes a person only in confronting God, specifically in the encounter with Jesus.[18]

Experience should not be regarded as a low-level human activity, inferior in quality and meaning to intellectual activity. Experience is not confined to the senses or to the appetites. Rather, experience constitutes the immersion of the total self into reality. Experience represents the entire self as a unit in intimate living contact with the milieu. The intellectual and spiritual activities of man, far from being above or beyond the act of experiencing, are in fact part and parcel of this experiencing. Indeed, in the act of experiencing, the intellect and the spirit attain their greatest and most fulsome coordination with the other components of the self; consequently it is in the act of experiencing that the intellect and the spirit can function the most truly and the most really. Thus present personal experience is not a motivational device in order that the class can the more easily pass on to intellectual and spiritual matters. In true religious instruction, personal experience is at the heart of the religious instruction enterprise.[19]

One important practical outcome of all of the above is that teaching is rendered most effective when it is centered in the realm of learning experiences rather than in the realm of subject content and product content. This is in no way to deny or to minimize the importance of Christian doctrine and dogmas in the religion class. On the contrary, when doctrine and dogmas are imbedded in the living contextual reality of experience, the learner is enabled to perceive them with a new freshness, incorporate them into his self-system with new vitality, and translate them into his pattern of behavior with new vigor. Doctrine is heightened and vivified by placing it in the contextual reality of experience. Doctrine is not given the death knell by placing it in the wider framework of experience; on the contrary, it is given the trumpet blast awakening it to life. There is no antithesis between doctrinal learnings and the experiential mode, since "experiencing has no existence apart from the subject matter experienced."[20]

The focal point of experience in religious instruction, therefore, does in no way dismiss doctrinal statements or knowledge outcomes as irrelevant or unimportant. The experience approach is, in Gerard Pottebaum's words, based instead "on the belief that each person's experience offers him the only opportunity to meet the God of our times, the living God. . . ."[21] God's self-revelation occurs in one's own personal experience. Consequently it is doctrine which must be taught in such a way that it is inserted into the learner's experience, rather than in the traditional way of using the learner's experience as the first stage of a pedagogical rocket thrusted at the outer space of doctrine, a stage to be discarded as soon as the rocket penetrates into the rarified regions of intellectual and spiritual activity. Gabriel Moran phrases it nicely when he speaks of learning biblical truths:

> The crucial question here is whether one is starting with real people and their real experience, elucidating that experience by an ever open and ever widening interpretation; or whether one begins with a set of truths that are self-interpretive and are imposed from the outside. And I would claim that a description of past events is — especially for a child — a set of propositional truths. A teacher with imagination can reconstruct a story from the past in a way that will catch the child's attention, but there is no way to make the events of some past life recorded in a story the facts of one's own life. The experience that Moses had of God may have been personal, concrete, and existential; but Moses is dead. That does not necessarily mean that what has been left by

Moses or about Moses is irrelevant today. As a child begins to discover himself in relation to others we would hope that a powerful means to understand his life will be found in what we know of Moses, Abraham, or Isaiah. But first the child has to be conscious to feel, to think, to choose, to love and be loved.[22]

Experiencing does not simply imply the learner's receptivity to the realities of the milieu. Experiencing also signifies the learner's creative processes vis-à-vis the milieu. The learner does not merely receive experience; he also makes experience and shapes the milieu. Thus the upward cycle of learning is, from a process dimension, a continuous reconstruction and reorganizing of experience and also of the milieu (to the extent this is possible). Because it engages the creative component of man, because it gives full play to the man-as-maker aspect of the human personality, the experience approach to religious instruction enables the religion class to be stimulating, envigorating, educative, and fun.[23] The experience mode can do much to make the religion class a movable feast.

Nowness

Religious instruction of the effective kind is that which is rooted in the now. In concrete terms religious instruction is itself life, and not a preparation for life. The religion class is a laboratory and a workshop for Christian living where students learn Christian living precisely by engaging in Christian living in the here-and-now learning situation.

One of the core principles in education, as I have just mentioned, is that the instructional process is not preparation for life, but is life itself. Yet it would appear that the majority of both specialists in, and practitioners of, religious instruction maintain the opposite position. These persons tend to affirm that the religious instruction lesson is a sort of training camp somehow removed from the secular world, a camp in which the students will be provided with the necessary weapons (usually doctrinal and other cognitive weapons) to equip them with that armamentarium which the teachers perceive as necessary to wage the Christian life in the future. Small wonder that religion classes are so frequently dull, irrelevant, and unmeaningful to the learners.

Nowness as a basic axis for religious instruction revolves around at least four basic vantage points: the pedagogical, the psychological, the philosophical, and the theological.

Pedagogically, religious instruction consists in present, here-and-now experiencing. One cannot experience the future, since the future does not yet exist. Religious instruction, to be effective, consists in taking pedagogical advantage of the needs and possibilities of the immediate present. Religious instruction means to truly and fully actualize the present moment in the learner's life so that the God within him and the God around him can meet and greet him, and in so doing help raise the person in whom this confluence uniquely occurs to new and higher self-fructification.

From the pedagogical point of view, the most effective way of preparing a learner for the future is to help him live as full a Christian life as possible in the present. The future, from one perspective, is the sum total of all an individual's nows. When preparation for future Christian living is made a focal point of religious instruction, then the existential and pedagogical potentialities are sacrificed to a suppositious future.

When this happens, the actual preparation for the future is missed or distorted. The ideal of using the present simply to get ready for the future contradicts itself. It omits, and even shuts out, the very conditions by which a person can be prepared for his future. We always live at the time we live and not at some other time, and only by extracting at each present time the full meaning of each present experience are we prepared for doing the same thing in the future. This is the only preparation which in the long run amounts to anything. All this means that attentive care must be devoted to the conditions which give each present experience worthwhile meaning. Instead of inferring that it doesn't make much difference what the present experience is as long as it is enjoyed, the conclusion is the exact opposite.[24]

To make the religion lesson a preparation for life rather than life itself is to sacrifice the present, and thereby render the lesson irrelevant in the perceptions of the learner. The focal point of the lesson being beyond the learner's present grasp, he must turn to other sources for learning. The street, companions, the mass media — all these unguided and sometimes miseducative activities — then become the locus where the student seeks to gain that kind of relevance and self-fulfillment which is supposed to be furnished by the religion class.

If perchance a learner were to die on graduation day, would all of his religion lessons up to that time have been a waste for him? We must answer this question in the affirmative if the religion lesson is viewed as a preparation for future life. But if the religion lesson is life itself, then each and every learning experience was fruitful and religiously enhancing. Perhaps this hypothetical case might smack of a *reductio ad absurdum*, nevertheless it does make the point.

Psychologically, a person lives in the present. It is the now which has meaning and relevance to him. The future does not exist for him except as a sort of projected world. Unless the learner "has been cowed into submissiveness, he wants to perceive the relation of religion to his personal and social problems now."[25] The student wants religion to be felt in his here-and-now experience.

From a psychological point of view, the "religious instruction as preparation" notion ignores and indeed denies the basic state of fullness which is present at every moment and in every stage of the person's developmental process. Implicit in the "preparation view" is the notion that the students in the religion class are not yet members in full standing in the living Christianity; the religion class exists in order to get these people ready for such full standing, according to this viewpoint. Thus the student is placed on the waiting list, so to speak; he is regarded as being in the candidate stage. This notion of "preparation" is particularly noxious when applied to children and youth, because it is positing adult religious behaviors as the standard against which the religious behaviors of the child or youth are to be judged. But maturity is not a *terminus ad quem*, a point beyond, a goal residing at some future stage. Rather, from the psychological point of view, maturity as a person and as a Christian is fully actualizing the self at the developmental point in which he is currently situated. Psychologically — and I suspect theologically as well — a child's religion is not defective for a child, but is in fact quite mature for him. If a child's religion suddenly were transformed into an adult's religion, that adult religion would be quite immature for him since it lacks congruence with the other sectors of his development. Carried to its logical consequence, "preparation" for adult religion or so-called "full religious behavior" is not possible for any Christian, since at every stage of his life the Christian is in preparation for the next stage and then for the beatific stage after the termination of his earthly life. To be a Christian is not to ignore the future, but to live fully in the present. To live constantly in "preparation" is never to truly live in the present; it is to withdraw from the present. This type of behavior is the mark of an individual who is not a fully-functioning person, who is immature, who has psychological problems. The present is a gift; it should be seized and lived to the brim.

From a *philosophical* standpoint, a person's nature cries out to live in the present, not in the future or in the past. When a person thinks or dreams about the future, it is his present self-condition which he projects into that future. He shapes his concept or dream of the future to fit his present needs, problems, desires. Similarly, a person's memory of past events is shaped and often distorted according to his present existential situation. Indeed, the very power of memory is not so much to transport the person back to the past as to carry the past forward to the realm of his present. Thomas Aquinas maintains that such is the glory of the memory, to make yesteryear live now, and so add to the psychological unity of the person over time.[26] Thus memory is a power which gives the person the gift to make all the past a present. From the philosophical point of view, is not the very eternity the Christian seeks a perpetual now?

Theologically the nature of revelation as God's present existential communication with man highlights the fact that religious instruction must be firmly planted in the present. It is in the present, not in the future, that God shares his life with man, that God unfolds himself in an ever-widening disclosure. It is because revelation is present in the present that it is supremely relevant to the life of each learner. Revelation and the learner meet at the only place where they can meet, in the present moment. Thus the most effective preparation the learner can make for the future is the living of a revelational life in the present, to borrow a phrase from Gabriel Moran.[27]

Like the person, the church too lives in the present rather than in the past or in the future. J. Donald Butler states it beautifully when he writes: "The actuality of the Church is the point at which revelation confronts each individual and each generation."[28] Christian living is done in communion with the church — the church broadly considered, of course. If the actuality of the church is to existentially reconcile the past, the present, and the future in the now, can the focus of religious instruction be any different?

In conclusion let me hasten to add that nowness is not to be identified with presentism. Presentism is that narrow and restrictive notion that nothing is of any intrinsic value except the present. Nowness accords great worth to the past and to the future. After all, the past is nothing more than the present that was, and the future is simply the present that will be. Because the past had and the future will have that fullness of life and revelation which is the special attribute and grace of the present, then both past and future ought to be esteemed and cherished. The point about nowness which I want to make in this discussion is that in terms of effective learning and living it is the now which serves as the watershed for educative growth.

From the educational standpoint, an awareness and a grasp of the past are imperative to fruitful Christian living in the present. By utilizing the past as a means rather than an end, religious instruction is saved from degenerating into antiquarianism — a state into which the exclusively past-oriented, totally bible-centered curricula of some fundamentalist Protestant religion classes have sunk. The past religious events recorded in the scriptures should not become ornaments or refuges or solaces; rather, these past events ought to be used to enlighten, enrich, and afford deeper meaning to the present.

The future also is not without deep significance for religious instruction and indeed for fruitful Christian living in the now. Surveying the relevant empirical studies, Jeffrey Keefe found that a lack of the concept and sense of the future was one of the factors most frequently found in the personality structure of persons about to commit suicide or who have been thwarted in a suicide attempt.[29] The problem in religious instruction too frequently has not been so much the importance of preparation for future Christian living as making this preparation a prime focus in the here-and-now learning situation.

In any case, whatever role is accorded in the religion lesson to preparation for future Christian living, a sense of circumspection and realism should be present throughout. After all, no one can know with any precision what the future will hold for him; this should be enough to temper the enthusiasm of those who would make the focus of the religion lesson one of "preparation." David Hunter expresses it very well: "We can focus our concerns and our purposes on the future as though we were preparing for some distant meeting with almighty God, where in a certain year of our life God will enter and we will be prepared to meet Him. The inescapable fact remains, however, that God is present *now* in our lives."[30]

Religious instruction, if truly Christian, is revelational, relevant, and real; in short, religious instruction is in the now. The learner is a Christian in process, and thus should be a processing Christian. It is this process which is a now thing, which joins the past and the future to the present.

Socialization

Socialization is that process by and through which a person is initiated into the life meanings and life patterns of interaction characterizing a particular group.[31] An individual is socialized into a particular culture or subculture through his participation in the activities of certain agencies, including the family, the peer-group, the school, and the church.

A major focus of religious instruction is to consciously facilitate the socialization of the individual into the church community in particular, and into the Christian fellowship-community in general, and finally into God's special fellowship.

An individual Christian lives in two deeply intertwined though different modes of Christian relationship, namely the mode called "church" and the mode called "God's fellowship." The church tends to be an institutionalized form of culture, though this is not necessarily the case.[32] Because of its typically institutionalized form, the church tends to be a society characterized by specific cultural and stylistic behavior patterns. The available empirical data suggest that a society's cultural beliefs and lifestyles are learned behaviors on the part of the individual, and become deeply embedded in the affective domain of his life.[33] One of the paramount foci of religious instruction is to assist in the church's general task of enculturating or acculturating the individual into the church society, so that by and through his participation in the life of the church he may attain that kind of Christian maturity most appropriate to his own unique personality. The religious instruction program, then, is one of the church's formally-erected agencies (or at least one of its approved modes) by which the individual is more readily socialized into the church society.

An important aspect of this enculturation or acculturation is the learning of those social roles peculiar to church society. By social role I do not mean simply skill in appropriate participation in church rites and liturgy, or the proper forms of ecclesiastical etiquette. Social role for a member of the church society also includes the incorporation into his or her own personal lifestyle of those behaviors which we can label "Christian," notably in the habitual performance of faith acts and love acts. Sociological investigations have revealed that one of the key constituents of social role is the expectancy on the part of both the person in a particular society and of others contacting that person to exhibit a particular behavioral pattern of living and acting.[34] Consequently, from both a theological and sociological perspective, a person can be said to be living his Christianhood to the extent that in his everyday life he is fulfilling his social role of behaving like a Christian. Because of the expectancy element inherent in social role, other persons expect a Christian to behave as a member of a church society, and are disappointed ("scandalized" is the theological term) when the Christian is not living out his social role.

In an ecumenical age, socialization into the society of a particular Christian denomination is not sufficient. Rather, ecumenically-oriented religious instruction socializes the individual simultaneously into a high-level, participatory membership of his own church and also into the broader fellowship of the church universal. Facilitating the individual's socialization into twin membership in his own particular Christian denomination and into the complex of Christendom as a whole represents one of the more challenging aspects of religious instruction for our time.

Concurrent with the task of socializing the individual into the church and indeed into Christendom at large, religious instruction also has the even deeper task of helping to facilitate the induction of the individual into that relational mode which can be termed "God's fellowship." Indeed, it is this deeply felt and lived personal relationship in his own pattern of behavior which is at the heart of the Christian lifestyle. While in the ideal order a person's participation in the church society and in God's fellowship is mutually complementary and indeed at the most profound level one and the same thing, nonetheless in the practical order it not infrequently happens that a person feels and perceives himself in a concrete existential situation in which the seeming demands of the two are pulling him in opposite behavioral directions. At particular times in their lives, some persons are deeply convinced that certain ecclesiastical regulations, fully approbated by the highest authoritative echelons of the church society, can and will hinder the quality and depth of their personal participation in God's fellowship. It might well be that in certain cases, sometimes in adolescence, sometimes in adulthood, the very induction into God's fellowship might lead to a lessening in the individual's overt participation in the church society (for example, staying away from worship services) or even in a withdrawal from formal membership in church society.[35] This existential and deeply-felt personal quandary represents a thorny and difficult theological problem, and falls outside the purview of our present study. I introduce this very real existential difficulty only to indicate that the process of socialization — or "house-breaking," as it is sometimes called — has a twin aspect. On the one hand, socialization into the institutional church means that the individual is eased into a society which has certain controlling, restricting, and hindering functions in terms of his range of acceptable behaviors. On the other hand, socialization into the institutional church has its constructive aspects in promoting personal growth, serving as a unique God-to-man mediational channel, and affording the individual all sorts of helps to ripen in his participation in God's fellowship. Socialization is both a shaping and a creative process, with the built-in tensions inherent in any growth-oriented social structure. God truly encounters man in a very special and unique way through the church society, yet in a certain sense *super ecclesiam Deus est.* Institutions, such as the institutional church, are very necessary to the furtherance of human development, for as the relevant empirical investigations have concluded, social relationships in a society are necessary for the person to become human,[36] to say nothing of becoming Christian. On the other hand, there can develop what Floyd Allport once termed "institutional idolatry," which when applied to religion means placing the purposes of the organization qua organization ahead of the religious development of the individual Christian.[37] It is an especial focus of religious instruction to facilitate in the learners the living of that dynamic equilibrium between participation in the church society and participation in God's personal fellowship which comprises the greatness and the turbulence of the Christian experience.

Precisely because it is an institution and a society, the church into which the individual is being socialized through the enterprise of religious instruction tends to be heavily occupied with the maintenance function. After all, one of the hallmarks of an institution and a society is that it contains within itself those elements necessary to continue its perpetuation regardless of whichever persons are situated in that society at any given time. To continue as a living society, the church must maintain its existence. On the other hand, the person who is being socialized into the church society has legitimate personal needs and modes of existence, some of which are enhanced by the church society, and some of which are eroded or destroyed by this institution. This tension, about which I have been speaking in the last paragraph, can partly be resolved by indicating the reconstructionist or prophetical function of religious instruction.

In other words, the focus of religious instruction as facilitating the socializing of the individual into the church society is incomplete without its complementary aspect of facilitating in that very individual the vision and the ability to widen the frontiers of that church society. Unless the church society incarnates the times and the men of the times, it will neither be timely nor Christian. As a society, the church will do little more than maintain itself. Therefore it remains for the individuals within that society, who possess the flesh-and-blood life which the institution does not possess, to push from within the society to ever newer dimensionalities. It is this push from within by members of the church that causes the conflict between the church society and individual members in that society. The individual's membership in the church society bids him to maintain the status quo, while at the same time it is his own personal uniqueness encountering God in a special noninstitutionalized personal fellowship that bids him sometimes and at certain points to depart and go beyond the parameters set by the church society. It is at this juncture that religious instruction becomes a deeply revelational thing, for here God contacts the individual personally. Also, in the economy of salvation, it is through this revelational contact with man that God is pushing his church ever forward toward Point Omega. It is in the individual, experiencing this tension of maintenance and reconstructionism, that revelation is being done. It is here we can see that revelation is a grace at once gorgeous and excruciating, because it sometimes brings the individual in conflict with the institutional church which he loves and cherishes. But this agony of personally-lived revelation and reconstructionism is a deeply educative thing, and represents a high point in the religious education and development of the individual Christian. To remain faithful both to the church society and to the God ever animating that society, while at the same time being authentic to self and to God as one meets God and self in God's fellowship, represents the dilemma and the promise of Christian existence. It is from this twin focus that the enterprise of religious instruction must never shrink by offering tinny solutions or pat answers, as has happened so often in the past. By making the little society in which religious instruction takes place — be that society the family, the school, the formal religion class, or an informal peer-group association — a true community into which the individual is at once socialized in a climate of freedom and individuation, the twin focus of fidelity and authenticity can be made to happen.

Kerygma

One of the most noteworthy features of contemporary religious instruction is the conscious effort to return to the new testament, particularly the gospels, in order to make modern religious pedagogy as faithful to, and as rich as, the religious pedagogy of Jesus and his immediate followers. One of the most fruitful discoveries of this return to the very historical sources of Christianity has been the kerygma. Aided by the findings of scripture scholars, religious educationists have found that the kerygma constitutes one of the chief focal points in the work of religious instruction as found in the teaching activities of Jesus and his apostles.[38]

A Greek word whose precise translation into English is not possible, kerygma means the joyful announcement of the good news about something vitally important and significant. Applied to religious instruction, it means the teaching of the joyous news of salvation. According to many scripture scholars, the kerygma constituted the introductory phase of the totality of the Apostles' three-stage teaching activity. The kerygma consisted in the proclamation of the glad tidings of salvation which came in the person of Jesus Christ.[39] The kerygma was used with non-Christians, and was intended to so inspire and motivate these individuals that in cooperation with God's grace they thereby would be converted to Christianity. The kerygmatic phase in the Apostolic teaching program was followed by a second stage, the catechetical phase. Catechesis, another Greek term, signifies oral instruction for beginners.[40] In catechesis the Apostles and their followers provided some instruction about the rudiments of the Christian religion, particularly about the moral code (although some doctrinal basics were introduced also). Catechesis was used in the case of those who had made the act of faith by virtue of the kerygma in cooperation with God's grace, so that they could begin their first steps in meaningfully living the Christian lifestyle.[41] The catechetical phase of the Apostles' religious pedagogy was capped by a third stage, the didascalic phase. Didascalia, also a Greek term, consisted in a fuller instruction in the elements of the Christian religion, with particular emphasis on doctrine. Didascalia was employed to assist the individual to come to a richer and more profound understanding of Christianity, and therefore to help him to live a deeper Christian life.[42]

The relation of kerygma to catechesis and to didascalia is nicely illustrated in Peter's sermon which immediately followed the descent of the Holy Spirit upon the Apostles at Pentecost (Acts 2:1-42). Peter's sermon was addressed to non-Christians — indeed to "devout Jews from every country under heaven" (Acts 2:5). In his lengthy sermon, Peter utilized the kerygma, telling his audience of the wondrous deeds of Jesus of Nazareth who died, rose again, and in whom salvation resides. The pedagogical aim of Peter's use of the kerygma was to elicit feelings of joy, admiration, and delight in these devout Jews, so that these individuals would be thereby facilitated to incorporate the process content and the product content of the good news into their own personal lives. Having encountered the kerygma, these devout Jews found that their "consciences were pricked" to the extent that they asked Peter what they should *do*, what behaviors they should utilize (Acts 2:37). Three thousand people were baptized that day, and the scripture concludes by saying that in the times which followed this event these three thousand persons were further taught by the Apostles (the catechetical phase and the didascalical phase).

The relation of catechesis to didascalia is, according to some scholars,[43] nicely delineated by both Paul (1 Corinthians 3:1-2) and by the author of the Epistle to the Hebrews (5:11-14). Each of these inspired writers refers to catechesis as "milk" which should be given to children prior to giving them solid food, namely didascalia. In both instances, the scripture indicates that while milk is necessary in the early stages of religious development, the individual should nonetheless advance to solid food as soon as feasible.

In the Apostolic period of the church, it often happened that a person was baptized immediately after he had made an act of faith which followed the kerygmatic phase. This, for example, was the case with Peter's sermon on Pentecost Day, and also with Philip and the courtier of Queen Candace (Acts 8:26-40).[44] However, with the advance of time in the era of Christian antiquity, the point at which a person was baptized gradually began to be deferred, and a special formal period of probation called the catechumenate was introduced. During the time of his catechumenate, the individual (who already had made his act of faith) was taught increasingly more of the essentials of Christianity. In the individual's catechumenate, doubtless the didascalia was added on to catechesis, since his catechumenate often lasted for as many as three years.

It should be emphasized that this three-stage teaching cycle of kerygma-catechesis-didascalia did not consist exclusively or even primarily in hortatory or intellectual learnings. The behavioral thrust of the kerygma used by Peter in his sermon on Pentecost Day can be seen in the response of the Jews when they asked Peter "What should we *do*?" (Acts 2:37). And after three thousand persons were converted (an overt behavior) that day, they subsequently continued to engage in religious behaviors in the company of the Apostles (Acts 2:42). Later on in Christian antiquity, when the formal catechumenate was introduced, the three years or so spent in this interval between one's act of faith and baptism was primarily a time in which the person was learning to behave like a Christian. To be sure, intellectually-oriented teaching about doctrine and morality was taking place during the catechumenate, but this instruction was intended to be directly incorporated into the developing Christian lifestyle of the catechumen.[45] This is a capital point often neglected in contemporary religious instruction. Behavior — inner and outer personal Christian lifestyle — is the goal of religious instruction, and to a great extent the means of religious instruction as well. Behavior, then, is not an entry vehicle to more efficiently get at intellectual learnings about doctrine or morals; rather, intellectual learning in religious instruction is valid and effective only to the degree in which it is immediately fused with the learner's inner and outer behavioral pattern in the actual learning situation itself.

As it is generally understood today, kerygma has three different but complementary meanings.[46] Kerygma can be considered as the product content of religious instruction, notably the subject matter of the good news as firmly planted and centered in Jesus the Christ. Thus Paul refers to the content of the gospel he preaches when he heralds Jesus (Romans 16:25). Secondly, kerygma can be regarded as the process content of religious instruction; that is, the becom*ing* like Jesus, the progressive awar*ing* of the Christian mystery, the form*ing* of attitudes and values in congruence with Jesus. Paul speaks of the gospel he preaches as itself revealing the mystery of Jesus (Romans 16:25). In 1 Corinthians 2:3-5, Paul writes of God's power itself, existentially present and living in the gospel the Apostle preaches, as being the principal content of his preaching — a splendid way of characterizing one mode of process content. Finally, kerygma can be taken as the very act of proclaiming the good news, the concrete teaching activity, the way in which the coming together of God and man is facilitated in this activity.[47]

The term "kerygma" is commonly linked to the words "heralding" and "proclaiming" as used in the new testament. But these two words are descriptive of the preaching function, rather than the more global and inclusive activity called religious instruction. In other words, I am suggesting that preaching is a kind or type of religious instruction, since preaching is only one mode of facilitating desired behavioral outcomes in learners. Consequently, "heralding" and "proclaiming" are appropriate to and quite possibly coextensive with preaching. It further follows that the approaches to and strategies of religious instruction are broader than "heralding" and "proclaiming." This explanation should serve to indicate why in this section I have regarded kerygma as an approach to religious instruction rather than simply an approach to preaching.

The year 1936 was a landmark year in the history of the concept of kerygma. It was in that year that two significant books appeared which discussed at some length the notion of kerygma and its seminal application to the nature and work of theology. On the Protestant side, C. H. Dodd, the English theologian, published his book, *The Apostolic Preaching and Its Developments*, which comprised three lectures he gave the previous year during the Michaelmas term at King's College, University of London.[48] In the Catholic sector, the Austrian theologian and liturgist, Josef Jungmann, published his *Die Frohbotschaft und unsere Glaubensverkündigung.*[49] It was Jungmann's work which caused the most furor, especially in Europe, where Catholic theologians of all sorts, especially the Germans and the Austrians, became embroiled in a bitter conflict. The heated controversy revolved around the question of whether kerygma is a separate theology in its own right as contrasted to and distinguished from the so-called "scientific theology." After a few years, in which the theologians wrote numerous books and articles — religious educationists did not seem to take part in this controversy — it was discovered that no one, not even Jungmann himself was advocating a "kerygmatic theology" as contradistinguished from "scientific theology." With this shaking discovery, theologians settled down to incorporate the kerygmatic dimension into "scientific theology," and with extra vigor kneaded the yeast of kerygmatic Christocentrism and the good news into their theological dough. Thanks in good measure to the kerygmatic approach, "scientific theology" has been ever more deeply relating revealed truth to life and to personal human experience.[50] This development occurred toward the beginning of the 1940's. Still later, kerygmatic theology was broadened to include the theological relationship of the proclamation of the good news to those aspects of "scientific theology" which lent themselves to an extension into pastoral care. With respect to religious instruction, this controversy points up the fact that even on the theological plane — as distinguished from the educational plane — there is a basic unity between dogma-moral itself and both the pastoral thrust of Christocentrism and the glad tidings of the good news.

As it applies specifically to religious instruction (rather than to theology), kerygma is a pedagogical approach rather than a particular teaching method. This is a cardinal point. In other words, kerygma is a spirit which animates the whole enterprise of religious instruction; it is not a specific technique. This sense of kerygma appears to be quite biblical. Despite the fact that the word kerygma does not have that degree of precision and clarity in the new testament as do certain other scriptural terms, it would appear that the word kerygma was employed in the new testament in "an almost technical sense" to signify the manner and approach in which the herald of the good news engaged in his proclamatory activity. [51] Kerygma is a sort of generalized style; hence it is not an attempt to return to the original pedagogical techniques used in Christian antiquity. To revert to these ancient particularized teaching techniques would be disastrous for contemporary religious instruction. Times have changed drastically since then, and so have people. The needs and exigencies of the church have also undergone profound alteration. Pedagogical strategies have substantially advanced since the old transmission or proclaiming pattern of teaching. But because it is person-oriented, because it is Christocentric, because it is joyous and zestful, because it is radicated in the good news of salvation, and because it is deeply related with the nowness of present-day living — because of all these things, the kerygmatic approach is as relevant to religious instruction now as it was at the dawn of the Christian era.

Due to its generalized nature, the kerygmatic approach penetrates all aspects of the work of religious instruction. In terms of the kerygma-catechesis-didascalia teaching cycle which I mentioned before, the kerygma as approach, as process (as distinguished from the theological concept of the kerygma as product), is found in all three stages of the cycle. While it is not precise to say that kerygma *is* the core of religious instruction, it is quite accurate to assert that kerygma *is* *at* the core of every phase of religious pedagogy. Kerygma, as Alfonso Nebreda has pointed out, represents one of the most dynamic aspects of religious instruction, and consequently is present at every stage of teaching. [52]

To be kerygmatic in one's approach to teaching is to be

scripturally based, liturgically oriented, existentially thrusted, experientially focused, personalistically directed, and Christologically pointed. It is precisely these processes, indeed the combination of these processes, which forms so much of the essential content of the good news. Content, then, is process. The kerygmatic approach to life, the kerygmatic process becomes one of the most important content learnings in the whole of the religious instruction enterprise. The kerygma is a process content rather than a product content. And herein lies much of its worth and significance, both existentially and pedagogically.

Stripped to its bare essentials, the kerygma, as applied to religious instruction, has two basic features, namely the joyous tidings of the good news and Christocentrism. The theme of the good news runs all through the scriptures. Isaiah had prophesied that the Christ would announce the good news and preach salvation (Isaiah 52:6-7). John the Baptist — "evangelizeto," that is — heralded the good news about the coming of the kingdom of God (Luke 4:18). All through the gospels, Jesus indicates that he is telling people the glad tidings of salvation. The second chapter of Acts, which I discussed previously in this section, showed how on Pentecost Day Peter kerygmatized to the devout Jews. Paul was very conscious that he was heralding the good news, and this theme runs throughout his epistles (for example, 1 Corinthians 15:3-4; 2 Timothy 4:17).[53] In our own time, contemporary theologians, some Protestant and Catholic, have rediscovered the primacy of the Incarnation and particularly of the Resurrection in terms of the kerygmatic joyful import of these two events. To these contemporary theologians, the passion and death of Jesus are intimately linked to the Resurrection and the Ascension, so that it is the Resurrection and Ascension which inform and give basic meaning to the passion and death.[54] It is the Resurrection which gives meaning to a Christian's faith (1 Corinthians 15:14) because it is in the Resurrection that not only the hope but even more importantly the germinal fullness of all future revelation is to be had. Bernard Cooke phrases it well when he states that perhaps the aspect of the Resurrection which touches most significantly on religious instruction "is the fact that it draws attention to the continuing revelation of the Father in the mystery of the risen Christ."[55]

The kerygma is deeply Christocentric; indeed, it is the person of Jesus that constitutes the source and fullness of the good news. What the kerygmatic approach does is to reawaken and refocus the task of religious instruction on the reality most fundamental to Christianity, namely Jesus as the center and direction of God's salvific activities. The kerygmatic approach thus facilitates the learners to respond to the central fact and value of Christian revelation. For too many centuries, Protestants and Catholics have been diffusing much of their religious instructional activities in the direction of specific doctrines and moral laws and even to folkloric aspects peculiar to one denomination or other. As Johannes Hofinger reminds us, religion teachers are "commissioned" — to appropriate his very important term — to teach not only specific doctrines, but more importantly to teach the kerygma which is the total mystery of Christ.[56] Indeed, Gerard Sloyan's review of the pertinent Protestant and Catholic theological research concluded that creedal statements were originally "recitals of sacred events in the history of the Christian people rather than mere 'historical propositions' as they were widely thought to have been." These creedal statements, Sloyan continues, are in actuality "formulated kerygmata," encoded joyous announcements.[57] In other words, creedal statements were originally intended to place aspects of the kerygma in codified form for concrete emphasis and pedagogical ease.

The kerygma is basically a process, the process of Christification, of the flowing of Jesus into the teaching act and into the lives of both learner and teacher in a continuing ongoing revelation which is educative and salvific. Kerygma is, above all, a process approach to, and a process outcome of, the enterprise of religious instruction.

Person

Religious instruction is based on, centered around, and aimed toward the human development and Christian actualization of the learner as a person.

Education has as one of its touchstones taking the person as he is. This is not only the basis for effective pedagogy; it also forms the foundation for a proper Christian respect of the person qua person. Focus on the integrity of the person as he is in present actuality in no way implies that religious instruction ignores the learner's future potentialities. Indeed, a prime axis of the work and mode of the enterprise of religious instruction is to provide the opportunities for the learner to be all the things he can be. Yet it is vital that religious instruction begin with the learner where he is, at his own unique point of development.

The history of salvation, Didier Piveteau reminds us, is not only the history of the chosen people but also the history of one's own personal lived existence.[58] It is in and through each person that revelation, and hence personal salvation, flows. Becoming human implies a self-actualizing process, a personalizing of self through deeply-felt experiencing, a living out of one's own existential thrust. Ross Snyder describes existential thrust very beautifully:

> Existential thrust first of all means that I intend to *live*; to be burgeoning energy, potential on its way to significant form; to experience creation's joyful cry, "I am"; to be a unique person and particularity, caring deeply about some things. Existential thrust suggests that I am a freedom invoking other freedoms, open hands, ears, eyes, mouth — rather than closing fingers . . . . Existential thrust is the movement to become authentic, to incarnate vividly the truth I am meant to be, live out of truth. For I know the truth only to the degree that I participate in it.[59]

To borrow a construct from Carl Rogers, a major task of religious instruction is to help the individual come to be in awareness that which he is in experience.[60] Religious instruction is a facilitational process whereby among other outcomes the developing person becomes his experience. In so doing the person achieves optimal congruence between his so-called inner and outer selves. He then operates as a fully functioning person, one in whom life's rhythms freely flow, and at once find their source and fulfillment. Such a person then becomes compatible, as it were, with God's total living revelation, and lives in his own self the joy and gladness and brimming-overness which constitute the Christian lifestyle.

How is this emphasis on personhood and existential subjectivity to be reconciled with the stress placed by many religious instruction specialists on the imperative that religious instruction be totally faithful to the word of God?[61] Fidelity in this context means complete adhesion to God's word. This was the classic emphasis in the traditional religious instruction enterprise in centuries gone by. It was this fidelity approach which gave rise, in the Roman Church at least, to that kind of religious instruction which revolved around the memorization by learners of specific doctrinal statements framed in precise wording and compiled in a logically-ordered formulary called the catechism. It was likewise the fidelity approach which characterized the core of the Munich Method which was the dominant form of Catholic religious instruction in Europe, particularly in the German-speaking countries, during the first half of the twentieth century. To be sure, advocates of the Munich Method insisted that during the central part of the lesson — called the "presentation stage" — the students should sit attentively, devotionally, and in complete and absolute silence, listening to the words of the teacher, so that they would receive the exact word of God without distortion.[62]   Another specialist in religious instruction states explicitly, "Fidelity is clearly the most important and the most characteristic virtue of a herald [religion teacher]. As he is sent to proclaim a message to others, his fidelity causes him to proclaim his message exactly, carefully, diligently . . . . We are not the masters of our message; we are not permitted to select the material according to our own tastes and personal devotion."[63]

The fidelity approach indicates that a prime goal of religious instruction is conformity rather than transformation or self-actualizing in one's own way. The process of religious instruction is thus conceived of as one of disciplinary training, alignment with verbal formulae instead of personal development. Yet it is my own belief, a contention strongly buttressed by contemporary theology — and even more important for the pedagogical endeavor, by empirical research findings on the nature of learning — that the focus of religious education ought to be on personal fulfillment. When this is truly on the way toward accomplishment, all other things will be added unto it. Now this is not to imply in any way a relativism. It is to indicate that God's revelation is not merely objective. Indeed the fullness of God's revelation is precisely intersubjectivity. Jesus is a subjectivity, not an objectivity. It is one's deep personal lived relationship with the subjectivity that is Jesus the Christ which forms true religion. If the Incarnation means anything, it means that revelation was made flesh and dwells among us. A person, and most especially the Person of Persons is a subjectivity, not a formula. To be a Christian is to be humanly — fleshly and spiritually — joined first to the Person, and second to all persons who by their very humanity participate to some degree in that Person.

There are at least four principal stumbling blocks in the fidelity approach, namely pedagogical, psychological, philosophical, and theological.

Pedagogically, one of the cardinal aspects of the teaching act is, as Aquinas so often observes, that all learning occurs according to the manner of the learner. It is the learner, not the teacher, who is the primary proximate intrinsic agent in the facilitation of learning.[64]   A learner, like any other human being, "can accept, act upon or realize a certain truth only if this truth corresponds to the level of his own development. If he cannot relate this truth to his experience, it will only be superimposed, pasted on and experienced as unreal."[65] Learning takes place where the learner "is at" — to use the existentially forceful Negro idiom. Thus as the overwhelming mass of research data suggests, learning occurs within the context of the learner's personality, need structure, problems, and developmental concerns.[66] To be effective, religious instruction must start at the learner's own point of development and self-actualization, and work from there toward facilitating his religious and existential growth, which will be both authentic to his own self and faithful to God. In the final analysis, the more an individual is truly authentic, the more will he tend to automatically grow in fidelity to the God of personal revelation. The empirical research data suggest that changes in behavior imposed on a society or on individuals from outside — for example, by the teacher — are especially unlikely to be accepted. Forced change from outside tends to result in overcompliance but covert resistance.[67] In short, what I am saying is that efficacious learning can be facilitated, not by telling the individual that such-and-such is God's word and he must be faithful to it, but instead by so structuring the learning situation whereby the individual is enabled to be faithful to his own experiencing. Once this happens, then the God flowing freely within the individual will be enabled as fully as possible to encounter the person at a deeply intersubjective level, that is the Person of God meeting at a point of contact with the human person. It is then that religious instruction will have pedagogically created the conditions for pervasive, meaningful, and true fidelity to the ongoing revelation of God.

From the educational point of view, the fidelity approach has set up a dichotomy between product content and person. It is the product content of specified doctrines which serves as the focal point for fidelity-oriented religious pedagogy. The key test of the efficacy of learning under this approach is the extent and depth to which the teacher "covers the ground." Consequently, the learner as person has to conform to the product content. Thus we have the situation of academic marks assigned to religion class, seeming to imply that a student attaining a 90% mark learned more religion in class than the student who receives an 82%. One might legitimately ask whether these academic marks are more a measure of the conformity of the student to the exigencies of the product content demands of the teacher than a measure of his overall religious learning. At a deeper level, the fidelity approach seems to ignore the basic fact that in the Christian heritage, product content is not a thing or an abstract set of doctrinal propositions, but instead, a Person. God qua Person is the prime product content, without which doctrinal product contents are tinny and hollow. Jesus is a Person and not a datum or a doctrinal proposition. Jesus died for persons, not for subject matter.

Finally, the fidelity approach virtually ignores the existence of process content, to say nothing of ignoring its primacy. The process of the individual's becoming religious by and through the activities of religious pedagogy is denigrated. With no supporting empirical data, it is assumed that a learner becomes religious primarily by acquiring a set of doctrinal propositions or by receiving from another some key insights into the intellectual understanding of these doctrines, to be followed up by conative acts faithful to these doctrinal propositions. But the process by which the learner accomplishes this all too frequently squeezes out of him the vital juices of religious awaring and valuing and living. Religious living for the learner thus becomes a sort of legal game: doctrinal propositions versus him. All too often, therefore, religion becomes a limitational constraint on a person instead of being the liberational process which Jesus indicated that it is.

Psychologically, the fidelity approach ignores and indeed flails one of the touchstones of all behavioral science, namely that each person while possessing certain of the same characteristics as other individuals, nonetheless is unique and different from all others. In totally ignoring the basic psychological fact of individual differences, the fidelity approach to religious instruction insists that learners, who naturally have different bents, be taught doctrines in the same way. This approach further suggests that true fidelity to God's word means that each individual conforms to revelation in precisely the same way, operationally defined as the way the teacher or the ruling cadre of the local institutional church perceives that such conformity best takes place for the populace. Yet modern psychology counts individual differences to be one of the most precious of all characteristics of humankind. The fidelity approach propounds an aim of religious instruction which tends to stunt the personal development of the learner vis-à-vis his own self and his lived relationship with God. Revelation is not uniform, but in an extraordinarily exquisite manner takes on the form of the psychological and existential requirements of the developing person.

A particularly noxious outgrowth of the fidelity approach, as far as children and youth are concerned, has been that adults typically assumed that their own habits, lifestyle and perception of God's word in fact constitute God's word. As a result, children and youth have been terribly confused and often soured on religion, because they are told in an existential and process way that fidelity to God's revelation ought not to be in terms of contacting Jesus at their own point of development but instead, of contacting him in a manner which adults had fashioned for themselves. Revelation has been cast into the mold of adult standards. Children and youth have been treated as little adults, and they have been given adult standards as exemplars. Fidelity-oriented religious educators assert that these children and youth, to the extent that they conform to these adult standards, are "mature" and "grown up." But as I indicated earlier in this chapter, from a psychological point of view, maturity is self-actualizing at one's own point of development; it is not the closeness of one's conformity to some external or adult standard of behavior.

It is interesting, and in fact quaint, to observe certain contemporary theologians and theologically-oriented religious educators simultaneously in sharp disagreement with the fidelity approach while at the same time stoutly maintaining that Christianity is an adult's religion rather than a children's religion.[68] From the standpoint of social science and of behavioral science, this assertion is sheer nonsense. Valid religion is as much a religion of children and youth as it is of adults and those already lapsed into dotage. Religion is the living of a relationship with God where the person "is at," at the person's own unique point of self-actualization. It is distinctly unhuman, if not indeed unchristian, to suggest that religion is not an affair for children and youth. Jesus himself decried such a *grand hauteur* on the part of the adults of his day who felt that Jesus's place was with adults and not with children. "Let the little children come unto me," Jesus said, "for the kingdom of heaven belongs to such as these" (Matthew 19:14). Religion is for everybody, where he is. To be sure, certain theologians and religious educators might someday wake up to discover that true lived revelational religion is being had more by individuals and classes of individuals which these savants asserted were incapable of so having, than by these men themselves.

Philosophically, the fidelity approach flounders on the nature of truth and the individual's adhesion to it. One of Gabriel Marcel's students once remarked to the noted twentieth-century French philosopher that he found a more profound elaboration of Marcel's concept of the nature of truth in the philosopher's plays and dramatic works than in his explicitly philosophical treatises on the subject. For Marcel this penetrating observation served to point up the fact that the essence and grandeur of truth, particularly for a Christian in his relation to God, is basically one's lived valuing relationship with God.[69] In one sense — to be sure, a secondary and derived sense — truth is the adequation of the mind with what actually exists in reality. But in a deeper and more human sense, truth is value; specifically, truth is person and particularly the Person that is Jesus. Truth — God's word — by virtue of the Incarnation, was truly made flesh and blood which even now dwells among us in concrete human situations and happenings. Perhaps one major reason why learners find religion teaching as proffered by adults to be so personally irrelevant (and hence of little truth-value to them) is that truth is recast in the intellectual formulational terms of abstract doctrinal propositions instead of being left in their pristine yet richer state of person and concrete. Only when religious pedagogy becomes person-oriented as the individual functions in a concrete situation will the learner grow in personal fidelity to the truth and the Truth. A person can never really know another individual; but he can truly love him. Likewise a person can never really know the Truth, but he can really love the Truth.

The fidelity approach to teaching God's word has as its primary axis the preservation and development of orthodoxy in the learner. Yet there is a vast difference between orthodoxy and conformism. Orthodoxy is always creative, personalistic, and therefore in a certain way at odds with, and in deviation from, a norm emanating from a verbal formula or from a human group.[70] Conformism, on the other hand, implies submission to a certain command emanating from either a group or from a person acting as a role functionary, which claims that it incarnates what must be thought and must be valued.[71] Considered from the aspect of revelation as a living growing personal relationship between Jesus and man, together with the responding which that man makes to Jesus, it would appear that it is orthodoxy and not conformism which represents true fidelity. In other words, what the fidelity approach does in actual pedagogical practice is to stifle fidelity by promoting conformism and suffocating orthodoxy. True fidelity is an open thing; it is not a closed system.

Theologically, the fidelity approach tends to minimize if not indeed strangle the human element in Christianity by making religion a business of adherence to precision of verbal formulae. Yet Christianity would appear to be precisely the opposite. Christianity is, among other things, an assembly of people, an assembly which transcends the conventional boundaries of time and space. Because it is with and for people, Christianity becomes truly lived Christianity to the extent that it is human. It is in the gospel of John that the most human of Christ's encounters and activities are recorded. This fact prompted the remark by one theologian that the gospel of John is the most divine because it is the most human. Fidelity to God's word is best attained by becoming truly authentic to oneself. This is not to remand to the rubbish heap all doctrinal pronouncements and encoded objectifications of God's revelation; instead it is to accord them their proper secondary but valuable role in the work of religious instruction. For too long have doctrinal formulae, whether overt as in yesteryear or covert as right now, been occupied with what the older ascetical theologians dubbed "pride of place" in religious instruction.

"Person is a gift," Josef Goldbrunner has remarked, "but it is also a task."[72] In the enterprise of religious instruction, person is a double task. Person is a task to the individual himself to successfully work through and accomplish, as appropriate, the various tasks of personal development which his own self-system as it interacts with his milieu imposes on him.[73] Person is a task to the religion teacher to so structure the learning situation that the learner's natural-supernatural development as a person remains central at every phase of the instructional process. Vis-à-vis the fidelity approach, this means that the primacy in religious instruction must on every count — pedagogical, psychological, philosophical, and theological — be placed on the psychological structure of the learner rather than on the logical structure of human formulations of God's revelation.

The emphasis on "person" as *a* focal point for religious instruction in no way implies that religious instruction is the same as religious counseling. As I will show in the next chapter, religious instruction, while sharing certain features with religious counseling, is nonetheless an essentially distinct activity within the total enterprise of religious education. Stress on the focal point of "person" does not mean that religious instruction is totally process-oriented or totally affective domain-oriented. Rather, the "person" as *a* focal point serves to emphasize the crucial fact that religious instruction has both process and product components and also has affective and cognitive components. Further, the person as person assumes a central place in the work of religious instruction.

CONCLUSION

The discussion in this chapter of six different focal points of religious instruction is not intended to be an exhaustive treatment of all the major foci of the teaching of religion. Rather, it is hoped that a treatment of the six focal points I selected will help throw into bold relief some of the major linchpins of religious instruction, and also set the stage for what follows in the remainder of this book.

The focal points discussed in this chapter serve — though not in the same way — as both ends and means in the task of religious instruction. As ends, they are kinds of developmental goals toward which the enterprise of religious instruction is thrusted. This is particularly valid for the focal point which I designated as "Christian living." As means, the focal points represent major ongoing axes which should pervade the pedagogical approach, pedagogical process, pedagogical strategies, and pedagogical methodologies used in the everyday work of religious instruction. These focal points help to facilitate effective teaching and also to be facilitated through effective teaching.

FOOTNOTES

1. Kahlil Gibran, *The Prophet* (New York: Knopf, 1923, reset 1953), p. 40.
2. Horace Bushnell, *Christian Nurture* (New Haven, Connecticut: Yale University Press, 1888), p. 7.
3. Marcel van Caster, *The Structure of Catechetics*, 2d ed., translated by Edward J. Dirkswager, Jr., Olga Guedetarian, and Nicolas Smith (New York: Herder and Herder, 1965), p. 38.
4. Charles Y. Glock, "On the Study of Religious Commitment," in *Religious Education*, research supplement, LVII, July-August, 1962, pp. s-98-s110.
5. See, for example, Johannes Hofinger, *The Art of Teaching Christian Doctrine: The Good News And Its Proclamation*, 2d ed. (Notre Dame, Indiana: University of Notre Dame Press, 1962), pp. 17, 33, and 70.
6. Herman Hendrickx, "Figures of the Church: Teaching Situations and Attitudes," in *Lumen Vitae*, XXIII, June, 1968, p. 314.

7. André Brien, "Catechetics as a Task for Our Age," in Johannes Hofinger, editor, *Teaching All Nations*, revised and partly translated by Clifford Howell (Freiburg, Germany: Herder, 1961), p. 7.
8. Marcel van Caster, *The Structure of Catechetics*, pp. 12-21.
9. It will be observed that I say here "religious *instruction*" rather than religious education or catechesis, terms which van Caster, a theologian, uses as the umbrella for his stages. My reason for this is that the term "instruction," as van Caster used it in his books and articles, and which he uses to characterize the first stage, is too narrowly defined by him. Van Caster tends to equate the instructional process with the transmission of knowledge from the teacher (sender) to the pupil (receiver). Doubtless van Caster's restricted and restrictive concept of instruction derives from the fact that he was trained as a theologian rather than as an educationist, and, therefore, is probably unaware of the findings of social science or of the teaching-learning process.
10. Josef Andreas Jungmann, *Handing on the Faith: A Manual of Catechetics*, translated and revised by A. N. Fuerst (New York: Herder and Herder, 1959), p. 2; see also Hans Lietzmann, *A History of the Early Church*, volume II, translated by Bertram Lee Woolf (Cleveland, Ohio: World Meridian, 1961), pp. 148-172.
11. See Asahel D. Woodruff, *Basic Concepts of Teaching*, concise edition (San Francisco: Chandler, 1961), pp. 115-158.
12. On this last point, see Antoine Vergote, "Religious Experience," in *Lumen Vitae*, XIX, June, 1964. p. 218.
13. Asahel D. Woodruff, *Basic Concepts of Teaching*, p. 222.
14. John Dewey, *Experience and Education* (New York: Macmillan, 1938), pp. 16-17.
15. Paul H. Vieth, editor, *The Church and Christian Education* (St. Louis: Bethany, 1946), p. 80.
16. It is here that I think Bernard Cooke misses the mark. Cooke's clinging to the teacher's words as the vehicle for classroom revelation would hinder the learner from actualizing the God-learner encounter in the classroom situation. Yet oddly enough, it is this personal encounter which forms the basis of Cooke's thesis. See Bernard Cooke, "Theology of the Word: Implications for Religious Instruction," in James Michael Lee and Patrick C. Rooney, editors, *Toward a Future for Religious Education* (Dayton, Ohio: Pflaum, 1970), pp. 138-153.
17. See, for example, P. de Letter, "The Encounter with God," in *Thought*, XXXVI, Spring, 1961, pp. 5-24.

18. Josef Goldbrunner, "Catechesis and Encounter," in Josef Goldbrunner, editor, *New Catechetical Methods* (Notre Dame, Indiana: University of Notre Dame Press, 1965), p. 30.
19. Christopher Kiesling brings this same point out nicely in his article "Liturgical Pedagogics," in James Michael Lee and Patrick C. Rooney, editors, *Toward a Future for Religious Education*, pp. 115-120.
20. John Dewey, *Philosophy and Civilization* (New York: Putnam, 1931), p. 26.
21. Gerard A. Pottebaum, "Where Is Your Doctrine?: The New Direction of Religious Education," in *New Book Review*, nv., nd., p. 9.
22. Gabriel Moran, *Catechesis of Revelation* (New York: Herder and Herder, 1966), pp. 46-47.
23. This is not to deny the receptivity aspect of experience or the importance of the learning of and the adherence to doctrine and dogma. Rather it is to put the spotlight on the creative and active aspect of experience.
24. John Dewey, *Experience and Education*, pp. 50-51.
25. Harold W. Bernard, *Adolescent Development in American Culture* (Yonkers, New York: Harcourt, Brace and World, 1957), p. 383.
26. For the exposition of this last point, I am indebted to W. Norris Clark who discussed it at length in his course on Thomistic epistemology during the 1959-1960 academic year at Fordham University.
27. Gabriel Moran, *Catechesis of Revelation*, p. 51.
28. J. Donald Butler, *Religious Education: The Foundations and Practice of Nurture* (New York: Harper & Row, 1962), p. 1.
29. Lecture delivered by Jeffrey Keefe to the faculty and students of the department of graduate studies in education, University of Notre Dame, July, 1967.
30. David R. Hunter, *Christian Education as Engagement* (New York: Seabury, 1963), p. 25.
31. Peter L. Berger *The Sacred Canopy: Elements of a Sociological Theory of Religion* (New York: Doubleday, 1967), p. 15; see also Donald E. Miller, "Religious Education as a Discipline: Christian Education as a Contextual Discipline," in *Religious Education*, LXII, September-October, 1967, p. 423.
32. Doubtless many traditional Christians, notably conservative Catholics, would disagree, contending that church is coextensive with institutionalized structure. However, I believe that to equate church with an institutionalized structure is to rob the church of much of its fluidity, elasticity, and embraceability. I suggest in this connection that conservatively-oriented Chris-

tians align their concept of the church society with that rich and encompassing reality called baptism of desire.

33. Bernard Berelson and Gary A. Steiner, *Human Behavior: An Inventory of Scientific Findings* (New York: Harcourt, Brace and World, 1964), pp. 643-649.

34. See Robert J. Havighurst and Bernice L. Neugarten, *Society and Education*, 3d ed. (Boston: Allyn and Bacon, 1967), p. 127.

35. As I explained in footnote 32, in cases of this type, I do not believe that such persons are therefore necessarily de facto outside the church society if they fall within the boundaries of baptism of desire, broadly considered. However, for the more conservatively oriented Christian, such persons would in all probability be regarded as outside the church (*extra ecclesiam*).

36. Havighurst and Neugarten, *Society and Education*, p. 125.

37. Floyd Henry Allport, *Institutional Behavior* (Chapel Hill, North Carolina: University of North Carolina Press, 1933), pp. 34-46.

38. Vincent Novak observes that in its pre-Christian forms, kerygma is even older than the Christian church, dating back to ancient Homeric literature. See Vincent M. Novak, "The Kerygma in Religious Education," in *Catholic School Journal*, LX, April, 1960, p. 41.

39. Josef Andreas Jungmann, *Handing on the Faith: A Manual of Catechetics*, p. 387.

40. This was the ecclesiastical use of this Greek term. In secular usage, catechesis meant "down," "to sound," "to resound."

41. See Francis Somerville, "What Does 'Kerygmatic' Mean?" in *Guide*, CLXI, October, 1961, pp. 8-9.

42. This threefold distinction of kerygma, catechesis, and didascalia was underscored and clarified by André Rétif in his 1948 doctoral dissertation, "*La Prédication kérygmatique dans les Actes des Apôtres*," presented and defended at the Gregorian University (Rome). A summary of some of the more salient conclusions of this dissertation can be found in the informative article by Rétif, "*Qu'est-ce que le Kérygme?*" in *Nouvelle Revue Théologique*, LXXI, 1949, pp. 910-922. Rétif's textual analysis of scripture in connection with the kerygma is of especial interest. Indeed, Rétif's analysis of the pertinent new testament texts indicates that while the three stages of kerygma, catechesis, and didascalia operationally described the whole of the Apostles' teaching activity, nonetheless the terminology of the scripture is sufficiently fluid to indicate that these three stages were not always demarked so clearly in actual practice. This is particularly true of the kerygma.

43. See, for example, F. X. Murphy, "Catechesis, I, (Early Christian)," in *New Catholic Encyclopedia*, Volume 3 (New York:

McGraw-Hill, 1967), p. 208.

44. Even in these two instances there possibly took place some catechesis as Peter and Philip announced and explained the good news of Jesus's death and resurrection.

45. Jules Lebreton and Jacques Zeiller, *The History of the Primitive Church*, Volume II, translated by Ernest C. Messinger (New York: Macmillan, 1947), pp. 692-696; Josef Andreas Jungmann, *Handing on the Faith: A Manual of Catechetics*, p. 2.

46. See, for example, Jules Laurence Moreau, "Kerygma," in Kendig Brubaker Cully, editor, *The Westminster Dictionary of Christian Education* (Philadelphia: Westminster, 1963), pp. 364-365; and E. F. Malone, "Kerygma: Dogmatic Theology," in *New Catholic Encyclopedia*, Volume 8, pp. 168-169.

47. It should be noted that in Europe particularly, this general agreement among Americans concerning the nature of kerygma is not universally shared. Domenico Grasso has nicely summed up the various interpretations of kerygma which the Continentals, notably the theologians rather than the religious educationists among them, have given to the term kerygma. See Domenico Grasso, *Proclaiming God's Message: A Study in the Theology of Preaching* (Notre Dame, Indiana: University of Notre Dame Press, 1965), pp. 243-248.

48. C. H. Dodd, *The Apostolic Preaching and Its Developments: Three Lectures* (London: Hodder and Stroughton, 1936, reset in 1944).

49. Josef Andreas Jungmann, *Die Frohbotschaft und unsere Glaubensverkündigung* (Regensburg, Deutschland: Pustet, 1936).

50. See Léon de Coninck, "La Théologie Kérygmatique," in *Lumen Vitae*, III, Janvier-Mars, 1948, pp. 103-115.

51. On this point, see F. X. Murphy, "Kerygma," in *The New Catholic Encyclopedia*, Volume 8, p. 167.

52. Alfonso M. Nebreda, *Kerygma in Crisis?* (Chicago: Loyola University Press, 1965), p. 65.

53. Vincent M. Novak, "The Kerygma in Religious Education," p. 41.

54. See Paul Hitz, *To Preach the Gospel*, translated by Rosemary Sheed (New York: Sheed & Ward, 1963), pp. 124-130.

55. Bernard Cooke, "Theology and Catechetical Renewal," in Johannes Hofinger and Theodore C. Stone, editors, *Pastoral Catechetics* (New York: Herder and Herder, 1964,), p. 89.

56. Johannes Hofinger, *The Art of Teaching Christian Doctrine: The Good News and Its Proclamation*, 2d ed. (Notre Dame, Indiana: University of Notre Dame Press, 1962), p. 52.

57. Gerard Sloyan, "What Should Children's Catechisms Be Like?" in Johannes Hofinger and Theodore Stone, editors, *Pastoral*

Catechetics, p. 34.

58. Didier Piveteau, "Biblical Pedagogics," in James Michael Lee and Patrick C. Rooney, editors, *Toward a Future for Religious Education*, pp. 101-107.

59. Ross Snyder, "Group Theory and Religious Education," in Marvin J. Taylor, editor, *An Introduction to Christian Education* (Nashville, Tennessee: Abingdon, 1966), p. 284.

60. Carl R. Rogers, *On Becoming a Person* (Boston: Houghton Mifflin, 1961), pp. 104-105.

61. This is particularly true of the European Roman Catholic specialists in religious instruction. See, for example, Johannes Hofinger, *The Art of Teaching Christian Doctrine: The Good News and Its Proclamation*, p. 200; and Josef Andreas Jungmann, *Handing on the Faith: A Manual of Catechetics*, p. 202.

62. *Ibid.*

63. Johannes Hofinger, *The Art of Teaching Christian Doctrine: The Good News and Its Proclamation*, p. 200.

64. On this point, see Thomas Aquinas, *De Veritate*, q. XI, a. 1.

65. Josef Goldbrunner, "Catechetical Method," in Josef Goldbrunner, editor, *New Catechetical Methods*, translated by M. Veronica Riedl (Notre Dame, Indiana: University of Notre Dame Press, 1965), p. 53.

66. See, for example, Lee J. Cronbach, *Educational Psychology*, 2d ed. (New York: Harcourt, Brace and World, 1963).

67. Bernard Berelson and Gary A. Steiner, *Human Behavior: An Inventory of Scientific Findings*, p. 614.

68. See, for example, Gabriel Moran, *Vision and Tactics* (New York: Herder and Herder, 1968).

69. Gabriel Marcel, *Le Mystère de l'Etre*, volume I, *Réflexion et Mystère* (Paris: Aubier, 1951), pp. 68-74.

70. It should be noted that I use the term "in a certain way." Orthodoxy is not a total deviation from the above-mentioned kind of norm, but rather a personalizing process which, per se, implies a living of this norm in a way at once similar to and unique from both abstract doctrinal propositions and a society's abstract formulation of that norm.

71. Gabriel Marcel, *Creative Fidelity*, translated by Robert Rosthal (New York: Farrar, Strauss, 1964), pp. 184-209.

72. Josef Goldbrunner, "Catechetical Method," p. 52.

73. See Robert J. Havighurst, *Developmental Tasks in Education*, 2d ed. (New York: McKay, 1952).

CHAPTER THREE

THE MANNER

*"In our era, the road to holiness
necessarily passes through the
world of action."*
— Dag Hammarskjöld[1]

INTRODUCTION

The process of religious instruction has certain characteristic features which specify it as a particular kind of activity. In a world deeply interconnected at every level of existence, it is impossible for any one mode of reality such as religious instruction to have facets each of which is totally different from all other sectors of existence. Notwithstanding, on the overall religious landscape, there is a certain sector whose contours set off and demark it as the enterprise of religious instruction. It is the manner in which these contours are shaped, it is the way in which these features hang together that constitute the theme of this chapter.

FACILITATION OF LEARNING

By facilitation I mean the process by which the significant variables in the learning situation are consciously and deliberatively structured so that desired learning outcomes tend to be induced. Facilitation is the enabling function in the work of instruction. Facilitation thus represents the process by and through which the significant variables (including the teacher) in the learning situation are promotive of learning in an individual. Facilitation is a full-fledged process in its own right. It is not a watering-down activity; it is not a kind of popularizing; it is not a greasing of the rails of learning; it is not another name for motivation.

As I have just mentioned, the teacher is one of the variables, and indeed usually the most significant variable in the facilitational endeavor. In terms of the teacher, facilitation can be said to describe the operation in the concrete of the complex of enabling behaviors which comprise his teaching activity. Facilitation implies a process which of its nature is not necessarily linked to one or another product content. In other words, facilitation is the enabling function which goes on no matter what product content or specific subject matter is being facilitated. Facilitation is not simply the teacher's "behavior repertoire," to use David Ryans's expression.[2] Rather, facilitation constitutes this behavioral repertoire *in action*. As far as the teacher variable in the learning situation is concerned, facilitation represents the efficacious timing of instructional efforts. In other words, it is teaching at the teachable moment. Robert Havighurst relates this timing of the teachable moment to the readiness of the learner. In Havighurst's view, readiness is simply the moment when the learner has reached a particular task level in the evolution of his needs and of his developmental self-system.[3]

Facilitation is a total process, the entire fluid entity of helping. It is not a kind of link between sender (teacher) and receiver (student), to use the image of the traditional conception of religious instruction. Facilitation is not a way of somehow "handing on" the content to be learned. Quite the opposite. Facilitation is the total helping process of enabling the individual to learn for himself all the various "contents," the process content as well as the product content, the affective content as well as the cognitive content, the nonverbal content as well as the verbal content. Facilitation is not a transfer of knowledge from the mind of the teacher to the mind of the students. Instead, facilitation is the deliberative arrangement of the conditions of learning whereby the individual is enabled to learn what he can learn in terms of where he is developmentally here and now. Facilitation, then, is at the very core of teaching.

It should be noted that teaching constitutes only one mode of facilitation. There are many other modes of facilitation, such as counseling facilitation, health facilitation, political facilitation, and so on. In Plato's terminology, teaching "participates" as a specific representation or mode of the overall facilitation process. In the instructional enterprise, the pedagogical act basically is a facilitating process which induces desired behavioral outcomes in the learner.

Facilitation implies that religious instruction, though always pointed toward the promotion of specific behavioral outcomes in learners, is nonetheless characterized by a large degree of free-swingingness on the part of the teacher. This free-swingingness is conducive to providing that kind of open and expansive learning climate which can give full range to the myriad ways in which God's grace and love work in the individual learner. It is a prime task of religious instruction to help in enabling the flow of God's grace into the life of the learner. The facilitation process, supple and free-flowing as it is, is uniquely geared to establishing the mobile conditions which are most apt for allowing God's grace to become operable within a given situation. This notion is in contrast to the fidelity approach with its emphasis on the direct verbal transmission of intellectual data and product content, with its stress on the pupil interacting only with the teacher (while the other learners could, at best, merely watch this interaction); thus the fidelity approach represents an instructional situation so restrictive and so cooped-in that God's grace can only slip through the cracks of the bolted-down pedagogical window.[4]

The facilitation process as it operates in the teaching-learning situation is a conscious and deliberative act. In other words, teaching represents a situation which is so carefully shaped as to constitute an environment in which the probability that the learner will acquire the desired outcome is brought to the highest possible point. Teaching is not an activity in which any variable should be left to chance; indeed, the more variables in the learning activity which are left to chance, the less probable it is that the desired learning outcomes will be produced. What I am saying, then, is that teaching is a deliberative act and as such is diametrically opposed to a formless "happening." A "happening" might be interesting; it might even be relevant, but it is not teaching. Whatever learning might occur during a "happening" typically results by accident. Let us hope that causing learning is not an accidental process. Nor is erecting a "happening" a prerequisite of a free-swinging lesson. As I mentioned in the preceding paragraph, the facilitational process itself, occurring as it does within a shaped environment, inherently involves a large degree of suppleness. This suppleness and free-swingingness result in part from the way in which the variables present within the learning environment constantly interact with each other, and also in part from the manner in which the teacher continually and deliberatively realigns these instructional variables during the lesson so as to enhance the probability of learning.

A word or two on the nature and function of variables might be in order here. A variable is a reality which assumes a different function or value according to (i.e., varying with) the kind of context in which it is situated. In social situations such as the instructional setting, the teacher, the learner, and the environmental factors are all variables. Thus, for example, Johnny (learner variable) behaves differently (behavior variable) vis-à-vis teacher "X" (teacher variable) in religion class (environment variable) than he does with another set of teachers, areas of study, and so forth. In other words, the teaching-learning situation comprises a set of interactive variables which assume different colorations, functions, and potencies after the manner in which they interact. Facilitation refers to the conscious deliberative process by which the teacher initially shapes and then implements the instructional variables to enable the desired learning outcome to come to pass.

Religious instruction is at once scientific and artistic. In its scientific aspect, it must be constantly rooted in the findings and principles of social science with regard to the way in which religious learning is facilitated and to the way in which behavior in the learner is modified along religious lines. Also, it must be continually nourished by the findings and the spirit and the ways of theological science. But religious instruction as an artistic activity consists in the actual skill and proficiency of facilitating desired behavioral outcomes in learners. The religion teacher in the field not only ought to be adequately grounded in the science of religious instruction, but also must possess to a sufficiently high level the proficiency skills involved in facilitating religious behaviors in learners.

If the quality of the enterprise of religious instruction has remained at a fairly low plane throughout the centuries, it is largely due to the fact that insufficient stress has been placed on the process and function of facilitation in the work of religious instruction. Almost all the efforts of theologians and religious educationists have centered around what to facilitate rather than on the facilitation process itself. While improvement in the theological ways of looking at and interpreting product content is helpful and essential to the task of religious instruction, nonetheless, the real breakthrough in significantly upgrading religious instruction will come about principally by converging our research and training efforts on that complex of facilitation activities which spell the success or failure of a concrete religion class. How most efficiently to facilitate learning should represent the central quest of both religious educationists and of religious educators. In the past, religious educationists as well as those theologians interested in religious instruction rarely considered the wide variety and complex interaction among the host of variables involved in the facilitation process. These specialists typically considered the product content or subject matter as the central variable, and all but banished consideration of the other variables in the teaching-learning-situations — variables which, in actual fact, are more significant and more central than product content in the facilitation of learning.[5] When indeed these specialists did consider the facilitation function, they usually subsumed it under the rubric of "motivation," wrote a few inspiring but vague words of exhortation to the teacher, and left the matter at that. But the facilitation of learning involves a host of variables, each of which acts and interacts with each other in different ways under different learning situations. It is primarily through proficiency in fashioning the complex of these variables into a situation which will facilitate learning that religious instruction will be rendered effective. It is this facilitation process, or what Klemens Tilmann terms "helping men to become Christians," which comprises the basic functional shape of the task of religious instruction.[6]

As I emphasized in the first chapter, the goal-oriented task of religious instruction is the facilitation of Christian living in learners. This very facilitation of Christian living is itself a valuable process content and learning outcome of the religious instruction act. In addition, the facilitation function produces process and product outcomes which follow from and extend the facilitation function. Process outcomes of this sort include the bringing of the learners to a more profound relationship with Jesus, helping them grow in their relationship with God and with others, gaining deeper Christian values and attitudes, and so forth.[7] Product outcomes also form a vital and essential component of the totality of that which the learner acquires in the religious education endeavor. The emphasis which I have been placing on the premium of process content at every stage of the religious education enterprise should not be taken as in any way a denigration of the pivotal importance of product outcomes. Rather, this accentuation is to accord product outcomes their rightful place in the galaxy of those things learned in formal or informal religious instruction activities. Product outcomes are indeed important; after all the teacher must facilitate a product as well as a process outcome. It is impossible to facilitate simply process.

The essential place of product outcomes in the work of religious instruction serves to illustrate one of the fundamental differences between religious instruction and religious counseling. As I indicated at the very outset of this book, there is a basic difference between the instructional function and the counseling function in the enterprise of education. Since the beginning of the 1960's, a keen dissatisfaction with the old ways of religious instruction, combined perhaps with a legitimate dynamic release of the inner need-structure and emotional restraints of many religion teachers, resulted in all too frequent substitution of religious counseling for religious instruction. One such substitution was the emergence of the so-called "encounter catechetics," which at bottom is a form of religious counseling. Religious counseling, while complementing the work of religious instruction, can never serve as a substitute for it. I should like to indicate just a few of the many ways in which religious instruction is sharply divergent from religious counseling on the axis of the facilitation function.[8]

Religious instruction aims at facilitating both product and process outcomes in a person, whereas religious counseling aims at facilitating process outcomes exclusively. There are definite product learnings essential to the task of religious instruction. Such learnings include the acquisition of appropriate religious knowledge, a grasp of religious meanings, an understanding of religious behavior, and so forth. Yet even in the process dimension, the facilitating roles of religious instruction and religious counseling differ. Religious counseling is totally and exclusively focused on facilitating the process whereby the client becomes a fully functioning person. On the other hand, religious instruction, while also focused on facilitating the process whereby the learner becomes a fully functioning person is in addition focused on enabling the individual to incorporate into his personal lifestyle certain behaviors which can be termed Christian in both the broad and strict sense of that term. In other words, unlike religious counseling, religious instruction takes the facilitation of a fully functioning person as *a* basic but not an exclusive task. Religious instruction, unlike religious counseling, facilitates the learner to become a fully functioning person as both an important behavioral outcome and also as a way of more effectively promoting the acquisition of other product and process outcomes.[9] Religious counseling starts with the person, works completely through him, and ends in him. Religious instruction starts with both the person and God's revelation, works through both of these, and ends in the person.

Religious instruction aims at facilitating self-actualization in the learner, as that self-actualization is related both to preplanned learning outcomes and to desired changes in behavior. Religious counseling aims at facilitating self-actualization in and through itself. There are no previously specified desirable changes in behavior in the counseling enterprise. Instead, counseling is focused entirely on helping the individual to develop in that direction where his own present potentialities are taking him.[10]

Religious instruction is judgmental in the sense that the norm for assessing its effectiveness is the degree to which desired changes in the learner's behavior actually took place. This implies that the teacher and the learner are constantly judging, evaluating, and working to improve the extent to which the learner is achieving these preset behavioral goals of the class or the lesson. Religious counseling is nonjudgmental since both the facilitator and the client totally and unconditionally accept the client, with absolutely no reference to any set of norms or expected behaviors other than the client's growing toward becoming a fully functioning person.

In religious instruction the situation plays a key role; it is the situation, with all its carefully structured learning stimuli, which will bring about the desired behavioral outcomes. The teacher represents only one — and sometimes not the most prominent or important — of the variables in the learning situation. In religious counseling, the situation is an insignificant and inconsequential aspect of the facilitation process. It is the depth and freedom and authenticity of the relationship between counselor and client which form the totality of the learning variables.

The contrasts I have made between religious instruction and religious counseling are intended to be suggestive rather than exhaustive of the differences between these two enabling processes. Further, it is not legitimate either to indicate that religious instruction is superior to religious counseling, or that religious counseling is more important than religious instruction. Each of these two kinds of facilitation activities is essential and complementary in the total enterprise of religious education. Each achieves a behavioral outcome in the learner which the other does not achieve, or at least does not achieve as well. To a certain extent there is a partial — but only a partial — overlapping in the goals, roles, and functions of religious instruction and religious counseling. This is quite natural and to be expected, since in all of flesh-and-blood living, no two things are ever mutually or totally exclusive. An effective and fruitful religious education program features both the instructional service and the counseling service utilized in a complementary and mutually enriching fashion by professionally prepared and competent facilitators.

BEHAVIORAL MODIFICATION

Human behavior, as defined by social scientists, denotes any activity of a person. Human behavior, then, is a broad term signifying anything which an individual does, including overt physical action, internal physiological and emotional processes, and implicit mental activity.[11] Behavior may be classed as overt or inner. Overt behavior is that kind of human activity which can be directly observed by another individual or by some sort of measuring instrument. Walking, singing, performing a deed — these are kinds of overt behavior. Inner behavior is that kind of human activity which cannot be directly observed by another individual or by some sort of measuring device. Thinking, perceiving, loving — these are examples of inner behavior.

Simply defined, learning is a change or modification in behavior.[12] The task of religious instruction is to facilitate learning in the individual. How then does the teacher truly know when and what the individual has learned? Only by observing a change or modification in the behavior of an individual along the lines which the teacher was attempting to facilitate. Change in overt behavior is relatively simple to assess. If we wish to teach a person who is unable to paint a picture of a sailing ship to actually paint such a picture, and that person does in fact paint this picture, we can directly observe that he has modified or changed his behavior from a state of nonskill to one of skill in painting this picture. Change in inner behavior, on the other hand, is far more difficult to assess. Suppose, for example, we wish to teach a person to increase his love of God. How do we accurately determine whether he has indeed changed his behavior in the direction of a positive increase in love of God? Obviously we cannot jump inside the person to find out. We can only infer that he has modified his inner behavior along this line by observing him perform certain overt acts which are typically correlated with a love of God, such as increase in attendance at church services, performing for his neighbors more deeds which can be labeled "charitable," and so on. Yet even here we cannot be totally certain that he has increased his love of God because he might be performing these acts for reasons quite different from the love of God, for example, to please the teacher and so get a higher mark, or to be admired by his peer group. The determination of whether learning has taken place, as well as the degree to which learning has taken place — particularly in the case of inner behavior — is basically an inference from the individual's exterior observable performance. We can never be absolutely sure that the individual has truly modified his behavior along the lines we have been attempting to facilitate. Such is the fallout of the inferential process. Yet the more closely we can validate that certain performance outcomes are closely correlated with the inferred learning, the more probably correct is our judgment that the person has learned what was intended to be learned. Eliciting performance or overt behavior in the learners is, consequently, of crucial importance in the work of religious instruction.

A major theme of this book is that *religious instruction consists in facilitating the modification of the learner's behavior along desired religious lines.* As I have previously indicated, behavior is a social-science term to indicate all activity of the human organism, both inner and overt. Hence behavioral modification along religious lines comes under the purview of the task of religious instruction in one way or another. Religious instruction has as a cardinal goal the modification of a learner's cognitive behavior so that he gains the appropriate religious knowledges and understandings and therefore can make an intellectual synthesis of faith and cognition in his own life. Religious instruction has as a second cardinal goal the modification of a learner's affective behavior so that he acquires the processes of awaring, valuing, and forming attitudes about religious and religious-related reality. Religious instruction has as a third cardinal goal the modification of the learner's product behavior so that he can attain an appropriate command of the relevant existential, theological, and theologically-related subject matter. Religious instruction has as a fourth cardinal goal the modification of the learner's process behavior, so that he can acquire the ongoing patterns, operations, and dynamics of thought, feeling, and action as related to religious living.

Religious instruction at its highest level consists in facilitating the modification of the learner's entire behavioral pattern along religious lines. In other words, religious instruction has as its central task the modification of the learner's inner and overt behaviors, the modification of his product and process behaviors, the modification of his cognitive and affective behaviors, and the modification of his lifestyle as he acts himself out in everyday living. In short, the basic role of religious instruction is to facilitate that total behavioral modification which can be termed "enhanced Christian living." It is the integration of the learner's more specified behaviors such as cognitive and affective behaviors into a more generalized Christian lifestyle which comprises total behavioral modification. Indeed, as Robert O'Gorman once reminded me, man's fundamental nature is such as to demand a behavioral or lifestyle expression for anything that is real in him. For the Christian, such an expression is, as it were, a double imperative for self-realization.

The objective of the overall enterprise of religious instruction is a behavioral outcome in terms of the learner's life. Only in this way can religious instruction have significance as an endeavor as well as a learner-oriented activity of enablement. Asahel Woodruff puts it nicely when he remarks that all significant major educational objectives consist of ways of behaving.[13] The kinds of learning experiences provided through religious instruction, therefore, should be selected on the basis of their efficacy in modifying the learner's behavior in a desired direction. This is underscored by the fact that learning is only an inference from observable behavior and from performance. Consequently unless the learner's performance is changed, a teacher or religious instruction facilitator cannot ascertain whether cognitions or affects, for example, have been truly learned. Religious instruction is aimed at a change not only in personal commitment but in personal overt lifestyle as well. A prime objective of religious instruction is an extension or "outering" of the learning process, to borrow an expressive phrase from Marshall McLuhan.[14]

Christian living is a behavioral thing. Further, Christian living is a total behavior pattern, an operationalized lifestyle. To serve as an enabler in the process of religious instruction is to seek to facilitate the modification of a learner's total Christian behavioral lifestyle in an advancing and enhancing manner. The religion teacher, in his most professionally-oriented reflective moments, asks himself: "What difference does my religion class make in the lives of the learners? Do the learners behave in a more Christian manner as a result of the learning experiences I am providing them?"

Even the most cursory glance at the gospels reveals that Jesus regarded himself as a facilitator of behavioral modification.[15] Further, Jesus continually identified his own lifestyle behaviorally rather than notionally. This is readily seen, for example, in the incident when the imprisoned John the Baptist sent his own disciples to find out from Jesus whether or not the Nazarene was truly the

Messias. John's disciples put the question straightforward to Jesus. Jesus's answer is most revealing. He does not give John's disciples a theological discourse on the nature of God. He does not even answer "Yes." Instead, Jesus says: "Go and tell John what your own eyes and ears have witnessed, how the blind see, the lame walk, how the lepers are made clean and the deaf are enabled to hear, how the dead are raised to life, and how the poor people have the gospel preached to them" (Matthew 11:6; also Luke 7:22). Jesus does not tell John's men what the nature of the Messias is, but rather what he is doing, how he is behaving. It is from Jesus's observable behaviors that John has to infer whether or not Jesus is indeed the awaited one. So too with the learner in the religious instruction enterprise; it is the total lifestyle and behavioral pattern which represent incarnated personalized Christianity.

The facilitation process is a neutral activity. That is to say, the facilitation process is not effective in its own right. It is effective only insofar as the behavioral modification which is facilitated effects the learner in the desired direction. Unless the behaviors which were intended to be facilitated are indeed facilitated, the facilitation process has become miseducative rather than educative. Thus for example, the teacher and a group of adult learners, in their preplanning sessions, have decided that one broad behavioral outcome to be facilitated by their two-year course of study is an increase in the learner's religious values as measured by the Religious Scale of the Allport-Vernon-Lindzey *Study of Values.* Using the standard pre-test-post-test technique, it is discovered that at the end of the two-year period of time the learner's behavior has indeed been modified, but in the wrong direction, namely of being less religious. Whereas a behavioral modification in the learner was facilitated, [16] the facilitation was not effective because the *desired* learning outcome (effect) was not brought to pass.

Religious instruction, then, consists in so structuring the learning situation that the modification of the learner's behavior along desired religious lines will be facilitated in the most fruitful and effective manner possible. Later in this chapter, I will return to this axial theme of "structuring the learning situation." For now, however, I wish to point out that the total situation itself, with all the many variables in that situation existentially interacting with the learner, represents the most effective and most fruitful kind of facilitation process in terms of bringing to pass the desired behavioral outcomes. Yet all too often, religious instruction activities are characterized by the exceedingly heavy stress placed on only one variable in the student's situational field, namely the teacher. But it is in the interaction with the total existential situation qua situation, and with the variables in that situation which are significant and meaningful to him, that the learner is most effectively facilitated to attain the desired behavioral outcomes. Just a cursory look at the relevant empirical research findings,[17] at the most significant educative moments in one's own personal experience, and finally at the way in which Jesus facilitated learning in the apostles, clearly indicates that behavioral modification is most effectively facilitated by deliberatively shaping the entire learning environment — not by constricting the learner's focus in this environment to the teacher alone.

Desired learning outcomes — that is, educational goals — are rendered effective to the extent that they are both framed and taught for in terms of observable behavior. Objectives in religious instruction remain on the theoretical and hoped-for levels until they have become actual learning outcomes in the life of the individual learner. Objectives form the rationale and *terminus ad quem* for the process of facilitating behavioral modification. But if specific performance outcomes are not caused in the learner through the instructional activity, then the objectives have not been realized or accomplished. Formal statements by church bodies and episcopal committees typically are replete with lofty and worthwhile learning objectives for religious instruction. It would be far more helpful to religion teachers and administrators in the field if these statements were recast into specific behavioral modifications and performance outcomes to be facilitated and achieved.

Performance or behavioral outcomes are indispensable to religious instruction because it is only by either directly observing or inferring from these outcomes that one can say with any sort of validity that learners have actually learned what was intended. Performance or behavioral outcomes in the cognitive sphere, while vital and indispensable in religious instruction, nevertheless should not comprise the sole criterion or goal. Christian lifestyle in terms of the learner's affective behaviors, nonverbal behaviors, and most notably in terms of his overt behaviors, should also be worked for and assessed. For far too long, religion teachers and administrators have assumed that a strong tendency, if not an actual one-to-one link, exists for an individual who has acquired desired cognitive behaviors to transfer these behaviors into other sectors of his life. Not since

Plato has any major thinker assumed that knowledge equals virtue or directly yields virtue. On the empirical level, the careful researches made by Hugh Hartshorne and Mark. A. May in their Character Education Inquiry project in the 1920's have pretty much laid to permanent rest the notion that a person either automatically or almost always transfers knowledge and understanding of religious doctrine and morals into his personal lifestyle.[18] On a more homespun level, I vividly recall an incident which came to my attention several years ago. It seems that a religion teacher in a Roman Catholic high school in a middle-sized midwestern industrial city had in his senior class a boy who throughout his high school career scored between 95% and 100% on his cognitively-based religion examinations. All his religion teachers agreed that at graduation this boy would receive the religion medal for outstanding performance in religion during his secondary school career. Early in the spring of his senior year, the school principal, reviewing the attendance records, by chance noticed that this youth had been absent from school each Friday since midway in his junior year. The senior grade adviser and the religion teacher were summoned to the principal's office, whereupon they advised the principal that they knew of the boy's habitual Friday absences but were not overly concerned because they assumed he was spending the day with his parents. Besides, the two teachers observed, a boy with such good marks in religion class surely would not be absent from class except for some worthy purpose. The principal contacted the youth's parents who expressed surprise because they had believed all along that their son was spending long weekends with the religious brothers who operated the high school. Intensive investigation revealed that early every Friday morning the boy would leave for another city in the state where he would spend the long weekend working with one of the largest rings of stolen automobiles in the midwest. Surely this story illustrates the point that the religion teacher cannot assume or suppose that the learner will transfer cognitive learnings into other areas of his personality structure and behavioral pattern.

A carefully conducted, large-scale research investigation under-taken by Andrew Greeley and Peter Rossi of Catholic adults who attended Catholic schools and of Catholic adults who had attended public schools indicated that the adults who attended Catholic schools seemed to score higher on the Greeley-Rossi test items on religious knowledge than those who did not attend Catholic schools.

However, on the Greeley-Rossi measures of the practice of the virtue of charity — which the investigators posited as the "essence of Christianity" — there was no significant difference in the measured charitable behaviors of the two groups of adults. Greeley and Rossi concluded that if the religiously-oriented instructional program of Catholic schools is "turning out people who are more diligent in the practice of love of neighbor, the fact is not confirmed by the evidence available to us."[19]

Ronald Johnstone made a well-executed empirical study of two large and representative groups of Missouri Synod Lutheran youth. One group was attending Lutheran schools while the other group was not attending such schools. Johnstone found that those youths who attended the Lutheran schools scored higher in a test on certain kinds of biblical knowledge and doctrinal understanding than did those youths who attended public schools. But the investigator also discovered that there appeared to be no significant differences between the broadly based Christian lifestyle of the two groups.[20]

The acquisition by the learner of cognitive religious outcomes does not of itself imply transfer to other aspects of his behavioral pattern or to the broad sweep of his lifestyle taken as a whole. Now this suggests that to be effective in terms of modifying the lifestyle of the learner along religious lines, the activity of religious instruction should be such that it consists of an amalgam of behavioral outcomes each of which reinforces the other. In other words, the religion class, whether formal or informal, should be so structured that a specified cognitive outcome, for example, will be learned in concert with an affective outcome and an overt behavioral outcome so that each outcome will expand and reinforce the others. Only through this multipronged approach is it possible to enable any one outcome to be transferred into all the sectors of the learner's lifestyle and behavioral pattern.

Perhaps the importance of what I have just stated can be pointed up by recalling an additional research finding of the Greeley-Rossi and the Johnstone empirical investigations. The Greeley-Rossi study found that there was a somewhat higher rate of attendance at church services and of reception of the sacraments by Catholic adults who had been enrolled in the religiously-oriented Catholic school instructional program as compared to those Catholic adults who had gone to public schools.[21] Similarly, Johnstone discovered that there was a somewhat elevated rate of attendance at church services by those Missouri Synod Lutheran youths who were enrolled in the

religiously-oriented Lutheran school instructional program as compared to those Lutheran youths who were attending public
schools.[22] Interestingly, the Greeley-Rossi study and the Johnstone
study both concluded that there was no significant difference in the
overall and essential Christian-living lifestyle of those persons who
had enrolled in the religiously-oriented church-related schools as
compared to those who attended the public schools. Yet it will be
recalled that the Greeley-Rossi study and the Johnstone study
reported a somewhat higher rate of religious knowledge among the
parochial school students as compared to those of the faith who had
not attended the parochial school. What, then, do these data suggest
relative to the findings on the one hand that persons attending
parochial schools have higher cognitive religious behaviors and higher
church attendance behaviors than persons of the faith attending
public schools, while on the other hand not differing significantly in
their overall Christian lifestyle and behavioral patterns from the
persons not attending parochial schools? These data imply that the
instructional activities in the parochial school were possibly such
that the cognitive behaviors and the church attendance behaviors
were not taught for in conjunction with other types of behaviors
such as affective behaviors and process behaviors. In other words, if
one behavior or a small set of behaviors is not taught in active
concert with the other significant behaviors in the learner's lifestyle
repertoire, there is a good probability that the original learned
behavior or small set of learned behaviors will remain in isolation in
the person's behavioral pattern instead of yeasting and reinforcing
other aspects of his total lifestyle.

One of the prime goals of religious instruction is to promote and
augment the transfer of learning. Transfer is "the application of
knowledge, skills, habits, attitudes or ideals acquired in one situation
to another situation for which they had not been specifically
learned."[23] The religion teacher aims at enabling the learner first to
transfer one specific behavioral outcome into the more generalized
pattern of his Christian lifestyle, and second to transfer this
generalized behavioral pattern into every situation he encounters in
life. My own review of the relevant empirical research concluded
that learners do not transfer automatically. Rather, transfer must be
a deliberate aim and ongoing pedagogical activity of the teacher and
the learning situation in general; in short, it must be consciously
worked for.[24] One of the most effective ways of accomplishing
transfer is to structure all the variables in the learning situation so

that they reinforce and expand each other in different but complementary manners. The function of the teacher is to so shape the learning situation that this complementary and expansive reinforcement on the part of all the variables converges to enhance the possibility of transfer. Transfer can be more effectively facilitated by the religion teacher structuring his teaching strategy in terms of learning experiences rather than in terms of content to be taught.[25] In other words, the *terminus a quo* of the class, as well as every point of the lesson's axis of ongoing development, should be radicated in the experiences which the learner is having and not on the content which the teacher wishes to teach. That is to say, the religion lesson should be architected from the inside out instead of from the outside in.[26] The act of religion teaching is at once an empirically research-based, intellectual, moral, and artistic enterprise of facilitating learning, and its goal is a progressively evolving operational unity of experience for the learner.

I should like to stress that behavior modification is not synonymous with psychological behaviorism[27] or Pavlovian conditioned reflex.[28] Behavior modification in religious instruction means the attempt to assist the learner to alter specific behaviors and indeed his entire lifestyle in a beneficial manner according both to the corpus of findings of the psychology of learning and to the Christian stance toward life. The use of the term "beneficial" serves to indicate that behavior modification is to be distinguished from certain types of totalitarian and enslaving manipulative activities such as brainwashing (which also seek to alter behavior, but in the interest of the manipulator rather than of the learner). The first control referent of the term "beneficial" is the corpus of findings of the psychology of learning, thus indicating that behavioral modification in religious instruction will be facilitated in accord with what is currently known and empirically verified about the way individuals actually learn and grow and mature. The second control referent of the term "beneficial" is the Christian stance toward life, thus indicating that behavioral modification in religious instruction will be facilitated in accord with the theological vision into the most fruitful kind of religious self-actualization.

Perhaps it might be helpful to give a rather dramatic example of how one person can modify the behavior of another by shaping and controlling the significant variables in the situation. Though this example is drawn from psychiatric rather than from instructional behavior modification, and though this example is not directly related to religious behavior modification, nonetheless I believe this illustration will serve to throw additional light on behavioral modification. A German psychotherapist named Katsch was treating a patient who complained of severe asthma attacks which took place regularly when the patient retired to bed with his wife. Psychotherapeutic sessions between Katsch and the patient had no effect on reducing the asthma attacks. However, these attacks ceased immediately and completely when Katsch altered one of the variables in the existential situation in which the attacks took place. What Katsch did was to remove a large picture of his patient's mother-in-law from its place on the wall. Apparently the mother-in-law played a key role in producing the conflict which manifested itself in the patient's asthma attacks.[29] Here we have a case of patient-enhancing behavioral modification effected through skillful restructuring of the learning situation.

The work of religious instruction is that of serving as a change agent in terms of both specific behaviors and overall Christian lifestyle of the learners. This change agent role is exercised through appropriate structuring of the learning situation so that behavioral modification in the learner is effected. Behavioral modification implies that objectives of religious instruction be conceptualized and framed behaviorally, and that the assessment of the degree to which the learner has acquired these objectives be made in terms of performance. There is a vast difference between learning and satisfaction. The religion teacher may feel the warm glow of satisfaction in believing that the learners' behavior has been modified. The learners might experience a deeply-felt sense of satisfaction in thinking that their own behavior has been modified in the desired direction. However, unless the learners can exhibit a definite intended learning in performance or behavior, there is little evidence to indicate that they have actually learned what was supposed to be learned. Conversely, a learner (or his teacher) might be dissatisfied with the class, but if the learner exhibits a definite learning in performance or in behavior, then there is solid reason to infer that he has actually learned. In other words, satisfaction or dissatisfaction is not necessarily a significant factor in assessing whether learning has taken place. It might be a clue — but either a leading or misleading clue. Performance is what counts.[30]

In his own religious instruction activities, Jesus continually framed his own role as teacher in behavioral or performance terms. Thus, for example, at the Last Supper, praying to the Father, Jesus said: "I have exalted your glory on earth, by accomplishing the task you gave me to do" (John 14:4). When describing the learning objectives for those who would be Christians, Jesus again states these objectives in terms of modifying behavior: "If any man wishes to be a follower of mine, let him renounce himself, and take up his cross, and follow me" (Matthew 16:24). Indeed, John the Baptist even went so far as to describe Jesus not in notional terms or in terms of an essence, but in behavioral terms: "Look, this is the lamb of God; look, this is he who takes away the sin of the world" (John 1:29).

OPERATIONALIZING

In the social and behavioral sciences, to operationalize is to make a concept an experience, or more precisely a specific kind of experience. Operationalizing, then, is existentially expressing in a specific behavior, or possibly in a bundle of specific behaviors, what a concept attempts to define in a generalization. A conceptual definition of sin might be that sin is a "transgression against God," or that sin is an evil act. On the other hand, an operational definition of sin might read something like: "man commits a sin when . . . he does such and such a specific behavior." The gospels report that Jesus continually operationalized in his religious instruction activities. Thus, for example, just before the Last Supper, Jesus told his apostles: "If anyone is to be my servant, he must follow my way; so shall my servant too be where I am" (John 12:26). The way which Jesus told his friends to follow consisted precisely in a set of concrete ways of behaving under a variety of circumstances. To be sure, the very word "following" connotes a behavioral pattern, a set of human operations. Certainly the significance of the earthly ministry of Jesus lies in the fact that it is a series of specific behaviors and bundles of behaviors, rather than a carefully formulated systematic set of doctrinal propositions. Jesus never wrote a systematic treatise on religious instruction or on theology; he simply operationalized Christian living in his everyday behaviors.

As it is applied to religious instruction, to operationalize is to highlight and to identify a specific performance from which religious learning can be inferred. To operationalize is to specify what precise behavioral activity the learner is engaged in. Further, operationalizing describes a performance or a behavioral outcome, rather than giving the content of the learning objective to be achieved. The following incident related in the gospel illustrates how Jesus operationalized the objective of personal eternal salvation:

And now a man came to him, and said, "Master, who is so good,
what must I do to win eternal life?" He said to him, "Why do you
come to me to ask of goodness? God is good, and he only. If you
wish to enter into life, keep the commandments." "Which
commandments?" he asked. Jesus said, "You shall not murder,
you shall not commit adultery, you shall not steal, you shall not
bear false witness. Honor your father and your mother, and love
your neighbor as yourself." "I have kept all these," the young
man told him, "ever since I grew up; where is it that I am
wanting?" Jesus said to him, "If you really want to be perfect, go
home and sell all that belongs to you; give it to the poor, so the
treasure you have shall be in heaven; then come back and follow
me" (Matthew 19:16-21).

In this activity of religiously instructing the young man through
the dialogue technique, Jesus tells the young man to do a concrete
behavioral act, to perform a highly specific task, namely to sell all
his possessions, give the money realized from the sale to the poor,
and then follow him. The behaviors which Jesus mentioned prior to
his admonition, while somewhat focused, nevertheless had a certain
note of generalization about them. Thus, for example, what specific
behaviors are involved in honoring one's father and mother? Jesus
operationalized Christian living vis-à-vis the man by suggesting to
him that he perform in a specific way; the objective of eternal life
for that man was operationalized by Jesus as selling his goods, giving
the proceeds to the poor, and then joining Jesus's little band of
apostles.

Operationalizing means that the teacher can describe what
specific behaviors the learner is here-and-now engaged in during any
one phase of his pursuit of attaining a desired learning objective. [31]
Applied to religious instruction, operationalizing signifies that until
the teacher can describe what the learner is doing as he "appre-
ciates" the virtue of charity or "practices" the virtue of charity, we
have not yet established a base for any valid assessment as to
whether or not the individual has learned the virtue of charity.
Learning, after all, is simply an inference from performance. As
recorded in the gospels, Jesus often operationalized in terms of
describing what specific behaviors his followers will be doing. At his
final meal with his apostles, Jesus remarked: "This is the greatest
love a man can show, that he lays down his life for his friends"
(John 15:13). Showing love for a friend is a generalized description
of a behavior. Dying for a friend operationalizes loving in a concrete,

specified, observable form. Laying down one's life describes what an individual is doing when he is showing love for his friend.

To operationalize is to translate into a precise measurable behavior some segment of a more general concept or of a more global behavioral pattern. To operationalize is to so describe the behavior as to establish the conditions for its measurable observation.[32] It is crucial to establish the conditions to make it possible to observe and measure the behavior, because only then can it be discovered whether in fact the learner has acquired the desired outcome. In a chemistry class, for example, when a pupil asserts that a particular substance is "hot," one cannot state with validity whether or not he has learned that this substance is hot, since what is hot for him might not be hot objectively. However, when the pupil frames his statement operationally — "This substance is boiling" — we can verify whether he has actually learned by observing and measuring the particular substance concerned. Jesus frequently operationalized in terms of observable, measurable learner behavior, as illustrated in the following parable:

> When a great multitude had gathered, and more came flocking to him out of the cities, he spoke to them in a parable. Here is the sower gone out to sow his seed. And as he sowed, there were some grains that fell beside the path, so that they were trodden underfoot, and the birds flew down and ate them. And others fell on the rocks, where they had withered as soon as they were up, because they had no moisture. And some fell among briars, and the briars grew up with them and smothered them. But others fell where the soil was good, and when these grew up they yielded a hundredfold. (Luke 8:4-8)

In each case the progress and fate of the grains could be observed and measured. From this observation, valid inferences on realization could be made.

Measurable observations of Christian living (the goal of religious instruction) are not simple or easy because of the many natural and supernatural variables present in the generalized behavior termed Christian living. For example, we may operationally assess the degree of an individual's learning of religious behaviors by measuring the increase in his score on the religious scale of the Allport-Vernon-Lindzey *Study of Values*. Yet it is common sense, as well as good empirical research methodology, to be aware that a valid assessment of the degree to which a person has advanced in Christian living must measure additional variables, such as his family behavior, his behavior with his peer group, and so on. Pastors, for example, typically define the religiosity of their congregations in operational terms, such as increase or decrease in church attendance or reception of the sacraments. However, everyone realizes that church attendance and sacramental reception are not necessarily valid representative samples of the overall religious lifestyle of the parishioners. In other words, these specific behaviors form a working hypothesis toward, rather than a valid index of, the more global religiosity of the congregation. What is urgently needed, therefore, is the development of a taxonomy of religious instruction objectives which can serve as the basis for obtaining valid operational answers as to the degree and intensity of the growth of learners in Christian living.

A taxonomy in the sense I am using it here is a scientific classification of the overall general objectives of religious instruction. What a taxonomy basically does is to classify in operational categories and terms the intended learning outcomes. The intended or desired behavioral modifications, not the actual learned behaviors, are what the taxonomy classifies. Curricular content or teacher behavior is not classified.

An effective taxonomy of instructional objectives for the religious domain has several characteristics. It is comprehensive; that is, it classifies the full range of religious behaviors. It differentiates in an ordered hierarchical manner the intended learning behaviors. It is logically developed and internally consistent. It is based on empirically verified facts and laws of human learning. Finally, it is a purely descriptive set of behavioral statements of religious instruction objectives represented in a relatively neutral fashion, so that both learners and teachers can operationalize these statements according to the exigencies of the individual learner, the group, and the local situation.

The development of a taxonomy of instructional objectives in the religious domain would serve several vital purposes. It would provide an orderly, sequential, operational, and progressively hierarchical classification of intended learning outcomes. It would set up valid criteria for religious learnings and render these learnings operational. It would establish a base for effective evaluation of the degree to which the learner's actual behavioral outcomes compare with the desired learning outcomes intended by the teacher, or by the teacher and the learner together. It would facilitate more effective teaching and teacher behaviors. Finally, it would reduce vague instructional objectives such as "learning faith" or "becoming more charitable" to specific operational behaviors, thus facilitating teaching, learning, and evaluation.

This last point is particularly worthy of elaboration. One reason for the relative ineffectiveness of contemporary religious instruction is the vagueness of its intended objectives. If the objectives are vague, it is difficult for learners to know exactly what they are to learn. Further, vague objectives do little more than obfuscate just what specific instructional behaviors the teacher is to employ in order to facilitate learning.

One of the principal priorities in religious instruction is to develop a valid and useful taxonomy of instructional objectives for the religious domain. Secular educationists have already developed two parallel taxonomies, one for the cognitive domain[33] and a second for the affective domain.[34] These two taxonomies have exerted a profound influence in operationalizing and significantly upgrading instructional objectives and curricula throughout the United States, chiefly in government schools at the elementary and secondary levels. A taxonomy for the religious domain would be difficult to develop. However, if the enterprise of religious instruction is to flourish, such a taxonomy ought to be constructed as rapidly as possible.

The supernatural element in religious instruction introduces a new and strong variable which at first blush would seem to place a difficult if not insuperable obstacle in the path of both operationalizing the objectives of religious instruction and of building a taxonomy of instructional objectives for the religious domain. The traditional theological view is that the best that religious instruction can accomplish is to lay the groundwork for an intermingling of God's revelatory activity in the learner's soul. Holiness is the activity of God working in a soul which cooperates with him. Religious instruction at its richest prepares a terrain which is favorable for this divine action. Now in one sense all this is quite true, but it is also true for any kind of learning. Thus Thomas Aquinas indicates that while God's activity is preeminent in all kinds of teaching and all kinds of learning (not in religious learning alone), nonetheless the effectiveness in the causing of learning by the scientifically-based performance of the educator cannot be denied on the ground that the workings of God are necessary at every stage in effecting learning in the individual.[35] To be sure, a special problem exists in the case of the learner's acquisition of religious behaviors as contrasted to the acquisition of what the older theologians termed his "secular or profane" behaviors. Nonetheless, it would appear that vis-à-vis God's teaching action in the person, the problem of a learner acquiring religious behaviors is basically a variant of, rather than being totally distinct from, the problem of learning behaviors in general, without respect to their religious or nonreligious character.

What I am suggesting, in other words, is that various kinds of learning vis-à-vis God's activity are not as discontinuous as might seem at first blush. Theologians — particularly pastoral theologians, moral theologians, and those theologians who turn their attention to religious instruction — typically devote considerable attention to the approaches, structures, and methods by which the faith can be effectively "handed on" (to borrow one of their favorite expressions). These theologians characteristically speak of such instructional behaviors as maintaining an existential stance with respect to the learner, expanding the borders of the learner's freedom, reducing emphasis on formulations so as to arrive more effectively at the gospel spirit, and utilizing the kerygmatic approach. Hence even the theologians, totally involved as they are in concern with and exploration of the supernatural dimension, indicate a need for somehow operationalizing in order to facilitate the acquisition of religious outcomes in learners.

Being social scientists, the religious educationist and the religious educator place heavy emphasis on verification in the learning process. In this connection André Godin reminds us that theologians and theologically-oriented religious educationists tend to "discuss with intelligence and depth the theological pertinence of a religious pedagogy, all without any reference at all to a demonstrated effectiveness of a particular instruction or a specific form of teaching or a pedagogical method on the religious level."[36] By its very nature as an educational activity, religious instruction must have reference to demonstrated effectiveness in terms of the religious behaviors caused.

One way out of the apparent problem posed for religious instruction by theologians is to view religion operationally. An operational perspective of religion has been overlooked by theologians, chiefly because the methodology of theological science — in contrast to the methodology of social science — regards religion notionally. Orlo Strunk has laid the groundwork for constructing an operational definition of religion with his statement: "Religion is an organization of cognitive-affective-conative factors, perceived by the individual as being religious in nature, and of being especially appropriate or inappropriate in achieving self-adequacy."[37] Among its many distinct advantages, an operational view of religion serves to provide a solid theoretical and conceptual foundation for the elaboration and development of a mature religious pedagogy.

To operationalize the definition or view of religion is not to desacralize it; instead it is to open up religion to even broader areas. It is to open up a whole new unexplored territory to theologians as well as to religious educationists and religious educators. To furnish an operational view or operational definition is not to suggest that such a view or definition is either the best view or the total definition. To be sure, the classic notional definition of religion as stated by the theologians gives us another rich insight into that reality we term religion. Views and definitions serve, after all, as searchlights to illumine a reality from various perspectives and vantage points. They also provide us with concepts which we can operationalize. A combination of both the notional and the operational concepts of religion complement each other in a harmonious fashion. While the notional definition of religion is in some ways helpful to religious instruction, I believe that an operational definition is more appropriate and more fruitful in that it provides a more nurturant soil for the development both of curricula and instructional approaches, strategies and methods to most effectively facilitate the modification of the learner's behavior along religious lines.

Perhaps Jesus himself provided a more operational concept of religion than any of us might have thought when he said: "I repeat, you will be able to tell them by their fruits" (Matthew 7:20).

Some additional light might possibly be shed on the theme of the previous paragraphs by briefly examining a few points which are basic to the methodology of social science, of which educational science is a derivative.[38] A concept is a word which expresses an abstraction formed by generalizing from particulars.[39] Concepts are formed out of the observations of certain related particular behaviors. Religion is an example of a concept. We cannot directly experience or observe another person's religion. We can only experience this or that particular behavior, from which we can make the generalized inference that these behaviors are religious and that therefore this person has religion. In education as in the other branches of social science, a concept is often made into a construct for purposes of facilitating scientific discovery and learning more about that which the concept is generalizing. A construct is a concept which is consciously invented or "constructed" to be useful to scientific inquiry and discovery. All constructs are concepts, but not all concepts are made into constructs. Religion as a construct, for example, is defined in such a way that it can be assessed to that degree to which this phenomenon can be measured. Thus, as an illustration, a subsidiary construct of the overall construct "religion" would be such-and-such a behavior which could be empirically observed and tested. One of the chief reasons for translating a concept such as religion into a construct is to thereby render the original concept "fruitful," a social-science term meaning both generative of newer and higher levels of discovery and generalization, and also useful in exploring the dimensions of the present level of the concept.

A notional definition defines a concept or a construct by using other descriptive words about it, in the fashion of the dictionary. Notional definitions tend to be inadequate when dealing with extremely simple phenomena such as the definition of "being," or when dealing with highly complex phenomena such as the definition of "religion." In other words, the closer a phenomenon is to the middle of the simple-complex continuum, the more adequate a notional definition tends to be. There has been considerable controversy down through the years on the notional definition of "religion" so that to this day there seems to be little consensus. [40] Notional definitions of religion tend to be vague and not too informative, as witness Léonce de Grandmaison's famous definition: "Religion is the relationship of man, individually and collectively, with God." [41]

An operational definition defines a concept or construct by indicating what actions or behaviors the word denotes or connotes. An operational definition specifies the activities or operations which perforce lend themselves to direct observation and measurement. An operational definition does not typically reflect the total richness of the reality it is attempting to describe; nevertheless it provides an illumination and a handle on concepts and constructs, especially on the more obscure and slippery kind. One good example of an operational definition of religion was given by the apostle James in his universal letter: "coming to the help of orphans and widows when they need it, and keeping oneself uncontaminated by the world" (James 1:27). [42] Operational definitions of religion, then, describe religion in terms of specific behaviors which can be labeled religious.

Operational definitions typically are phrased in the classic "if-then" mode of social science. For example, if out of ultimate conviction a person goes to church frequently and helps his neighbor, then he can be said to be religious. Jesus himself operationally defined followership in this "if-then" mode when he said to his disciples: "If anyone wants to be a follower of mine, [then] let him renounce himself and take up his cross and follow me" (Matthew 16:24).

May Brodbeck further says of operational definitions:

> Scientific terms are defined, not in isolation, as in the dictionary, but by stating observable conditions· in which a sentence containing the term is true or false. Instead of defining the word by itself . . . it is defined by giving the conditions for the truth of a sentence in which the term occurs. Such definitions are called *operational* for they frequently state what must be done in order to make certain observations. For instance, in order to determine a child's I.Q., we must first administer a test of a specific kind, then observe his performance on the test, and finally make certain calculations. *All* of these conditions define the meaning of I.Q., as it appears in the sentence "John has an I.Q. of 115."[43]

Educational objectives, Benjamin Bloom reminds us, are statements of desired changes in the thoughts, actions, or feelings of students which a particular course or educational program can bring about.[44] A principal benefit to be derived from operationalizing educational objectives is that, by describing learning outcomes in terms of specifying the procedure through which these outcomes are to be brought about, effective approaches and effective strategies to facilitate learning are thereby suggested to curriculum builders and teachers alike. An educational objective, to be efficacious, must be capable of being translated into a method of cooperating with the activities of the learner. An efficacious educational objective suggests the kind of curriculum, learning environment, and teaching strategy needed to liberate and organize the learner's capacities.[45] Operationalizing educational objectives represents the most effective manner of facilitating the realization of these objectives in the learner's behavioral pattern. The relevant empirical research has shown that an act of teaching most significantly modifies behavior when it is targeted toward producing a specific operationally defined result consisting of a particular behavior which forms one aspect of curriculum content. The converse — or perhaps more accurately, the corollary — of this is that the specifically defined result is achieved when a student goes through whatever particular learning experience is required to produce that desired result.[46] Operationalizing of an educational objective specifies the type of learning experience in performance terms, and hence is crucial to facilitate optimally the realization of the desired learning outcomes.

SHAPING THE LEARNING ENVIRONMENT

Even at its highest level, religious instruction of itself cannot directly produce or effect Christian living in the learner. But, as Iris Cully reminds us, religious instruction does contribute toward or against the possibility of effecting Christian living.[47] In other words, the task of religious instruction is to provide the experience in which Christian learning can take place and in which the individual can acquire behaviors which we may legitimately term "Christian." The work of all the facilitational elements of religious instruction — curriculum, program, teacher, and so on — is to introduce new learning opportunities into the individual's field of experience. The learner's field of experience, that is to say the learning environment, consists of all the elements in the learning situation with which he somehow interacts. The task of religious instruction is to so restructure the learner's field of experience that at pivot points in terms of his learning "some new element enters the environment which changes the whole picture of the field for the individual."[48] Religious instruction, therefore, consists in the shaping of the learning environment by which the facilitation of behavioral modification in the individual is most significantly effected and enhanced.

In the religious instruction enterprise, there are many environmental vectors intersecting at the learner's field of experience (or phenomenal field, as some psychologists prefer to call it). The institutional environment is the organizational setting in which religious instruction is taking place, for example, a church-related school, a Sunday school or CCD class, an informal educational group, a family-centered program, and so on. The curricular environment consists in the design, range, scope, continuity, sequence, and integration of the course of study. The instructional environment is the network of facilitational patterns and moves which the teacher utilizes in the actual learning situation. The materials environment relates to those instructional and parainstructional objects and aids which the learner utilizes in the course of his acquiring the desired learning outcomes. The physical environment refers to the actual place in which the teaching-learning process occurs, such as a classroom, a church, the living room of one's home. Finally, the human environment comprises the particular individuals and set of individuals who are involved in the teaching-learning experience at any one time. The learner's field of experience is such as to include all these environmental variables simultaneously. Each of these environmental variables taken separately, as well as the combination of them acting in concert, has a profound effect on the kind of learning which will take place. It is the task of the total religious instruction enterprise, and of the teacher in particular, to structure these environmental variables in such a way that what will result is an environment so shaped that learning outcomes will be optimally effected. *It is this structuring of the learning situation to most effectively facilitate the modification of behavior along religious lines which constitutes the very heart of the religious instruction process.*

As we have seen, the environment to be shaped is a complex and variegated one. The learning environment, globally considered, is that set of conditions in which the teaching-learning act occurs. It is the business of the religious instruction enterprise to establish that kind of environment which is optimally conducive to the facilitation of the desired learning outcomes. While the first precondition for effective learning is to place the learner in a shaped environment, this of itself is not sufficient to effect the intended modification of behavior. Everything depends on how the teacher structures the elements and combination of elements in that shaped environment to produce the learning outcome.

The shaping of the learning environment and the structuring of the learning situations within the environment must, of course, be radicated in the learner's phenomenal field. From a psychological point of view, the shaped environment is nothing other than what the learner perceives it to be. It is this perception which in a psychological sense creates the environment in which the learner interacts. To be effective, therefore, the environment must be so structured as to take into primary consideration the learner and where he is both as a person and as a learner-in-this-particular-situation. To shape a learning environment is to specially prepare a milieu with the learner in mind.

The gospels are replete with examples of Jesus shaping the learning environment to facilitate desired outcomes — all with the learners primarily in mind. It might be helpful to examine the following gospel narrative from the vantage point of a shaped learning environment:

> Now about eight days after this had been said, he took with him Peter and John and James and went up the mountain to pray. As he prayed, the aspect of his face was changed and his clothing became brilliant as lightning. Suddenly there were two men there talking to him; they were Moses and Elijah appearing in glory, and they were speaking of his death which he was about to accomplish in Jerusalem. Peter and his companions were heavy with sleep, but they kept awake and saw his glory and the two men standing with him. As these were leaving him, Peter said to Jesus, "Master, it is wonderful for us to be here; so let us make three tents, one for you, one for Moses and one for Elijah." He did not know what he was saying. As he spoke, a cloud came and covered them with a shadow, and when they went into the cloud the disciples were afraid. And a voice came from the cloud saying, "This is my Son, the Chosen One. Listen to him." And after the voice had spoken, Jesus was found alone. The disciples kept silence and, at that time, told no one what they had seen. (Luke 9:26-36)

He carefully structured all the elements in the learning situation. He went up to a mountain so as to avoid factors which might distract the attention of the apostles. He arranged for his person and his garments to blaze as lightning, indicating power and grace. He saw to it that two of the greatest old testament prophets conversed with him so that the tradition and authority of these two men would add weight to his already lofty stature in the perceptions of the apostles. He arranged for the conversation centered around his impending death in Jerusalem, indicating both approbation of himself by the two prophets and a prediction not uncommonly associated with the prophetical role. He designed it so that a cloud would overshadow him to give yet more approbation to his personal stature, since the apostles knew full well that in the old testament especially great revelations by God were not infrequently given in clouds on the mountain. Finally, he arranged the situation so that there would be a verbal reinforcer in the voice which came from the cloud. What was the intended behavioral outcome of the transfiguration lesson? Doubtless one key intended outcome was a deepening of the awareness of the apostles of the greatness and divinity of Jesus — an outcome admirably facilitated through the shaping of that learning environment we know today as the transfiguration.

Any environment teems with life experiences which may become learning experiences for the individual. Yet it is self-evident that not all life experiences gained in a particular environment are of equal worth in effecting desired changes in the individual. It thus remains for the religious instruction program in general, and for the teacher in particular, to so shape the environment that the learner engages in those kinds of experiences which represent optimal and fruitful learning for him. This is the facilitational role of the teacher; this is the function of structuring the learning situation. The program and the teacher shape the environment from one of relatively chance activities for the individual, in terms of effecting desired outcomes, to one of providing those experiences most conducive to bringing about these behavioral modifications.

What I am suggesting is that in the final analysis all that either the religious instruction enterprise or the teacher is able to do is to so shape the learning environment as to heighten and indeed maximize the possibility of desirable learning outcomes to take place. It is the total shaped environment, and the learner's particularized interaction with that environment which promote this acquisition of desired changes. I underscore this point because all too frequently in the history and the practice of religious instruction, unduly excessive emphasis has been placed on one or other variable in the learning situation — for example, on the teacher or the textbook or the product content of the "message" — at the expense of the impact of the total environment. If teaching is viewed as a process which is interactive with all the variables within the shaped environment, then it is patently foolish and indeed educationally unsound to account for learning events solely in terms of one or other variable in that situation, as for example, the teacher or the textbook or even God's grace for that matter. Instead, these learning events must be regarded as outcomes in which pupil variables, interacting dynamically with a host of environment variables, play an important role.[49]
In other words, all the variables in the total environment must be structured into a situation which can become change-producing in terms of the learner's behaviors. The gospels are replete with examples of Jesus utilizing all the variables in the total environment to produce change in those he wishes to teach. The following scriptural narrative may serve to highlight this point.

Looking up, Jesus saw the crowds approaching and said to Philip, "Where can we buy some bread for these people to eat?" He only said this to test Philip; he himself knew exactly what he was going to do. Philip answered, "Two hundred denarii would only buy enough to give them a small piece each." One of his disciples, Andrew, Simon Peter's brother, said, "There is a small boy here with five barley loaves and two fish; but what is that between so many?" Jesus said to them, "Make the people sit down." There was plenty of grass there, and as many as five thousand men sat down. Then Jesus took the loaves, gave thanks, and gave them out to all who were sitting ready; he then did the same with the fish, giving out as much as was wanted. When they had eaten enough he said to the disciples, "Pick up the pieces left over, so that nothing gets wasted." So they picked them up, and filled twelve hampers with scraps left over from the meal of five barley loaves. The people, seeing this sign that he had given, said, "This really is the prophet who is to come into the world." (John 6:5-14)

A close examination reveals how skillfully Jesus structured all the variables in this situation to so shape the environment that the desired learning outcome would be facilitated. He selected a locality which was comfortable and in which all the learners could see each other and so be impressed by the enormity of the problem. He introduced a dilemma to Philip. He had the apostles and possibly others distribute the food so that with each new distribution to yet another person, the multiplication phenomenon would be reinforced in the perceptual field of each of the five thousand men. He used another reinforcer when he had the disciples gather up the fragments. The learning situation was particularly effective because it was congruent with a deeply-felt need of the five-thousand men: they were hungry. Through skillfully structuring the learning situation, Jesus brought about the desired behavioral change; the learners affirmed that Jesus was a prophet and even wished to further operationalize this affirmation by making him king. But Jesus's time had not yet arrived, so he fled by himself to the hills. Did Jesus consciously and deliberatively shape the learning environment to produce the desired changes? John supplies the answer when he wrote that Jesus himself "knew exactly what he was going to do" (John 6:6).

The crucial importance of the total environment in facilitating changed behavior is borne out by a host of empirical investigations on various types of populations. John Bowlby's celebrated extensive review of the relevant research from around the world concludes that the effect on the psychological maturation of the infant during its first year of life was greatly influenced by whether or not it was reared in an institutional environment or in a family environment. [50] A later empirical research investigation by Sally Provence and Rose Lipton confirms Bowlby's findings and bears out their hypothesis that "adequate development and learning in the first year come about through an interaction of the infant's unborn maturing systems and the forces of the environment."[51]   In other words, different total environments, whether between family environments and institutional environments, or between different kinds of home environments, have a profound effect on the kind and degree of personality development of the infant. So strong is the influence of total environment on the developing organism that even animals, which are less emotionally and socially[52] sensitive than human beings, are greatly influenced by the kind of early environment in which they are reared.[53]   An interesting side note in this latter connection is an experimental investigation by Donald O. Hebb, a university professor in Canada. Suspecting that his rats reared in small cages at the university laboratory displayed behavioral effects of living in that kind of environment, Hebb took some of them into his home and allowed them to be brought up as pets. This not only greatly increased their social contacts with people, but also afforded them a great variety of physical objects to explore and a much more physically expanded area in which to live. When these rats were returned to the laboratory as adults and tested in the Hebb-Williams maze, they performed much better than did the control laboratory rats reared in the laboratory cages.[54]

Experimental research on human adults offers additional support to the conclusion that the environment in its totality has a significant effect on behavior. Much of this research is carried on by the military to ascertain what effects a change in environment has in making a prisoner more willing to reveal information. A considerable portion of this research has centered around the effects of reduced environmental stimulation on human behavior. The research has concluded that placing an individual in a barren cell devoid of any differentiated environmental stimuli tends to make the prisoner more susceptible and responsible to the influence of the inter-rogator.[55]

I have cited the gospel narrative of the loaves and the fishes, and also have given a quick overview of the pertinent empirical researches to briefly demonstrate that the total environment does play an important role in modifying human behavior in desired directions. A contrast between the activities of Jesus with the five thousand persons and the activities of a military interrogator indicates that the influence of the total environment may be either positive or negative. In this connection, Romuald Zaniewski observes that the total environment as an objective reality exercises a positive influence when it facilitates the person to modify his behavior in a direction which furthers his own personal, social, psychological, or spiritual growth. On the other hand, the total environment exercises a negative influence when it acts as a force which enables the person to modify his behavior in a direction which impairs his own personal, social, psychological, or spiritual growth.[56] The important point to note is that it is the total environment qua environment which has such a critical impact on behavior modification. As I emphasized throughout the early part of this book, it is the task of the instructional program and particularly of the teacher to so shape this learning environment that it will facilitate changes in the learner in desirable and positive directions. All too often theorists and practitioners of religious instruction place excessive emphasis on one variable in the total learning environment — typically the teacher or the textbook or the "message" of good news. I am not denying that at selected pivot points of the teaching-learning act, this or that variable in the environment might be more significant than another variable in the facilitation of learning. What I am trying to emphasize is that it is the total environment which is the most significant aspect in the enablement of learning. Indeed, the teacher variable or the textbook variable or any other variable receives meaning and sustenance precisely as it is radicated in and related to its environment, and as it is reinforced or extinguished by environmental press.

Emphasis on the total environment, therefore, is quite at odds with the prevalent notion in Protestant and particularly in Catholic religious education circles that religious instruction is basically proclaiming the good news, or in the words of one theologian, presenting revelation to the young.[57] Such an emphasis on "proclaiming" or "presenting" ignores and denies the influence of the total environment and places undue and exclusive stress on the teacher variable. To be sure, exclusive stress on the teacher variable tends of itself to create a total environment in which all other living aspects of the milieu are extinguished and the teacher-presentation variable becomes the learner's total environment. Such a cooping-up process ignores the tremendous facilitational influence of the total environment and is pedagogically parallel to the previously-described efforts of military interrogators to behavioristically condition the individual by depriving him of all environmental influences other than himself. The task of the religious instruction program and of the teacher is to expand and enrich the individual's total learning environment. In this way the conditions conducive to optimal learner growth will have been deliberatively shaped, and the learner can be helped to interact with those sectors of the total learning environment which optimally facilitate his own growth in the desired direction.

A LABORATORY FOR CHRISTIAN LIVING

To shape the learning environment is at bottom to make the classroom (or wherever religious instruction is taking place) a laboratory in which students learn to live and to continually enhance their living as Christians. The learning situation qua laboratory clearly implies that it is in a social situation that the learner forges and hammers out in a deeply existential manner his own personal form of operationalizing the revelation experience in his own life. To be effective, religion should be learned in that kind of personalized interactive milieu which we can term a laboratory. The laboratory setting helps to facilitate the fusion in the learner's concrete experience of all the cognitive, affective, and conative functions of his personality into a consistent and mutually reinforcing overall behavioral pattern. The goal of religious instruction is Christian living; such a goal can only be effected if the students are placed in a lived and living learning situation.

The entity we call "learning laboratory" connotes stress on several constituent elements. A learning laboratory is characterized by primary experience. The learner learns in a laboratory through primary experience rather than through secondary experience. He learns charitable behaviors by practicing charitable behaviors in a shaped environment, not by simply learning about charitable behaviors from the teacher's mouth or from the textbook. A learning laboratory is characterized by its situational emphasis. A situation connotes the presence of a goodly number of elements either interacting with each other or poised to interact with some other element or indeed, with all the other elements in the situation. The laboratory is an actual existential situation so deliberatively structured that all of the persons, objects, and materials in that situation act as complementary and reinforcing vectors to induce a desired learning outcome. A learning laboratory is characterized by a wide range of activity. Activity, whether cognitive or affective or overt, is one of the hallmarks of a laboratory, whether it be an engineering laboratory working on the effects of stress on building materials, or a managerial laboratory working at Mission Control on the final countdown of a rocket launch, or a learning laboratory working on acquiring some specified behavioral outcome. Finally, a learning laboratory is characterized by its person-centeredness. The shaped learning situation is an environment so deliberatively contrived that it induces learning of the most personalizable sort.

A learning laboratory therefore stands at the opposite end of the pedagogical pole from the old "presenting the message" or "heralding the good news" emphasis which for centuries has been the dominant model in religious instruction theory and practice. A lecture approach, whether in pure or modified form, represents the antithesis of a laboratory approach. The discussion method stands only at the vestibule of the learning laboratory, since in discussion the activity is usually restricted to cognitive activity and the elements of the situation are typically so restricted in breadth and range as to include only words and possibly nonverbal behaviors, with a textbook thrown in for good measure.

The principal thrust in the learning laboratory invention is that it facilitates the existential fusion in the learner's life of believing and living. In the laboratory, the learner is provided with structured opportunities to live his beliefs — and one of the most effective ways to understand both one's beliefs and the consequences of these beliefs is to live them out. For centuries Christians have maintained that what and how an individual believes will affect his life. Modern psychology, on the other hand, has discovered that how one lives one's life profoundly affects his belief system. Further, as Paul van Buren observes, Christian believers "frequently disagree about the precise consequences of believing when it comes to specific decisions. This disagreement appears to have led many Christians to conclude the relationship between believing and living is so vague or general that nothing specific can be said or even that faith has no concrete ethical consequences at all.[58] Belief and practice can be brought into a mutually reinforcing congruence only by existentially facilitating their fusion in the crucible of lived experience. The learning laboratory is precisely this crucible. When all is said and done, the only effective learning method is that of primary experience both lived and personalized. Religious instruction is concerned not simply with how to think about things, but even more fundamentally with how to experience them.[59]

Cognitive learnings comprise an important segment of the total fabric of desired behavioral outcomes for the religion class. The learning laboratory does not minimize the significance of cognitive learnings in religious instruction. Indeed, the structured learning laboratory represents a pedagogical activity which, because of its existential, situational, lived nature represents a signal instructional opportunity for enhancing the probability that cognitive outcomes will be acquired by the learners. Even more than this, the learning laboratory is intrinsically promotive of effecting a here-and-now fusion of the learner's cognitive outcomes and his lifestyle pattern. In short, the learning laboratory augments the probability that the individual will transfer cognitive gains into his overall lifestyle.

The learning laboratory structurally facilitates an engagement between the learner and God-as-he-is-in-another-person, and also an engagement between the learner and God-as-he-is-in-himself. Surely at bottom the Christian religion is the personal lived engagement between God and man in a mutually flowing interpenetrating rhythm. I use the word "engagement" here after the manner in which David Hunter employs it.[60] Hunter uses the term "engagement" as an intertwining, a mutual involvement, a response in which there is a flow of something of self into the other, all in terms of the deeply personal man-to-God, God-to-man mutually lived relationship. Engagement "refers to the experience we are having or ought to be having as Christians; namely our changing and unchanging encounter with God, our response to His action; of if we are not conscious of encounter with God, it refers simply to God's confrontation of us."[61]   At the opposite pole of engagement is detachment, which Hunter distinguishes from the monastic use of the term. "Engagement is the uniting, the reconciling action of God in which we may be caught up. Detachment is the separating, fragmenting action of man by which we try to shield ourselves from the pervasive activity of God."[62] Concretized as a laboratory situation, religious instruction facilitates the student to live Christian engagement to a high degree right in the learning setting itself. The learning laboratory by definition provides the conditions whereby the individual can engage in God's revelational activity. Often this engagement is the open lived relationship with other persons in the learning situation. If the divine indwelling has any meaning and relevance, it is that God abides in each man according to the uniqueness of that individual. To encounter a person is to encounter the person and the God in that person without separating the two. This engagement, Randolph Crump Miller observes, "like Jacob's wrestling with God, may be seen like a violent encounter, or like Jeremiah's experience, it may be called obedience, or like Pentecost, it may be the opening of the revelation to many others."[63] Precisely because it is a laboratory situation, the kind of religion class I am advocating is in a uniquely favored position to enhance this kind of revelational engagement, as well as a host of other types of learning behaviors which flesh out and amplify revelational engagement.

In the religious instruction literature of the 1940's and 1950's, particularly in Europe, great stress was placed on the religion class being so arranged that it would lead to and culminate in a prayer at the end of the lesson. Such an approach clearly misses the mark in terms of the continuous and ongoing nature of revelation and engagement. It is bad pedagogy and even worse theology to suggest that the lesson lead learners systematically to prayer as the finale of the class: every moment of the religious instruction class is a prayer in action, is an engagement of God with man in a revelational dynamic. The religion lesson should be shaped as a learning laboratory precisely because the laboratory structure is most conducive to the arrangement of those conditions which offer the greatest promise for the realization and maximizing of the revelational engagement.

"Every individual has grown up," remarks John Dewey, "and always must grow up in a social medium. His responses grow intelligent, or gain meaning simply because he lives and acts in a medium of accepted meanings and values."[64] What the laboratory structure accomplishes is the shaping in a concrete way of those conditions which can effect desired behavioral modifications more efficiently precisely because these conditions have been deliberatively structured with the goal of producing those modifications. The learning laboratory, then, *is* the shaped environment. As such, the laboratory provides a host of conditions promotive of optimal and productive interaction and fusion into the learner's lifestyle of the many disparate and seemingly unconnected elements which he encounters in the relatively unstructured environment that is life.

I would take issue with Marcel van Caster who suggests that Christian practice in daily life provides a subject for religious instruction which should not be neglected.[65] Quite the contrary: religious instruction should be totally and essentially Christian practice in daily life — daily classroom life or daily life, wherever the teaching-learning act is occurring. One cannot say that what happens outside the religion lesson is life, and what occurs in the lesson is something other than life. The religion lesson, through the laboratory structure, is first and foremost a mode of life. It is a mode of life which has been deliberatively shaped to provide a kind of living which represents a focused and more enhanced kind of Christian living than a learner can find in the more randomized experiences in life outside the laboratory. The laboratory mode is pedagogically superior to the lecture or discussion mode because while the last two offer the learners only the verbal part of life, the laboratory places them in a milieu in which all of life is represented, but in a structured form.

The religious instruction class — I do not say classroom — is a microcosm of society. To the extent that the classroom society and the larger society are isomorphic, to that extent will the smaller class society fulfill its function of socializing the learners into the wider church society and Christian fellowship. With its conditions so structured that it does indeed contain in minifashion the representative elements of the church society and the broader Christian fellowship in a manner conducive to effect the desired learning, the laboratory mode represents the most fruitful direction for religious pedagogy to take.

Because the religion class ought to be isomorphic at a minilevel with the church society and with the society of Christian fellowship at large, the learners should be involved in much more than merely cognitive behaviors. Cognitive behaviors, while forming a part of the life of the larger society of the church and Christian fellowship, do indeed form precisely that: only a part. To be truly isomorphic with the larger society, the little society which is the class should provide the individuals with those conditions whereby they will be able to experience in a learning-oriented fashion all those productive behaviors that represent the larger church and Christian society at their finest levels. Only in this way can religious instruction realize its twin role of being at once a socializing and a prophetic or futuristic force. It is the learning laboratory which represents the pedagogical structure eminently suited to the actualization of this twin role.

Over and above being a society, the religion class is — or at least should be — a community. A community implies communion, a communion of believers in that kind of pedagogically-focused Christian fellowship which we call religion class. The religious instruction activity does not stand apart from the Christian community or the fellowship of believers; rather it represents a task-oriented and specifically goal-directed kind of Christian community. The religious instruction enterprise is not coextensive with community. In other words, where there exists a Christian community there does not therefore necessarily exist a formal or informal religion class. It is the pedagogical thrust toward certain instructional goals, and the pedagogical facilitation of the accomplishment of these instructional goals which differentiate the religious instruction enterprise from other forms of Christian community. On the other hand, however, to the extent that the religion class is itself not a fully-functioning Christian community, at least *in via*, to that extent does it fail to negotiate one of its primary instructional tasks. Herein lies one crucial difference between the religion class and classes in other so-called "subject matter areas." Unlike most "subject matter areas," religious instruction has as one of its primary process outcomes the formation of a living community and the deepening of the bond of fellowship among the members of the instructional group. Thus Roger Shinn can write that one of the key objectives of religious instruction "is to draw individuals into the functional reality of a living Christian fellowship."[66]

This orientation of the religion class toward being a functional Christian community is in congruence with the nurture-model of Christian instruction so popular with Protestants. This congruence is clearly suggested by Donald Butler who regards Christian nurture as "an action by which men are brought to share the kind of being the church has."[67] Unless the religious instruction group is living a church life in both the restricted and broad sense of the term, the learners cannot be expected to acquire that prime goal of religious instruction, namely Christian living.

In one sense, a person becomes a Christian within a Christian community.[68] A fish becomes a fish within the milieu of water. The water nourishes the fish, provides the conditions by which it might function adequately, and opens to it new extensions of itself. The more fully the religion class is a functioning Christian community, the more fully will the learner be able to develop and to forge for himself the *habitus* of Christian living within the necessary contextual framework of the people of God. By providing the learner with progressively deepening experiences of Christian community and fellowship, the religion class initiates the learner into more meaningful participation with the wider church community of his own denomination and into the even wider community of broadly ecumenical Christian fellowship. The learning laboratory, with its emphasis on interaction of the student with the totality of goal-oriented variables in the entire structured situation, is obviously more conducive to the attainment of desired learning outcomes than is the teacher-learner or textbook-learner emphasis of the old "presentation" or "heralding" modes of religious instruction.

One of the hallmarks of a functioning community is interactive experiencing by the members of the group. Gabriel Moran suggests that where revelation happens is in the learner's experience both of and within his present community.[69] In the act of this revelational experience, the learner grows in grace and also in his acquisition of meaning about both Christian existence and Christian existing. It is in the milieu of that functioning Christian minicommunity we call the religion class that the learner is helped to progressively mature in his ongoing intersubjective relationship with his fellowman and with God himself. Through this interpersonal participatory life, the Christian lives fully the ongoing revelational experience which is divine life in the world.[70]

One aspect of community which should not be neglected is that of openness to persons outside of the group. Historically, there seems to have been a recurrent tendency among Christian minicommunities to substitute cultism for genuine community. Not infrequently has it happened in past centuries — and in our own era as well — that community living and community spirit have degenerated into a neognosticism. This type of ingroupism, with its clam-like stance to the outer world, exerts a constrictive influence on the members of the group. Cultism is destructive both of true community functioning and of effective religious instruction. The religious instruction program and also the teacher should so structure the variables within the learning laboratory that the learners as a group are not set apart from the world as a narrow entity. The Christian community that is the religion class does indeed have a prophetical and reconstructionist role to play vis-à-vis the larger Christian congregation and community. But this prophetical and reconstructionist role is ill-served by the group turning excessively in on itself in the fashion of a neognostic cult. The yeast must be in open and free contact with the dough if the leavening process is to be achieved.

FOOTNOTES

1. Dag Hammarskjöld, *Markings*, translated by Leif Sjöberg and W. H. Auden (New York: Knopf, 1965), p. 122.
2. David G. Ryans, "Teacher Behavior Theory and Research: Implications for Teacher Education," in *Journal of Teacher Education*, XIV, September, 1963, p. 274.
3. Robert J. Havighurst, *Developmental Tasks in Education*, 2d ed. (New York: McKay, 1952), p. 5.
4. Advocates of the fidelity approach might reprove me for having a too narrow concept of God's grace which, they might suggest, would come through the very panes of glass in the metaphorical window used in my example. God's grace, to be sure, does not readily lend itself to human imagery, but in so far as it might, what I am suggesting is that God's grace has a better chance of reaching and affecting the learner if the pedagogical window is open rather than bolted securely closed.
5. See, for example, Johannes Hofinger, *The Art of Teaching Christian Doctrine: The Good News and Its Proclamation*, 2d ed. (Notre Dame, Indiana: University of Notre Dame Press, 1962); also James D. Smart, *The Teaching Ministry of the Church* (Philadelphia: Westminster, 1954).
6. Klemens Tilmann, "On Helping Men to Become Christians: A Revaluation of Our Catechetical Pastoral Efforts," in *Lumen Vitae*, XXIII, June, 1968, p. 218.
7. See James B. Fulmer, "Preaching and Christian Education," in *Religious Education*, LXI, March-April, 1966, p. 130.
8. Because of limitations of space, my treatment of the distinctive natures and functions of religious instruction and religious counseling is somewhat oversimplified. For full-length treatments of the teaching function and the guidance-counseling function as they relate to the overall enterprise of religious education, see James Michael Lee, *Principles and Methods of Secondary Education* (New York: McGraw-Hill Catholic Series in Education, 1963); see also James Michael Lee and Nathaniel J. Pallone, *Guidance and Counseling in Schools: Foundations and Processes* (New York: McGraw-Hill Catholic Series in Education, 1966).
9. See Adrian L. van Kaam, "Counseling from the Viewpoint of Existential Psychology," in *Harvard Educational Review*, XXXII, April, 1962, pp. 403-415.

10. See Carl R. Rogers, *On Becoming a Person* (Boston: Houghton Mifflin, 1961), pp. 31-196.
11. Carter V. Good, editor, *Dictionary of Education*, 2d ed. (New York: McGraw-Hill, 1959), p. 55.
12. Actually, an accurate definition of learning is somewhat more complex. I shall discuss the nature and ways of human learning more fully in volume II of a projected three-volume series on religious instruction of which the present book comprises volume I.
13. Asahel D. Woodruff, *Basic Concepts of Teaching*, concise edition (San Francisco: Chandler, 1961), p. 57.
14. Marshall McLuhan, *Understanding Media: The Extensions of Man* (New York: McGraw-Hill, 1964), p. 152. While McLuhan used this phrase in a different context, nonetheless it seems eminently applicable to the present discussion.
15. A word about my use of the scriptures is in order. The validity of my use of the scriptures is not at all dependent upon an interpretation of them which is literal or allegorical, which is Bultmannian or Barthian, which is *historisch* or *geschichtlich*. I am taking the scriptures I cite at face value as stories, with no reference as to whether these stories are pure myths, allegorical wrappings of a basic truth, or the literal truth itself. In other words, the stories or sentences precisely *qua* stories and sentences have pedagogical import; in this context, the scriptural or doctrinal exegesis of the scriptural story or sentence is not relevant.
16. Methodologically I am positing in this example that all the intervening variables were properly controlled.
17. See, for example, Lee J. Cronbach, *Educational Psychology*, 2d edition (New York: Harcourt, Brace and World, 1963).
18. For a concise summary of the three-volume report of the Character Education Inquiry, see Hugh Hartshorne and Mark A. May, "A Summary of the Work of the Character Education Inquiry," in *Religious Education*, XXV, September, 1930, pp. 607-619 and also October, 1930, pp. 754-762.
19. Andrew M. Greeley and Peter H. Rossi, *The Education of American Catholics* (Chicago: Aldine, 1966), pp. 60-67.
20. Ronald L. Johnstone, *The Effectiveness of Lutheran Elementary and Secondary Schools as Agencies of Christian Education* (St. Louis: Concordia, 1966), pp. 104, 140-143.
21. Andrew M. Greeley and Peter H. Rossi, *The Education of Catholic Americans*, pp. 53-76.
22. Ronald L. Johnstone, *The Effectiveness of Lutheran Elementary and Secondary Schools as Agencies of Christian Education*, pp. 67-84.

23. Walter B. Kolesnik, *Mental Discipline in Modern Education* (Madison, Wisconsin: University of Wisconsin Press, 1958), p. 5.
24. James Michael Lee, *Principles and Methods of Secondary Education*, p. 134.
25. James Michael Lee, "The *Teaching* of Religion," in James Michael Lee and Patrick C. Rooney, editors, *Toward a Future for Religious Education* (Dayton, Ohio: Pflaum, 1970), pp. 63-64.
26. This term "architected" in terms of building a lesson first came to my attention when it was used by Esther D. Flashner in her attempt to operationally describe the way the most gifted and effective teacher in her department consciously and deliberatively evolved her classroom lessons.
27. See, for example, John Broadus Watson, *Psychology from the Standpoint of a Behaviorist* (Philadelphia: Lippincott, 1919).
28. See, for example, Ivan Petrovich Pavlov, *Conditioned Reflexes* (London: Oxford University Press, 1927).
29. This study by Katsch is reported in H. J. Eyseneck, "The Nature of Behavior Therapy," in H. J. Eyseneck, *Experiments in Behavior Therapy* (New York: Macmillan, 1964), p. 3. Commenting on this Katsch study, Eyseneck remarks that "it is difficult to see how control groups would provide better and more impressive evidence of the correctness of this hypothesis [of the causative role of the picture of the mother-in-law] than does the experimental control exercised by Katsch in this case."
30. The only exception to what I have written in this paragraph occurs when satisfaction itself constitutes a desired behavioral outcome of the lesson. I am indebted to Robert O'Gorman for calling my attention to this point.
31. On the whole topic of operationalizing instructional objectives, see Robert F. Mager, *Preparing Instructional Objectives* (Palo Alto, California: Fearon, 1962).
32. For an elaboration on this point, see Fred N. Kerlinger, *Foundations of Behavioral Research: Educational and Psychological Inquiry* (New York: Holt, Rinehart and Winston, 1964), pp. 33-38.
33. Benjamin S. Bloom et al., *Taxonomy of Educational Objectives: Handbook I: Cognitive Domain* (New York: McKay, 1956).
34. David R. Krathwohl, Benjamin S. Bloom, and Bertram B. Masia, *Taxonomy of Educational Objectives: Handbook II: Affective Domain* (New York: McKay, 1964).
35. Thomas Aquinas, *De Veritate*, q.11, a.1, ad.1.
36. André Godin, "Importance and Difficulty of Scientific Research in Religious Education: The Problem of the 'Criterion,'" in *Religious Education, Research Supplement*, LVII, July-August,

1962, p. s-166.

37. Orlo Strunk, Jr., *Religion: A Psychological Interpretation* (Nashville, Tennessee: Abingdon, 1962), p. 22.

38. For a fuller explanation, see May Brodbeck, "Logic and Scientific Method in Research on Teaching," in N. L. Gage, editor, *Handbook of Research on Teaching* (Chicago: Rand McNally, 1963), pp. 44-93, and especially pp. 48-59.

39. Henri Grenier, a philosopher in the neo-Scholastic tradition, defines a concept as "the representation which the intellect expresses in itself, and in which we perceive a thing." See Henri Grenier, *Thomistic Philosophy: Logic*, volume I (Charlottetown, Canada: St. Dunstan's University Press, 1948), p. 26.

40. See, for example, Stanley A. Cook, "Religion," in James Hastings, general editor, *Encyclopedia of Religion and Ethics*, volume IX (New York: Scribner's, 1928), pp. 662-663; Virgilius Ferm, "Religion, the Problem of Definition," in Virgilius Ferm, general editor, *An Encyclopedia of Religion* (New York: Philosophical Library), pp. 646-647; E. Magnin, "Religion," in A. Vacant, E. Mangenot, and E. Amann, editors, *Dictionnaire de Théologie Catholique*, tome XIII, pt. 2 (Paris: Letouzey et Ané, 1937), columns 2182-2187.

41. Quoted in *ibid.*, column 2186 (translation mine).

42. The first part of this definition is more operational than is the second part.

43. May Brodbeck, "Logic and Scientific Method in Research on Teaching," p. 49.

44. Benjamin S. Bloom, "Testing Cognitive Ability and Achievement," in N. L. Gage, editor, *Handbook of Research on Teaching*, p. 389.

45. John Dewey, *Democracy and Education* (New York: Macmillan, 1916), pp. 126-127.

46. Asahel D. Woodruff, *Basic Concepts of Teaching*, concise edition, p. 30.

47. Iris V. Cully, "Christian Education: Instruction and Nurture," in *Religious Education*, LXI, January-February, 1966, p. 8.

48. See Ernest Ligon, *Dimensions of Character* (New York: Macmillan, 1956), p. 12.

49. See N. L. Gage, Philip J. Runkel, and B. B. Chatterjee, *Equilibrium Theory and Behavior Change: An Experiment in Feedback from Pupils to Teachers* (Urbana, Illinois: Bureau of Educational Research, College of Education, University of Illinois, 1960), p. 3.

50. John Bowlby, *Maternal Care and Mental Health* (Geneva, Switzerland: World Health Organization, 1952).

51. Sally Provence and Rose C. Lipton, *Infants in Institutions* (New

York: International Universities Press, 1962), pp. 161-162.

52. I use the terms "emotionally" and "socially" here in the wide sense to include animal responses.

53. For a review of some pertinent experimental research investigations on this point, see Daniel G. Freedman, Charlotte B. Loring, and Robert M. Martin, "Emotional Behavior and Personality Development," in Yvonne Brackbill, *Infancy and Early Childhood* (New York: Free Press, 1967), p. 481.

54. Donald O. Hebb, "The Effects of Early Experience on Problem-Solving at Maturity," paper presented at the annual meeting of the American Psychological Association, September 11, 1947.

55. Philip E. Kubzansky, "The Effects of Reduced Environmental Stimulation on Human Behavior," in Albert D. Biderman and Herbert Zimmer, *The Manipulation of Human Behavior* (New York: Wiley, 1961), pp. 52-55. For the religious educator who, like myself, believes in a profoundly humanistically oriented instructional program, I would like to add the following generalized conclusion from the studies on the effects of reduced environmental stimulation on human behavior: "The purposes that men have in seeking to control, or to influence, the behavior of others involve the distinctively human capabilities of men and their significance for one another. The major fallacy of the totalitarian interrogator grows out of a poor appreciation of this fact. Some of the chapters [in the book] here indicate that there are limits to which the ability of a source to reveal information can be separated from his willingness to do so." Albert D. Biderman and Herbert Zimmer, *The Manipulation of Human Behavior*, p. 7.

56. Romuald Zaniewski, *Les Théories des Milieux et la Pédagogie Mésologique: Introduction Générale à l'Etude du Milieu* (Tournai, Belgique: Castermann, 1951), pp. 30-31.

57. Gabriel Moran, *Catechesis of Revelation* (New York: Herder and Herder, 1966), p. 132.

58. Paul M. van Buren, "Linguistic Philosophy and Religious Education: Christian Education *Post Mortem Dei*," in *Religious Education*, LX, January-February, 1965, p. 9.

59. E. M. Adams, "Recapturing the Moral and Religious Dimensions in Education," in *Religious Education* LXIII, September-October, 1968, p. 391.

60. David R. Hunter, *Christian Education as Engagement* (New York: Seabury, 1962).

61. *Ibid.*, p. 7.

62. *Ibid.*, p. 8.

63. Randolph Crump Miller, "From Where I Sit: Some Issues in Christian Education," in *Religious Education*, LX, March-April,

1965 p. 99.
64. John Dewey, *Democracy and Education*, p. 344. While I believe that this quotation from Dewey bears great relevance for religious instruction, I cannot concur with his conclusion that mind is simply what the self achieves in its reflexively interactive encounters with external reality.
65. Marcel van Caster, *The Structure of Catechetics*, 2d edition, translated by Edward J. Dirkswager, Jr., Olga Guedetarian, and Nicolas Smith (New York: Herder and Herder, 1965), p. 162.
66. Roger L. Shinn, *The Educational Mission of Our Church* (Philadelphia: United Church Press, 1962).
67. J. Donald Butler, *Religious Education: The Foundations and Practice of Nurture* (New York: Harper & Row, 1962), p. 21.
68. Randolph Crump Miller, *Christian Nurture and the Church* (New York: Scribner's, 1961), p. 17.
69. Gabriel Moran, *Catechesis of Revelation*, p. 145.
70. Marcel van Caster dubs this type of learning as the initiation stage of religious instruction. Marcel van Caster, *The Structure of Catechetics*, pp. 12-21.

CHAPTER FOUR

RELIGIOUS INSTRUCTION AS A DISCIPLINE

*"It is a wise father that knows
his own child."*
    — William Shakespeare[1]

With an intensity mounting over the years, religious education in general and religious instruction in particular are increasingly facing an identity crisis. What *is* religious instruction? What kind of professional person is a religion teacher? Is religious instruction distinctive as a discipline and as a profession?[2] What are the special characteristics which mark off religious instruction from other activities? This identity crisis is significant because a field of endeavor like religious instruction needs to be delimited within some kind of parameters if it is to achieve any sort of focused outcome or effective result. Systematic cultivation and enrichment of that which falls within these parameters is necessary if the work of religious instruction is to attain maturity and become optimally effective.

In this short chapter I am going to focus my attention on an examination of whether religious instruction is truly a discipline. I am doing this in full consciousness that virtually all of the discussion heretofore has been directed toward the question of whether religious education — rather than religious instruction — is a discipline. I am centering my examination on religious instruction primarily because this is what forms the converging point of this entire book. Besides, Protestant and Catholic theorists who write on religious education typically use this term loosely as being coextensive with religious instruction. Rarely do these theorists equate religious education with either religious counseling or religious personnel services. To be sure, the conclusions of our probe into whether religious instruction is a discipline will *a fortiori* be applicable to religious education, since religious instruction is more sharply focused and is situated within more clearly delimited parameters.

By discipline I mean the smallest integral irreducible body of knowledge composed of systematized facts, laws, and theories. An example of a discipline is psychology. There are, of course, various branches of psychology such as abnormal psychology, educational psychology, adolescent psychology, and so forth. However, these constitute branches of the discipline of psychology; they are not distinct disciplines in their own right because they do not possess that integralness which characterizes the body of subject matter called psychology. I use the term "discipline" in contrast to the term "science." By science I mean that combination of interrelated disciplines which are bundled together into a single, broadly distinctive, common set of systematized interactive facts, laws, and theories. An example of a science is that broad area of inquiry called "social science." The field of psychology, then, constitutes one of the disciplines which form the corpus of social science. To borrow an analogy from natural science, a discipline is to an element as a science is to a molecule.[3] A science functions like a system, with the discipline acting as a subsystem within the larger system.

Marc Belth suggests four criteria which serve to distinguish one discipline from another.[4] First, each discipline operates at a distinct level of abstraction relative to the concepts with which it deals. For example, it is a task of psychology to collect systematic observations, build laws, and develop theories used to form explanations of the ways in which the human organism behaves in an interactive environment. It is the task of sociology, on the other hand, to collect systematic observations, build laws, and develop theories used to form explanations of human social grouping and behavior. (Psychology and sociology are disciplines within the broad system of social science.) Second, each discipline is thrusted toward a distinctly different kind of objective. The objective of psychology is to penetrate the interactive relationships of the human organism and his environment in order to learn more about the way in which this kind of organism operates and will operate. The objective of sociology is to investigate the ways in which groups behave, in which individuals interact within groups, and in which groups interact with other groups so as to learn more about the ways in which individuals and groups operate and will operate in a group situation. "Acceptance of an objective," Belth writes, "depends on agreement upon an operation intrinsic to the discipline."[5] Third, one discipline can be distinguished from another by its methodology and modes of inquiry. In a basic sense, there are three fundamental kinds of methodology: namely, mathematical, empirical, and speculative. But in another sense, there are as many fundamental kinds of methodology as there are generic sciences. Since there are probably not too many types of generic sciences, the issue of distinctive methodological types does not get out of hand.[6] Disciplines tend to employ one or other basic methodology to the degree that this methodology is characteristic of the type of generic science under which a particular discipline falls. Thus, for example, psychology utilizes predominantly an empirical inductive method, while theology makes use of a predominantly speculative deductive method. Fourth, each discipline is limited and evaluated by distinctive types and manifestations of certain moral rules. It is this basic set of rules which enables each discipline to perform its proper function in the manner appropriate to its level of abstraction and distinctive objectives. These rules not only focus the activity of the discipline but also serve as evaluative-corrective criteria. For example, psychology cannot study the human organism in a way which would defeat the basic purposes of this organism, such as by establishing a controlled situation in which the human subject would have to commit suicide in order that the experiment could be successfully completed.

Viewed in the light of these four criteria, religious instruction surely is not a discipline. It is not an area of inquiry or a branch of knowledge in its own right. The level of abstraction at which it operates is not basically distinctive, but instead incorporates within it levels of abstraction characteristic of several other disciplines. The goal of religious instruction is the facilitation of Christian living, a goal which of necessity incorporates the insights and activities of several disciplines, rather than comprising in itself one discipline alone. Its methodology, while primarily empirical, nonetheless contains much of the speculative, particularly in the theological aspects of religious instruction. Finally, the moral rules which serve to intrinsically limit and evaluate religious instruction are, again, drawn from diverse disciplines; thus, for example, the theological ingredient of religious instruction imposes the rule of remaining within the Christian context while the educational component suggests the restraint of keeping all the learner's experiences educative rather than miseducative or even chancy. Moreover, in the current approaches to religious instruction there seems to be scant effort to work out the principles of formulation, methodology of study, scope of content, direction of activity, and evaluative-corrective norms — all within a broad framework of a systematized, taxonomic set of principles and procedures. This is true at the practical level, whether in the Sunday school, CCD, or parochial school modes. This is also true at the theoretical level, as judged by the writings of persons like Randolph Crump Miller, James D. Smart, David Hunter, Gabriel Moran, Gerard Sloyan, and Mary Perkins Ryan.[7] From the above examination of the extent to which religious instruction meets the criteria of a discipline, it is possible to assert that religious instruction does not possess that integralness, that distinctiveness, and that specificity which would set it off as a separate discipline in its own right.

It is not to the point to argue that in the modern era there are no pure disciplines remaining. At a low level of theoretical development, it is possible to make mutually exclusive distinctions among psychology, anthropology, and sociology. But at the higher levels, analysis clearly shows that each of these three disciplines, all of which study man from a distinctive initial vantage point, tends to overlap in some degree.[8] Even to describe in clearly delimited terms the parameters of a single discipline is becoming more difficult in light of the increasingly higher levels of theoretical and abstractional sophistication of the various disciplines and subdisciplines. At these higher levels, there is a tendency for one discipline to shade into another. Apropos of this, Marc Belth has highlighted "the difficulty of distinguishing the physicist's study of the basis of his operations as a physicist from the philosophy of science."[9] The main point is that there is enough in the functions, objectives, methodologies, and moral rules of the discrete disciplines to validly say that these are indeed distinct disciplines. A practitioner of one discipline does indeed gain valuable insights for the development and enrichment of his own discipline by venturing forth into other disciplines. One might argue that such venturesomeness is necessary for the fulsome development of a distinctive discipline.[10] But this is a far cry from denying that there are disciplines distinct in their own right.

Earlier in this chapter I indicated that a field of endeavor like religious instruction needs to be delimited within some kind of parameters if it is to achieve any sort of focused outcome and fruitful result. Awareness of the parameters within which religious instruction is operating — in order that this area can be carefully cultivated and systematically nourished — is essential if religious instruction is to be rescued from overextension and therefore from triviality. But if religious instruction is not a discipline, how can it possibly be delimited within those parameters so necessary to insure its proper focus and optimum growth? It is patently silly to maintain, as some attempt to do, that religious instruction is a derivative discipline[11] since "derivative discipline" is a contradiction of terms. Nor is it fundamentally fruitful or helpful to distinguish, as Kingsley Price does, between the theory of education and the practice of education.[12]

The solution to the dilemma of the parameters of religious instruction seems to lie somewhere other than in attempting to squeeze it into the specificity inherent in a discrete discipline. Religious instruction is not a distinct discipline; rather it is a meeting place for *certain kinds* of disciplines. What I am suggesting is that the clue to the discovery of the parameters of religious instruction lies not in attempting to delineate it as a discipline but instead to see under what kind of broader science it falls. By asking the question: "Does religious instruction fall within the category of natural science, mathematical science, social science, theological science, and so forth?" we will be able to more clearly ascertain the objectives, boundaries, methodology, and activities proper to religious instruction as distinct from other types of human enterprises.

At this juncture, the objection might be raised: "Does the pinpointing of religious instruction as falling within the scope of one or another broad science really matter? After all, is not the enterprise of religious instruction actually held together by a common endeavor, an actual situation?" My answer is that this kind of identification matters, and matters terribly. Without a clear notion of where religious instruction belongs in the constellation of broad sciences, it would be well nigh impossible to foster its mature development and growth. Without an adequately clear notion of methodology, boundaries, objectives, and appropriate activities, religious instruction becomes an amorphous, blurred, directionless, and therefore necessarily goal-blunted enterprise. Situating religious instruction within its rightful broad science will provide this adequately clear notion of methodology, boundaries, objectives, and appropriate activities.

How do we determine which science provides the proper home for religious instruction? I would suggest that such a determination is made by critically examining the distinctive and unique kinds of activities which go to make up the work of religious instruction. Such determination is made by investigating which kinds of disciplines tend to predominate in the ongoing operation of the teaching of religion. If we find that these activities tend to be reflective of certain kinds of disciplines, and these disciplines tend to fall under the grouping of one science rather than another, then we can say that religious instruction is a type of this or that science. Now it is fairly obvious that the two chief contenders among the broad sciences as the rightful home of religious instruction are theological science and social science. I shall briefly but carefully examine the nature and work of theological science and of social science in Chapters Five and Six respectively. Following this, I shall examine the activities which comprise religious instruction, and see in which broad science they seem to fit best. I shall also test whether the methods and operations of theological science or of social science are most promotive of the realization of the goals of religious instruction. The conclusion of this critical investigation will be that *religious instruction is a kind of social science and not a kind of theological science.* This conclusion is of the utmost importance in the practical order, because if implemented, it will cause a fundamental redirection in the theory of religious instruction and will result as well in a significant sharpening and enhancement of the actual concrete practice of the teaching of religion.

FOOTNOTES

1. William Shakespeare, *The Merchant of Venice*, Act II, Scene 2, line 72. I am here quoting from the First Folio, which scholars generally acknowledge to be the nearest in point of time, with certain qualifications, to Shakespeare's own hand. Hence the citation reads "Line 72." Other editions cite different lines for this passage, for example, line 80 or line 83. I have also rendered the First Folio spelling into modern usage.
2. The journal *Religious Education* devoted most of its September-October, 1967, issue to the consideration of whether religious education is a discipline.
3. All analogies limp. I hope this one does not limp so severely as to confuse the issue. There are some aspects in the element-molecule structure and relationship which are not relevant to, and indeed are perhaps in a certain manner marked contrast to, the discipline-science relationship.
4. Marc Belth, *Education as a Discipline* (Boston: Allyn and

Bacon, 1965), pp. 6-15.

5. *Ibid.*, p. 11.

6. The question of establishing what is and what is not a generic science has been a thorny one throughout the centuries, and it is well outside the scope of this chapter to even minimally treat of this point. Vincent Edward Smith, for example, following Aristotle and Aquinas, concluded that there are six generic sciences: logic, metaphysics, mathematics, natural science, theology, and ethics. See Vincent Edward Smith, *The School Examined: Its Aim and Content* (Milwaukee: Bruce, 1960), pp. 70-82. Other philosophers and scientists throughout the ages have agreed or disagreed in varying degrees.

7. See J. Gordon Chamberlin, *Freedom and Faith: New Approaches to Christian Education* (Philadelphia: Westminster, 1965), pp. 19-20.

8. See R. S. Peters, "Comments," in John Walton and James L. Kuethe, editors, *The Discipline of Education* (Madison, Wisconsin: University of Wisconsin Press, 1963), p. 17.

9. Marc Belth, *Education as a Discipline*, p. 16. To illustrate his point, Belth invited comparison of the writings of Norman Campbell, a physicist, and Ernst Nagel, a philosopher of science, specifically in Campbell's book *Foundations of Science* (New York: Dover, 1957, part 1, and in Nagel's volume *The Structure of Science* (New York: Harcourt, Brace and World, 1961).

10. See Robert C. Worley, "Noetic Models and Church Education," in *Religious Education*, LXIII, July-August, 1968, p. 270.

11. For a proffering of this position of "derivative discipline," see Leonard A. Sibley, Jr., "Religious Education as a Discipline: Report of the Listening Team," in *Religious Education*, LXII, September-October, 1967, p. 429.

12. Price suggests that the theory of education can constitute a legitimate discipline in its own right, whereas the practice of teaching basically is a borrowing from a host of disciplines. Such a distinction seems unwarranted and indeed forced, as can be easily seen by applying this distinction to disciplines such as psychology. Different "practices" tend to form branches of a single discipline. Kingsley Price, "Discipline in Teaching in Its Study and in Its Theory," in John Walton and James L. Kuethe, editors, *The Discipline of Education*, p. 38.

CHAPTER FIVE

THE WORK OF THEOLOGY

"I also have a flower."
"We do not record flowers,"
said the geographer.
"Why is that? The flower is the
most beautiful thing on my planet!"
"We do not record them,"
said the geographer,
"because they are ephemeral."
"What does that mean —
'ephemeral'?"

"Geographies," said the geographer, "are the books which,
of all books, are most concerned
with matters of consequence.
They never become old-fa-
shioned. It is very rarely that a
mountain changes its position.
It is very rarely that an ocean
empties itself of its waters.
We write of eternal things."

— Antoine de Saint-Exupéry[1]

INTRODUCTION
In the last two thousand years, probably no period has witnessed
more confusion and groping in theology than the present time. While
it is something of an exaggeration to assert that there are today as
many theologies as there are theologians, nonetheless it is true that
there exists today a bewildering array of Protestant and Catholic
theological opinion. John Macquarrie's book contains over one hundred chapters, each devoted to a differing major conception of the
nature and function of theology as enunciated in the twentieth
century.[2] Morton Trippe Kelsey, a Protestant religious educationist,
finds five essentially different theologies current today: (1) Thomistic and Neo-Thomistic; (2) liberal, dating from the early part of the
twentieth century as exemplified by Adolf von Harnack; (3) fundamentalist, typically dispensational and conservative, of which Karl
Barth is the refinement; (4) existential, particularly of the kind
exemplified by Rudolf Bultmann and his disciples, out of which the
death-of-God movement arose; (5) experiential, as illustrated by the
higher-order Pentecostals.[3] Most Catholic theologians would probably bridle at Kelsey for placing all current Catholic theologizing
within the Thomist or Neo-Thomist camp. To be sure there is a host
of different major theological types prevalent in modern Catholicism, ranging from a Neo-Augustinianism through an existential
form through a phenomenological variety through an evolutionary
kind and so forth. Whatever stranglehold Thomism might have had

on Catholic theology is broken.

In one sense, then, it is more accurate to speak of theologies than of theology in terms of the current state of the field. Yet the pivotal point to remember, I think, is that while there is a vast panoply of different kinds of theology, nonetheless each of these kinds has a certain nature and does a particular type of work which sets it off from other major areas of inquiry, such as physics or mathematics or social science. Sometimes this point becomes lost in the almost overwhelming mists of confusion which beset contemporary theologizing.

This chapter will delineate in broad strokes, first, the general parameters of theology which set it off as a distinctive field of endeavor, and second, the ways in which theologians work in the course of their theologizing. This procedure will doubtless be unsatisfying for many theologians since they will possibly think that I have slighted their own school of thought. For purposes of this chapter, I lump together Protestant, Orthodox, and Catholic theologizing, although my background in and leaning toward a Catholic kind of theology inevitably seeps through. I do not overtly treat of non-Christian theology, since it is not relevant to this book.

In order to provide as impartial and as broad a sweep of the field as possible, I am utilizing two principal procedures in this chapter. First, I am dividing theological methodologies into sets of contrasting pairs. These sets of pairs are intended to be exhaustive in terms of the various divergent theological methodologies currently employed. Virtually every theology uses one term of one or more of the sets in its work of inquiry. Second, I am using as neutral an approach to the field as possible. With these objectives in mind, I am resorting to a stylistically systematic approach reminiscent of a textbook which will make this chapter as well as the one which follows it stand out from the rest of the book.

In any sphere of human activity, from playing football to photography to theology, a knowledge of fundamental methodology is absolutely indispensable. Too often theological students and inexperienced religious educators cast rigorous methodology to the winds in the name of being relevant or au courant. There is no irreconcilability between relevance and a thorough grounding in the fundamentals. Indeed, I would argue that no serious theologizing and no serious religious instruction can be done apart from thorough training in the fundamentals of theological methodology and instructional methodology. It may be important to deviate from the fundamentals from time to time to be relevant and instructionally effective; however, such deviation is only fruitful when a person first knows what these fundamentals are. When a European nobleman trained in the graces breaks this or that rule of table manners, the effect still remains smooth; not so when a boor breaks the same rule. Some excessively exuberant admirers of the Catholic "new theology" believe that all the fundamentals are unduly restrictive and archaic, overlooking the fact that one of their heroes, Karl Rahner, served as the fifth in the series of redactors of the *Enchiridion Symbolorum*. Some Protestant ministers, all enthusiastic over post-Bultmannism and death-of-God theology, forget that Rudolf Bultmann was extremely well grounded in theological and biblical methodology from his earliest professional years.

The fundamentals of theologizing are independent of any stance of "old" or "new" theology, or of "conservative" or "liberal" theology. Every kind of theology, old or new, represents some form or living facet of the basic entity we call theology. Further, every kind of theology, "conservative" or "liberal," uses one or another kind of methodological procedure described in this chapter.

What this chapter does is to furnish a few of the fundamentals of the nature and work of theology. An understanding of these fundamentals will be of signal assistance to us in ascertaining whether religious instruction is a form of theology or a form of social science.

THE NATURE OF THEOLOGICAL SCIENCE

Definition of Theology

Etymologically, theology means the science or study of God. M. D. Chenu defines theology as "a participation in God's own knowledge of himself."[4] Virgilius Ferm has termed theology the area of inquiry "which concerns the question of God and God's relationship to the world."[5]

On another plane, G. F. van Ackeren has indicated that theology consists in "the methodological elaboration of the truths of divine revelation by reason enlightened by faith."[6] This double constitutive aspect of theology, namely, faith and revelation (to which Catholics add a third, that is, the magisterium) is highlighted by Yves Congar who observes that theology possesses a unique formal object *quod* and *quo* in that it seeks to inquire into the mystery of the revealed God insofar as God can be known by the activity of reason utilizing faith as the point of departure.[7] It is the task of theological inquiry to penetrate and give intelligible expression to God as he has revealed himself in Word and deed — already accepted in faith for his own sake.[8]

According to the overwhelming majority of Protestant and Catholic theologians, this relation between theology and faith is of such a character that true theologizing cannot be done apart from a previous and present faith act. Theology as a methodological investigation "presupposes Christian faith and always proceeds in the light of this faith to its goal of understanding."[9] Theology is thus that intellectual activity which is served by faith and which also serves faith. Anselm's definition of faith is classic in terms of the relationship between theology and faith: "*fides quaerens intellectum*," that is, faith seeking understanding.[10] Theology involves the fullness of faith grown mature in the conscious and methodological attainment of its goal. The work of theology, in M. D. Chenu's pregnant words, consists from beginning to end in the quest to attain "a beatifying knowledge of God and a full life of grace in the world."[11]

The relation of theology to revelation also is very intimate. Karl Rahner and Herbert Vorgrimler have indicated that theology represents "essentially the conscious effort of the Christian to hearken to the actual verbal revelation which God has promulgated in history, to acquire a knowledge of it by the methods of scholarship and to reflect upon its implications."[12] I would expand this notion of revelation to include not only the past verbal revelations of God in history, but also God's ongoing revelatory activities in the here-and-now. Revelation is not just in the past; it lives in the present as well. Further, revelation is not restricted to words in the bible only; it occurs also in the deeds of our daily lives. This is not to minimize the primacy of the place of the scriptures; rather it is to accord to God's revelation the dimensionalities proper to it. *Vox temporis, vox Dei.* While theology does not produce biblical revelation but instead presupposes it, nonetheless theology cannot be too sharply distinguished from revelation since revelation was and is promulgated in human terms.

Besides faith and revelation, there is, in Catholic theology at least, a third constitutive and terminal element in theology, namely the magisterium. It should be underscored, however, that this construct holds true only for Roman Catholics, though some of the Protestant confessions would to some extent maintain that the teaching authority of the church is a relevant factor in theological inquiry.

Karl Rahner and Herbert Vorgrimler contend that the magisterium is a necessary presupposition for theological inquiry, because it is in the living magisterium that the church faithfully preserves the revealed word of God. All theology involves an "undistorted hearing" of God's word with a view to salvation: it is the magisterium which has as one of its chief goals the authentic interpretation of this word of God unto salvation.[13] It should be observed, however, that a new interpretation of the magisterium is slowly evolving. One of the central features of this new interpretation is the dawning realization that the magisterium is perhaps wider in scope than was heretofore imagined. Nevertheless, both the older and the newer Catholic theologies insist on the magisterium as a presupposition to theological inquiry.

Many Protestant theologians, while understandably not directly concerned with the relationship of theology to magisterium except possibly in a negative way, nonetheless do maintain that there is an indispensable relationship between theology and the church. James Smart, for example, conceives of theology as "simply the church taking with complete seriousness the question of its own existence and inquiring with the utmost thoroughness at what point it is failing to be the church of God."[14] Karl Barth proposes an interesting distinction when he states that while "dogmatics" is a theological inquiry, theology proper is a function of the church. Theology is done, according to Barth, in two ways: when the church confesses God through her existence in the action of each individual believer, and when she existentially speaks of God through her special action as a community of believers.[15]

The act of theological inquiry, according to many Catholic theologians, brings the theologian into intimate converse with God, since this converse is indissolubly linked with faith, with revelation, and with the magisterium or church. To do theological inquiry, then, is to engage in "divine communion"; it is this converse and communion with God which comes with theological inquiry that, according to many theologians, "confers upon faith its divine existence."[16] In this view theological inquiry is continuously interpenetrated by and suffused with God. Albert the Great phrases it nicely when he writes: *"Theologia a Deo docetur, Deum docet, et ad Deum ducit."*[17] It is for this reason that many theologians, particularly of the old school, insist on referring to theology as "sacred theology."

Human knowledge about God can arise from revelation freely

given by God and received by man in faith, or simply from a rational analysis of the created world using unaided human reason within a broad framework of experience. The first of these kinds of knowledge of God is called theology while the second is termed theodicy (sometimes called natural theology). It is obvious that certain truths in theology, such as the Trinity or the Incarnation, are unknowable by human reason alone; such truths can only be known through God's revelation and received by man in faith. Theology and theodicy differ radically from one another in terms of both material object and methodology. The material object of theology is God's revealed mystery, while the material object of theodicy is simply the created world.[18] The methodology of theology is reason enlightened by faith, while the methodology of theodicy is unaided reason alone.[19] Unlike the work of theodicy, theology is continuously done within faith. Therefore, according to many theologians, while the work of theology brings the theologian into communion with God, the work of theodicy does not cause this relationship to exist for the theodician. Theodicy basically differs from theology, then, in three major respects: it is not done in faith, it does not utilize revelation, and it is not concerned with the magisterium or with the church. Theology and theodicy are to be properly regarded as complementary rather than as antithetical activities. In one sense theodicy can be conceived of as the vestibule of theology; yet in another sense this relational explanation is overfacile, since it fails to accord to theodicy sufficient independence and dignity.

TYPES OF THEOLOGY

A threefold division of theology is quite frequently made by Protestant and Catholic theologians.[20] These three major divisions, each of which has branches, are positive theology, speculative theology, and practical theology.

Positive Theology

Positive theology examines the Christian religion insofar as it has been revealed both in its own terms and within the cultural and nutritive context in which the meaning of these terms was brought to intelligibility.[21] The functions of positive theology, therefore, are to discover and explain, first, the development of revelation itself within the context of the bible; second, the meaning and truths of revelation within their original historical contexts; and finally, the true development in these meanings and truths from the close of biblical revelation down to the present time. Positive theology tends to be greatly concerned with historical growth. The two principal branches of positive theology are biblical theology and ecclesiastical theology. Theologians maintain that specializations of biblical theology typically include isagogics, biblical history, exegesis, and hermeneutics. The most significant specializations of ecclesiastical theology are patristics, church history, and ecclesiology.

Speculative Theology

Speculative theology examines the intelligibility of the ultimate terms of revealed truths, as far as can be humanly discerned in the light of faith. The functions of speculative theology, therefore, are to discover and explain in a systematic fashion, first, the relationship of these truths and mysteries to things about the world which are known by unaided reason; second, the interconnection among the truths and mysteries themselves; and third, the implications of these mysteries for the natural end of man, broadly considered. Speculative theology is sometimes referred to as systematic theology or doctrinal theology. Speculative theology tends to utilize analysis and deduction to a large degree. There are two principal branches of speculative theology, namely dogmatic theology and moral theology. Dogmatic theology has many specializations including soteriology, Christology, and eschatology. Specializations within moral theology include mystical theology, ascetical theology, and morals.

Practical Theology

Practical theology examines the relation between God's revelation and man's response to that revelation in terms of living out his life as a Christian. The functions of practical theology, therefore, are to discover and explain, first, the conditions of faith and grace present in the dynamic synapse of revelation and the person's living out his life as a Christian, and second, the relationship of the conditions attendant upon this synapse to the care of souls (*cura animarum*). Practical theology is sometimes referred to as pastoral theology. There are three branches of practical theology, one for each of the three essential functions of the church, namely, the priestly function, the teaching function, and the governing function. The primary specialization within the theology of church worship is that of liturgical theology. Theologians believe that among the specializations within the theology of church teaching are homiletics, evangelistics, missiology, and religious education. The major specialization within the branch of theology of church government is canon law.

It should be emphasized that while there are different types of theology, it nonetheless represents basically one single activity of which there are several divisions and branches which are deeply interrelated at every level. While each of the divisions of theology has a somewhat different material object, all have the same formal object.[22] From the Middle Ages onward, practical theology became more and more separated from both positive and speculative theology. The first half of the twentieth century witnessed a reversal of this movement, particularly as a result of the liturgical, pastoral, and kerygmatic renaissance which took place at that time. Moreover, theologians began to disagree with the centuries-old notion, inherited from the Thomistic school, that practical theology or positive theology has any less theological standing or intrinsic worth than speculative theology.[23] But the movement toward effective reunification of the theological divisions really gained momentum in the second half of the twentieth century with the strong theological thrust toward the social gospel and toward the relevancy of Christianity for the working out of a man's existence in the secular city.

I have presented this brief review of the skeletal structure of theology to indicate the proper place of religious education within the broad theological framework as perceived by theologians. It is crucial to observe, however, that these divisions of theology, together with their branches and specializations, represent the constructs of theologians. That is to say, it has been the theologians themselves who have deduced and determined that church history, for example, belongs to the general area of positive theology and that religious education is properly a specialization within pastoral theology. I am underscoring this point because it is not accurate to assert that simply because theologians on their own have decided that one area of inquiry or activity is a type of theology it is therefore necessarily so. Labelling an area of inquiry or activity as one thing or another does not automatically make it that thing. Indeed, the major work of this chapter and the following two chapters is to inquire whether religious instruction is primarily a branch of theology or of social science.

THEOLOGY AND FAITH

Far more difficult than theology to pinpoint is faith.[24] To be sure, there is a considerable difference not only between the Protestant and Catholic notions of faith, but also among Protestant and Catholic theologians as well. At the risk of gravely oversimplifying the complex notion of faith, I should like to identify four elements which appear to represent somewhat of a distillation of the thinking of contemporary theologians on the notion of faith. These elements are not given in any sort of sequential order, whether of causality or of temporality or of importance.

First, faith is an encounter between God and man. In this encounter it is God and only God who takes and maintains the initiative. This encounter engages two free and unique persons, God and man, in a free-flowing embrace.[25] In faith, man is caught up, as it were, in the vortex of divine action in which God is simultaneously the center and the whirl of the vortex. In faith, man encounters God totally on God's terms, yet also exquisitely, totally according to the nature and mode of the individual person. Faith engages man not only in the incomprehensible mystery of God, but even more in a sharing of the very life of God himself.[26] Thus faith, in a sense, constitutes the beginning of that ultimate engagement of the believer in the beatific vision itself.

Second, faith is a total, unqualified, and free assent on the part of the whole man to God. Theologians have typically indicated two kinds of human assent in the faith act, namely notional assent and existential assent. Notional assent implies that man's intellectual powers confess and affirm unconditionally the content of revelation. This notional assent is not given because the person cognitively agrees that the content of revelation is true because of the intrinsic nature of this content. On the contrary, this assent is given by an individual totally on the authority of God precisely because He affirms the revelation content to be true.[27] Faith is a kind of knowing, yet curiously, faith as knowledge begins at the point where human knowledge leaves off because unaided it can go no farther. Notional assent given on the basis of human knowledge always remains conditional, since human knowledge per se cannot yield absolute certainty. In contrast, notional assent given in the light of faith knowledge is always absolutely certain because it is God himself — Absolute Certainty — who is at once the source and object of this knowledge. The absolute certainty of faith knowledge "stems from the supernatural character of its foundation (divine revelation) and its principle (divine grace) which correspond to one another. Faith is infallible because it shares supernaturally in the infallibility of God."[28] Obviously, that to which the individual gives notional assent in the act of faith surpasses the capabilities of unaided human knowledge; consequently God's grace is present in a special way in the particular and abiding faith act. Modern theologians have been according increasing emphasis to the existential aspect of assent. In faith, the person does not give notional assent alone; more crucially, he gives existential assent, the saying of the "yes" with the whole of his being. Existential assent is a deeply personal thing: it is the total act of unconditional human trust by one person (the believer) in another person, Jesus.[29] To have faith is to stake one's whole life on Jesus Christ, on what he says and what he does. The believer places his whole human confidence in Jesus, not because of the rational evidence Jesus has given, but because of who Jesus is.

Third, faith involves a total commitment of the person to the whole of Christian revelation, both written and ongoing. This commitment is also an unconditional one; it is man's living response to Jesus's call, "Come follow me." Faith as commitment differs from purely human commitment because it involves the person's natural *and* supernatural dimensionalities in the living out of Christian revelation in an appropriate manner.

Finally, faith is a compact between God and man. In this compact man submits his whole present self and future destiny, as far as he is able, in an act of self-surrender to God; God, for his part, brings the individual into a state of living fellowship with Him in Jesus. Yet it should be noted that this statement, like all other statements about God, is to be considered analogically in terms of human compacts; consequently the statement suffers from the weakness of all analogies. God is deeply in both terms of the compact, not merely in the second term, since it is God who gives the supernatural grace to motivate and to enable the individual to make the self-surrender which is man's term in the compact.

Paul Tillich's concept of faith is of a somewhat different order of being than the concept of faith I have just indicated. For Tillich, faith is "the state of being grasped by the Spiritual Presence and opened to the transcendent unity of unambiguous life. In relation to the christological assertion, one could say that faith is the state of being grasped by the New Being as it is manifest in Jesus as the Christ."[30] This description of faith bears little resemblance to the older conceptions of faith which had as their basic components the intellect, will, and feeling. Indeed, declares Tillich, a statement such as, "God exists," is not an assertion of faith, but a cognitive proposition grounded in insufficient evidence. According to Tillich, faith includes the following elements: being "opened up" by the Spiritual Presence; accepting this opening up in awareness of the infinite gap which exists between the divine and human spirits, expecting final participation in the transcendental unity of unambiguous life. Of the second element, Tillich notes that a courageous standing in the Spiritual Presence is a requisite characteristic of the person living in faith.

I have spent the last few pages discussing the act of faith with the purpose of indicating that while faith is distinct from theology, it nevertheless plays an important and essential role in theologizing. It is characteristic of theologians to assert that faith constitutes the indispensable starting point for theologizing, because to theologize is to depend on faith in the sense that theology presupposes faith. [31] Faith acts as a powerful motivational force: in M. D. Chenu's words, faith excites in a person, particularly in theologians, "an ardent, an insatiable desire to discover and attain that [Supreme] cause and to obtain from it a science, the science of God in himself and in his designs."[32] Further, theology depends on faith as a starting point insofar as it is the content of faith,[33] which presents to theology, first, a set of propositions and a spirit as initial givens, and second, that continuity with faith and with the God of faith which constitutes the milieu in which theology must begin and continue. Yet faith is not simply a preliminary, a prelude, a necessary launching pad external to the ongoing work of the theologian. On the contrary, faith forms both the starting point and the ongoing, life-giving environment for the work of theology. At every level, theology is tethered to faith and suffused with faith. In other words, theologians assert that theologizing cannot be done apart from continuous faith acts by the theologian or the one theologizing. The use of theological methods and apparatus apart from faith might constitute an interesting investigation of phenomena, but it is not theology. Theology cannot be done without conscious acceptance of and continuous obedience to the self-revealing God as he discloses himself to the theologian both through his own unique person-to-Person communication and through the teachings of the church broadly considered. Further, theological investigation into the divine nature and its manifestations cannot be done without a conscious sharing by the theologian in that life of God which is called faith; a theologian can know of this realm only to the extent that God allows him to share. Theology is, in one sense, the testimony of the

Spirit with the theologian; this testimony calls for belief, which is essentially a personal act.[34] Karl Barth phrases this powerfully when he writes: ". . . dogmatics is possible only as an act of faith, when we refer to prayer as the attitude apart from which dogmatic work is impossible."[35]

To theologize is mainly to elaborate on the content of faith, to transform the content of faith from a personal experience of God's revelation into a universal expression of that experience in a form which can be generalized and hence shared by all men. Theology takes the individualized faith of one man which is supremely valid for that individual, and attempts to cast it into an intelligible form which can be communicated to other men, so that the original individualized faith-experience will thereby become valid for other men to the extent that it reinforces or enhances their own life.

IS THEOLOGY A SCIENCE?

In the previous chapter, I defined science as that combination of interrelated disciplines which are bundled together into a single, broadly distinctive common set of systematized interactive facts, laws, and theories. It would seem that theology meets these criteria requisite of a science. I have shown that there are three kinds of theological disciplines, namely positive theology, speculative theology, and practical theology, each characterized by its own distinctive form and methodology. Within each of these theological disciplines are, as I have already indicated, different branches. As a science represents the consolidation of interrelated and basically similar disciplines into a unified confederation, so does theology serve vis-à-vis the disciplines of positive theology, speculative theology, and practical theology. Theology has its own progressively widening set of explanatory facts, laws, and theories, all of which are woven together in a carefully developed system. This system is distinct from other broad fact-law-theory systems in that it is directed toward the ordering into intelligibility of the mysteries of divine revelation.

The chief characteristic which makes theology a science unique from the other generic sciences is that all the data investigated are explained with reference to God, either because they are God himself or because they are related to God as their beginning and their end.[36] Theology does indeed proceed according to the ways of human knowing, and perforce follows the laws which govern all forms of human knowledge. In the way its object first presents itself for study, in its primary principles, and in its methods of investigation, theology is a science quite distinct from what theologians like to term "profane sciences."[37] Particularly in its method of verification does theology differ from the other sciences. No other science utilizes God's word per se, or supernatural faith, or the magisterium as primary evidence. Not a few scholars in the other sciences claim that because of its peculiar (for the "profane" sciences) object of study, because of *terminus a quo* and *terminus ad quem*, and particularly because of its unique method of verification, theology therefore cannot lay claim to the title of science. This view would appear to be overly restrictive and narrow. It is the sheerest tunnel vision to deny scientific status to other areas of inquiry or activity just because the object of the methodology of these areas differs from that generic science in which oneself is engaged. The scientific spirit or the true parameters of a genuine science can no more be exclusively identified with experimental categories and method than with Aristotelian categories and method. Yet in all candor, it must be conceded that because of its dimensionalities in faith, in revelation, and in the 'magisterium, theology is a science unique from all other sciences. Karl Barth's viewpoint in this regard is sobering. Barth believes that theology as a distinct science is best justified on the basis of practical considerations. These practical considerations are three in number. First, by accepting the label "science," theology confesses its solidarity with other areas of this kind in their unified objective of rendering the unknown and unfelt world more intelligible and more fulfilling. Second, by refusing to abandon the construct of "science" to the "profane areas," theology thereby enters its necessary protest against the all too prevalent view that science is of its very nature a "heathen" affair. Finally, by accepting the designation of "science," theology thereby signifies that the work of the other sciences, "profane" though they may be, nonetheless is vitally complementary to theologizing, and is conjoined with theology at the appropriate level in the work and in the being of the church.[38]

Three basic arguments have been historically advanced in support of the statement that theology is not a science. The first argument is that since theology has the supernatural as its subject matter and also to a certain degree as its methodology, therefore its realm is perforce outside the scope of science. The prime weakness in this argument lies in its assumption that science studies special kinds of phenomena exclusively. On the contrary, all of reality, both natural and supernatural, falls within the purview of science. The second argument is that the creedal commitment which binds the theologian at every, level of his work makes true scientific effort impossible. True science, it is asserted, must be totally free in its investigation of phenomena.[39] In the church's magisterial and pastoral capacity, there rests the inner necessity to remain the vigilant guardian of the Word of God. In this regard, theologians typically hold that to theologize is to ever remain merely the loyal subject of the church.[40] This argument, while appealing in many respects, nonetheless is inadequate, since it is in the nature of every science to have limitations which fall outside of it and deprive it of total autonomy. Thus the natural sciences are not declared to be nonsciences because of the outside limitation which the body politic (or indeed the scientific community itself) places on investigation of the effects of lethal biological or chemical stimulants on involuntary human subjects. The final argument is that the use of faith as both a necessary precondition to theologizing, and also as a primary method of verification causes theology to fall outside the category of "science." God, the object of theological investigation, can only be attained in the light of faith, and then only through a glass darkly. Further, the act of faith demands a certain kind of subjective relationship which falls outside the scope of the purely objective character of science. Also, facts in science are verified in some sort of testable or demonstrable fashion, rather than merely on the say-so of faith. Upon closer scrutiny, this argument tends to break down. To deny faith an investigative or probative character is to beg the question. There are many modes of investigation; no adequate case can be made for the assertion that all of these must be rational or intuitive. Moreover, to state there is a necessary incompatibility between a subjective relationship and the objective character of science is to deny much of scientific method its nutrition. A psychologist who is deeply in love with his wife might thereby gain deeper insights into the research on love which he is doing in his experimental investigation than were he not in love. This is particularly true at the scientific stage involving interpretation of the data. Finally, every kind of science utilizes faith. Though this faith is natural faith, nonetheless it still remains faith in the validity of a guiding principle outside one's own science. The social scientist takes it on faith that man can truly know phenomena outside himself — a fact he takes on faith from the epistemologist. In exploring phenomena from his own vantage point, the physicist takes it on faith that numbers and their various interrelationships are indeed valid — a fact that he takes on faith from the mathematician. Far from debilitating the investigative work of science, faith, whether natural or supernatural, acts as a condition which is at once necessary and enriching to scientific activity.

THEOLOGICAL METHODOLOGY

The double process of investigation and verification is at the heart of any scientific methodology. I will devote most of this section to a brief treatment of theological investigation and follow it with a very short analysis of the role of verification in theological science.

The external source impinging on theological methodology is divine revelation; the internal source is reason illumined by supernatural faith. Within this broad and distinct methodological framework there are specific methods which are utilized conjointly in theological investigation. These methods can be conveniently systematized into three sets of pairs. Each of the terms in a pair is contrary to the other; taken together as a pair they form a categorical set. These three sets are reason and intuition; personal and impersonal; speculative and empirical. These pairs are not mutually exclusive.

Rational and Intuitional Methods

Reason is the gathering into the mind of the intelligible forms of reality and the subsequent judgment of and reasoning about these forms by means of a successive interplay among the various functions of the mind. In theology, the forms of reasoning typically employed are: deduction, axioms, analogy, fittingness, and reduction.

Deduction is the process of reasoning in which we conclude from a general law or from a premise to a particular instance of that law or premise. In one sense deduction is a method distinct unto itself; in another sense, however, deduction is a synonym for the collection of rational methods which proceed from a broad universal to a lesser universal or to a particular. At this time I am using deduction in the second sense. In any event, the deductive process is employed at nearly every stage of the rational activity in theology. Through deduction theology proceeds by syllogistic reasoning to the middle term, thereby arriving at demonstrable theological conclusions. The general law or premise which serves as the starting point for deductive reasoning in theology might be a datum of revelation, or a content object of faith, or a doctrinal definition by the magisterium. Sometimes these take on the outward appearance of a general law; other times they might be stated in such a way that one might think that these are individual instances and therefore unsuited to serve as the initial term of a deductive process. However, it is the unique property of the data of revelation and of faith and of the magisterium that they are not instances or individuals, but instead are actually universals. A datum of revelation is a general law for all men. Jesus is Jesus for all men and for all times.

An *axiom* is a proposition regarded as a self-evident truth. Theologians tend to use axiomatic reasoning with respect to judgments of a very general sort. These judgments cannot be proven, but instead are accepted because of their general explanatory power. Axioms oftentimes provide meanings inaccessible by other methods. Indeed, axioms frequently tend to govern a theologian's reasonings at the very deepest level. For example, in his own theological investigations, Thomas Aquinas made frequent use of the axiom "grace does not destroy nature, but rather perfects it" — yet never once does he attempt to prove this axiom (which is why it is an axiom).

Analogy is the process of reasoning by which we infer to an unknown, certain properties or characteristics on the basis of a degree of their resemblance to the known. Analogical reasoning is undoubtedly more crucial in theology than in any other science, due to the nature of God as transcendent and outside the range of direct human experience. The rational justification for the use of analogical reasoning in theology is that all effects are somehow in their cause, and so the world can be regarded as a reflection or a footprint of God. Whatever characteristics in the order of perfection can be found in creation can therefore by analogy be said to be characteristic of God to the infinite degree. God is said to be infinitely good because men possess goodness. The use of analogy corresponds to the classical *via positiva* in the theological method. Analogical reasoning is a slippery vehicle, one fraught with dangers from a use of unbridled imagination or excessive enthusiasm. The use of analogical reasoning, notably the analogy of proportionality, though laden with peril, nonetheless is an invaluable methodological tool for arriving at conclusions inaccessible by other mental efforts.

Fittingness is the process of reasoning by which a conclusion is reached simply because this conclusion seems to belong appropriately and harmoniously within the total configurational pattern of the reality under investigation. An example of a theological conclusion reached through the argument of fittingness is that it was "fitting" to the highest degree that the mother of Jesus, true God as well as true man, should be exempt from original sin. Fittingness is not a rational proof in the classic logical mode. Notwithstanding, it is in a deep sense rational in that it represents a discovery of the subtle inward relationship of reality. In this sense, fittingness shares somewhat in the intuitive mode of reasoning which I shall discuss shortly.

Reduction is the process of reasoning by which the content of a datum is analyzed in terms of its necessary presuppositions, in terms of the conditions which render it intelligible.[41] Thus reduction is a process converse to deduction. A celebrated illustration of the use of reductive analysis is that of the five ways of Thomas Aquinas. [42] Aquinas here uses reduction to weave a whole dialectic of essence and existence around the bobbin of ontological sufficiency and deficiency; that is, that essence and existence are distinct in the creature, thereby constituting his ontological deficiency, whereas they are united in God.[43] Reduction is an apt methodological tool for analyzing the dialectic of being and oneness. Reduction is a method of transcendental reflection. It goes to the very core of the first principles to seek a richer understanding of them. At its most fulsome, reduction represents a straightforward concentrated piercing by the mind to simplest existence. In such an action, a point is reached "where the intelligence functions, formally, as if it were itself transcendent and no longer like reason alone."[44] Thus, in one sense, reduction serves as a sort of bridge between the broader methodologies of ratiocination and intuition.

Intuition is the direct and immediate apprehension of the object by the mind without any intermediary. Intuition is as fully a mode of knowing as is reasoning; indeed, in some ways it is a higher mode. Sarvepalli Radhakrishnan remarks that intuitive knowledge is not nonrational; it is only nonconceptual.[45] Oriental theologians tend to rely heavily on intuitive knowledge whereas occidental theologians have historically tended to place great stress on reasoning. In theology, three forms of intuition are employed: intuitive cognition, insight, and mysticism.

Intuitive cognition is the immediate grasp by the mind of an object without any conscious reasoning or inferential process. Intuitive cognition consists in apprehending a reality all at once, rather than step-by-step. Intuitive cognition is not independent from, but instead emphatically dependent upon, thought (as distinct from reasoning). What is intuited is recognized, not created, by us. That is to say, what is intuited is not produced by the act of intuition itself. Intuitive cognition differs from mysticism in that mysticism is not only richer in accompanying affective content but is also an elevational force which takes the self totally out of the person uniting it to the object in an all-consuming manner.

Insight is the immediate and penetrating act of intelligent apprehension in which the mind grasps the deeper connectedness and meaning of phenomena as these phenomena are related both to their own inward structure and to broader arrangements within reality.[46] Insight is the placing of the full set of phenomena in any given range into a unique explanatory perspective. The sudden discovery by the reader of the solution to the mystery in a detective novel, or the manner in which Archimedes found his famous law represent two examples of insight.[47] Insight differs from intuitive cognition in that the latter is a direct and immediate grasp of the relationship and meaning of phenomena. Insight has the function of unifying and organizing. Every insight is both *a priori* and synthetic. Five characteristics can be identified concerning the cognitive act that is insight: insight comes as a release to the tension of inquiry; it arrives suddenly and unexpectedly; it is a function of inner conditions rather than outer circumstances; it pivots between the concrete and the abstract; it passes into the habitual texture of one's mental operations.

Mysticism is the consciousness of an ineffable intuitive experience of oneness with God as he is in himself. Mysticism represents virtually a total experience on the part of the one in the mystical state. Though the mystical experience is deeply interwoven with feelings (and is usually communicated to others in words or expressions with rich feeling content), it is also a mode of knowing. Because the content of the experience is simple, direct, nonconceptual, and ineffable, it is impossible for the mystic to communicate in words the knowledge he gained through this experience. Consequently this knowledge is usually communicated through symbolism rich in imagery and allegory. Mysticism is the most clear-cut and most dramatic form of intuition. Because mysticism is a direct experience, it unites the subject (the person) with the object (God) in a most intimate manner. Mysticism is a kind of divine revelation given to a person in a contemplative and intense experience. There are various levels or stages of mystical experiences, each of which yields an appropriate kind and commensurate degree of knowledge.[48] The direct, transcendent contact with God in mysticism is unique and provides theological knowledge attainable in no other way. A prime double task of theology in dealing with data gained from mystical experience is both to sort out the cognitive content from the affective content[49] and to distinguish true mystical knowledge from that gained in pathological states or in overexcited moments.

Personal and Impersonal Methods

The second set of methodological pairs utilized in theological investigation is that of personal and impersonal methods.

Personal investigation is that method of discovering and understanding a reality through intimate human self-involvement. In this century, the personal method has gained widespread acceptance due to the impact of phenomenology and existentialism. There are two principal modes of personal investigation in theology: natural life-experience and living faith. The natural life-experience mode stresses the necessity for the theologian to sit squarely in the middle of the river of life. By immersing himself in the variegated waters of firsthand experience, the theologian can grasp existentially the myriad facets of God's revelation as it oozes through every atom of existence. Much of the significant theologizing today is done wittingly or unwittingly in novels and in film rather than in the conventional monograph — a testimony to the growing importance of the personal methodology. The second mode of personal investigation is that of constant communication with God through the life of faith. Indeed, it is precisely the knowledge and understanding gained through this kind of communication that makes theologizing, at appropriate levels of depth and range, possible to people of all talents and walks of life. It is this kind of personal methodology which supplies theological understanding to the greatest theologian, and to the simple parish clergyman, and to the little old woman keeping the Word of God as best she can. To be sure, most theologians go so far as to assert that theologizing is impossible without remaining in a continuous state of inner communication with God in faith — immersed, as it were, in the lifestream of faith. After all, the data of theology are received through revelation — not only the revelation of the bible and tradition and the magisterium (or church) but through the personal content revealed in the actuality of living faith. Commenting on the internal laws of theology, Thomas Aquinas holds that the data and principles of theology, while *relativus* on the part of God who infuses, must become *orativus* on the part of the person receiving them. "It is in prayer and adoration, and in the profoundest sense of the word devotion, that theology, the understanding of the word of God, is born and lives."[50]

Impersonal investigation is the method of discovering and understanding a reality through a systematic objective study of phenomena. This method utilizes reasoning and intuition to come to discovery and understanding, rather than drawing on personal lived total firsthand experience for this purpose. Impersonal methodology represents the exterior operations of theologizing, while personal methodology constitutes the interior workings. Impersonal theology might be termed a thinking theology whereas personal theology can be called a praying theology. Impersonal theologizing, though perhaps less humanly appealing than personal theologizing, nonetheless is of crucial importance to theological investigation. As with any science, one must continually have recourse to systematic gathering of relevant data which are built into laws and theories to gain any sort of understanding and meaning. In ancient times, the milkmaid laughed at Thales who was so absorbed in observing the stars with a view to understanding them more deeply that he could not see the well right at his feet. There is a place for both milkmaids and for Thales in the work of theological investigation.[51] Personalistic and impersonalistic methodology are not opposed to each other: they are instead complementary.

Speculative and Empirical Methods

The third set of methodological pairs utilized in theological investigation is that of the speculative and empirical methods.

The *speculative method* is that process of knowing in which phenomena are investigated and examined from a mental point of view, and are verified by use of mentally-derived and mentally-validated principles. Speculation utilizes the manipulation of ideas as its virtually exclusive *modus operandi*. It relies very heavily on the metaphysical rules of logic. Much of speculation emanates from careful and systematic meditating and pondering on a problem, often in reflective awareness. Consequently speculation has at times been characterized as "armchair science" or "rocking-chair knowledge." The data used in speculation can be derived either in an *a priori* or *a posteriori* manner. The speculative method uses both the inductive and the deductive approach, though its prime method is distinctly deductive. This is not only true of *a priori* data but also with *a posteriori* data. Even in reasoning from effects to cause in attempting to rationally adduce the existence of God, the theological scientist does so in light of much *a priori* data, such as the relevant content of faith and the content of revelation.

The *empirical method* is that process of knowing in which phenomena are investigated through procedures gained from and tested in experience. Empirical methodology is focused on the use of systematically observable, testable, and replicable procedures. The data themselves are manipulated in such a fashion that they can be tested in a quantitative way. In the testable event, empirical methodology emphasizes the controlled observation, the replicable phenomenon, and quantitative inference, whereas speculation tends to work primarily with the reasoning and intuitive processes. Empirical methodology is based exclusively on *a posteriori* procedures and tends to use the inductive approach to investigation. In the first half of the twentieth century, there was a segment within theological science, notably among the Protestant theologians, who became deeply interested in what they termed "empirical theology." One of the central attempts of the proponents of empirical theology was to utilize empirical methodology to examine more carefully the data of religious perception and of faith as it is personally experienced.[52] The work of the so-called Chicago school of empirical theology represented, in one respect, a high-water mark in the development of empirical theology.[53] In the late 1960's, some Catholic theologians began to suggest the use of aspects of the empirical method in investigating the premises and data of moral theology.[54]

Verification

Thus far in this section, I have been devoting my attention primarily to the nature and function of investigation in the work of theology. Now I should like to briefly discuss the process of verification as it operates in theological science. I did, of course, introduce a consideration of verification at several points throughout my discussion of theological investigation. At this juncture, however, I wish to treat this aspect of theological science in a compact unitary manner.

Verification is the process of establishing the truth, the accuracy — and in appropriate cases, the reality — of both the conclusion(s) of the investigation as well as the very process of reaching the conclusion(s). In theology there are five primary methods of verification: scripture, tradition, magisterium (or church, in the case of the Protestants), faith, and natural logic. The first four pertain to the supernatural dimension; the last belongs to the natural realm.

Scripture forms a basic type of verification in theology. For example, it is the revealed word of God in the scriptures which verifies the event of the Resurrection. Because the event is revealed in the bible, it is *ipso facto* verified.[55] Less easy of such clear-cut verification is the more expansive type of revelation of which contemporary theologians are speaking.[56] The slippery aspect of the verification process in both of these kinds of revelation is the interpretation of the revealed data. How is the raw datum of the Resurrection to be interpreted? Further, what does it mean both to me and to the life of Christians in general? How is the original eucharist event to be interpreted? Will not this datum take on as many significantly different interpretations as there are major groups of individual interpreters? Why is it that distinguished scholars of different denominations, and even within the same denomination, interpret scripture so differently? Scripture scholars, of course, have identified scientific procedures appropriate to their task. As is typical in any science, most of these procedures are accepted as valid by theologians of different persuasions, while some procedures are rejected and other new procedures are suggested. Yet sharp disagreements on scriptural meaning and interpretation remain, despite the use of scientific procedures. Now all this suggests that in the verification process in theology, the various procedures of verification mentioned previously interact both with one another and as a group to produce in the end a final act of verification. Each of these verification procedures, then, acts as a control, a corrective, and a beacon in arriving at the final verification. Or is the hard fact of the matter, that at bottom it is faith and the magisterium which are the principal verifiers in the operational order?

Tradition also acts as an important mode of verification. In theology, tradition is a means whereby God communicates his revelation to man in ways other than by writing. Tradition is ultimately derived from the oral preaching by Jesus and the apostles insofar as these oral communications were preserved and continued by their friends and disciples in oral, written, institutionalized, or artifacted form. Tradition is not simply an oral substitute for written teaching, to supplement what in some way was not included in the bible. Rather, tradition has its own self-sufficiency even in cases where both scripture and tradition deal with the same content. The so-called "deposit" of Christian revelation is not merely a message qua data; it constitutes a whole Christian way of life.

Tradition is either verbal or existential. Verbal tradition is that which is expressed originally in spoken form, although it might have been reduced to writing at some point in time. Existential tradition is that life and activity of the church by which she embodies and presents the whole redemptive mystery, for example, in the liturgy.[57] Some theologians envisage tradition as a mode of the church's awareness, comprising objective and subjective aspects. According to this notion, the role of tradition in the church is analogous to the role played by awareness in the person's mental life.[58]

In terms of origin, theology has typically identified three types of tradition, namely, divine, apostolic, and ecclesiastical. God and Jesus are the bearers of divine tradition; the apostles initiated apostolic tradition; while the church, particularly illumined by the Holy Spirit, initiated ecclesiastical tradition in the apostolic period.

Tradition is not a conservative force but rather a force which promotes continuity and authenticity of the original basic Christian message and life with Christian life in succeeding eras. Genuine tradition helps to maintain the original spirit and life and message of Jesus and the apostles. Tradition, like scripture, contains that basic corpus of revelation which is so essential to a church continuous in time with the days of Jesus because it contains within itself rich potentialities for the incarnation of that spirit and life into the existential realities of every age. Tradition, then, is not a bulwark against change; it is instead a fluid reservoir (fed by the springs of historical continuity with the revelation initiated by Jesus and the apostles) by which change can be made congruent with revelation.

Theological science utilizes tradition as a mode of verification; however, there are considerable intrinsic and extrinsic difficulties in employing tradition as a verification tool. First of all, there seem to be significant disagreements among theologians as to the parameters of tradition. Oscar Cullmann, for example, maintains that oral tradition has normative value only until approximately 150 A.D.; yet Irenaeus, writing about the year 180, affirmed the necessity of tradition as a verifier of the content of theology. When the popes down through the centuries issued significant doctrinal pronouncements, such as the *ex cathedra* definition of the Immaculate

Conception, tradition is typically adduced as a vital form of verification of the authenticity of the doctrine. Yet some of the church's leading theologians, including Thomas Aquinas, have stated that this doctrine, while believed by many of the faithful, nevertheless does not represent authentic tradition. This suggests that a significant methodological problem intrudes itself in the use of tradition as a verification procedure. For example, what are the criteria for asserting that such and such represents actual tradition, as contrasted to pious and otherwise praiseworthy accumulations of the ages? It would seem in the final analysis that tradition is what the magisterium says it is. If this be the case, then the use of tradition as a verification procedure is of greater assistance as a corroborative verifier than as a powerful verifier in its own right.

The *magisterium* in the Catholic confession, or the church in the Protestant persuasion, serves as a process of verification and also a corrective on revelation and traditions. What the magisterium, or "teaching church," holds and declares, according to theological science, has verifying power in terms of the identification and interpretation of revealed truths. How this verification by magisterium or church takes place, and indeed what is the constituent scope of the magisterium or the church is still to some degree a controverted point among theologians;[59] yet there seems general agreement that the magisterium and the church act as significant agents in theological verification.

Faith is one of the hinges on which verification in theology swings most. The theologian is constantly verifying the methodology and the conclusions of his scientific work against the content of his faith. "How does this work square with what he knows, and particularly with what he has experienced in that intimate and superabundant living relationship with God which is termed faith?" — this is a question the theologian is continually posing to himself. It is faith which supplies the light and the power which make a man's theologizing possible. It is faith which gives worth and meaning to his theologizing. Therefore, faith stands at the heart of the verification process in theological science. Faith is to stake one's life on Jesus, and theologizing is to stake one's scientific activities on faith. Faith is to commit oneself totally to Jesus, and theologizing is to commit one's scientific investigations to faith. It is his standing in faith which assures the theologian that his theological explorations are congruent with the divine reality. Theology is a science of evidence, and faith by its very nature supplies this evidence. The theologian believes in the word of God, and it is this very word of God which constitutes the object of theology.

Let us examine, for example, the way in which theological science attains, at bottom, verification of the fact of the resurrection of Jesus. The historian would utilize as the axis of his verification procedures, the fact that there were eyewitnesses to the empty tomb, the fact that Jesus was actually seen by many persons after his witnessed entombment, and so forth. For a theological scientist, this procedure operates only as a supporting verifier. The fundamental verification procedure, when all is said and done, is the faith which the theologian has in the word of God as revealed in the scripture. After all, there is a yawning gap which prevents any kind of scientist from passing from the historical plane to the supernatural plane. In this verificational passage from natural to supernatural, it is Beatrice, not Virgil, who is the primary force.

While verification by faith is the best of verifiers from the subjective standpoint, it is not without its explanatory difficulties from the objective standpoint. Since faith is a personal relationship between the believer and Jesus, every person has at once the same kind of faith and a different shading of that faith (esse et talis). The process of verification of its very nature implies that what is being verified will be true for all men depending upon the level of force and validity of that verification. For example, the thesis that two parts of hydrogen when combined with one part of oxygen under given conditions results in water can be verified for all men. However, the extremely sharp divergence on the part of theological scientists as to their conclusions surely indicates a serious problem in terms of verification. Particularly acute for Catholic theologians is the problem of disagreement with the magisterium on theological conclusions. Since the magisterium and the theologians are both situated deeply in the life of faith, theoretically there should be no difference in their conclusions. But the magisterium has had a long history of condemning heretics, and in our own time of denouncing proponents of "novel opinions" and tenets claimed to be at variance with the magisterium. To be sure, the magisterium asserts that when the conclusions which a theologian reaches are not in agreement with the magisterium, then the theologian has a duty to "form his conscience and his conclusions in a right manner," that is to say, in harmony with the magisterium. In verification, then, is fides super ecclesiam, or is the ecclesia broader than the magisterium, or indeed is the composition of magisterium itself broader than those hierarchs who are typically considered to comprise the magisterium? All this has serious implications for the notion and strength and quality of verification in theological science, and indeed for the validity of theology as a science.

Finally, the use of *natural logic* according to the structure and principles of this logic acts as a verifier in theological science. In this regard, quite a few theologians are wont to remark that the procedures of natural logic — whether deduction, reduction, intuition, or the rest — act more as a negative check on theological investigation than as a verifier in the proper sense of that term. Still in a way, every act of verification serves as a negative check. Natural and supernatural phenomena are in harmony; there is no double truth or double universe. Consequently the proper utilization of natural logic, according to the scientific rules and laws governing the validity of the different methods involved, does surely serve as a mode of theological verification.

In the preceding pages, I have indicated that there are five principal verification procedures used in theological science: scripture, tradition, magisterium (or church), faith, and natural logic. It will be readily apparent that all but one of these verifiers are of a supernatural character. This suggests that the prime mode of verification in theology is supernatural.[60] In fact, even natural logic, the only nonsupernatural mode, is utilized in such a manner as always to square with the supernatural verifiers; if it strays, then it is declared either substantively or methodologically inaccurate.

Correlative to this point is the fact that at bottom verification in theological science is almost exclusively made from authority — the authority of God speaking through scripture, tradition, the magisterium, or faith. Thomas Aquinas phrases it succinctly: "The science of sacred theology is most appropriately based on the argument from authority because its principles are had through revelation. Consequently it is necessary to believe on the authority of those to whom the revelation has been given. In no way does this detract from the worth of theological science for though the argument based on human authority is the weakest of all, nevertheless the argument based on the authority of divine revelation constitutes the strongest of all possible arguments."[61]

THEOLOGICAL METHODOLOGY AND FAITH

Now that I have given an overview of theological methodology, I think it would be well to examine briefly the relationship of faith to theological method. In general, faith has three basic rules vis-à-vis theological method: faith is a theological method; faith shapes theological method; faith suffuses theological method.

I have already discussed in sufficient detail — at least for the purposes of this chapter — the way in which faith serves as a theological method. But faith also acts to significantly shape theological method. As G. F. van Ackeren phrases it, "in trying to understand the mysteries believed by faith, the question is not whether the mysteries are true, . . . but why or how they are true."[62] In other words, the theologian in his investigative and verificatory activities utilizes faith as a living filter.

Faith suffuses theological activity both at the objective and the subjective levels. At the objective level, faith acts to illumine and transform all the mental operations involved in theologizing. Through the suffusing action of faith, the operations of the human mind and spirit in theologizing are brought to the supernatural plane, while still remaining exquisitely human in the full sense of that term. Faith enables a theologian to accord supernatural assent to a supernatural truth. Faith brings to theologizing a reverential and obediential aspect, since faith represents an act of communion of theologian with God, especially when the theologian is theologizing. At the subjective level, faith bestows a personal and therefore an enriching element rarely found in the other generic sciences. Flooded with the intense illumination and personal contact with God that is faith, the theologian qua person enters intimately into his theologizing. M. D. Chenu remarks that in certain moments of grace, faith becomes "a sort of intoxication" to the theologian, arising from the rarified and inebriating nature of the mystery of the divine object of his scientific activities. Apropos of this, Chenu cites John Damascene who remarked that the theologian is "swept off his feet in the vast sea of the divine substance, for the more fully he partakes of this Life [by theologizing in conspectu fidei], the more he feels it to be beyond his grasp on a level he can never reach."[63] Surely the scope and intensity of this subjective element, as it is present in theological science, is scarcely, if ever, present in the work of the other generic sciences.

Is it possible for a nonbeliever, that is one not in experiential communion with God in faith, to do theology? The overwhelming body of Catholic and orthodox Protestant theologians firmly assert that theology can be done only by a person who is living the life of faith while he is doing his theology. Theology can never be simply and exclusively a *theologia speculativus*; it must always be at the same time a *theologia orativus*.

To summarize and conclude this section on theological methodology, it can be said that theological science is primarily speculative rather than empirical; primarily deductive rather than inductive; primarily supernatural rather than natural; primarily rational rather than intuitive. Further, theological methodology contains within it a strong personal element and a significant mystical constituent as well. Divine authority, external to the other sciences, is for theology part of the very fiber of the object of its study and of its mode of verification also. Theology depends on faith, uses faith, and is suffused by faith. Theology presupposes faith, is illumined by faith, and works toward understanding faith by means of faith enlightening understanding. Most theologians hold that one cannot theologize apart from a life of faith. In one sense, this faith-theology relationship is circular and hence presents to theology a basic problem of verification and of scientificness.

The advancement and further refinement of theological methodology can be significantly enhanced by the development of theoretical models.[64] Models make it possible to grasp the interactional unity of the whole of methodology, which in turn tends to give birth to new ways of conceptualization and theorizing. The social and natural sciences have found that model building has proved of great value in augmenting their own theorizing and subsequent relational investigations.

FOOTNOTES

1. Antoine de Saint Exupéry, *The Little Prince*, translated by Katherine Woods (New York: Harcourt, Brace and World, 1943), p. 54.
2. John Macquarrie, *Twentieth-Century Religious Thought* (New York: Harper & Row, 1963).
3. Morton Trippe Kelsey, letter to me dated July 6, 1970.
4. M. D. Chenu, *Is Theology a Science?*, translated by A. H. N. Green-Armytage (New York: Hawthorn, 1964), p. 24.
5. Virgilius Ferm, *A Protestant Dictionary* (New York: Philosophical Library, 1951), p. 254.
6. G. F. van Ackeren, "Theology," in *New Catholic Encyclopedia*, volume XIV (New York: McGraw-Hill, 1967), p. 39.
7. M.-J. Congar, "Théologie," in A. Vacant, E. Mangenot, and E. Amann, editors, *Dictionnaire de Théologie Catholique*, tome

XV (Paris: Letouzey et Ané, 1946), column 494.

8. Paul Hitz, "Théologie et Catéchèse," in *Nouvelle Revue Théologique*, LXVIII, November, 1955, pp. 908-909.

9. G. F. van Ackeren, "Theology," p. 39.

10. Anselm, *Proslogion, proemium.*

11. M. D. Chenu, *Is Theology a Science?* p. 63.

12. Karl Rahner and Herbert Vorgrimler, *Theological Dictionary*, edited by Cornelius Ernst, translated by Richard Strachan (New York: Herder and Herder, 1965), p. 456.

13. *Ibid.*

14. James D. Smart, *The Teaching Ministry of the Church* (Philadelphia: Westminster, 1954), p. 33.

15. Karl Barth, *Church Dogmatics: The Doctrine of the Word of God*, volume I, part 1, translated by G. T. Thomson (Edinburgh: T & T. Clark, 1936), p. 1.

16. M. D. Chenu, *Is Theology a Science?* p. 92.

17. Cited in Paul Glorieux, *Introduction à l'Etude du Dogme* (Paris: Vitrail, 1948), p. 13.

18. Henricus Denzinger et Adolfus Schönmetzer, editores, *Enchiridion Symbolorum*, editio XXXII (Barcelona, España: Herder, 1963), p. 591 (Vaticanus I, sessio 3, cap. 3, no. 1795).

19. For an elaboration of this point, see M.-J. Congar, "Théologie," columns 447-462.

20. It should be noted that not every Protestant or Catholic theologian admits of this threefold distinction. Some, like Paul Tillich, for example, hold to a twofold distinction. Further, some theologians differ slightly in the placing of one or other branch of theology with a particular major division. However, the threefold distinction among divisions and the placing of branches within selected divisions tends to be representative of the broad sweep of Christian theologians.

21. On the notion of intelligibility in the discussion of the types of theology, see J. Thornhill, "Methodology (Theology)," in *New Catholic Encyclopedia*, volume IX, pp. 756-757.

22. Thomas Aquinas, *Summa Theologica*, I, q. 1, a. 4.

23. See, for example, Paul Tillich, *Systematic Theology*, volume I (Chicago: University of Chicago Press, 1951), p. 33.

24. I am here treating of the act of faith rather than the virtue of faith or the notion of faith.

25. Eugène Joly, *What Is Faith?*, translated by Illtyd Trethowan (New York: Hawthorn, 1958), pp. 44-52.

26. In their description of this encounter of God and man in faith, I find that Karl Rahner and Herbert Vorgrimler tend to stress encounter more as notional than as existential participation. See Karl Rahner and Herbert Vorgrimler, *Theological Dictionary* p. 157.

27. The celebrated definition of faith given by Vatican I succinctly encapsulates this concept. *"Hanc vero fidem,... virtutem esse supernaturalem, qua, Dei aspirante et adjuvante gratia, ab ex revelata vera esse credimus, non propter intrinsecam rerum veritatem naturali rationis lumine perspectam, sed propter auctoritatem ipsius Dei revelantis, qui nec falli nec fallere potest."* Henricus Denzinger et Adolfus Schönmetzer, editores, *Enchiridion Symbolorum*, p. 589 (Vaticanus I, sessio 3, cap. 3, no. 1789).

28. Juan Alfaro, "II. Faith," in Karl Rahner et al., editors, *Sacramentum Mundi*, volume II (New York: Herder and Herder, 1968), p. 319. Paradoxically, while faith is objectively certain, it is subjectively obscure.

29. See Henry Bars, *Faith, Hope and Charity*, translated by P. J. Hepburne Scott (New York: Hawthorn, 1961), pp. 15-17.

30. Paul Tillich, *Systematic Theology*, volume III, p. 131.

31. Morton Trippe Kelsey holds that theology presupposes religious experience rather than faith. For Kelsey, a Jungian-oriented Protestant religious educationist teaching in the religious education program at the University of Notre Dame, faith is a somewhat vague and meaningless word. He prefers the concept "religious experience" and all which this concept implies.

32. M. D. Chenu, *Is Theology a Science?* p. 31.

33. Theologians use this term "content of faith" not to indicate inert data, but to indicate the dynamic fourfold constituents of the faith relationship which I have previously sketched.

34. M. D. Chenu, *Is Theology a Science?* pp. 32-33.

35. Karl Barth, *Church Dogmatics: The Doctrine of the Word of God*, p. 25.

36. Thomas Aquinas, *Summa Theologica*, I, q. 1, a. 7.

37. The term "profane sciences" is even used by modern theologians in the context I am here employing it. See Karl Rahner and Herbert Vorgrimler, *Theological Dictionary*, pp. 456-457.

38. Karl Barth, *Church Dogmatics: The Doctrine of the Word of God*, pp. 4-11.

39. Paul Ramsey, *Religion* (Englewood Cliffs, New Jersey: Prentice-Hall, 1965), p. viii.

40. See, for example, M. D. Chenu, *Is Theology a Science?* p. 125.

41. Compare this definition with that of P. Coffey: "Reduction ... [is] the process of so rearranging the premises [of a syllogism] that the same conclusion still follows from them but now in a different [syllogistic] mode — whether of the same or of a different figure." P. Coffey, *The Science of Logic*, volume I (London: Longmans, Green, 1918), p. 335. I am following Chenu very closely in my discussion of reduction. M. D. Chenu,

Is Theology a Science? pp.72-75.

42. Thomas Aquinas, *Summa Theologica*, I, q. 2, a. 3.

43. M. D. Chenu, *Is Theology a Science?* p. 73.

44. *Ibid.*, p. 72.

45. S. Radhakrishnan, *An Idealist View of Life*, revised edition (London: Allen, 1937), p. 153.

46. Insight, in the sense I am utilizing it here, is distinct from the psychological construct of insight as employed by the Gestaltists. See Willard D. Ellis, editor, *Source Book of Gestalt Psychology* (New York: Harcourt, Brace, 1938); Ash Gobar, *Philosophic Foundations of Genetic Psychology and Gestalt Psychology* (The Hague, Netherlands: Nijhoff, 1968); George W. Hartmann, *Gestalt Psychology* (New York: Ronald, 1938); Wolfgang Köhler, *Gestalt Psychology* (New York: Liveright, 1947).

47. These examples are given by Bernard Lonergan, the most celebrated contemporary proponent of the method of insight. My treatment of insight here is exclusively derived from Lonergan's seminal book *Insight*, revised edition (New York: Philosophical Library, 1958).

48. On this point, see Cuthbert Butler, *Western Mysticism* (London: Constable, 1922), pp. 5-19.

49. See Heribert Fischer, "Mysticism," in Karl Rahner et al., editors, *Sacramentum Mundi*, pp. 137-138, and p. 141.

50. M. D. Chenu, *Is Theology a Science?* p. 41.

51. I am indebted to Frederick Crowe for this apt analogy. See F. W. Crowe, "On the Method of Theology," in *Theological Studies*, XXIII, December, 1962, p. 638.

52. As an example of such a proposal, see Douglas Clyde McIntosh, *Theology as an Empirical Science* (New York: Macmillan, 1919), pp. 106-107.

53. See Bernard E. Meland, *The Future of Empirical Theology* (Chicago: University of Chicago Press, 1969).

54. See, for example, Charles Curran, "Social Ethics and Method in Moral Theology," in *Continuum*, VII, Winter-Spring, 1969, pp. 50-62.

55. Bultmannians would qualify this statement in their terms of kerygma and myth. See Rudolf Bultmann, "New Testament and Mythology," in Hans Werner Bartsch, editor, *Kerygma and Myth: A Theological Debate*, translated by Reginald H. Fuller (London: S.P.C.K., 1957), pp. 1-44.

56. See, for example, Gabriel Moran, *Theology of Revelation* (New York: Herder and Herder, 1966).

57. J. A. Fichtner, "Tradition (in Theology)," in *New Catholic Encyclopedia*, volume XIV, p. 225.

58. For a discussion of this point, see Yves Congar, *The Meaning of Tradition*, translated by A. N. Woodrow (New York: Hawthorn, 1964), pp. 76-78.
59. See, for example, Hans Küng, *Structures of the Church*, translated by Salvator Attanasio (New York: Nelson, 1964); also Karl Rahner, "Magisterium," in Karl Rahner et al., *Sacramentum Mundi*, volume III, pp. 352-355.
60. In terms of many twentieth-century Protestant theologians, this statement would have to be significantly qualified. For the Bultmannians and quite a few of the post-Bultmannians, the terms "mythological" and "supernatural" tend to be interchangeable. See Robert D. Knudsen, "Rudolf Bultmann," in Philip Edgcumbe Hughes, editor, *Creative Minds in Contemporary Theology* (Grand Rapids, Michigan: Eerdmans, 1966), pp. 158-159.
61. Thomas Aquinas, *Summa Theologica*, I, q. 1, a. 8, ad 2. Translation mine.
62. G. F. van Ackeren, "Theology," p. 41.
63. M. D. Chenu, *Is Theology a Science?* p. 36.
64. See Ewert Cousins, "Models and the Future of Theology," in *Continuum*, VII, Winter-Spring, 1969, pp. 78-92.

CHAPTER SIX

THE WORK OF SOCIAL SCIENCE

"And he was showing Pierre a globe. This globe was a living, quivering ball, with no definite limits. Its whole surface consisted of drops, closely cohering together. And those drops were all in motion, and changing, several passing into one, and then one splitting up again into many. Every drop seemed striving to spread, to take up more space, but the others, pressing upon it, sometimes absorbed it, sometimes melted into it."

— Leo Tolstoy[1]

INTRODUCTION

I have frequently seen it happen that people interested in the social-science approach to religious instruction wish to know the nature and function of social science itself. These individuals believe, and rightly so, that an understanding of the soil in which this approach to religious instruction is rooted will enhance and enrich their own religion teaching.

The purpose of this chapter, then, is to provide a brief overview of the basic principles of social science so that teachers and curriculum builders desirous of employing the social-science approach to religious instruction can use the information supplied herein as a wellspring. If religious instruction is to move forward in a social-science direction, it is vital that the concepts contained in this chapter be understood and integrated into the teacher's professional lifestyle. Even those religious educators who might not yet be ready to accept the social-science approach should possess an understanding of social science itself, since it is on the scientific axis rather than on the theological plane that most of the modern world operates. To understand the modern world, one must first understand the nature and work of social science.

This chapter is situated within the broader context of a book on religious instruction. Consequently it will be of greatest advantage to the reader if he will constantly relate what is written to the enterprise of religious instruction. For example, in reading the section on prediction, one might relate the social-science notion of the prediction of future behavior to the work of religious instruction (to structure the learning situation is to cause, that is, to actualize a prediction that a desired outcome will be attained). Or again, in reading the section on social-science research methodology, one might connect this kind of research procedure to religion teaching (to validly ascertain whether a religion class is effective, the teacher or curriculum builder will have to employ research techniques).

This chapter compresses into a relatively small space what typically takes an entire book to treat. To do this, I employ a tightly-written literary style, in some ways reminiscent of a textbook. In this regard, the present chapter and the preceding one stand out from the rest of the book.

An even minimally adequate understanding of the social-science approach to religious instruction rests on the information in this chapter. Further, much of what follows in this book hinges on a grasp of this chapter.

THE NATURE OF SOCIAL SCIENCE

Social science is a generic term for the collection of those disciplines which are focused on the detailed, systematic, and empirical study of human beings and their interrelations with individuals, groups, and institutions. Research in the social sciences consists of systematic, controlled, empirical, and critical investigation of hypothetical propositions about the presumed relations of human beings and the complex of variables with which they interact. The findings of this type of research lead to that kind of discovery and explanation which naturally flow from social science.

The scope of the social sciences in terms of constituent disciplines remains a controverted point. Some specialists prefer to make a distinction among what they name the social sciences, the semisocial sciences, and the sciences with social implications.[2] Because of the relative newness of the social sciences, and because of the lack of clarity concerning which are or are not the social sciences, I will not attempt such a distinction. Rather, let me simply indicate those disciplines I include under the generic name "social sciences": anthropology, economics, education, geography, history, law, political science, psychiatry, psychology, and sociology. Sometimes the term "behavioral science" is used synonymously with "social science"; other times, "behavioral science" is used to signify a group of disciplines including psychology and psychiatry which form a generic subdivision of social science. My own usage will follow the latter nomenclature. Finally, it should be noted that social science is not the same as sociology. Indeed, sociology is itself a discipline falling within the broader category of social science.

The confederation of disciplines within the rubric "social science" does in fact constitute a single science. These disciplines share the same subject matter (the behavior of men) and the same methodology (empirical and natural-scientific). In addition, as George Homans has pointed out, they employ the same body of general explanatory principles, although some social scientists might take issue with this point.[3]

As is typical of any generic science, social science does possess its own technical vocabulary. To those not knowledgeable in social science, or to the layman in general, the use of such specialized words might seem to constitute needless jargon. But jargon is the use of pretentious and outlandish terminology which has an obfuscatory rather than a clarifying function.[4] Technical terminology, on the other hand, represents the attempt to give a precision and a clarifying power to a word which ordinary usage does not so endow on a word or term. The natural sciences have the most advanced set of technical terms, as even a casual follower of the space program is aware. Medicine is replete with technical terminology: "Nurse, what did the biopsy reveal?" Theology contains a wealth of technical terminology whose meaning is unknown to anyone except those familiar in some way with that science. Words like "grace," "eucharist," "incarnation," "epiphany," and so forth are all technical terms. Technical terms in social science, then, are not jargon used to impress the uninitiated, nor are they just a difficult way of stating common sense. Rather, these terms make it possible to convey in the shortest, most precise way meanings which will readily be understood by others conversant with the field.[5]

Social science itself, as well as its constituent disciplines, utilizes both pure and applied research. This point is well worth remembering because so many people outside the social sciences seem to think that social science is concerned exclusively with empirical data-gathering and testing. Theorizing plays a crucial and indispensable part in the work of social science. Indeed, it may be argued that data-gathering and testing are done so that theories which are more fruitful and more explanatory might emerge. Further, theory also constitutes one of the important points of departure for data-gathering and testing. To be sure, the great advances within social science tend to be made by the theorists who gather and integrate the data into new forms and thrusts of explanation. Sigmund Freud, Carl Jung, Talcott Parsons, Erik Erikson, John Dewey, to name a few, were all data-oriented theorists.

As I indicated earlier in this chapter, any science, whether theological science or social science or natural science, has two prime functions, namely discovery and explanation. In social science, discovery consists of stating and testing the more or less general relationships between properties of the phenomenon under investigation. These relationships were unknown or unrecognized before research revealed them. Important and crucial though discovery is in the work of science, more valuable still is the offering of general explanations of and within the phenomena studied. Such explanations typically take the form of theories. In education, for example, instead of attempting to explain the different ways in which teachers and learners interact in a classroom setting, the educationist seeks general explanations which encompass and link together all these interactive behaviors.

SOME CHARACTERISTICS OF SOCIAL SCIENCE

Empirical

Social science is empirical in the sense in which I have used this term in the chapter on theological methodology. Social science is characterized by close adherence to observable data so that whatever conclusion is reached from the investigation follows naturally from the observable procedure rather than from sources which are speculative, authoritative, or uncontrolled. The formulation of laws and theories is based on empirically discovered and verified data, and indeed these laws and theories are themselves verified as far as possible on empirical grounds.

One of the hallmarks of social science is its constant nourishment from the real, concrete, existential world. Social science is concerned with the exploration of individual and group behavioral activities. Therefore if social science is to be valid, it must continuously be in touch with the actual observed behavioral patterns of individuals and groups. Social science therefore cannot legitimately *speculate about* what is taking place in the behavioral patterns of individuals and groups; rather, social science must continually explore and examine as directly as practicable these patterns of behavior. This exploration is carried out by empirical research of divers kinds — research designed to reflect and assess as accurately as possible the actual ongoing behaviors of persons and groups.[6] Social science "does something with," rather than simply "looking at" its subject matter.[7] All social-science concepts about persons, groups, or things must be defined and worked out of observable characteristics.[8]

Central to the empirical method is the testing of the data gathered from the controlled observation of the phenomena under study. For example, we may observe that a man eats frequently. But this datum does not tell us why the man is eating. Is he eating because he is hungry, or because he is anxious? To find the answer, a social scientist proposes a tentative hypothesis which seems to most effectively explain the existent data; he then sets about to erect a situation in which the conditions would be so controlled as to provide an empirically verifiable test of this hypothesis. Of course, the man in the street also tests his hypothesis, but typically he tests it in a selective fashion which frequently represents ways of confirming his hypothesis. To illustrate: if a religiously devout person believes that churchgoers tend to be racially fairminded, he will often filter out from his perceptual field those instances in which he sees a church-going person express a bigoted attitude toward a person of another race, while allowing expressions of nonbigoted racial attitudes on the part of church-going persons to enter his perceptual field. The social scientist, on the other hand, will insert empirical controls all along the line so that the data he gathers reflect accurately the objective state of the phenomenon under investigation. (Incidentally, empirical research has concluded that churchgoers tend to be more racially prejudiced than non-churchgoers.[9]) Evidence in social science is obtained by careful testing of the data to determine the accuracy of hypotheses about the data and the range of their validity.[10] For example, American Protestant theologians in the seventeeth and eighteenth centuries, and well into the nineteenth century, tended to believe in the depravity of man. Parents and teachers of that time implemented these data in their own relationships with children by assuming that negative reinforcement (punishment) was a more effective stimulus to learning than was positive reinforcement (reward). In the mid-1920's, Elizabeth Hurlock, a social scientist, empirically tested this assumption and found that quite the opposite is true: when employed over a period of time, positive reinforcement (reward) produces greater gain in learning than does either negative reinforcement (punishment) or no reinforcement at all.[11] Subsequent social scientists have replicated this study under different conditions, and the results have generally confirmed Hurlock's findings. Religious educators typically assumed that bible stories represented an effective way of inducing symbolic learning at a low level in children. The celebrated empirical research investigation by Ronald Goldman concluded that before the age of ten or twelve, such bible stories result in great confusion and misinterpretation of symbolic material on the part of the young learners.[12]

Empirical testing is not the same as experimental testing. To be sure, experimental testing, that is testing of human subjects in the laboratory or in other controlled environments, represents only one way of empirical testing. All sorts of empirical testing devices exist, many of them of the paper-and-pencil variety, such as, for example, the Minnesota Multiphasic Personality Inventory used to assess whether or not a subject has a personality dysfunction. Questionnaires and survey research constitute other kinds of empirical nonexperimental testing procedures. For example, Andrew Greeley and Peter Rossi conducted a survey research investigation on two groups of adult Catholics: a selected group of average, representative Catholics, and a group of Catholics identified by the researchers as being the "intellectual and liberal elite." One surprising conclusion of this study was that a significantly higher percentage of the intellectual and liberal elite group than the average group rated religious instruction as the principal advantage of the Catholic school.[13]

Quantitative

Social science is oriented toward quantitative treatment of the data. Quantification is the process of assigning numerical values to observations which are commonly qualitative. Quantification is important because it enables the investigator to be more precise in measuring both the data and the differences between and among various classes of related data. For example, an individual's quantitative score on an empirically-derived and validated attitude scale yields more precise, more informative, and more predictive data than does the statement: "This individual has strong positive ecumenical attitudes." Also, quantified results on this attitude scale will reveal the extent of significant correlations and differences among the several subscales within this instrument, thus giving a deeper meaning to the person's tested ecumenical attitudes.

Replicable

Social science research is replicable, that is, it is reproducible under the conditions given in the original investigation.[14] Social science features openness of inquiry; another scholar can test the finding by seeking to reproduce it. Social science research does not depend on the personal sensibilities or personal vision into reality, or personal faith-life unique to the researcher; instead, any scientist, regardless of his personality or his faith commitment, can reproduce the original investigation.

Public

Social science is public, and the results and methods are both communicable and communicated. The final report of the research investigation contains a detailed description of the conditions, the methodology down to the smallest detail, the results, the conclusions, and sometimes the interpretation of the data. Consequently any competent person can examine and evaluate the researcher's methodology, even going so far as to reproduce the original experiment or other research design initially employed. I recall a sociologist of religion once reading the report of a research investigation conducted by a colleague from another part of the country. This sociologist asked his colleague to send him the original computer cards on which the colleague's data were recorded so that he might rerun the cards using other statistical formulae in order to ascertain whether his colleague's methodology — and therefore his conclusions — were correct.

Objective

Social science is objective. Any hypothesis, however cherished, which a social scientist holds, must constantly be checked by what Fred Kerlinger terms "the court of empirical inquiry and test."[15] During each step of the investigation, from the systematic observation through the gathering of findings down to the formulation of conclusions, the social scientist is bound to follow the data, no matter how they fall. The work of social science is such that in its path toward attaining knowledge it employs continuous self-correction from both internal and external sources. There are built-in checks all along the way. These checks are so structured that they act to filter from the investigation any bias or contamination coming from a source outside the data themselves. Indeed, even if an experiment or other type of empirical test seems to confirm or deny the researcher's original working hypothesis, he will test out any promising alternative hypotheses which might cast a shadow of doubt on the original hypothesis. Moreover, these built-in checks are rooted as far as possible in reality lying outside the social scientist and his personal beliefs, perceptions, values, and emotions. Social science is founded on empirical or objective evidence. The results of social science investigation are always confronted by the results of other empirical and experimental tests.[16] Further, the internal methodology of the investigation is subject to the protracted scrutiny of statistical and other objective considerations.

One of the chief ways in which social science maintains its objective character is through the systematic application of rigorous controls. It is this constant use of standardized controls which makes empirical evidence gained in social science more valid than empirical evidence arrived at by the man in the street. For example, it was reported that a certain Jesuit priest in his mid-70's was summoned to the office of the local archbishop to explain the basis for the priest's rejection of the papal encyclical on birth control. The priest's response was direct and forthright: "On the basis of forty-two years of hearing confessions."[17] The priest here used empirical evidence to support his hypothesis, but because of the absence of controls there was no way for an outside observer to check on the objectivity — and therefore the validity — of the priest's data. Was the priest falsifying to sustain his hypothesis? Did the priest, because he believes in the legitimacy of birth control, unconsciously block out of his perception many instances in his confession experience in which the papal view would be upheld? Did the penitents form a representative sample of Catholics at large? What was the psychological state of these penitents? How accurate were the data which the penitents were reporting to the priest? I am raising these questions not to suggest that this priest was wrong — or even right — but rather to indicate that his evidence lacked objectivity and therefore in itself lacked the weight which a social science investigation of phenomena would normally have. It is the purpose of methodological controls to provide social science with that level of objectivity which is of a higher order than the empirical evidence adduced by the man in the street.

Empirical control represents the attempt to regulate every important factor hypothesized to exert or in fact actually exerting an influence on the precise object under investigation. Ideally, no significant factor should remain uncontrolled. To achieve this goal, the important variables must be isolated, described, utilized, or rendered inoperable during the observation, data-gathering, and testing phases of the investigation. Throughout the interpretation phase, these variables must be taken into account. In empirical research two types of nonmutually exclusive kinds of control are utilized, namely statistical control and experimental control. Statistical control represents indirect control over the variables while experimental control utilizes direct control procedures. Statistical control refers to the process of working with "quantitative data gathered from samples of observations in order to study and compare sources of variance of phenomena, to help make decisions to accept or reject hypothesized relations between the phenomena so studied, and to aid in making reliable inferences from observations."[18] Experimental control is "the attempt to equalize, by direct methods, the effects of one or more extraneous factors on the criterion measures of an experiment."[19]

An example might serve to illustrate the use of control procedures in social science research. We wish to find whether method x is more effective than method y in teaching the bible to youth of high school age. The first thing we do is to select a desired outcome which will be of a power sufficiently discriminatory to establish the difference in effectiveness (should any exist) of method x versus method y. Then we operationalize the intended outcome so that it can be put into a form suited to quantitative measure, as far as this can be done. The next step is to set up two learning groups, the characteristics of both groups being as nearly alike as possible in all respects, for example, identical distributions on intelligence, on attitudinal achievement, religiosity scales, similar socioeconomic backgrounds, and so forth. In other words, everything is held constant as far as possible except that which is being tested. The teacher now utilizes method x for the first group of learners and method y for the second group. After an appropriate number of teaching sessions, the two groups of students are given a test designed to accurately assess their gain in learning, in terms of the desired learning outcome. The data gathered from this test are then statistically treated to ascertain reliability, validity, relation, and variance — all in order to reveal whether there is any significant difference in effectiveness between the two teaching methods, and if so, what kinds of differences there are. I think this example, oversimplified as it is, nevertheless illustrates most of the controls which the social scientist utilizes in his research.

It is manifestly impossible to control all the variables in a piece of empirical research. In the case of those variables which for one or more reasons (usually stemming from practical considerations) cannot be controlled for, assumptions are substituted for the control. Such assumptions are most valid when they are derived from the results of comparable empirical research. The prime advantage of control, apart from the fact that empirical research is impossible in its absence, is that it gives to social science research a functional order and regulation which enable the investigator and indeed the general public at large to have a critical confidence in research results.

The proper use of controls facilitates rather than guarantees objectivity in empirical research. It is patently impossible to design an empirical method in social science which completely controls for all the variables, particularly the subjective variable.[20] Further, at the very heart of the process of social science lies the formulation of hypotheses and theories which are the fruits of the individual scientist's interpretation and speculation about the data.[21] Social science consists in more than data-gathering. However, the method of rigorous controls in observation, data collection, and statistical treatment does in fact act as a significant filter on the intrusion of subjective elements which might contaminate the objectivity of the phenomena under investigation.

Value-free

Social science is value-free. Social science is concerned with an impartial investigation and explanation of phenomena, without regard for any system of thought or group of people which would assign value judgments to either the phenomena or to the conclusions of the research. Consequently there is no room in social science for such value-oriented words as "good" or "excellent"; instead value-free words such as "effective" or "fruitful" or "useful" are used. Hence, after examining a religion teacher's lesson, a social scientist's conclusion would be that this was an effective or an ineffective lesson in terms of the particular variables he was observing.

Problems in social science are not moral or ethical questions. Social science tries to find out, for example, what is the most effective way to teach the bible to adults who come from disadvantaged areas. Social science investigates whether there is a correlation between attendance at a religion class and juvenile delinquency. The social scientist does not begin his investigation by stating, for example, that the dialogue homily is better than the more traditional sermon, or that the introduction of liturgical participation in religion class is better than separating the cognitive aspects of religion from the liturgical act. Such propositions are articles of belief, not impartial hypotheses to be studied and tested. In social science, these questions, proposed as value judgments, have to be restated. Such restatements would indicate an hypothesized relationship between the variables and an operational definition of the variables so as to permit a testing of the hypothesized relationship.

Because it is value-free, social science is not normative. Social science does not make statements concerning what ought to be or what should be. Social science is in no way normative vis-à-vis values. Social science simply makes statements about what is, as discovered from empirical observation and testing of the phenomena. In social science, the term "validity" does not refer to congruence with statements emanating from some outside authority (for example, the magisterium, the state) or from some source external to the phenomenon itself (for example, scripture, federal law). Validity in general social-science method refers to that characteristic of a concept whereby it is said to yield successful predictions.[22] Validity has a more restricted meaning in specific social-science methodology.

The state of being value-free and nonnormative in no way implies that social science is not concerned with values or norms. Indeed, much if not most of contemporary social-science research is focused on the investigation of values in one form or other. The relationship of social science to values is that values constitute the phenomena which social science studies. But unlike theology, for example, social science does not assign values or normative judgments to these phenomena. When a social scientist investigates a person's behavior in such-and-such a situation, he does so not to ascertain whether that behavior is good or bad (for example, heretical, immoral), but rather to learn the functional relationship of the conditions which caused this phenomenon and how under given circumstances the individual's behavior can be modified or reinforced (prediction). Social science, of course, accepts certain benchmark values as a necessary framework within which it operates in a value-free way. For example, in examining the relative effectiveness of teaching method x compared to teaching method y, the social scientist accepts certain previous moral values, such as avoidance of physical harm to a student, as a preplanned part of the research design. Christian social scientists similarly work within a given framework of values. However clear-cut in theory the relevance of a value code is as a framework within which social science works in a value-free methodological fashion, in practice problems continually crop up. Suppose, for example, a social scientist wishes to test the effectiveness in the religion class of a unit which is centered around the sinfulness of stealing. Would it be immoral, in terms of the Christian value code within which a Christian social scientist is working, to set up the research design in such a way that youths are presented with an opportunity to steal something in an in-laboratory or out-of-laboratory setting? A satisfactory solution to this problem would consume many pages, and is outside the direct scope of my discussion here. I raise the issue simply to indicate that the application of the value-framework principle is not always a clear-cut matter for the social scientist.

Conditional

Social science is conditional. Social science explanations hold true only for a certain range of phenomena, and are applicable only when specified conditions are realized. The phenomena which social science investigates are not pure processes devoid of content, devoid of existential specificity, devoid of context. The very existence of a particular phenomenon is deeply imbedded in some sort of a context, as are the interactions of any phenomenon with other phenomena.[23] For example, the investigation of the comparative effectiveness of teaching method x vis-à-vis teaching method y is made in a particularized cultural setting (country, region, city, part of city), in a particularized milieu (a school situation), with particularized groups of people (students, fifteen-year-olds, teachers, women). Strictly speaking, the findings of the research are applicable only to the particular group studied, and only in those circumstances.

The conditionality of social science gives no occasion for depair or disappointment. To be sure, it is accurate to assert that nothing is true in social science "except under certain circumstances." However, the findings of one research study can be generalized to other situations in which the conditions are similar to those present in the original verified setting. The more nearly identical an unresearched area is to the area tested, the more valid will be the generalization of the findings. Social science is not an exact science; it is a science of approximations, as perforce are all kinds of inquiries into human behavior. Approximations in social science are stated in terms of probabilities — the whole world works on probability. By use of careful methodology, social science can indicate the degree of probability to which such-and-such a finding can be generalized to other situations. Let us say, for example, there has been an empirical investigation into the relative effectiveness of four different kinds of teaching methods for improving understanding of the bible on the part of fifteen-year-old boys and girls from a low income district in New York City. It is probable that the findings of this study can be generalized to the same kind of teaching-learning situations in other big cities. It is even possible that the findings can be generalized to the same kind of teaching-learning situation in smaller cities. On the other hand, the more dissimilar is the situation to which the original findings are being extrapolated, the less is the generalizability of the original investigation. Only subsequent related research in other settings will ever truly validate the generalizability of the original study. Conditionality, Abraham Kaplan observes, has to do with the restricted circumstances in which the tested data suggest sound explanations, being limited to those in which it is relevant and related.[24] It is the task of social science as a total science to systematically accumulate enough data in a sufficiently wide variety of circumstances to be able to validly generalize about broad conditions and interactions of human behavior. This has already been done in the case of quite a few heavily-researched sectors of human behavior.[25]

Prediction

Social science is aimed at prediction. In other words, social science sets out to discover what specific set of variables interacts in such a way that the outcome of this interaction can be accurately forecast. To illustrate: research on the nature of religious behavior is significant to social science not so much for discovering the nature of religious behavior as for being able to predict what set of circumstances must be brought together for religious behavior to be produced. The discovery of what will tend to bring about religious behavior is, in May Brodbeck's terms, "to find a set of symptoms which, without additions or deletions, will enter into laws, that is, enable prediction of other behavior."[26] In terms of religious instruction, the social scientist wishes to learn which classroom conditions serve as accurate predictors that such-and-such a desired learning outcome will be achieved. Once this is known, the teacher can then so structure the learning situation that these conditions are present and operable.

Prediction is an inference to the forecast of future behavior, made on the basis of past performance in a setting where certain conditions were functioning. Consequently prediction of future behavior is only legitimate and accurate to the extent that the set of conditions present in the predicted-to behavior was also present in that past setting on which the prediction is based. Illustrative of this is the instrument developed by Milton Rokeach to measure an individual's level of dogmatism. In testing his instrument Rokeach discovered that, as predicted, Catholic students in Michigan obtained significantly higher D (for dogmatism) scores on his instrument than did Protestant students. However, these results did not hold up in New York.[27] One of the principal reasons for the lack of predictability to the New York sample is, of course, that the milieux — a vital condition — in Michigan and in New York differ significantly. In expanding the predictability of any instrument or teaching strategy, the social scientist tests his original findings on as many individuals and groups under as many conditions as possible. In this way he can discover the extensions and limits of predictability — and often in the process he can so modify the original instrument or strategy that it can be utilized to predict a particular response in a yet greater number of sets of conditions.

Explanation

Social science seeks explanation. For social science, explanation is the process of making phenomena intelligible vis-à-vis their context within a larger body of systematic and coherent relationships. A social scientist seeks to know and to prove the how and the why of phenomena in order to be able to predict the conditions under which a specified behavior can or will be brought forth. To seek an explanation for an event is to seek a generalization which can be applied to similar kinds of phenomena. Therefore to state an explanation is to state a scientific law, and in some cases to suggest a broad theory.

Explanation is to be distinguished from result, from analysis, and from interpretation. A result is a statement of the summarized observations. Analysis is the ordering and categorizing of these observations (data) in order to be in a position to answer the initiating research problem.[28] Analysis is the structuring of the data in such a way that these data will more readily provide an answer to the research question. Interpretation is the act of assigning meaning to the analyzed result. Interpretation comes through making inferences pertinent to the research relations under investigation, and then drawing conclusions about these relations. Interpretation can be made in one or both of two ways. Interpretation can be made of the results and their relation within the research investigation itself. This kind of interpretation flows almost automatically from the analysis of the data. A second kind of interpretation is that in which the analyzed results of this research investigation are compared with the analyzed results of relevant investigations conducted either by other researchers or by oneself. It must be noted that analysis and interpretation are made through use of the rigorous canons of valid empirical methodology so as to exclude as far as possible any contamination by subjective forces. Explanation is the subsuming of the correlated conclusions of many related research investigations into a more generalized and generalizable law.

An example might clarify the point. We wish to investigate the effect of a teacher-centered versus a student-centered instructional methodology in modifying a specified religious attitude in a particular group of youth. The methodology of the study is a relatively unsophisticated one. We divide the youth into three subgroups, either on a totally random basis or on as close a matching of personality characteristics as possible. One subgroup of youth are taught in a deliberatively teacher-centered fashion, the second subgroup in a deliberatively student-centered fashion, and the third subgroup without any specific attention to teacher-centeredness or student-centeredness. The first two subgroups form the experimental groups, the last subgroup, the control group. We control for constancy of all the variables except that for which we are testing. We administer a standardized attitude test before the beginning of the experiment and again after its termination. The results of the investigation reveal particular scores on the pretest and posttest attitudes for each of the three groups. Analysis of the data indicates that a greater modification of student attitude in the desired direction took place in the student-centered subgroup than in the teacher-centered subgroup. A further analysis reveals that the attitudes of those youth in the student-centered group who were identified on a psychology inventory as permissive were more greatly modified than those youth in this same group who were identified as authoritarian. Interpretation of these data analyses concludes that student-centered behavior by the teacher is more effective for this group of youth in modifying their attitudes in the desired direction than is teacher-centered behavior, and further, that student-centered behavior by teachers is particularly effective with students whose personalities can be described as permissive. This interpretation is widened and reinforced by comparing the conclusions of this study with those of similar studies, and noting the strong positive correlation between the conclusions. These interpretations suggest several tentative explanations, such as (1) that specified teacher behaviors are effective in modifying student behavior, or (2) that there is a relationship between teacher behavior and the personality of students vis-à-vis inducing desirable learning outcomes.

Explanation is intimately connected with prediction. One of the most important reasons for the existence of social-science explanation is its prediction of what conditions will bring about a specified or a desired behavior. In his attempt to clarify the functional relationship between explanation and predictability in physics, Hans Reichenbach employs the term "postdictability" to characterize explanation, and "predictability" to characterize prediction. William McEwen suggests that Reichenbach's distinction might prove fruitful for social science.[29] An explanation is as fruitful as the generalizability it possesses. This generalizability is frequently termed "explanatory power."

Social-science explanation differs most significantly from theological explanation or from metaphysical explanation in that the former represents generalization from empirically tested relations among phenomena. To explain juvenile delinquency on the basis of the youth's lack of cooperation with divine grace is to offer a theological explanation. A social scientist seeks the explanation for juvenile delinquency from the interaction of such variables as family life and cohesion, physiological factors, sociocultural milieu, economic setting, and so forth.

GENERAL METHOD OF SOCIAL SCIENCE

Induction

Induction is the process of reasoning in which we conclude from a group of particular instances to a general law. In one sense induction is a methodology distinct unto itself; in another sense, however, it is a synonym for the collection of rational methods which proceed from particulars to universals. At this time I am using induction in the second sense. The inductive process is the fundamental rational procedure employed in social science. On the basis of individual bits of data, the social scientist induces an hypothesis to explain the relation of these data to one another, or the relation of this set of data to other sets of data. Then the social scientist subjects the data to rigorous empirical tests, all of which tend to have an inductive character. From the measured results of these tests, he verifies or rejects his working hypothesis, induces explanations, and evolves predictions.

Because of its empirical nature, social science quite obviously has the inductive rather than the deductive approach as its prime axis. As Henri Grenier notes, the deductive syllogism is based on the connection of its three terms (concepts or notions) and consequently belongs to the purely intelligible order. Induction, on the contrary, works toward proving that a predicate is identified with a universal subject because it is identified with the singulars of an enumeration; therefore the inductive syllogism passes from the sensible order to the intelligible order. The conclusion of an induction expresses a law of nature or a law that is derived from experience. The conclusion of a deductive syllogism typically expresses a truth which is known from principles. Consequently induction is the rational process proper to empirical knowledge while deduction is the rational process proper to speculative knowledge.[30]

Whatever deductive processes might be utilized in social science are utilized in reasoning about those general hypotheses and laws which were discovered and verified by inductive methodology.

Deduction

As I noted in the previous chapter, deduction is the process of reasoning whereby we conclude from a general law or from a premise to a particular instance of that law or premise. In one sense, deduction is a method distinct unto itself; in another sense, however, deduction is a synonym for the collection of rational methods which proceed from universals to a lesser universal or to a particular. At this time I am using deduction in the second sense.

Most social scientists contend that deductive reasoning is utilized in the following phases of social science: elaborating on hypotheses, offering explanations, making predictions.

Fred Kerlinger maintains that once the social scientist has fashioned a working hypothesis from the data, he then deduces to specific probable consequences of this hypothesis. In this deductive process, the social scientist arrives at a problem quite different from the one with which he originally began. Indeed, the hypothesis itself might need refinement or amplification as a result of the implications deduced from it.[31] The use of the hypothesis in social science constitutes a major difference between the pure use of inductive reasoning and the scientific approach. In pure induction the investigator first makes his observations and then organizes the data gained. In the scientific approach, the investigator deductively reasons what he will find if an hypothesis is true, and then systematically makes controlled observations in order to confirm or fail to confirm the hypothesis. The scientific method is typically regarded as a process involving five successive steps: (1) moving inductively from observation (by the investigator himself or other prior investigators) to an hypothesis; (2) proceeding deductively from the hypothesis to the logical implications of the hypothesis, that is, deducing that certain consequences will follow if an hypothesized relationship is true; (3) testing the hypothesis by empirically gathering relevant data; (4) confirming or rejecting the hypothesis; (5) placing the hypothesis in a wider context of a general law.

Most social scientists, then, hold that the process of explanation in social science consists in placing the individual analyzed results of the investigation(s) in a deductive system in terms of which these results assume meaning.[32] George Homans writes "explanation is the deduction of empirical propositions from more general ones." [33] In other words, the explanation of a finding, whether a generalization or a proposition about a single event, is at bottom the process of showing that the finding follows as a logical conclusion or a deduction from one or more general propositions under specified given conditions. For Homans, the proposition to be explained (the *explicandum*) is deduced and derived from other propositions, the whole set forming a deductive system. A law may be explained by deducing it from other laws.[34] Karl Popper is of the opinion that offering a causal explanation of a result or an event is to deduce a statement which describes that result or event — using as the premises of the deduction one or more empirically-derived universal laws, together with certain singular statements (the given conditions).[35] Israel Scheffler sharpens the discussion when he notes that "despite the fact that explanatory premises are not themselves deducible from available evidence, explanation may consistently be held to be a matter of deducing from such premises descriptions of the events to be explained."[36]

Prediction, in the view of most social scientists, is making a prophecy by deductively inferring it from the particular facts and laws already known and verified. It is precisely this deductive connection between statements which shows why observations confirm or refute hypotheses. If a prediction deduced from a set of premises turns out to be true, then naturally the generalization is thereby further confirmed. If, on the other hand, the prediction turns out to be false, then either the generalization or some individual fact used in making the prediction must be false. Since there is less likelihood that the fact is false, the failure of a prediction typically indicates that the generalization is thereby refuted.[37]

Social science methodology is typically regarded as being an eclectic combination of the inductive and the deductive processes. The hybrid designation "inductive-deductive" is commonly employed to indicate both the primacy of the inductive over the deductive in the work of social science, as well as combinative character.[38] No science — with the possible exception of mathematical science — is either purely inductive or purely deductive. Though one of the two methods of reasoning predominates to a greater or lesser extent, nonetheless both are present in any situation. Exclusive use of induction would result in the accumulation of isolated bits of knowledge and information. It is through deduction that these bits are placed into a wider explanatory system — although even here induction plays a part. In social science the inductive process predominates; however it predominates according to the combinative procedure called the inductive-deductive process, that is, the scientific method. In this connection it might be well to recall Herbert Feigl's remark that many logical empiricists have traditionally tended to misclassify certain rather basic synthetic statements as "really analytic."[39]

Concept

In an apt analogy, May Brodbeck states that the words of ordinary speech correspond to the concepts of science, and the sentences correspond to its definitions, to its statements of individual facts, to its laws. Certain sets of sentences correspond to the theories of science.[40] As I have previously indicated, a concept is a word which expresses an abstraction formed by generalizing from particulars.

Concepts are formed out of observations of certain related particular behaviors. "Religion," "culture," and "intelligence" are examples of concepts. Concepts comprise the indispensable and irreducible elements which go to make up theoretical explanations in social science. Indeed, the development and the validity of scientific theory are contingent upon the accuracy and type of conceptual apparatus which is used. In its work of investigation social science utilizes two basic kinds of concepts, namely substantive and methodological. Substantive concepts, sometimes called phenomenal concepts, are those which related to the subject matter being investigated. Methodological concepts, sometimes known as procedural concepts, are those which have to do with the investigation process itself. Both of these classes of concepts are essential to the work of social science, yet each leads to generically different types of theory. In its work of explanation, social science tends to utilize concepts which are relational or functional rather than those which represent classificatory or property terms. Functional concepts are typically more useful and more fruitful in social science explanation than are classificatory concepts.[41]

Because social science utilizes concepts as one of its basic building blocks toward more penetrating investigation and more comprehensive explanation, there is the danger of identifying the concept with the phenomenon. A concept is simply an abstraction made for the purpose of more fruitful investigation and explanation; it is not the concrete phenomenon itself. Failure to recognize this point results in reification, that is, treating these abstractions (concepts) as if they were real phenomena. Concepts exist in the logical order, not in the phenomenal order. For example, some persons seem to worship religion (a concept) rather than perform those specific behaviors from which the concept "religion" is capable of being induced.

Definition

A definition is a set of words which states what a reality is. A definition indicates the conditions which are both necessary and sufficient for the applicability of the term being defined. A definition is always a tautology, since the left-hand side of the definition has no independent meaning, but represents only a code word for the right-hand side. In social science, a reality can be defined in any one or more of three sets of ways, depending on the referent. Definitions can be either real or nominal, notional or operational, operating or nonoperating.

A *real definition* is a statement of the essential characteristics of a reality. A real definition equates the word defined with some objectively existing reality. "Man is a rational animal" is a real definition. A real definition, therefore, is a proposition which is either true or false. Robert Bierstedt suggests that a real definition possesses three important properties: it states that two expressions, each of which has an independent meaning, are equivalent to each other; it has truth claims; it can serve as a valid premise in inferential reasoning.[42] A *nominal definition* is the assigning of a meaning to a term on an arbitrary basis. By arbitrary I mean that there is no necessary ontological ground for equating the two terms in the definition proposition. "Hot" might be nominally defined as the state of a substance when it has attained a certain temperature level measured by degrees centigrade. The designation of such-and-such a temperature level carries with it a certain arbitrariness.

Real definitions have both ontological and logical consequences, whereas nominal definitions have only logical consequences. Because a nominal definition is only logical and verbal rather than founded in objective reality, it has no inherent claims to truth. Why is it, then, that social science so frequently employs nominal definitions? Nominal definitions are frequently more accurate than real definitions, thus for example, the nominal definition of "hot" is more precise than its real definition. Nominal definitions serve as shorthand for the introduction of new and more precise technical terms into the language as in the case of the word "centigrade." Nominal definitions tend to be operational in format and therefore are more suited to the work of social science than the more metaphysically-oriented real definitions. Finally, nominal definitions are judged by their utility function while real definitions are judged by their ontological truth value. Social science is not concerned with investigating or explaining truth in an ontological fashion. It is concerned with the usefulness of concepts, definitions, and so forth in explaining more comprehensively and deeply the phenomena under investigation.

A *notional definition* defines a concept or a construct by using other descriptive words about it, in the fashion of the dictionary. An *operational definition* defines a concept or construct by indicating what actions or behaviors the word denotes or connotes. Notional definitions tend to be positively correlated to real definitions; operational definitions tend to be positively correlated with nominal definitions. I have treated the nature and distinction of notional and operational definitions in Chapter Two, consequently it would be repetitious to go into this here.

George Homans has suggested that the set "operating definitions and nonoperating definitions" be more widely employed in social science methodology. He defines an *operating definition* as the specification of the significant variable(s) which appear in the testable proposition embodied in the definition. A *nonoperating definition* obviously is the converse. As an illustration of a nonoperating definition, Homans offers a standard definition of role: "the behavior expected of a person occupying a particular social position." Homans prefers to think of a nonoperating definition as an "orienting statement" rather than as a definition.[43]

Definitions play a significant part in the work of social science. Definitions operate to clarify and distinguish the various constituent elements under investigation. While a definition does not form the basis of reasoning in the inductive sciences, it nevertheless does point out the course of investigation.

Fact

A fact, in social science, is an empirically observed and tested phenomenon. Facts are established, not simply discovered. In other words, adequate testing and verifying procedures must be employed to ascertain whether or not such-and-such is a fact. For example, we might state as a fact that John is a religious youth. But we cannot state this as a fact until we have empirically tested whether this is indeed a fact; such testing would come about by systematically observing, recording, measuring, and assessing John's behaviors, and finally comparing these data with some validated standard of distinctively religious behaviors.

In social science we are frequently unable to attach the term "fact" to any reality simply by observing it. It is impossible, for instance, to directly observe a child's I.Q. Further, we are frequently unable to attach the term "fact" to any reality merely by one observation of it. By observing a youth only once, we cannot legitimately declare it a fact that the youth is or is not religious. An individual fact is only significant and fruitful in social science in so far as it is connected with other facts.

Facts are not laws; rather, facts are instances of laws. Indeed, the basic rhythm of inductive science is that facts can yield laws and laws can yield theories. It is the task of the social scientist to discover the conditions under which collections of facts can yield a law, and collections of laws can suggest a theory.

Law

A law is a statement of an order or the relation of phenomena which, as far as is known, is invariable under the given conditions. A law, then, is a generalization or a universal statement connecting individual or general facts. It is an expression of a regularity. It describes a constancy, that is, with one or more facts being always connected with another fact or set of facts as far as can be ascertained. For example, the more alike are the marriage partners, the more likely will be their marital adjustment and happiness.[44] A generalization or universal "is such by virtue of its form, stating that all things having a certain character also have another, or whenever we have the first we also have the second."[45]

A generalization is the result of the logical operation of induction. A law is born directly from logic rather than from direct observation. Consequently it is possible for a law in social science to turn out to be false. After all, it is not feasible to investigate all of a law's instances. Because of this fragility inherent in all generalizations, a law is also an hypothesis. A major work of social science is the recurrent testing of these hypotheses to verify or reject them. In this testing of hypotheses, that which eventuates is not just verification or rejection but sometimes a further refinement of and advance on the original law. Such discoveries form one of the more exciting aspects of social science methodology.

A law is ipso facto an explanation in that it elucidates the meaning of phenomena and relations among phenomena. Further, a law is also ipso facto a predictor since it predicts what will happen when certain phenomena are brought together under given conditions.

Not every bona fide universal statement is a law. Summarizing the work of such logicians of science as Ernest Nagel, Carl Hempel, and others, Abraham Kaplan lists five requirements which a generalization must possess in order to be considered a law: (1) the generalization must be truly universal, without restriction as to time and space; (2) the generalization must not be vacuously true, in other words, true only because nothing satisfies the conditions stated, unless the generalization is derivable from other laws; (3) the evidence for the generalization must not coincide with the range of its application; (4) the generalization must be derivable from other laws, that is, it must play a part in a scientific theory (otherwise what is obtained is a so-called "empirical generalization" rather than a law); (5) a generalization must be true.[46]

A law is interrelated to a concept. Indeed, a concept is significant only if it enters into a law. In other words, a concept is significant only to the extent to which something is known about the way in which it is connected with other things. To know this connection is to know what effects a concept has, when it occurs, or how it changes.

Theory

A theory is a set of interrelated facts and laws which present a systematic view of phenomena by specifying relations among variables in order to explain and predict the phenomena.[47] An example of the formulation of a theory might deal with the failure of a ten-year-old child to learn religion. The significant variables involved in formulating a theory to explain why the child is failing to learn religion might include family attitudes toward religion, peer group influences, anxiety, degree of interest in school, the methods used in teaching religion, social class membership, age, and so on. Significant facts might include that the child's family manifests disinterest in religion, his peer group tends to maintain an irreverent stance toward religion, the teaching methods are primarily verbal and teacher-centered, and so on. Laws which enter the picture might include: if the family holds one kind of attitude toward religion, then the young offspring will tend to hold this same attitude; if the attitude of the peer group reinforces a deep-seated attitude held by the family, then the effect will be to reinforce that attitude in the young offspring of that family; if the teaching method is primarily verbal, then the effect on influencing nonverbal learner behavior is significantly reduced. The theory accumulates interrelated facts and laws, specifies relations among the variables, and attempts to so systematize them that a general explanation which will cover the child's failure to learn will emerge. Instead of attempting to explain every single behavior of the child, the social scientist attempts to formulate general explanations which will encompass and link together many different behaviors.

Methodology in social science is not a set of rules for discovery; it represents instead a certain way of formulating constructs, confirming hypotheses, and above all, of constructing theories. Indeed, it can be argued that the main task of social science is to formulate theories.

Theory has several key functions in the work of social science. Theory acts as an orientation by narrowing and focusing the range of the facts and laws to be investigated. Theory assists in conceptualization and classification, and in so doing facilitates the organizing and systematizing functions of social science qua science. Theory summarizes in a compact yet fulsome way the various facts and laws which comprise the object of the investigation. Theory explains the relationship between the significant variables relating to the object under investigation, and indicates broadly why kinds of phenomena like those investigated behave in a certain fashion. Theory serves to act as a predictor to new situations basically related to the set of facts and laws which it has explained. Finally, theory points to gaps in knowledge and to areas not previously or adequately explored or explained.[48]

In some respects the most important function of theory is that of explanation. A theory provides the broadest possible explanation of phenomena in the most economical fashion. Consequently theory serves as the most fruitful kind of predictor in social science. A theory is not something abstruse and unrelated to phenomena; rather, at bottom, a theory of phenomena is an explanation of these phenomena. Hence nothing that is not an explanation is worthy to be called a theory. Conversely, to seek an explanation of phenomena is to ultimately develop a theory about these phenomena.[49] One major goal of social science is to so broaden the explanatory power of a theory that in the end there will remain the smallest number of possible theories, each possessing the widest explanatory power.

Because a theory is a broad explanation, most social scientists claim that a theory represents a broad principle from which specific explanations and predictions can be deduced. A theory, then, initiates deductive reasoning from itself.

A theory arranges that which we know into a system in order to more effectively mine the meaning locked in the facts and particularly in the laws. A theory, from one aspect, is a connected set of laws. A theory attempts to make sense of what would otherwise be mute empirically-derived facts and laws. A theory thus provides meaning, and in providing meaning, attests to the truth. Just as a law is not only confirmed by the factual data but also in turn helps bestow factual status on the data, so a theory is not only supported by verified laws but also plays a role in establishing them. A theory is said to be fruitful to the extent that many, different, and tenable hypotheses can be derived from it.

Theory is not somehow opposed to fact. Only to the scientifically uninformed person does theory connote abstruseness, etherealness, or an up-in-the-clouds mentality as contrasted to the real world of facts and concrete reality. Theory and fact are in constant dynamic interaction and interplay. A theory is, among other things, an expressed relationship among facts, the ordering of facts in a meaningful fashion. Facts in social science are empirically verifiable observations, and are typically not harvested at random. Theory suggests where, how, and why such-and-such a phenomenon can be located and converted into a fact. A theory defines the kinds of facts which are to be extracted and abstracted. A theory helps us to predict facts. Facts, for their part, play a key role in theory. Facts have a central role in initiating theory. Facts lead to the verification, reformulation, modification, or rejection of an existing theory. Facts aid in redefining and clarifying theory. At every stage of the work of social science, fact, law, and theory are dynamically interacting. If a theory is not deeply interconnected with facts, if a theory is up in the clouds, this is a certain indication that what is being discussed is some statement other than a theory.

Model

A model is a system of interrelated facts and laws subsumed in one theory which serves as a functional description of the reality being investigated. A model is closely related to a theory.[50] Abraham Kaplan states that the term "model" refers to the style in which a theory is couched.[51] A model is a kind of embodiment of a structural analogy. This embodiment might take the form of a set of symbols, or it might be presented in an isomorphic shape.

A model acts as an approach to more fruitfully explore special relationships existing among various connective elements within a theory. In one view, a model attempts to operationalize a theory while still remaining in the cognitive, speculative, abstract, generalized state. By reshaping a theory into a model, social scientists hope to extract from a theory significant inferences which might otherwise remain hidden from notice. Model building is believed to be one of the most promising ways in which social science can make significant new discoveries and formulate more useful explanations.

Verification

Thus far in this larger section I have been treating of the process of investigation in the social sciences. Now I should like to turn my attention briefly to the process of verification. Verification is the process of establishing the truth of what is stated. Verification is proof by and from evidence. Consequently verification implies a kind of finality. In the social sciences, verification is primarily empirical. In one sense, verification may be said to constitute the way in which social science tests its findings. A fact, a law, or a theory must always be tested and verified in empirically-oriented social science. Framing a statement to be tested into a hypothetical statement is one of the principal ways in which social science goes about its specific process of verification. As to its general process of verification, five basic ways can be identified.[52] These basic ways of verification are the method of agreement, the method of difference, the joint method of agreement and difference, the method of residues, and the method of concomitant variations.

The *method of agreement* states that if two or more instances of the phenomenon under investigation have one and only one circumstance in common, the one circumstance in which alone all the instances agree constitutes the cause (or effect) of the phenomenon. This method, while helpful, nonetheless is not very rigorous. Consequently any conclusions drawn from the use of the method of agreement must remain tentative. It is not possible to observe all the circumstances affecting an individual in his daily life; therefore, there might be more than one circumstance common to the phenomenon under investigation. For example, if a religion teacher notices that in five different lessons during the month of March when Johnny learned very efficiently, she was wearing the same green dress, then the teacher might begin to conclude that wearing the green dress constituted an indispensable factor in causing this learning in Johnny. It is possible that the green dress might indeed have been indispensable for producing the efficient learning; but it is also possible that on each of these five days the teacher used the same kind of effective teaching method. In order for the method of agreement to prove efficacious as a verifier, the teacher would have to be very complete in her recording of all the classroom circumstances impinging on Johnny during those five days, and from this total observation ascertain whether or not her wearing of the green dress proved to be the one and only one significant circumstance which those five days had in common for Johnny.

The *method of difference* states that if an instance in which the phenomenon under investigation does occur, and an instance in

which this phenomenon does not occur both have every circumstance in common except one, that one occurring only in the former
— then the circumstance in which alone the two instances differ is
the effect, or the cause, or an indispensable part of the cause of the
phenomenon. For example, the religion teacher might arrange
classroom conditions so that every time she wore the green dress she
would utilize teaching methods x, y, and z. Concomitantly she
would employ these teaching methods at times other than when she
was wearing the green dress. She would control for all the other
significant variables in the classroom situation. If she found that
Johnny learned most efficiently when she used teaching method
y,whether or not she was at that time wearing the green dress, and if
she also discovered that when she was wearing the green dress
Johnny did not learn very efficiently when she employed teaching
methods x and z, she could conclude that it was teaching method y,
not the green dress, which was the cause of Johnny's effective
learning. Both the method of agreement and the method of
difference have as their core the use of the process of elimination.
The method of difference is eminently suited to a controlled
experiment. In one respect the method of difference constitutes the
heart of experimental verification.

The *joint method of agreement and difference* states that if two
or more instances in which the phenomenon occurs have one and
only one circumstance in common, while two or more instances in
which this phenomenon does not occur have nothing in common
except the absence of that circumstance, then the circumstance in
which alone the two sets of circumstances differ is the effect or the
cause or an indispensable part of the cause of the phenomenon. The
joint method of agreement and difference is frequently employed as
a substitute when for one or more reasons direct experimentation is
not possible or feasible. The joint method of agreement and
difference has higher verifying power than the method of agreement
but lower verifying power than the method of difference. The latter
is so because the conclusions of an experimental investigation are
intrinsically more verifiable than the conclusions of empirical but
nonexperimental investigation.

The *method of residues* states that if one sifts out from any
phenomenon all parts which are known from previous inductions to
constitute the effects of certain antecedents, then the residue of the
phenomenon is the effect of the remaining antecedents. The method
of residues rests on previous knowledge rather than on direct

experimentation or on present empirical phenomena. The use of the method of residues has been quite helpful in natural science because of the goodly number of its empirically established laws. Social science, being a relatively new science, does not yet contain that number of empirically established laws large enough to enable the method of residues to be employed on a wide scale.

The *method of concomitant variations* states that if a phenomenon varies in some manner whenever another phenomenon varies in a particular manner, then the first phenomenon is either a cause or an effect of that other phenomenon, or is connected with that other phenomenon through some form of causation. Let us say, for example, that a religion teacher uses a particular instructional method in teaching the same lesson on brotherhood to ten groups of young people. These youths are as closely matched as possible except in one major variable, namely that five of the groups are boys and the other five are girls. We discover a certain variance in the effectiveness of the instructional method between the all-boy groups and the all-girl groups. The use of measurement and statistics in analyzing the pattern of intergroup and intragroup variance would have the general method of concomitant variations as a verification check. Contemporary social science utilizes to a significant degree the method of concomitant variations, particularly in the verification of its measurement usages and its statistical treatments. Social science features a great deal of measurement of variables, measurement of correlation, and measurement of variance. The basis for the verification of these measurements rests on the method of concomitant variations.

SPECIFIC METHODOLOGY OF SOCIAL SCIENCE

"The more one emphasizes organization as a mark of science," John Dewey writes, "then the more he is committed to a recognition of the primacy of method in the definition of science. For method defines the organization in virtue of which science is science."[53] Modern natural and social science aim at producing systematic explanations grounded in, controllable by, and verified out of empirically based evidence. This is not to say that all of the social sciences achieve this goal in the highest possible degree; however, it is to imply that this ideal pervades the social sciences. General method, of which I dealt in the last section, forms the broad framework in which social science proceeds. Specific methodology which forms the burden of the remainder of this chapter represents the concrete ways in which social science goes about its business.

The broad categories in which social science methodology is carried out can be reduced to five temporally sequential steps. [54] These steps are: problem, hypothesis, testing, verification, and interpretation.

Problem

The social scientist typically begins his investigation as a result of some perceived obstacle blocking his understanding of the explanation of some phenomenon. He wonders why something is as it is, or why someone behaves as he does. His first activity consists in struggling to clarify and sharpen the problem into a simple, clear, and relatively complete form. Joseph Schwab has suggested that one effective way of accomplishing this is to ask a "telling question," that is, one which "tells" on the phenomenon and facilitates inquiry. [55] When at last he has hammered the problem into manageable form, it will generally take the form of an interrogative statement inquiring into the relationship which exists between two or more variables. The answer to this question comprises the goal of his research.

Fred Kerlinger observes that fruitful and useful problems are characterized by three criteria. [56] First, a problem should express a relation between two or more variables. Thus a typical problem would be phrased like: How are A and B related to C? Second, the problem should be stated clearly and unequivocally, and preferably in question form. Third, the interrogative problem statement should be such as to imply possibilities of empirical testing. Hence philosophical and theological questions per se are excluded. For example, the problem statement, "How is original sin transmitted from one generation to another?" precludes empirical testing.

Perhaps a hypothetical case will serve to illustrate the process of clarifying and stating a useful problem. I have noticed that youths in a variety of religion classroom and nonclassroom settings do not seem to transfer into their daily behavior certain moral principles acquired in the learning situation. I am puzzled and distressed by this. I formulate my problem: "Does formal religion teaching have any effect on a youth's moral behavior?"

Hypothesis

An hypothesis is a conjectural statement of the relation between two or more variables. It is a tentative assumed conclusion made in order to draw out and to empirically test consequences. An hypothesis is always framed as a declarative sentence. An hypothesis is a tentatively suggested answer to a problem, such as the problem mentioned in the previous paragraph. An hypothesis looks forward and leads to an empirical test that will determine its validity.

Fred Kerlinger notes that the hypothesis is "the most powerful tool man has invented" to achieve dependable empirical knowledge. An hypothesis leads to that kind of empirical validation necessary for verified understanding of phenomena and their interrelationships. In one way an hypothesis is an explanation, one which can be verified — or rejected. An hypothesis is a prediction. It stipulates that if x occurs, then y will also occur. In other words, y is predicted from x. Even when an hypothesis is rejected it has power since negative findings reduce the range of possible explanations and sometimes suggest fruitful new hypotheses. To be sure, the social scientist cannot distinguish positive from negative evidence unless he employs an hypothesis. Kerlinger highlights three fundamental reasons for the importance of the hypothesis in social-science investigation. First, it is the working instrument of theory. Second, an hypothesis can be tested and shown to be probably true or probably false. Isolated facts cannot be tested; only relations can be tested. And an hypothesis is an expressed relation between two facts. Third, the hypothesis enables man to get outside himself, to gain objectivity.[57]

An hypothesis is termed tenable if it is confirmed; in this case it is called a proposition. An hypothesis is termed valid if it is deducible; in this case it is called a theorem. A system of tenable hypotheses is basically an inductive system, while a system of valid hypotheses is essentially a deductive system. An inductive-deductive system such as social science is one in which valid hypotheses are tenable, and none, or almost none, are untenable. An hypothesis describes a phenomenon if the phenomenon confirms the hypothesis. A theory explains a phenomenon if it implies an hypothesis that describes the phenomenon. A low-level hypothesis describes while a high-level hypothesis explains.[58]

At least seven characteristics of a usable hypothesis can be identified. The usable hypothesis is clearly defined, preferably in operational terms. Second, the usable hypothesis states relations between variables. Third, the usable hypothesis has empirical referents. No usable hypothesis can embody empirically untestable metaphysical and theological judgments. Fourth, the usable hypothesis carries clear implications for testing the stated relations between (among) the variables. Fifth, the usable hypothesis is specific. All its operations and predictions are spelled out in some detail. Sixth, the usable hypothesis is related to available and appropriate research techniques. Finally, the usable hypothesis is linked to theory. The hypothesis is formulated within a clear theoretical framework. In one sense, an hypothesis is a form of scientific law, and hence it is vital that it be intimately related both to theory as well as to fact.[59]

Perhaps a continuation of the hypothetical case used in the previous section on problem clarification will illustrate the task of hypothesis formulation. Aware of the nature of theories of teaching and cognizant of the relevant research data, I generate the following hypothesis: "A religion class which is so structured that the students existentially live out in the classroom situation what they are learning cognitively will result in a higher incidence of transfer of moral behaviors to out-of-class life than will religion classes which are conducted in an exclusively cognitive manner." The variables in this hypothesis are teaching method and learner achievement. The hypothesis can be tested empirically through observed student behavior. The prediction is spelled out in terms of moral behaviors, rather than in terms of behavior, generally speaking. The hypothesis is linked to learning theory and to research data on effecting learning (notably the data on immediate and mutually-enhancing rein-forcement).

Testing

Testing refers to the complex of procedures used to determine the truth or falsity of an hypothesis. Testing an hypothesis in the social sciences is done in an empirical manner, that is, by observation and/or experimentation. An hypothesis is not tested directly. That is to say, a social scientist does not test the variables themselves, but rather he tests the relation between the variables. In our example of the hypothesized effect of a specific kind of teaching methodology on pupil learning, what we are putting to the empirical test is the presumed relation between teaching methodology and pupil learning.

In testing an hypothesis, a social scientist goes through at least four distinct operations: constructing a research design, conducting the test proper, collecting the data, and treating the data.

Research Design. The term "research design" refers to the pattern or framework or structural organization used in selecting, planning, and carrying forward the empirical investigation. Design does not affect the content of the investigation so much as it does the way in which the content is arranged to facilitate the effective prosecution of the research. The manner in which the research is structured has much to do with the degree to which the goals of the investigation will both fruitfully and validly be attained. An effective research design indicates the investigative strategies which will be employed in carrying forward the empirical inquiry.

The prime purpose of a research design is to provide answers to the research question(s), specifically to the question(s) implied in the hypothesis to be tested. What is being tested is the relation between two or more variables in the hypothesis; therefore the research design represents an investigative invention "designed" to make adequate tests of the presumed relation. This is accomplished principally by controlling variance. Design represents a set of instructions on gathering and analyzing the data in certain ways. In other words, research design functions as a control mechanism. Accordingly, the investigator attempts "(1) to maximize the variance of the variable or variables in his substantive research hypothesis, (2) to control the variance of extraneous or 'unwanted' variables that may have an effect on his experimental outcomes but in which he is not interested, and (3) to minimize the error or random variance, including so-called errors of measurement."[60]

In the broadest terms, there are four research designs used in the social sciences: the experiment, the survey, the case study, and ex post facto research.

The *experiment* is the trial of a planned procedure accompanied by control of conditions and/or controlled variation of conditions together with observation of results for the purpose of discovering relations and assessing the validity of a given hypothesis. In any experiment there are always two factors present: control of some variable(s), and systematic measured observation of the results. The experiment, then, consists in assigning subjects [61] to an environment in which the conditions are systematically controlled; in such an environment, the phenomenon under investigation is brought to intervene in the environment so as to ascertain what effects, if any, are produced by this intervention.[62] Indeed, control over all aspects of the experiment is a necessary condition for success. The investigator must always be vigilant in uncovering any aspect not under control and to make the necessary environmental or statistical adjustments to neutralize these uncontrolled conditions. For example, Robert Rosenthal's extensive researches have shown that even the most tightly controlled experiments sometimes are contaminated by the unintended intrusion of experimenter expectancy.[63]

More than any other kind of empirical research activity, the experiment is paramount because of its greater methodological rigor, its greater precision, and its greater objectivity. Yet what makes the experimental method the most valid and the most favored by social scientists is above all its efficiency in testing an hypothesis; in other words, intentional intervention of a phenomenon in a controlled environment constitutes the scientific method which most readily disentangles cause-effect relationships and exposes them to clear view.[64] At bottom, the experiment consists in one form or other of a comparison of two sets of circumstances, all of which match each other as exactly as possible in every respect except one.[65] Consequently any differences resulting in either group must be a result of the differentiating variable operating in these matched environments.

The experimental environment is a specially selected milieu which features observation of the phenomena under controlled condition. Both the environment and the subjects are selected in such a careful way as will best insure that all the conditions in the experiment are indeed controlled. Carter Good has identified four principal categories in the experimental environment which must be subject to controlled conditions: characteristics of the subjects; manipulation of the environment; selection of the parts; and management of the procedural elements. Salient characteristics of the subjects which must be controlled for include age, sex, socioeconomic background, level of schooling, maturity, intelligence, culture, social activities, and physiological factors. Relevant aspects of the experimental environment which are manipulated according to the nature and goals of the experiment include mechanical means (for example soundproofing a room), electrical means (for example, generating a specific kind of noise), and pharmacological means. Prominent parts of the experiment to be chosen include the selection of subjects, selection of materials, and the selection of data. Notable among the procedural elements to be managed include equal exposure of the subject to the experimental conditions; minimizing the contribution of the spatial arrangement of procedural factors; minimizing the contribution of temporal factors within the experimental situation; minimizing the influence of factors emanating from the order of experimental conditions through their random assignment to subjects.[66]

The design of the research experiment can take a number of different forms. The social scientist selects that form most appropriate to the optimal prosecution of his research goal. George Mouly has identified four basic kinds of experimental designs, each varying in complexity and adequacy: the single-group design, the parallel-group design, the rotation-group design, and factorial designs.[67] The single-group design consists in observing the effects of some variable(s) on a single group under two different sets of conditions. In other words, a group is subjected successively to an experimental intervention and to a control intervention for equivalent periods of time. A comparison is then made of the outcomes. Perhaps a further continuation of the example I used in my discussion of problem and hypothesis might be helpful here. A single group of selected students in a religion class is tested for achievement in both a cognitive knowledge of a selected moral behavior and in terms of students' actualization of this knowledge into their out-of-class activities. The teacher teaches the students the cognitive aspects and products of this moral behavior. The group is tested once again along the two lines I have previously indicated, and the respective gains are noted. Then the experimenter allows for a period of transition. Once again he tests the group on the same two lines, that is, cognitive knowledge and subsequent out-of-class moral behavior. Then the teacher teaches the students in such a way that in the actual class setting they live out the cognitive and existential dimensions of the moral behavior so as to attain an experiential fusing of the two. The group is tested once more to ascertain the gain. Finally, the gains resulting from each of the teaching methods are compared, and the original hypothesis is either verified or rejected. The single-group design is the most elementary and least rigorous of all experimental designs. Some social scientists go so far as to call it a semiexperimental design. In many ways it is empirically inadequate.

The parallel- or equivalent-group design is that experimental technique in which two or more groups, matched as equivalently as possible, are subjected to an experimental intervention and to a control intervention and the results are compared. This experimental design is sometimes referred to as the "classical experimental design," and represents an objectification of the method of difference I discussed earlier. In our example, two groups of matched students are selected for the experiment. The teacher teaches the first group only the cognitive aspects and products of the moral behavior selected, while with the second group she teaches in such a way that in the actual class setting the students are caused to live out the existential aspects of the moral behavior in addition to learning the cognitive knowledges associated with this behavior. The two groups of students are tested on the extent to which they actualize these moral behaviors in their out-of-class life, and the results are compared. There are several variations of this design.

The rotation-group design is that experimental technique in which the experimental group and the control group rotate at different intervals. Thus each group is subjected to the experimental intervention and to the control intervention. A comparison is made at the end of the experiment as to the relative gains made by each of the two groups. The rotation-group design represents a variation of the single-group design. It has, however, the advantage of being somewhat more rigorous than the single-group design. Yet it still falls far short of the rigor and adequacy of the parallel-group design. In our example, two groups of students would be taught by the two teaching methods I have indicated. After the conclusion of the instruction, the out-of-class behaviors of each group would be recorded. The groups then switch and the teaching methodologies are also reversed. The out-of-class behaviors of both groups are again tested, and the results of this test and the test utilized in the first half of the experiment are compared and analyzed.

Factorial designs are those which permit the simultaneous evaluation of the effects of a number of factors taken singly and in interaction with one another. The factorial design, sometimes termed multivariate analysis, differs most significantly from the three previously mentioned experimental designs in that these three are concerned solely with the observation of the relation of a single variable (teaching method) to learning achievement. The social scientist might wish to also investigate in the same experiment the effects of some other variable such as style of teaching (for example, teacher-centered versus student-centered classes) on the learning of actualized moral behaviors. Factorial designs are of signal assistance here.

Experiments are conducted either in the laboratory or in a natural environment. The chief advantage of the laboratory setting is that it permits a greater control over the physical variables associated directly or indirectly with the experiment. The laboratory milieu enhances the ability of the investigator and his research associates to watch the experiment. Also, the laboratory is typically equipped with those devices necessary to record salient aspects of the experiment. However, in many experiments, notably those involving very large groups or those in which the natural milieu constitutes a necessary condition for the experiment, the natural environment is used as the experimental setting. The natural environment, while often not as fully under the experimenter's control as the laboratory, nonetheless does not suffer from the chief limitation of the laboratory, namely artificiality. Some attempts are being made to create a laboratory setting which will simulate as closely as possible the natural environment so as to reap the benefits of both milieux. An example of this, hopefully, is the religious instruction laboratory which I established in 1970 at the University of Notre Dame. This laboratory is an actual classroom, fitted with three television cameras and videotape recorders to secure a total coverage of classroom episodes for later clinical analysis. A one-way vision screen permits the investigator and his graduate assistants to observe the experiment as it is actually being conducted.

The *survey* is an investigation of large and/or small populations or universes by selecting and studying samples chosen from these populations in order to ascertain the relative incidence, distribution, and interrelations of selected sociopsychological or status variables.[68] These variables typically consist of facts, attitudes, values, and opinions. Herbert Hyman has indentified two major types of survey research: the descriptive survey and the explanatory survey.[69] A descriptive survey is one which simply describes some phenomenon. A survey of the personality characteristics of religion teachers exemplifies this type of survey. An explanatory survey is one which explores the relationship between two or more phenomena and their hypothesized cause(s).[70] The explanatory survey represents a more sophisticated and a more behavioral type of investigation than does the descriptive survey.

The population studied in the sample may comprise either the total population to be studied (called the universe) or a sample of the total population. Because it is often not feasible to study the whole population, for example, all religion teachers in the United States, or all Lutheran pastors, a survey frequently is made of a sample of the total population. Of paramount methodological importance in selecting the sample is that it be representative of the total population. In other words, the sample must be isomorphic to the total population to be investigated.

Since social science has at its methodological base the use of controlled rather than uncontrolled observation, the survey technique is characterized by procedural controls both in research design and in execution. These controls are manifest at three critical stages of the survey: sampling, instrumentation, and treatment.

Sampling "is the process by which a relatively small number of individuals or measures of individuals, objects or events, is selected and analyzed in order to find out something about the entire population or universe from which it was selected."[71] Any one of three principal techniques is employed in selecting the sample: simple random sampling, stratified random sampling, and interval sampling. The purpose of each technique is to insure that the sample is as nearly isomorphic to the universe as possible. Simple random sampling is the process of selecting the portion of the universe on a purely chance basis. The principle underlying randomization is that every member of a population has an equal chance of being selected. Therefore members with certain distinguishing characteristics, such as male or female, Catholic or Protestant, will, if selected, probably be counterbalanced in the long run by the selection of other members of the opposite quantity or quality of such distinguishing characteristics. In collecting a random sample, the investigator can use any one of many so-called "table of random numbers" specifically developed by statisticians for this purpose. Stratified random sampling is the process of selecting the portion of the universe on the basis of dividing the universe into subpopulations, or strata, which are proportional to the size and composition of the universe. A random sample is then taken from each of these strata. The main objective in stratification is to secure a more reliable sample than might be the case in simple random sampling. Obviously, the basic composition of the universe must first be known in order to make a stratified random sampling. Interval sampling, as its name implies, is the process of selecting a portion of the universe on the basis of regular intervals occurring in a series of one sort or another, for example, an alphabetical listing. Thus the investigator might choose every fifth name from a list. This technique can be used only on finite universes where complete listings are available.[72]

The two most widely used instruments in survey research are the mailed questionnaire and the interview. These instruments are administered to all persons in the sample. Both the mailed questionnaire and the interview typically consist of two sections, the first which asks basic questions such as the respondent's age, birthplace, sex, and so on, and the second which is devoted chiefly to those items selected and validated for the purpose of eliciting responses on the subject matter to be surveyed, for example, the attitudes of religion teachers on teacher-centered instructional techniques. Compared to the interview, the mailed questionnaire is easier, quicker, and more economical. However, it is less reliable than the interview. Further, the percentage of return from the mailed questionnaire is significantly less than the percentage of response from an interview.[73]

The survey instrument, whether mailed or put into an interview situation, is carefully structured in terms of the validity and reliability of its content. Statistical methods are used in this regard. Typically the instrument is pretested before it is finally administered to the sample population or to the universe.[74]

The *case study* is a research method "whereby data are collected and studied which depict any phase of a, or an entire, life process of a unit in its various interrelationships and in its cultural setting. The unit studied may be a person, a family, a social group, a social institution, a community or a nation."[75] The purpose of the case study is to probe the "unit" intensively and in depth in order to identify the antecedents hypothesized to be directly or indirectly causative of the occurrence of a given phenomenon, such as frequent stealing. Whereas the survey is essentially research in breadth, the case study represents research in depth.[76] William Goode and Paul Hatt contend that the case study represents more of an approach than a specific technique. They claim that the case study represents a way of organizing sociopsychological data in such a way that the unitary character of the psychosocial object under investigation is preserved.[77]

Data in a case study are collected from historical records; census data; life histories; autobiographies; interviews with persons close to the event, person, or "unit" under investigation; counseling sessions; and so on. Once the data are gathered, the original hypothesis is tested. (When the "unit" studied is a person, the hypothesis is called a diagnosis.) The methods of testing the hypothesis are not nearly so rigorous as in the experiment or in the social survey. For example, if we are making a case study on a boy who commits frequent thefts, we may hypothetically diagnose the cause of this phenomenon as his low self-image. We test this hypothesis by attempting to raise the level of his self-image and then ascertaining whether or not his deviant behavior continues. If the deviant behavior does continue we know that the hypothesis can be safely rejected. If, however, the deviant behavior ceases, our hypothesis is supported but by no means confirmed since there may be hidden causative variables associated with self-image which are responsible for his deviant behavior. Further analysis of the data is therefore necessary.

Ex post facto research is that which seeks to discover the relation of present existing phenomena with their antecedent(s). Ex post facto research therefore differs from experimental research in that in the latter the experimenter creates or examines the hypothesized relation of antecedent and consequent as it is now occurring under controlled conditions, whereas in the former the antecedent in the hypothesized relation has already occurred. In an experiment the antecedent is controlled; in ex post facto research the antecedent is not controlled. Due to this lack of control of the antecedent, the results of ex post facto research have not the same level of confidence as have the results of experimental research. Indeed, George Mouly goes so far as to assert that in ex post facto research the evidence merely illustrates the hypothesis rather than confirming or rejecting it as is the case in the experimental design.[78]

Despite its lack of methodological rigor, ex post facto research is valuable to social science, particularly in cases where the antecedents have occurred and cannot be replicated. Thus, for example, in ascertaining the hypothesized relation of cigarette smoking to lung cancer, ex post facto research with humans was necessary because immediate experimentation with human subjects was manifestly impossible. Such ex post facto research was supplemented with experimental research on animal subjects. Ex post facto research on the relation of cigarette smoking to lung cancer illustrates that ex post facto research, survey research, and case studies are often undertaken concomitantly as part of one overall research design.

Collection of the data. Social science focuses on the systematic observation of phenomena. Once these phenomena have been observed, data must be carefully collected so that the hypothesized relation between two or more phenomena can be tested. Indeed, one of the functions of the research design is to structurally facilitate the collection of data pertinent to the investigation. There are at least four basic methods used singly or in combination to collect the pertinent data: direct observation, tests and inventories, interviews, and records.[79]

Direct observation of the phenomenon can be made by the social scientist, either as a participant or as a nonparticipant. Experimental research design frequently calls for direct observation by the investigator in one form or other. In some kinds of sociological research the investigator acts as a participant. He might, for example, join a factory assembly line to assess the attitudes of what the French term the "dechristianized masses."

Tests and inventories, and also *questionnaires* are so closely related that there is some doubt as to the existence of any substantial distinction among them. A test is a scientifically prepared instrument designed to objectively assess some skill or performance of the individual. One example of a test would be a paper-and-pencil instrument designed to assess the individual's achievement in acquiring selected knowledges in religion. An intelligence test represents another type of test. An inventory is typically regarded as that kind of test in which the subject responds to items pertaining rather directly to himself. For example, a personality instrument measuring responses to such questions as, "How frequently do you have serious doubts of faith?" would be regarded as an inventory. A questionnaire usually refers to an instrument in which the individual answers questions about some personally held attitude, value, or belief. Persons taking tests are commonly called "subjects"; those completing inventories and questionnaires are referred to as "respondents." Tests and inventories are standardized so that the results will be valid and reliable.

An *interview* may assume any one of four different forms: the structured interview, the semistructured interview, the unstructured interview, and the free-association interview. A structured interview is one in which the set of responses which the individual can make is entirely controlled by the format, the wording, and the sequence of questions. In a structured interview both the content and the procedures of response are prescribed, coded, and standardized in advance. For example, a typical item might read: "When do you think the Christian denominations will merge: within the next five years, within the next ten years, before the year 2000, within the next hundred years, or never?" A semistructured interview is one in which the format, wording, and sequence of the questions are controlled in advance, but where the wording of the response is left to the individual respondent. The semistructured interview aims at combining a certain amount of standardization with the more open and free individual response. For example, a typical item might read: "When do you think the Christian denominations will merge?" The unstructured interview is one in which the questions have a general focus but the responses are in no way controlled, structured, or directed. There is no list of questions; instead there is a broad outline of topics to be covered. The wording, sequence, and intensity of the questioning are left to the interviewer's discretion; ordinarily they are tailored to each interview in order to obtain that kind of data most meaningful to each respondent. Generally speaking, there is no preset instrument for this kind of interview. The free-association interview is one in which the interviewer refrains from all structure, even to the extent of not asking any direct questions whatsoever, thus freeing the respondent to report anything that may come into his consciousness. Ideally, even ordinarily assumed constraints of convention are removed, such as logical sequence, rules of grammar, and so forth. The depth interview is typically employed in psychotherapy and psychoanalysis.

Records are accounts of past phenomena. Records might be official, such as census data, or unofficial, such as an account of a counseling interview. Records might be written, such as baptism data in the parish registry, or unwritten, such as a statue in a fourth-century church. Records are valuable to the social scientist in that they furnish him with data about phenomena which are unavailable for original investigation.

Treatment of the Data. The quantitative nature of social science makes the treatment of the data gained from the observed phenomena primarily quantitative in form. This is not to imply an exclusion of nonquantitative analysis, such as in certain kinds of psychological research; rather, it is to place primary stress on the quantitative aspect.

Data in social science are treated by quantitative measurement. By this I mean that the observed data are given numerical values which are then subjected to quantitative manipulation and analysis. Measurement, therefore, represents quantitative coding of the pertinent aspects of the observed phenomena. During the operations of measurement, statistics play a key role. Broadly speaking, statistics are of two types: descriptive statistics and inferential statistics. Descriptive statistics are those which summarize and synthesize in numerical form the observed phenomena. Examples of descriptive statistics include the mean, the standard deviation, and coefficients of correlation. Inferential statistics are those which yield a generalization to the universe from the sample investigated.

Inferential statistics give measures of probability. Examples of inferential statistics include statistical significance and analysis of variance.[80]

The two most important criteria for effective measurement are validity and reliability. Validity is that property of an instrument which insures its measuring what it purports to measure. For example, a test purporting to identify those boys who will go into the Christian ministry is valid to the extent that it predicts those subjects who in fact do enter the ministry. Reliability is that property of an instrument which insures that there is consistency in the measurement of whatever the instrument purports to measure. The above mentioned test is reliable to the extent that the subject receives approximately the same score in March as he did the preceding January, assuming all other conditions remained approximately the same.

Verification

On the basis of the tests applied to the hypothesis, conclusions are drawn. These conclusions must be verified. The process of verification does not take place simply at the end of the testing procedure; it occurs as well at every stage of the testing. The controls built in by the research design, together with the controls involved in the measurement stage, provide continuous verification all along the line. The final verification of the conclusions is typically directed toward a proper disentanglement of the various causes together with a confirmation that x is indeed the cause of y. To this end, replication of the investigation is sometimes in order to ascertain whether the "proved" relations between the variables do occur again (at least within a reasonable range) under the given conditions. Also, the data are sometimes reanalyzed to determine whether other causes can possibly account for the relation of variables. For example, an investigation of high school seniors attending Sunday school might reveal that those who scored the highest on achievement tests measuring cognitive knowledge of religious truths tended to be higher church attenders than matched students who scored significantly lower on such a test. The conclusion drawn is that there is a causative correlation between cognitive gain in religious knowledge and church attendance. However, a reanalysis of the data indicates that the first group of youths come from families which are more religious than the families of the second group. Consequently, while there is indeed a correlation between religious knowledge and church attendance, this correlation is not causative; what is probably causative is the attitude toward religion of the family to which the youths belong.

Interpretation

Interpretation is the process by which the investigator discovers the meaning and applicability of his research conclusions. As I observed earlier in this chapter, interpretation can be made in one or both of two ways. Interpretation can be made of the conclusions and their relation within the research investigation itself. Or interpretation can be made of the relation of the conclusions of the investigation to the conclusions of other investigations. A basic principle governing interpretation is that of adhering as closely as possible to the original data. Also, the law of parsimony applies: interpretations should aim at giving the most simple explanation possible. For example, if an intelligent youth scores low on a religion achievement test, it is inappropriate to interpret this datum as a sign that the youth is irreligious; the boy might have been fatigued or anxious when he took the test. Moreover, the investigator should not overgeneralize from his sample population to other populations which share only tenuously related or unrelated characteristics with the sample investigated. What might be a valid interpretation for a group of sixteen-year-old urban youths might not be a valid interpretation for a group of sixteen-year-old rural youths. Finally, the investigator should take every methodological precaution to prevent contamination of his interpretation by any subjective element. It is the phenomenon and its relations which are being investigated, not the researcher's notion of or expectancy for the phenomenon. Disciplined inquiry, when properly used, teams constructively with imagination, as Lee Cronbach and Patrick Suppes have remarked.[81] But the use of imagination occurs after the conclusions and interpretations of the investigation have been drawn. Research is one thing, development quite another. Development does indeed extend and fructify research. Nonetheless, development is not research. Not social-science research anyway.

FOOTNOTES

1. Leo Tolstoy, *War and Peace*, translated by Constance Garnett (New York: Bantam, 1956), p. 586.
2. David L. Sills, "Introduction," in David L. Sills, editor,

International Encyclopedia of the Social Sciences (New York: Macmillan and The Free Press, 1968), pp. xxi-xxiii.

3. George C. Homans, *The Nature of Social Science* (New York: Harcourt, Brace and World, 1967), p. 3.

4. James Michael Lee, "Jargon, Stereotypes, and Plain Talk," in *The Clearing House*, XXXIII, March, 1959, pp. 390-392.

5. William J. Goode and Paul K. Hatt, *Methods in Social Research* (New York: McGraw-Hill, 1952), p. 44.

6. See James Michael Lee, "Social Science Catechetics," in *Today's Catholic Teacher*, November, 1969, pp. 23-27.

7. John Madge, *The Tools of Social Science* (Garden City, New York: Doubleday Anchor, 1965), p. 293.

8. May Brodbeck, "Logic and Scientific Method in Research on Teaching," in N. L. Gage, editor, *Handbook of Research on Teaching* (Chicago: Rand McNally, 1963), p. 55.

9. Milton Rokeach, "Faith, Hope and Bigotry," in *Psychology Today*, III, April, 1970, p. 33; Robert C. L. Brannon, "Gimme That Old Time Racism," in *ibid.*, p. 42.

10. Ernest Nagel, *The Structure of Science* (New York: Harcourt, Brace and World, 1961), p. 12.

11. Elizabeth Hurlock, "An Evaluation of Certain Incentives Used in Schoolwork," in *Journal of Educational Psychology*, XVI, March, 1925, pp. 145-159.

12. Ronald Goldman, *Religious Thinking from Childhood to Adolescence* (New York: Humanities Press, 1964).

13. Andrew M. Greeley and Peter H. Rossi, *The Education of Catholic Americans* (Chicago: Aldine, 1966), pp. 206-214.

14. See Johan Galtung, *Theory and Methods of Social Research* (New York: Columbia University Press, 1967), pp. 464-465.

15. Fred N. Kerlinger, *Foundations of Behavioral Research* (New York: Holt, Rinehart and Winston, 1964), p. 13.

16. Karl R. Popper, "Unity of Method in the Natural and Social Sciences," in David Braybrooke, editor, *Philosophical Problems of the Social Sciences* (New York: Macmillan, 1965), p. 34.

17. Vincent J. Lovett, "Confusion and Pain Wrack the Priesthood," in *National Catholic Reporter*, December 10, 1969, p. 1.

18. Fred N. Kerlinger, *Foundations of Behavioral Research*, p. 148.

19. Carter V. Good, editor, *Dictionary of Education*, 2d ed. (New York: McGraw-Hill, 1959), p. 129.

20. John Madge, *The Tools of Social Science*, p. 12.

21. It is beyond the scope of this chapter to treat of the *Verstehen* school of social-science methodology. Let me simply note that the Verstehenists assert that there is a fundamental distinction between the method of social science and that of natural science. This distinction results from the subject matter of social

science, namely man and his experience. Consequently, the Verstehenists assert, the social scientist must utilize his own personal reflective experience to a significantly larger degree than is possible in natural science. The use of personal reflective experience by the investigator must operate within the parameters of objectivity and hence be subject to a variety of empirical and logical controls. Objectivity remains paramount — the investigator's reflective experience represents an attempt to make the objective more objective by adapting it to the object under investigation, namely man and his experience. The *Verstehen* school is not dominant within the field of social science. See Alfred Schutz, *Collected Papers: The Problem of Social Reality*, volume I, edited by Maurice Natanson (The Hague, Netherlands: Nijhoff, 1962); Leonard Krimerman, editor, *The Nature and Scope of Social Science* (New York: Appleton-Century-Crofts, 1969); Peter Winch, *The Idea of a Social Science* (New York: Humanities Press, 1958).

22. May Brodbeck, "Logic and Scientific Method in Research on Teaching," p. 53.

23. Muzafer Sherif, "Theoretical Analysis of the Individual-Group Relationship in a Social Situation," in Gordon J. DiRenzo, editor, *Concepts, Theory, and Explanation in the Behavioral Sciences* (New York: Random House, 1966), p. 59.

24. Abraham Kaplan, *The Conduct of Inquiry: Methodology for Behavioral Science* (San Francisco: Chandler, 1964), p. 352.

25. See Bernard Berelson and Gary A. Steiner, *Human Behavior: An Inventory of Scientific Findings* (New York: Harcourt, Brace and World, 1964).

26. May Brodbeck, "Logic and Scientific Method in Research on Teaching," p. 54.

27. Milton Rokeach, *The Open and Closed Mind* (New York: Basic Books, 1960).

28. Statistical treatment of the data is sometimes referred to as "analysis" or "analysis of the data." The use of analysis in this connection is in the restricted sense of the term. Strictly speaking, statistics represents a form of treatment of the data, rather than analysis of the data properly so-called.

29. William P. McEwen, *The Problem of Scientific Knowledge* (Totowa, New Jersey: Bedminster, 1963), p. 439.

30. Henri Grenier, *Thomistic Philosophy* volume I, *Logic*. (Charlottestown, P.E.I., Canada: St. Dunstan's University Press, 1950), p. 111.

31. Fred N. Kerlinger, *Foundations of Behavioral Research*, pp. 14-16.

32. Carter V. Good, editor, *Dictionary of Education*, p. 217.

33. George C Homans, *The Nature of Social Science*, p. 31.
34. May Brodbeck, "Logic and Scientific Method in Research on Teaching," p. 68.
35. Karl R. Popper, *The Logic of Scientific Discovery* (New York: Basic Books, 1959), p. 59.
36. Israel Scheffler, *The Anatomy of Inquiry* (New York: Knopf, 1963), p. 28. Italics deleted.
37. May Brodbeck, "Logic and Scientific Method in Research on Teaching," p. 68.
38. See Johan Galtung, *Theory and Methods of Social Research*, p. 454.
39. Herbert Feigl, "Some Major Issues and Developments in the philosophy of Science of Logical Empiricism", in Herbert Feigl and Michael Scriven, editors, *Minnesota Studies in the Philosophy of Science*, volume I (Minneapolis, Minn.: University of Minnesota Press, 1956), p. 8. See also pp. 12-22.
40. May Brodbeck, "Logic and Scientific Method in Research on Teaching," p. 44.
41. See Gordon J. DiRenzo, "Editor's Introduction," in Gordon J. DiRenzo, editor, *Concepts, Theory, and Explanation in the Behavioral Sciences*, pp. 3-5.
42. Robert Bierstedt, "Nominal and Real Definitions in Sociological Theory," in Llewellyn Gross, editor, *Symposium on Sociological Theory* (Evanston, Ill.: Row, Peterson, 1959), pp. 127-128. Bierstedt defines a real definition as a proposition announcing the conventional intension of a concept.
43. George Homans, *The Nature of Social Science*, pp. 10-11.
44. Bernard Berelson and Gary A. Steiner, *Human Behavior: An Inventory of Scientific Findings*, p. 310.
45. May Brodbeck, "Logic and Scientific Method in Research on Teaching," p. 56.
46. Abraham Kaplan, *The Conduct of Inquiry*, pp. 91-92.
47. See Fred N. Kerlinger, *Foundations of Behavioral Research*, pp. 10-11.
48. William J. Goode and Paul K. Hatt, *Methods in Social Research*, pp. 9-12.
49. On this last point, see Marc Belth, *Education As a Discipline* (Boston: Allyn and Bacon, 1965), p. 139.
50. Indeed, sometimes in the social-science literature, the words "model" and "theory" are used synonymously.
51. Abraham Kaplan, *The Conduct of Inquiry*, p. 263. Kaplan identifies three such styles, namely the symbolic, the postulational, and the formal.
52. While I am here following the rather well-established canons of the general process of verification in social science, I will base

180   THE WORK OF SOCIAL SCIENCE

my discussion on that of John Madge in his *The Tools of Social Science* pp. 52-57.

53. John Dewey, *Democracy and Education* (New York: Macmillan, 1916), p. 244.
54. For purposes of clarification, I have modified and altered the celebrated paradigm of problematical inquiry given by John Dewey in his book *How We Think* (Boston: Heath, 1933).
55. Joseph J. Schwab, "Structure of the Disciplines: Meaning and Significance," in G.W. Ford and Lawrence Pugno, editors, *The Structure of Knowledge and the Curriculum* (Chicago: Rand McNally, 1964), pp. 1-30.
56. Fred N. Kerlinger, *Foundations of Behavioral Research*, pp. 19-20.
57. *Ibid.*, pp. 22 and 27-38.
58. Johan Galtung, *Theory and Methods of Social Research*, p. 453.
59. See William J. Goode and Paul K. Hatt, *Methods in Social Research*, pp. 67-70.
60. Fred N. Kerlinger, *Foundations of Behavioral Research*, p. 280.
61. In an experiment the term "subject" refers to the human or animal which is being tested or "subjected" to the experiment.
62. For this phrase "assigning subjects to conditions" I am indebted to William A. Scott and Michael Wertheimer, *Introduction to Psychological Research* (New York: Wiley, 1962).
63. Robert Rosenthal, *Experimenter Effects in Behavioral Research* (New York: Appleton-Century-Crofts, 1966).
64. Bernard Berelson and Gary A. Steiner, *Human Behavior: An Inventory of Scientific Findings*, p. 19.
65. John Madge, *The Tools of Social Science*, p. 291.
66. Carter V. Good, *Introduction to Educational Research*, 2d edition (New York: Appleton-Century-Crofts, 1963), pp. 447-449.
67. George Mouly, *The Science of Educational Research* (New York: American Book, 1963), pp. 340-350.
68. Fred N. Kerlinger, *Foundations of Behavioral Research*, p. 393.
69. Herbert Hyman, *Survey Design and Analysis* (Glencoe, Ill.: The Free Press, 1955), pp. 66-89.
70. The phenomena here constitute the dependent variable(s); the cause(s) constitute(s) the independent variable(s).
71. Francis G. Cornell, "Sampling Methods," in Chester W. Harris, editor, *Encyclopedia of Educational Research*, 3d edition (New York: Macmillan, 1960), p. 1181.
72. For a discussion of principles and procedures of sampling, see Leslie Kish, *Survey Sampling* (New York: Wiley, 1965); also Calvin F. Schmid, "Basic Statistical Concepts and Techniques," in Pauline V. Young, *Scientific Social Surveys and Research*

(Englewood Cliffs, N.J.: Prentice Hall, 1966), pp. 325-334.

73. Mildred Parten, *Surveys, Polls, and Samples* (New York: Cooper Square, 1966).

74. C. A. Moser, *Survey Methods in Social Investigation* (New York: Humanities Press, 1958).

75. Quoted in Wilson Gee, *Social Science Research Methods* (New York: Appleton-Century-Crofts, 1950), p. 242.

76. Armand J. Galfo and Karl Miller, *Interpreting Education Research* (Dubuque, Iowa: Brown, 1965), pp. 15-16.

77. William J. Goode and Paul K. Hatt, *Methods of Social Research*, pp. 330-331.

78. George Mouly, *The Science of Educational Research*, pp. 335-336.

79. I am here following in a somewhat modified fashion, the delineation made by Bernard Berelson and Gary A. Steiner, *Human Behavior: An Inventory of Scientific Findings*, pp. 28-34.

80. George Mouly, *The Science of Educational Research*, pp. 143-150.

81. Lee J. Cronbach and Patrick Suppes, editors, *Research for Tomorrow's Schools* (New York: Macmillan, 1969), p. 172.

CHAPTER SEVEN

RELIGIOUS INSTRUCTION AS SOCIAL SCIENCE

"You're the illogical one, Meyer.
You want omelettes for breakfast,
but you don't want to crack the eggs."
— Morris L. West[1]

INTRODUCTION
I spent the last two chapters treating of the nature and methodology of both theological science and social science in order to lay the groundwork for an exploration of the question: "Is religious instruction a branch of theological science or a branch of social science?" The answer to this question is of paramount practical importance because on it depend the entire axis and thrust of every aspect of the work of religious instruction. Thus, for example, if we state that religious instruction is a branch of theological science, the preparation of religion teachers will take the form of a primary, if not at times an exclusive, emphasis on deepening the trainees' theological insights and understanding. If, on the other hand, we take the position that religious instruction is a branch of social science, the preparation of religion teachers will revolve around the improvement of those understandings and skills which will enable the trainees to most effectively facilitate desired religious behaviors in learners. In this chapter I intend to reintroduce some of those properties of social science which I discussed in Chapter Six, in order to ascertain whether or not religious instruction can be properly said to be a branch of social science. Naturally, I will not now go over each property at length, nor for that matter will I include all the properties of social science. I will present only as much material as is required to illumine the basic point. It is my hope that from the two foregoing chapters the reader has extracted enough information to

enable him to make for himself a more lengthy examination of the implications and consequences which result from the placing of religious instruction within the confines of either theological science or social science.

A Contextual Note

In seeking to ascertain whether religious instruction is a theological science or a social science, it might well be that the very phrase "religious instruction" offers a clue. It will be noted that "religious" is the adjective and "instruction" is the noun. In other words, the term "religious" specifies the kind of instruction that is done. Religious instruction, then, is situated within the total context of instruction, whether instruction is viewed vertically (early childhood instruction, elementary school instruction, secondary school instruction, university instruction, instruction for the professions, instruction for adults)[2] or horizontally (science instruction, reading instruction, social studies instruction, language instruction).

The substantive noun "instruction" bears witness that religious instruction is characterized by the same objectives, processes, and operational principles as other kinds of instruction, while at the same time being particularized as a certain kind or form of instruction. Perhaps an analogy drawn from philosophy might be helpful here. In the Aristotelian tradition, any substance is conceived as having both being (esse) and specificity (talis). Thus, a particular substance shares with all other substances similarities which are most fundamental and most ordaining, while also stamped with features which particularize it as this kind of thing rather than that kind. Esse provides the existential and ordaining framework for talis, much as instruction provides the existential and ordaining framework for the way in which religion operates in this context.

What I am suggesting is that there is a vast difference between religious instruction and instructional religion. Religious instruction is the process of facilitating behavioral modification in learners along religious lines. Instructional religion is the process by which the exercise of religion has educational outcomes as by-products. In a certain theological sense, of course, all instruction is religious and all religion is instructional, and so the ontological distinction between religious instruction and instructional religion is not watertight. In an organically interrelated world, there is considerable overlapping with everything. Yet there is a difference between a church service which is an act of religion and a classroom situation which is an act of instruction. The activities carried out in a church service are shaped primarily by the fact that worship participation constitutes an act of religion whereas the activities of a classroom setting are shaped primarily by the fact that class participation constitutes an act of instruction. Religious instruction and instructional religion alike aim at facilitating a change in behavior; however, the way in which each of these enterprises goes about its facilitation process varies considerably depending on whether the activity is substantively religion or substantively instruction. Any way one wishes to slice it, a church is a church and not a classroom, and a classroom is a classroom and not a church. Indeed, the lack of awareness of this fundamental distinction on the part of both clergy and teachers has resulted in church services sometimes being operated as classes, and classes being turned into prayer meetings.

At this time I do not wish to treat at any length the interrelationship of theology and instruction since these two are joined in the ongoing work of religious instruction. I shall devote all of Chapter Eight to this topic. I wish simply to indicate that in religious instruction, religion is done within the general context and ground of the instructional process. In other words, I am suggesting that the very phrase "religious instruction" *eo ipso* connotes that religious instruction belongs to social science rather than to theological science.

THE EMPIRICAL CHARACTER
OF RELIGIOUS INSTRUCTION

One of the chief characteristics of social science, it will be recalled, is its empirical base. Social science, then, is oriented toward working with observable phenomena in such a way that conclusions about the present and future operations of these phenomena are empirically tested and verified. Theological science, on the other hand, tends to operate primarily within a speculative rather than an empirical framework. Of course, theological science is in as close a contact with *a posteriori* data as possible; nonetheless it does not utilize any empirical or objective controls to ascertain the validity and reliability of these *a posteriori* data. Thus Philip Phenix can remark that whereas social-science theorists like Gordon Allport and Rollo May have a disciplined and empirically-verified knowledge of human nature and its integrative drives, theologians such as Johann Metz merely have *a priori* dogmatic premises about human nature.[3]

Put another way, theological science makes statements about

human behavior which speculatively follow from certain basic principles but which, from the standpoint of empirical testing and verification, are untested assumptions. An example will perhaps serve to illustrate this point. Ecclesiastical leaders of most Christian churches, from the Roman Church to the Anglican Church to the Lutheran Church and so on, have down through the centuries asserted that the clerical and religious role of itself bears witness to Jesus and his lifeway, and brings about a closer relationship of the clergyman or religious with his or her spiritual children. A social-science orientation suggests that this is a statement about human behavior, which until empirically tested remains at the level of an assumption. As a matter of fact, there is some empirical evidence which indicates that the theological statement about the behavioral effect of a clerical or religious role is not true. Peter Grande's experimental investigation is relevant in this connection. Grande studied the behavioral rapport of adolescents in Catholic secondary schools who were counseled by two different groups of counselors who had the same professional training. One group of counselors were laymen; the other group was composed exclusively of clergymen and religious. The investigator found that the rapport achieved by the youths with the lay counselors was superior to that with the clerical or religious counselors. One conclusion of the study was that the youth's awareness that the counselor is a clergyman or religious *eo ipso* lessens the degree of rapport achieved with the counselor. In other words, the religious role seems to act as a barrier inhibiting rapport and indeed inhibiting the client's communication of some personality characteristics.[4] As I have mentioned elsewhere,[5] the personality of the counselor after a period of time becomes more functionally important to the client than does his status role; in this way clergymen and religious can indeed achieve effective rapport with their clients. However, this does not at all nullify the fact that theological statements about the positive behavioral effect of the religious role remain at the level of assumptions. The reason is that theological science is intrinsically inadequate to probe the behavioral cause-effect relationship existing between two or more observable human transactional patterns. Speculation can provide a possible clue into why a person behaves in a particular manner; however, it remains for empirical methodology to test and verify this clue. Theological speculation is particularly helpful when some or all of the phenomena under investigation are supernatural in character, and therefore not amenable to empirical methodology.

Religious instruction has as a major concern the discernment of the kind of curriculum and pedagogical methodologies which cause effective learning to take place. Perhaps a contrast between the theological approach and the social-science approach to this problem might be useful in our discussion. Throughout the second half of the nineteenth century, the catechism of the theologian Joseph Deharbe was the most important single vehicle for religious instruction in the Catholic Church in Germany. The pedagogical principle from which Deharbe was operating was that "the most sublime, comprehensive and significant truths are the most abstract truths and can only be taught as such."[6] One of the most influential religious educators in Germany and Austria in the twentieth century has been the theologian Josef Jungmann who writes: "As a result of the careful ordering of these associated parts (in the catechism) the good news character of the dogmatic structure will be made apparent. Through unswerving concentration on what is taught the chances are that the children will remember the basic facts of the Christian faith, even under the most unfavorable circumstances."[7] Argus Communications, theologically-oriented publishers of *Choose Life*, a popular series of so-called "religion non-textbooks" in the 1960's and 1970's, declare that this series " . . . begins where revelation happens in the student's experience . . . The materials meet the young person where he is. They draw upon everyday experiences of ordinary life: the spoken word, the newspaper headline, the Madison Avenue gimmick, the sophisticated catch-phrase, the tongue-in-cheek editorial, the serious scholar's report, the sights and sounds that are all around us — the world of the 'now' generation."[8]

A social-science perspective of these statements by Deharbe, Jungmann, and Argus is that they are interesting assumptions which remain assumptions until some hard empirical data can be adduced for their support. The statements of all three sources are declarations about concrete human behaviors. What is the empirical evidence to corroborate Deharbe's claim that abstract truths are the most sublime of all truths, and indeed can be taught only in an abstract form? Did Deharbe or anyone else test the truth or falsity of this assumption by finding out how, in reality, children do in fact learn? What is the empirical support for Jungmann's assertion that a careful ordering of the curriculum around a logical axis will indeed make the kerygmatic thrust of dogmatic truths apparent to the learners? Also, what evidence does Jungmann advance to bolster his affirmation that "unswerving concentration on what is taught" will help insure that the child will learn what the curriculum makers intend for him to learn? What empirical investigations have been made to ascertain if real-life children actually do acquire from a curriculum structure what Jungmann states flatly they will acquire? Where are the hard data to confirm Argus's *a priori* assumption that its instructional materials begin where revelation happens in the student's experience? How does Argus know when revelation happens in a young person's experience? Argus also claims that its materials meet the young person where he is. Are there any empirical data to support the contention that the "sophisticated catch-phrase," or the "tongue-in-cheek editorial," the "Madison Avenue gimmick," or indeed the "serious scholar's report" are where the youth in a rural backwoods community is existentially at? How culture-fair is the Argus series? What empirical research has Argus employed even in such a methodologically primitive category as insuring that the vocabulary and concepts used are consonant with the empirically-verified norms of the adolescent population at which the series is aimed?

It may well be that the *a priori* assumptions made by theologians and theologically-oriented religious educators are true. The point I am attempting to make is that the task of religious instruction is to enhance the probability of the individual's acquiring the desired learning outcome. In order to maximize this probability, we must have data which indicate how learning takes place, and what pedagogical conditions optimally promote this learning. This is fundamentally the work of social science. Effective religious instruction cannot operate on untested assumptions.

To be sure, untested assumptions abound in the literature. It would not be surprising if religion teachers, dependent as they are on leadership from the specialists, operate their own pedagogy on the basis of these untested assumptions rather than on the basis of what has been empirically validated. Despite the mass of hard data on child and adolescent development, it is astonishing to discover how many religious instruction writers employ untested assumptions about child and adolescent development instead of seeking to test their assumptions either experimentally or by a comparison with the extant empirical data. A few examples will suffice to concretize the point. Anna Barbara, an American religion teacher at the secondary level, declares that "psychologically, the adolescent is ripe for eschatology."[9] Barbara's statement represents a generalization about adolescent behavior — but where are her empirical data to indicate whether her generalization is valid or not? Perhaps she gleaned her generalization from the high school youth whom she taught. If this is so, her statement remains at the hypothetical level only, since she has not tested it within the context of methodological controls. Pierre Ranwez, a European theologian with an interest in religious instruction, states that obedience is the child's first virtue, and that obedience practiced in love constitutes the basic Christian attitude.[10] The second part of his statement is a theological affirmation, while the first part is a declaration of child development. Where are the empirical data to confirm Ranwez's generalization that obedience is the child's first virtue? Certainly most child psychologists would disagree on the basis of the relevant empirical research findings.[11] While Ranwez's assumption is rejected by the hard data, there is evidence to indicate that as late as the early 1960's, Catholic clergy tended to base their parochial school programs on this assumption. Thus, for example, Gerhard Lenski's empirical study revealed that eighty-one percent of the Catholic clergy investigated ranked obedience as far more important than intellectual autonomy as a key learning outcome in the school.[12] Randolph Crump Miller, one of America's leading theologically-oriented Protestant religious educators, writes that the primary school child "wants to be a member of the Church and know that he is recognized as such. At seven, he will like the Church's worship as an aid to his inner life. He will be sufficiently aware of death to ask questions about it."[13] What data exist to confirm that the primary school child wants to be a member of the church? Why does not Miller adduce hard data to support his contention that at seven, the child likes the church's worship as an aid to his inner life? What does the research say on the primary school child's concept of death?

In highlighting the importance of empirically-verified data for the work of religious instruction, I am not suggesting that social science provides the entire framework for religious instruction. To be sure, the work of the supernatural constitutes a central variable in the enterprise of religious instruction. However, the supernatural cannot be measured by empirical procedures. Indeed, theological science itself seems hard pressed to make any sort of accurate assessment of the supernatural effects of religious instruction. But the evaluation and improvement of a particular religion class or religion curriculum are dependent upon the degree to which the learner's behavior is being modified along desired religious lines. Consequently some sort of judgment must be made about the relative effectiveness of teaching method x compared with teaching method y, or of curriculum a compared with curriculum b. It is proper to assume, I think, that an increase in faith and charity and other supernatural virtues will cause a related change in the religious behavior of the learner to the extent that he has acquired one or more of these supernatural qualities. If supernatural enhancement has no visible effect on one's daily living, perhaps the Christian religion is in vain. Empirical methodology, then, is useful in assessing the religious effects on the learner's life of one or other teaching method or curriculum structure or instructional materials. From the data, we may make a legitimate inference as to the augmentation of this or that supernatural quality in the learner. For example, if we study two groups of matched youths, being taught by different instructional methods, and observe over a protracted period of time that Group A practices love of neighbor more than Group B does, then we may infer that the instructional method used with Group A is more effective that the method used with Group B in producing those behaviors identified with the virtue of charity.

VERIFICATION IN RELIGIOUS INSTRUCTION

In theology, verification for propositions comes from faith or from the bible or from tradition, or from natural reasoning, or from the magisterium (or the church). In other words, verification comes from a speculative, authoritative source which in an important way lies external to the phenomena. In M. D. Chenu's words, " . . . theology, being the child of faith, can only exist in submission to the Word of God, in loyalty to its mysteries, in obedience to its dogmas and consequently in the absence of any evidence for its basic principles."[14] In social science, on the other hand, verification for propositions comes from controlled observation and empirical testing of the phenomena and their relation, according to the method of difference or one of the other general methods. Let us look at a typical religious instruction activity in order to ascertain which method of verification is most appropriate. A teacher in a certain religion class wishes to have his students learn to relate the Christian teaching of love of neighbor to their everyday life. How does this teacher verify that he has succeeded in his attempt? Will the magisterium provide him with an accurate answer? Of what help are scripture and tradition in assessing the effectiveness of the lesson? Does faith somehow provide the answer to the lesson's level of success? Or perhaps is it necessary to use empirical methods to ascertain the degree to which these students are in fact relating their class learnings to their out-of-class life?

An empirical study conducted by Milton Rokeach, a social scientist, will possibly illustrate this point. This investigator explored the relation between an individual's religious values and the degree of his compassionate social outlook. From the viewpoint of theological science, there would obviously be a high correlation, since the person having more expressly religious values would presumably be living a richer life of faith; further, such a person is in closer contact with the bible, and his elevated level of church attendance and fidelity to the magisterium (or church) would serve in addition to produce a high correlation. Rokeach's carefully-conducted attitudinal survey of over 1,000 adult Americans in a national sample revealed that religious values are more or less irrelevant as guides in ascertaining the degree of compassionate social outlook. Indeed, Rokeach noted that the findings suggest a pervasive social outlook among those with high religious values which seems incompatible and often opposite to the compassion taught in the Sermon on the Mount. For example, the respondents were asked whether they had felt anger on learning the news of Martin Luther King's murder, or whether the assassination had made them "think about the many tragic things that have happened to Negroes and that this was just another one of them." Those persons who scored highest on religious values, notably in their emphasis on salvation as a prime Christian value, were insensitive to such feelings — "it never occurred to me." On the other hand, those not so salvation-minded were most likely to have experienced such reactions of compassion.[15] Rokeach's investigation confirms and extends earlier social-science findings that an individual's belief in Christian teachings often bears no relation to his concern with Christian moral practice.

Jesus frequently made use of empirical verifiers to confirm the truth and validity of his teachings for those to whom he was giving religious instruction. Again and again we read in the gospels something akin to what he told the nobleman whose son lay sick at Capernaum: "You must see signs and miracles happen, or you will not believe" (John 4: 48). Jesus, then, employed empirically observable and testable experiences to act as verifiers for the supernatural cause-effect relation which he stated as true. The use of such verifiers, obviously, accomplished a pedagogical purpose. An illustration of Jesus's use of empirical verifiers in his work of religious instruction is as follows:

> When he returned to Capernaum some time later, word went round that he was back; and so many people collected that there was no room left, even in front of the door. He was preaching the word to them when some people came bringing him a paralytic carried by four men, but as the crowd made it impossible to get the man to him, they stripped the roof over the place where Jesus was; and when they had made an opening, they lowered the stretcher on which the paralytic lay. Seeing their faith, Jesus said to the paralytic, "My child, your sins are forgiven." Now some scribes were sitting there, and they thought to themselves, "How can this man talk like that? He is blaspheming. Who can forgive sins but God?" Jesus, inwardly aware that this was what they were thinking, said to them, "Why do you have these thoughts in your hearts? Which of these is easier: to say to the paralytic, 'Your sins are forgiven,' or to say, 'Get up, pick up your stretcher and walk?' But to prove to you that the Son of Man has authority on earth to forgive sins" — he said to the paralytic — "I order you: get up, pick up your stretcher, and go off home." And the man got up, picked up his stretcher at once and walked out in front of everyone, so that they were all astounded and praised God saying, "We have never seen anything like this." (Mark 2:1-12).

What I am suggesting in this section, and indeed in this entire chapter, is that social science is far more helpful than is theological science in verifying both the level and effectiveness of religious instruction. In fact, theological science by its very nature is not equipped to verify the level or effectiveness of the teaching-learning process.

T. W. Dean writes that confronted with the mysteries of the world, man feels a positive need to acknowledge the transcendence of God.[16] How would theological science verify this to be the fact that Dean says it is? Some theologians might hold that such a need represents a wishful projection on the part of man. Others might note that confrontation with the mysteries of the world leads man to seek the God within rather than the God "up there." And so forth. Dean is making a statement about human behavior — psychological behavior, to be precise. Attempts to verify this behavior by theological science result in all sorts of conflicting speculative theories.

The German theologians who gave birth to the Munich Method for religious instruction based much of their approach on the notion that understandings give rise to convictions and to improved religious attitudes.[17] Once again, theologians are making statements which by their very nature cannot be verified by the methodology proper to theological science. To be sure, social-science research investigations have concluded that understandings do not necessarily give rise to convictions, and when they do so, it is within the framework of selected conditions. There are other more powerful ways of effecting convictions than by improving understanding. Perhaps an example will reinforce my point. One social-science researcher found in his study that penitentiary inmates and college students, when asked to rank the ten commandments in the order of importance to themselves, came to a high degree of similarity in their responses.[18] The college students had a deeper understanding of the ten commandments than did the penitentiary inmates. However, this higher level of understanding of the ten commandments on the part of the college students did not result in their having convictions about the relative personal worth of these commandments which were substantially different from those of the penitentiary inmates.

Catholic theologians for centuries have strongly believed in the efficacy of retreats to significantly alter the attitudes and convictions of those individuals making the retreat. These theologians have further asserted that a closed retreat is more effective in altering attitudes and convictions than is an open retreat.[19] The special retreat masters as well as parish clergymen have repeatedly testified that significant changes were wrought in the attitudes, values, and lives of those making the retreats. But in recent decades, other retreat masters and clergymen have reported that retreats had relatively little effect on the retreatants. Is theological methodology capable of assessing this contradictory evidence and establishing the truth or falsity of one of these statements? Thomas Hennessey decided to employ the tools of social science to learn the answer and so make a verification. Hennessey's study dealt with the changes and with the permanence of changes in the religious ideals of Catholic high school students following a closed retreat. He investigated an experimental group of these youths in a closed three-day retreat and a control group in an open three-day retreat. Hennessey's data indicated a pronounced improvement in the former group as compared with the latter in expressed religious ideals at the conclusion of the respective retreats. Five months later, however, there were no statistical differences between the groups in the area of religious ideals; in fact, the religious attitudes of students were just about as they had been before the retreat. Whereas the attitudes had not been altered, religious practices such as church attendance had improved in the experimental group.[20]

THE PLACE OF PREDICTION
IN RELIGIOUS INSTRUCTION

One of the primary aims of social science is to predict future behavior or occurrences on the basis of laws derived from empirically observed and verified phenomena. Prediction of the learner's behavior is of paramount importance in religious instruction; indeed, it might be said that a cardinal objective of all pedagogical activity is to modify the learner's behavior along desired lines. The religion teacher operates on the probability that a certain product content and a certain instructional process will cause a desired learning outcome in the student. For example, in his attempt to teach students to appreciate the Christian value of suffering, the teacher will utilize teaching method x in preference to method y because he predicts method x will be more effective in this case.

This kind of prediction is uniquely the work of social science and not of theological science. It is social science that is methodologically equipped to empirically ascertain which set of pedagogical variables interacts in such a way that the learning outcome of this interaction can be accurately forecast by the teacher or by the appropriate educational authorities. To predict that desired learning outcomes will take place in students, the social scientist tests which conditions must exist and how these conditions must be shaped in order to forecast that an individual will effectively learn one particular thing rather than either another thing or nothing at all. It is the work of social science, not of theological science, to evolve both laws of teaching and laws of learning from empirically verified facts. And it is by the judicious use of these empirically derived laws that the religion teacher goes about his work of facilitating learning as optimally as possible. One important function of a law of learning is to enable the teacher to choose that pedagogical approach and strategy which will most effectively bring about the desired learning outcome. Thus the law essentially has a predictive function. For example, it is a law of learning that positive reinforcement results in significantly higher retention of learned material than no reinforcement. Hence if an adolescent learns that compassion is a deeply Christian virtue, the teacher will attempt to reinforce this learning by some positive reward. In doing so, the teacher is guided by yet another law of learning, namely, that the more immediate is the reinforcement of the learned behavior, the higher is the retention. In selecting the suitable kind of immediate reinforcement, the teacher acts on still another law of learning, namely that peer-group reinforcement is more effective for adolescents than is reinforcement from the teacher.

Let us say that a teacher is working with a group of parents in evolving a preschool religious education program for their toddlers. What should he suggest concerning the punishment of their little ones for various kinds of offenses? A conservative theologian might urge fair but rigorous punishment, in keeping with the biblical maxim, "Do not withhold correction from a child, for if you strike him he shall not die. You shall beat him with the rod and deliver his soul from hell."[21] A liberal theologian might counsel a more moderate approach. A social scientist, on the other hand, would find out what the empirical research has to report on the effects of punishment and nonpunishment on the present and future conduct of children. He would discover among other things that the more severely children are punished for aggression by their mothers, the more aggressive they become during their preschool years.[22] By using the tools of this science, the social scientist occupies a more favored position in predicting future behavior than does the theologian employing the tools of his science.

Perhaps another example will illustrate the point I am making. Beginning with the Council of Trent, Catholic theologians and indeed the magisterium itself forcefully have stated that an environment totally isolated from the world provides the most effective training milieu for its future priests. The theologians at the Second Vatican Council reversed this centuries-old position, predicting that an environment providing contact with the world and with so-called "secular persons" would produce a more effective priest. Using their own research tools, social scientists have made independent research investigations into the comparative results of isolated versus nonisolated seminary environments in predicting the effectiveness of future priests trained in each of these milieux. John Murray attempted to assess the influence which traditional seminary training exerted on personality. Murray found an increase in psychological deviancy during the seminary years, and a sharp regression toward the normal after ordination when the young men perforce left the confines of the isolated seminary setting.[23] Richard

Vaughan investigated the personality change in students who lived in traditional isolated Roman Catholic seminaries versus those who lived in university-based Roman Catholic seminaries. Vaughan's study examined four groups of seminarians, two of which lived either on a university campus in separate boarding facilities or in a residential seminary while attending all their classes on a university campus. The other two groups were domiciled in the traditional isolated seminary milieu. Each group was tested twice by the investigator: once before entering the seminary and again after completing from one to nine years as seminarians. All four groups received the first two years of their training in an isolated seminary setting. Groups B and C attended classes for one year at a university. Group A spent the entire time in a traditional isolated seminary as did Group D also; however, Group D began teaching after six or seven years of training. Vaughan's study concluded that "those students who received all their training in the traditional seminary environment showed the greatest shift in the direction of abnormality." He further found that whereas changing the location of training from the traditional isolated seminary setting to a university campus failed to offset the effects of previous self-centered training in the case of junior college seminarians, it did so to a degree in the case of the more mature university seminarians.[24] Surely the social science research conducted by such men as Murray and Vaughan serves as more reliable predictors than do the pronouncements of theologians vis-à-vis the effect on student personality of traditional isolated seminary environments versus university-based seminary milieux.

To be an effective teacher is to so shape the learning environment that its conditions will be optimally conducive to the attainment of a desired learning outcome. Unless the teacher consciously and deliberatively shapes the instructional environment, he will not be able to predict the learning outcome. Lacking this, teaching is reduced to chance, to some sort of vague get-together. It is the purpose of social science to furnish the teacher with those hard data, those facts, and those laws which enhance the probability that the students will learn what is meant to be learned. The attitude of a theologian toward the work of prediction in religious instruction is quite the opposite, as the following quotation from Gabriel Moran demonstrates: "The Spirit works where He wills and how He wills, and it is not for man to control Him. The catechist, like the apostle, invites man to respond to God, but when, where, and under what conditions is not for the catechist to decide. What the catechist can do is show what a Christian life is by living one."[25]   In terms of religious instruction, I believe Moran's view misses the mark. The pedagogical problem is not controlling the actions of the Spirit, but rather shaping the learning conditions in such a way that the Spirit will be enabled to most fruitfully operate. Indeed, I suspect it is bad theology to imply that no intimate connection exists between the supernatural world and the natural world. If the scriptures show anything, they show that God's holy men were constantly engaged in a struggle to so shape political, social, cultural, environmental, and pedagogical conditions so that the Spirit could act in an effective manner. The notion of willy-nilly chance promoting the effective operation of the Spirit seems quite foreign to the activities recounted in the bible.

Hard empirical data, then, together with empirically-derived laws enable the teacher and curriculum builder to predict which variables will most effectively achieve the learning of desired outcomes under given conditions. This procedure is of its nature proper to social science rather than to theological science, as is illustrated by the following quotation from a European theologian interested in religious instruction: "The catechist himself should not begin with God and then treat of Christ, the Church, the sacraments and the moral law. He should begin rather with the sacramental life, discuss our attitudes toward it and the frustrations we experience, and only then delve into those matters which cast light and clarity on Christian living."[26]   What this theologian is doing is attempting to predict the order in which topics should be introduced in the curriculum to optimally promote learning. His decision on the ordering was made on theological grounds. But on what basis does theological science predict that such-and-such a curricular ordering does indeed result in facilitating learning? Does the whole matter of determining what does or does not facilitate learning properly fall within the competence of theological science? Or is such a determination more in line with the work of social science which has as its axis the critical testing and verifying of past causative factors in the teaching-learning process so that, as a consequence, we can predict what will happen when similar kinds of teaching-learning activities take place?

THE CONDITIONALITY OF RELIGIOUS INSTRUCTION

The teaching-learning process always takes place within some kind of existential context. Interactive relations among phenomena never occur in isolation. A person learns a particular product or process because all the conditions necessary to cause this learning are present and interacting in such a way as to produce a particular learning outcome. If any of the conditions change, then it is possible that the learning might not be produced. For example, a young person might be able to readily learn the meaning of a particular scriptural passage in a class taught early in the day, but experience considerable difficulty in grasping the meaning when the class is taught after his lunch period. In this case, time is a significant condition which, when altered, affects the rate and quality of learning.

It would seem that social scientists tend to be more deeply aware of the results of altering contextual conditions than do theological scientists. The reasons for this do not seem to have been explored to any degree of depth. Perhaps it is because conditionality forms such an intimate part of the investigative method of social science. In any event, the greater sensitivity to conditionality on the part of social scientists enables them to explain and predict more accurately than the theologian those conditions which promote or hinder religious learning. An example might illustrate this point. Angela Dolores Goldbeck, a religion teacher who bases her pedagogy on theological science, writes as follows: "Talking with God, discussing the joys and sorrows, the painful process of growing up, and other problems with this Friend, has to be done in the quiet of one's own heart. Therefore, a time should be provided after the religion lesson, with 'heads down' on folded arms, to think of something heard or enjoyed during that lesson .... Needless to say, a real personal love for Christ, and through him of the Father and the Holy Spirit, is one of the major consequences of this growth in informal meditation for God can never be outdone in generosity."[27] Goldbeck's position on the effectiveness of a "heads down" meditative period might hold true with the children in her particular class. However, suppose the conditions were changed so that Goldbeck's pupils came from a different social class, or that they belonged to a totally different culture, or that they were brain-damaged, and so forth. Under such altered conditions, the effectiveness of her teaching method may or may not hold true. In other words, the effectiveness of her method, strictly speaking, cannot be generalized to other than her own group of children; broadly speaking, statements about the effectiveness of her method can be generalized to situations in which the population and the other conditions are similar to the original situation. (Parenthetically, a social scientist would pose several serious questions to Goldbeck on the basis of her statements. What substantiating data does Goldbeck have for her statement that talking with God has to be done in the quiet of one's own heart? What data does Goldbeck adduce to show that her lesson was indeed effective in terms of promoting real personal love for Christ? In this connection, Goldbeck supports her position that the "heads down" method is effective because God can never be outdone in generosity. Is this adequate verification for the effectiveness of the "heads down" method? Operationally defined, what are Goldbeck's criteria for real personal love for Christ?)

Social scientists have learned from the data that there is a host of conditions which, when altered, significantly change the interactive relations in any given context. It has been found, for example, that crime is more prevalent among men, persons from low socioeconomic groups, certain minority groups, urban dwellers, and the less religious, than among women, persons from high socioeconomic groups, majority group members, rural dwellers, and the more religious.[28] In other words, a person's sex, socioeconomic group, membership in minority or majority group, place of residence, and religiosity are all conditions which significantly influence the rate of his criminality or probable criminality. Similarly, it has been found that school life and school performance are also greatly influenced by a host of conditions, including the learner's sex, socioeconomic environment, familial setting, and so forth.[29] Indeed, it has been found that the school environment itself represents an important condition serving to stimulate or stifle learning.[30] A review of the pertinent empirical research concludes that even such a relatively "minor" condition as group size can affect the performance and learning of members of the group.[31]

What I am suggesting is that it is the work of social science rather than the work of theological science to supply the facts and the laws indicating the causal relationship of a collection of conditions upon learning. The teacher acts as a social scientist, not as a theologian, when he makes the decision that the deployment of one teaching strategy (condition) in preference to another teaching strategy (condition) will bring about the desired learning outcome. And it is this act of structuring the conditions in such a way as to bring about desired learning which is the very essence of religious instruction.

REPLICATION IN RELIGIOUS INSTRUCTION
The religion teacher is continuously seeking to increase the

effectiveness of his pedagogical activity. In the process of doing this, he continuously seeks empirical tests to ascertain whether some pedagogical approach or strategy which seemed effective in the past is still effective. Or again, he seeks to test whether the conditions in his present instructional setting are sufficiently similar to those prior instructional milieux in which teaching method x has consistently been found by social scientists to be more effective than teaching method y. In other words, to maintain and improve his instructional effectiveness, the religion teacher in his own way is seeking to replicate the conditions which either he himself or social scientists have found will insure that the students attain desired learning outcomes.

Research conducted by social scientists on teaching effectiveness or on learning outcomes tends to have more objective validity and reliability than do "homemade" empirical tests constructed by the religion teacher in his particular setting. Therefore, the religion teacher will naturally be in close contact with the relevant research data so that he might replicate in his own classroom those conditions which social-science investigations have demonstrated bring about effective learning. Let me give two examples of how a religion teacher might go about this. In the 1930's and 1940's, there was much experimentation in public schools on the effectiveness of the so-called Core curriculum. The Core curriculum is one which centers around interdisciplinary problems of both eternal and personal concern. Subject matter is brought into the learning situation as it is needed to solve the problem being studied, without respect to precise subject-matter boundaries. Thus, for example, a study of the problem of social injustice might bring in such diverse subject areas as the history of the American Negro, music of the slaves, literature on man's inhumanity to man, religious writings on the topic, surveys of black attitudes, and so forth. The conclusions of carefully conducted research investigations into the learning outcomes derived from Core as compared with those derived from subject-centered classes have almost consistently revealed the superiority of Core. The results of the Eight-Year Study, for example, showed that students from schools with a Core curriculum scored higher in college than did matched students from schools utilizing the traditional design.[32] Wayne Wrightstone's report of a study comparing students in experimental Core classes with matched pupils from the traditional curriculum in New York City high schools discovered that Core pupils received significantly higher scores in all subjects except Latin grammar.[33] Results of other studies on Core came to much the same conclusions.[34] Reviewing all this research on the Core curriculum, the religion teacher in a particular church-related high school decides that he would like to enhance student learning by embarking on a Core curriculum. Working with the teachers, students, parents association, and school officials he secures enough students to form an experimental group of youth who will opt for the Core curriculum. Then he sets about to create conditions which are sufficiently similar to the instructional and curricular conditions of the original experiments. Next, he replicates the Core program, with the assurance that there is a strong probability that he will achieve results similar to those obtained in the earlier experiments. In other words, this religion teacher is using the replicability of social science to improve the instructional program.

Whereas my first example centers around the replication of an experiment, my second example will be based on replication of a survey to improve the instructional program. In 1961 Gerhard Lenski reported the results of a carefully-conducted piece of survey research which concluded that the Catholic schools investigated appeared not to be developing those attitudes, beliefs, values, and intellectual orientations which make it possible for individuals to enjoy working.[35] A religion teacher in a Protestant school setting might wonder if Lenski's findings could also point to one outcome of his own school program. Or a Catholic religion teacher might be eager to learn whether Lenski's 1961 data are applicable to his school during the current year. Both of these teachers can administer Lenski's instrument, either in its original form or in a revised version, to ascertain the impact of the school program on work attitudes. By replicating Lenski's survey, utilizing a social-science approach, these religion teachers can separate what is fact from what is fiction or what is wishful thinking on the part of teachers, school officials, and parents.

THE FUNCTION OF OBJECTIVITY
IN RELIGIOUS INSTRUCTION

All along the line, the religion teacher must make sure that each individual is really learning what the teacher, the individual himself, and the rest of the group perceive he is learning. Just because a teacher or a parent believes that an individual has acquired a specified learning outcome is no proof that the individual has indeed acquired that outcome. In other words, the teacher must objectively verify the extent to which the individual has acquired the desired learning outcome. The process of objective verification of learning outcomes is more suited to the work of empirically-oriented social science than to that of theological science. In the process of objectively verifying the acquisition of learning outcomes, the religion teacher utilizes as many controls as possible to insure a filtering out of subjective bias or expectancy on his part. Thus, for example, he administers a standardized test to an individual, or he uses objectively derived measuring instruments to assess the degree to which the individual has operationalized the hypothesized learning outcome in his life. To illustrate: the religion teacher believes that method x is superior to method y in causing a particular learning outcome. How does the teacher really know that his students are achieving a higher rate of learning as a result of method x? Perhaps the teacher has a conscious or unconscious emotional preference for method x. Possibly the students prefer method x because it is more enjoyable and they express greater satisfaction with this method (learner satisfaction may or may not be related to the degree of learning which has taken place). Objective criteria are needed to establish the reality of the situation.

Some illustrations might serve to throw additional light on this point. Billy Graham believes he has accomplished a great deal of permanent behavior modification along religious lines for the crowds who have attended his prayer gatherings. Yet an objective empirical follow-up study discovered little if any such change among a significant percentage of those who attended Graham's services.[36]

Daniel Brown, a theologically-oriented university professor, has proposed a method which he personally perceives as effective for teaching the old testament to college students. His method is to concentrate on one area of the Israel phenomenon, "thus reducing the material to what can be properly handled in a semester and doing so as a privileged example of a living tradition, a tradition continuing today, which the student can enter into and make his own, thus bringing out the true relevance of the old testament to his personal life." While he does not spell out his specific pedagogical methodology, it seems safe to infer that Brown relies pretty much on lectures, assigned readings, written assignments, and an examination.[37] From a social-science viewpoint, Brown's perception of the effectiveness of his teaching methodology poses several serious problems relating to objective criteria. Are Brown's students learning as effectively as Brown perceives they are? After all, *to be* is not the same as *to be perceived*. What are the criteria Brown uses for assessing whether or not his evaluation of their written assignments and final examination is truly objective? In other words, what objective controls are built into the evaluation procedure to insure that Brown does or does not consciously or unconsciously compose and/or evaluate the assignments and the test in such a way as to be perceived by him as justifying his judgment about the effectiveness of his class? What objective evidence does Brown bring forward to verify that his method is more effective than other teaching methods in causing learning? Assuming for a moment that Brown's method is instructionally effective in his own case, what objective criteria does he employ to generalize that this pedagogical method is effective for all other teachers as well?

Randolph Crump Miller, a theologically-oriented Protestant specialist in religious education, writes: "In most cases, it is my opinion that eighth- and ninth-graders will attack content that is external to themselves. This is why a course on old testament is sound procedure. It is history, which many of them enjoy."[38] The personal opinion of so experienced a religious education specialist as Miller surely carries weight; however, there is considerably more validity to empirically-derived objective verification. There is indeed empirical research to support Miller's belief that external content is not too meaningful to eighth- and ninth-graders; these data constitute a more sound and objective verifier than does Miller's subjective opinion. A course in old testament itself is sound procedure if it is appropriate to the maturational level of the eighth- and ninth-graders in question. Objective evidence on the psychological stages of these children, rather than one's personal opinion, should serve as the basis for assessing the effectiveness of a course on old testament.

Throughout the world in recent years, there has been a great deal of anxiety on the part of older people in particular that sexual practices, notably among young adults, are deteriorating considerably from the "good old days." Theologians and religious educators have voiced concern in this area. But the social scientist asks the question: What is the objective verification that sexual practice today is considerably more permissive than in the "good old days"? In France in the 1960's, some social scientists sought an objective answer to this question. It is an empirically verified fact that the period of human gestation is normally nine months. By the use of statistical methods, it is possible to infer with reasonable accuracy the degree of deviation from this mean point. The French social scientists then examined parish records for a three-hundred year period, from the mid-seventeenth century up until the year of their study. They compared the day-month-year of a couple's marriage with the day-month-year of the birth of their first child. If the interval was significantly less than nine months (with statistical allowances for the probability of a nonnormal gestation period), the social scientists inferred there was sexual permissiveness. The conclusion was that no matter what major variable was taken into account — war or peace, famine or plenty, eighteenth or twentieth century, and so forth — the rate[39] of inferred premarital pregnancy tended to be approximately the same. Such a study provides objective rather than impressionistic data.

All sciences are characterized by a certain degree of objectivity. Yet it seems safe to assert that social science of its very nature represents a greater attempt than that made by theological science to insure a total objectivity. Theologians declare that theology inevitably bears the mark of its time. Theology is influenced by the period in which it is done, and in turn seeks to influence that period as well. This does not mean that theological science is shaped totally by an era, but rather that the way in which it is done reflects to a significant extent the Zeitgeist.[40] One need only think of the biblical and theological interpretations of slavery and the black man formulated in different epochs or in different parts of the world to see the influence of the Zeitgeist on theologizing. Further, as Theodor Filthaut observes, the Zeitgeist has exerted considerable impact on the content and shape of any kind of religious instruction which is primarily theological in derivation.[41] Indeed, as M. D. Chenu has reminded us, theology takes on very different colors when viewed by different minds.[42] We have the Augustinian school and the Thomist school, the Protestant school and the Catholic school, the fundamentalist school and the liberal school, and so on. To be sure, when after painstaking care, a theologian assembles his data he really is not objectively free to draw any conclusions which the data themselves suggest. In the final analysis, it is not the objective analysis of the data which is the decisive factor (as in the case of social science) but rather some force outside the data themselves. For Catholics, it is fundamentally the magisterium which determines the parameters within which the data may be analyzed and interpreted.[43] Paul Tillich nicely sums up the forces external to the data which are decisive in any Protestant analysis and interpretation of the data:

> In every assumedly scientific theology there is a point where
> individual experience, traditional valuation, and personal commit-
> ment must decide the issue. This point, often hidden to the
> authors of such theologies, is obvious to those who look at them
> with other experiences and other commitments. If an inductive
> approach is employed, one must ask in what direction the writer
> looked for his material. And if the answer is that he looks in
> every experience, one must ask what characteristic of reality or
> experience is the empirical basis of his theology. Whatever the
> answer may be, an a priori of experience and valuation is implied.
> The same is true of a deductive approach, as developed in classical
> idealism. The ultimate principles in idealist theology are rational
> expressions of an ultimate concern; like all metaphysical ulti-
> mates, they are religious ultimates at the same time. A theology
> derived from them is determined by the hidden theology implied
> in them. In both the empirical and the metaphysical approaches
> [to theology], as well as in the much more numerous cases of
> their mixture, it can be observed that the a priori which directs
> the induction and the deduction is a type of mystical
> experience.[44]

Social science utilizes empirical controls all along the way to insure objectivity. In so doing, it is very helpful to the work of religious instruction. To facilitate learning in a black child, for example, it is crucial that we know in an objective manner how this black child does in fact learn. Our theology of the black child is not of itself a vital factor in facilitating desired learning outcomes in him; such a theology becomes a significant process variable only when it somehow interacts with other variables which affect learning. Thus, for example, if one holds a theology that blackness is an external manifestation of divine displeasure, then this theology becomes a significant process variable only to the extent that such a theology results in the teacher's behaving in a hostile or derogatory fashion toward the child (behaviors proved to correlate negatively with the facilitation of learning).

THE QUANTITATIVE ASPECT
OF RELIGIOUS INSTRUCTION

Religious instruction aims at facilitating Christian living in the learner's total behavioral pattern. Consequently, it is important that the teacher and the student have some clear idea of the extent to which a particular Christian behavior is being facilitated. It is the purpose of quantification to provide both teacher and learner with some measure of precision as to the degree and extent to which the desired learning outcomes are being achieved. Indeed, the very concept of effective learning connotes some sort of quantified measure, crude or refined, by which an individual can assess whether or not he is actually attaining the desired behavioral outcomes. A religion teacher might say to himself that pedagogical method x is more effective than method y. However, unless there is some sort of quantitative measure to differentiate the effectiveness of the two methods, it is not possible to objectively assert that method x is more effective than method y. Further, this religion teacher will wish to ascertain how much more effective method x is, so that he can make wise instructional decisions. Suppose, for example, that the implementation of method x demands a great deal more time, effort, and financial expense than does method y. An analysis of the results of each method reveals method x is indeed the more effective, but only by a few percentage points. Such quantitative data can help the teacher judge whether all the extra time, effort, and financial expense involved in method x pay the proportionate learning dividends.

Social-science survey research done on American students has concluded that men consistently score higher on tests of theoretical, political, and economic values, whereas women score higher on tests of religious, social, and aesthetic values.[45] This kind of quantified data is of significant assistance to the religion teacher in helping him differentiate his instructional activities. Further, by delving deeper into the data, the religion teacher can learn the degree to which women score higher than men on religious values. The amount of instructional differentiation which the teacher must provide in order to insure effective learning of religious values by his male and female students will vary according to the level of difference in the scores on the religious values scale.

One of the claims made by teachers and educational officials of Sunday school programs and church-related schools is that the students in these learning experiences acquire personal religious models who can serve as concrete ideals with whom to identify in fashioning their own Christian living. This is a claim; but what are the factual data? Here again quantitative measures can indicate the extent to which such personal religious models do act as concrete ideals for the learners. In this way, the teachers and educational officials can assess with some degree of accuracy the effectiveness of their religion programs in the area of providing personal religious models for the students. A 1957 study by Robert Morocco revealed that sixty-two percent of the students in Catholic secondary schools chose a religious personage as their primary personal ideal. The most frequently mentioned names were Fulton Sheen (a prominent bishop and popular television personality of the time) and the blessed mother Mary — Jesus was named by only nine students.[46]

Quantification is proper to social science rather than to theological science. Indeed, when theological science incorporated quantification into its work, various unfortunate results came about. For example, in the Catholic Church, God's mercy was placed in quantified form by a theological system called indulgences. Thus an individual could gain an indulgence of seven years and seven quarantines for performing this act, or an indulgence of six years for doing another act. Again, some moral theologians appeared to be employing quantitative or quasi-quantitative procedures in ascertaining how far an individual could go before he passed from the state of venial sin to that of mortal sin.

While theologically-oriented specialists in religious instruction would doubtless deny its social-science character, nonetheless their writings often reflect an implicit quantification of which they might be unaware. Thus, for example, Johannes Hofinger writes: "From the standpoint of religious pedagogy . . . a dialogue Mass is preferable even to a sung or solemn high Mass. This is not a question of the highest form of celebration, objectively speaking, but of the form of the Mass most fitted to give our children and young people a proper understanding of the teaching and the meaning of the Mass, and one which will help them to participate as intensively and meaningfully as possible."[47] Hofinger is here implying that children and young people learn more (quantitative) from a dialogue Mass than from a sung or solemn high Mass. All comparisons in the degree or level of pedagogical effectiveness perforce are in expressed or implied quantitative terms. (Parenthetically, I might note that Hofinger does not offer any hard data to support his contention that a dialogue Mass is a more effective pedagogical vehicle for children and young people than is a sung or solemn high Mass. Theological presuppositions are no substitute for empirically verified data in this regard.)

I should add that I do not mean to suggest in this section that religious instruction is at bottom quantitative, or that all religious instruction can be quantitatively measured. What I am saying is that the assessment and improvement of religious instruction must as far as possible utilize quantitative procedures if it is to provide valid and reliable indications and measures of the degree of its effectiveness.

VALUE-FREEDOM IN RELIGIOUS INSTRUCTION

It will be recalled from the last chapter that one of the characteristics of social science is that it is value-free. In other words, it does not assign value judgments to the results of its activity. A theological scientist, for example, might categorize a particular act as sinful or heretical, while a social scientist would categorize the same act as a personality malfunction or a socially disruptive activity.

For religious instruction, value-freedom means that the teaching process itself can facilitate behavioral modification toward one system of values more or less as readily as toward a different system of values. In other words, the process of producing learning outcomes can take place regardless of the values the teacher wishes the individual to attain. For example, a teacher in a Methodist Sunday school will use many of the same general pedagogical techniques to facilitate Methodist-type behaviors in his students as a Catholic CCD teacher will employ in facilitating Catholic-type behaviors in his students.

For religious instruction, value-freedom means that the process or effectiveness of behavioral modification is not normally subjected to theological judgments. For example, the magisterium or church or faith is not competent to judge whether teaching method x is more effective than teaching method y in facilitating a particular charitable behavior in the learner. Nor is theological science competent to judge the manner in which a person learns. For example, basing his evidence on the opinion of theologians, Josef Goldbrunner asserts that a "child acts only from an ethics of obedience and not out of personal decision."[48] Such psychological judgments clearly fall outside the scope of theological methodology and theological science in general.

When I say that religious instruction is value-free, I am not suggesting that religious instruction is unconcerned with values. Quite the contrary: both the process and product outcomes of religious instruction are themselves values. Christian living, the goal of religious instruction, is a supreme value. Moreover, religious instruction accepts the benchmark values of Christianity as the framework within which it operates. Hence religious instruction cannot violate any Christian principles in its work of behavioral modification. It is in this domain of values that a synapse is effected between the process of religious instruction and theological science. One of the crucial roles which theological science plays in the work of religious instruction is to provide the parameters and the overall direction within which and toward which the process of religious instruction works. I will discuss this point at greater length in the next chapter.

It is precisely in this matter of accepting and facilitating theological value structures that religious instruction differs sharply from religious counseling. The religion teacher's function is to facilitate certain desired values in the learner, while the work of the religious counselor is to accept unconditionally the client's values no matter how erroneous they may be.[49] The counselor's personal religious convictions, or the tenets of the religious denomination sponsoring the relationship he is having with his client, must not interfere with the client's self-actualizing.[50] For example, if an adolescent explains that he is having guilt feelings about masturbation, attributing such feelings to felt conflicts between his physio-psychological needs and his Roman Catholic religion, the counselor does not seize the opportunity to discuss the morality of masturbation.[51] He simply listens and reacts in a neutral way, without making any value judgment one way or the other, but merely expressing unconditional positive regard for the client as a person without accepting or supporting the client's beliefs qua beliefs. Religious counseling is concerned with value but primarily the value of the person self-actualizing and the incorporation by the client into his own self-system of those values he perceives will promote his own self-actualization.[52] Religious instruction, on the other hand, aims at the conscious and deliberative modification of desired values on the part of the learner.

THE FACILITATION PROCESS
IN RELIGIOUS INSTRUCTION

The facilitation process in religious instruction is a uniquely social-science activity. Facilitation is the enabling function; it is the process by which the learner is helped to modify his behavior in desired directions. Facilitation is the arrangement of instructional conditions so as to optimally promote learning. Properly and essentially considered, facilitation is a content-free process; however, the way in which learning is facilitated in a particular religious class does, of course, take on some of the coloring of the specified outcome to be facilitated. Theological science does not afford significant assistance in the ways to facilitate behavioral modification; rather it lends assistance to the work of religious instruction by suggesting fruitful directions toward which the behavior might be modified.

A failure on the part of theologians to recognize the social-science character of the facilitation process in religious instruction has led to some silly and pietistic statements. The following might be considered representative: "The human teacher is always subordinate to the Holy Spirit in the catechizing of the child . . . Catechesis is not an event between the catechist and the child, but between God and the child."[53] Indeed such statements smack of ontologism and angelism. Religious instruction is not a mystical experience; it is first and foremost an interaction between the learner and the conditions which have been consciously and deliberatively shaped in such a way that he will acquire the desired learning outcomes. Of course, God resides in all things, including the religion lesson. But history has shown that God works through human and other natural agents in causing the behaviors he wishes. Until religious instruction is demythologized of the prevalent attitude reflected in such statements as I have just cited, I believe it will remain quagmired in the same overpresumptuous reliance on God and overneglect of human and natural resources which have caused such nonprofessionalism in the field for centuries. God cannot — and I suspect will not — be dragged in by the heels to make every religion class a paragon of behavioral facilitation. I rather believe that God works in and through the natural order. In religious instruction this means that educational experiences must be planned carefully and implemented skilfully if they are to have the intended effects on the learner.[54]

The cumulative effect of all sorts of variables operating within the learning situation is what causes the individual to learn one thing rather than another. It is within the competency of social science to isolate those variables which are most productive of learning, and so structure them that the desired learning outcome is achieved. This conscious control and deliberative structuring of the learning situation is at the heart of the facilitation process. Because both the scientific discernment of the significant instructional variables which affect learning, and also the arrangement of these variables to produce effective learning fall outside the competency of theological science, theologically-oriented religious educators have had to stumble around and guess how a lesson could be structured to facilitate the desired learning outcomes. The results of this theological speculation sometimes have been mistaken and other times irrelevant. For example, Johannes Hofinger states flatly that the most effective way of facilitating young children in the primary school grades to enter more completely into a living union with Jesus is through a biblical-historical approach, which leads to Jesus through the telling of the story of salvation. To buttress his contention, Hofinger cites this method as the way in which Paul attempted to facilitate religious learnings in his speech in the synagogue of the Pisidian Antioch, and the way in which Augustine urged religious instruction to be facilitated. To further support his position, Hofinger adduces theological arguments including that of the history of salvation's being at the center of the joyous Christian message.[55]

There are obvious minor flaws in Hofinger's arguments. For example, Paul's audience at Antioch were all adults, as were most of those whom Augustine had in mind — and adults learn quite differently from children, as common sense, to say nothing of social-science data, indicates. But the major weakness in any attempt to make theology do the work of facilitation is that theological science *eo ipso* is not geared to the facilitation of behavioral modification. It is clearly outside the province of theological science to discover and predict the psychological and instructional conditions under which children learn. For example, how is theology equipped to predict the effects of television versus classroom discussion in shaping the attitudes of learners? Indeed, in the case of Hofinger's contention there are some hard data which suggest that the biblical-historical method is inappropriate and ineffective in facilitating in young children the very learning outcomes which Hofinger says will result.[56]

By virtue of the kind of science it is, social science occupies a uniquely favored position to discover, explain, and predict the effect of a host of instructional variables which facilitate or impede the attainment of desirable learning outcomes. For example, social science has discovered that the very words use; by a teacher or other person in communicating with another individual do significantly facilitate or impede the acquisition of the content and coloration of the message. The research investigation conducted by William Verplanck illustrates this. Verplanck's experiment was carried out in a series of ordinary conversations between two people: the subject who was not informed in any way that he was taking part in an experiment and the experimenter. Twenty-four subjects participated. Each experimenter engaged the subject in conversation on a variety of topics for at least one-half hour. The half-hour was divided into three discrete periods of ten minutes each. During the first ten-minute period, the experimenter engaged in normal conversation, and recorded the rate of the subject's opinion output. A comparative baseline of the subject's rate of opinion utterance was thereby established. During the second ten-minute period, the experimenter positively reinforced every opinion-statement made by the subject. This positive reinforcement was effected by the experimenter's verbally agreeing with every opinion stated by the subject, or by making a nodding or smiling affirmation if he could not verbally interrupt. In the last of the three ten-minute periods the experimenter tried to extinguish all the subject's opinion-statements. He did this by withdrawing all reinforcement, that is, by failing to respond at all in the case of some subjects or by negative reinforcement, that is, by disagreeing with every opinion-statement in the case of other subjects. The results of the study are as informative as they are dramatic. The subjects' rate of speaking during the entire half-hour period did not change. However, what did change markedly was the amount of opinion-statements made by the subjects. All twenty-four subjects showed an increase in the relative frequency of opinion-statements during the second time period, that is, when the experimenter was positively reinforcing their opinion-statements. On the other hand, twenty-one of the twenty-four subjects showed a decrease in the relative frequency of opinion-statements during the third time period, namely, when the experimenter was extinguishing their opinion-statements by withholding all reinforcements or by disagreeing with them.[57] The significance of the Verplanck study for religious instruction is that it again illustrates that student behavior is in fact shaped by significant variables within the teacher's repertoire of instructional behaviors. In the work of religious instruction, surely it is God who gives the increase, but it must be the learning situation which plants, and the teacher who waters. To facilitate is both to plant and to water.

BEHAVIOR MODIFICATION
AND RELIGIOUS INSTRUCTION

Religious instruction works toward effecting in the learner a behavioral modification along religious lines. Such behavioral modifications might be in the area of cognition affectivity or more globally, the learner's lifestyle. Basically, learning is a change in behavior; therefore, the modification of an individual's behavior is an operational way of expressing learning. The scriptures abound with incidents in which Jesus modified an individual's behavior. He taught Peter to have faith and John to have humility. He effected the conversion of the Samaritan woman at the well and enabled his companions on the road to Emmaus to gain insight. In short, Jesus went around doing good, that is, in one way or another modifying the behavior of all who would learn from him.

In order to effectively modify behavior, the religion teacher or curriculum builder must first, know the conditions which bring about behavior change and second, arrange for the concrete structuring of these conditions in such a way that the learner's behavior is in fact modified in the desired direction. Consequently, the religion teacher and the curriculum builder must be conversant with the empirical data on how a learner actually learns, and how to facilitate that kind of behavioral modification which is really possible, given the existential conditions of the learner. In other words, in the work of causing behavior modification in the learner, the teacher is a practicing social scientist.

While theological science is useful in suggesting directions toward which the learner's behavior can be fruitfully modified, it is the work of social science which actually secures and effects the behavior modification itself. For example, there has been dispute among theologians throughout the centuries as to the most propitious moment for first communion, and whether a child should make first communion in the company of his peer-group or of his parents. The duration of this theological dispute and the variegation of opinions serve as an indication that a real solution to this question is not within the scope of theological science. Social-science investigation can reveal the actual facts of the psychological maturation, readiness, and development of children of different age levels, together with the kinds of interactions they have with parents and peer-group members. On this basis, a decision can be intelligently made as to the moment and the accompanying group most propitious for the reception of first communion.

Both theologians and theologically-oriented religious educators tend to develop curricula for religious instruction programs from the standpoint of the logical development of theological science. A social scientist, on the other hand, tends to develop his curricula from the existential situation of the learner — how he does in fact learn, the conditions conducive to facilitating learning, and so forth. A theologian like Marcel van Caster suggests that in the teaching of the eschatological dimension of Christianity, the religion teacher should "take as his starting-point the fact of Christ's resurrection; put the Christian's death explicitly in relation to the death of Christ and the meaning of his death."[58] A social scientist would take as his starting point the way in which the particular group of individuals he is teaching do in fact learn. Their age level, psychophysiological needs, socioeconomic background, cultural milieu — all these have been shown by the hard data to bear a very significant relationship to the way in which learning actually occurs. It may well be that the empirical data suggest that the resurrection is an inappropriate starting point, or again, the data might reveal that the resurrection does represent an effective starting point in terms of where the learners are existentially at. What I am saying is that a priori assumptions about religious instruction, no matter how sound they might be from the standpoint of theological science, do not of themselves suggest the most effective mode of facilitating behavioral modification for this or that group of learners.

SHAPING THE LEARNING ENVIRONMENT
TO PROMOTE RELIGIOUS INSTRUCTION

It is the total environment in which the teaching-learning process takes place, and not simply any one variable within that environment such as the teacher or the curriculum, which works toward producing the desired learning outcomes. The task of the religion teacher is to skilfully shape the learning environment so that all the conditions will work together to cause the intended behavioral modification. The religion teacher as a practicing social scientist controls and shapes all the variables which are known to exert a significant influence on the acquisition of learning outcomes — pedagogical strategy, materials, curriculum, socioemotional climate, institutional setting, physical and human environment, and so on. In a very fundamental sense, teaching can be defined as structuring the learning situation in such a way that the environmental variables within that shaped situation interact to cause learning. Because of the difference in their respective natures, it is within the scope of social science — not theological science — first to identify those variables which cause learning, second to structure those variables in a situational fashion so as to bring about the desired learning, and finally to assess whether or not the desired behavioral modification actually occurred.

In that theological science by its nature is not equipped to structure environmental variables to bring about the desired modifications in behavior, its efforts in this direction have been on a hit-or-miss basis. This is in sharp contrast to a social-science approach to the problem; social science is geared to reduce chance to a minimum in the cause and prediction of behavior. Perhaps an example will illustrate the results which follow from hit-or-miss efforts when theologians rather than social scientists are put in charge of shaping the learning environment. Novitiates and convents for the training of women religious represent learning environments shaped by theologically-oriented persons in such a way as to bring about desired behavioral modifications in the young women living within their confines. Social-science data have revealed that this kind of environment has scored a direct "hit" rather than a "miss" in terms of producing the desired behavioral modification. Thus, for example, Marie Francis Kenoyer conducted a careful empirical study of two groups of matched Catholic girls, one of which had entered the religious life and the other which remained in the lay life. Both groups were matched prior to group A's entering the convent or novitiate. After a number of years had elapsed, Kenoyer employed psychological assessment devices to compare the two groups of girls. The study found that the girls in religious life perceived themselves as more submissive, more self-abasement-oriented, more in need of being dominated, and more shy than the matched group of lay women. Kenoyer concluded that this difference in personality traits was due to the effect of the convent environment on group A.[59]

Other instances can be related to indicate that environments shaped by theologically-oriented individuals failed to produce the anticipated learning outcomes. Let me give one illustrative case. Catholic theologians and theologically-oriented religious authorities have for centuries decried coeducation of youth. Pius XI stated flatly that coeducation frequently was based on naturalism and a denial of original sin. Surveying creation from the vantage point of theological science, Pius noted that divine and natural law indicate tha coeducation of youth is highly deleterious to the natural and supernatural development of young men and women.[60] The Pian prohibition on coeducation of youth was reinforced in a 1958 instructio of the Sacred Congregation of Religious which states from a theological position that coeducation in Catholic high schools is permissible only in localities where the bishop deems this evil gravely necessary. In such situations, the Sacred Congregation has listed specific precautions which must be taken, for example, boys and girls must be housed in different classrooms or at least on opposite sides of the same classroom where separate classrooms are not possible, and they must enter and leave the school at different times. Religious are not permitted to conduct coeducational secondary schools. Further, religious who teach in these schools must be men or women whose virtue has been proved by experience — a provision which probably excludes young religious from teaching in such schools.[61] Despite these weighty theological viewpoints, social-science data have not indicated harmful effects of coeducational environments on the development or religious behavior of youth. [62] Indeed, there are some data which suggest that segregation of the sexes at the secondary and university levels has unfortunate behavioral results. For example, the study by Alice Wessell and Mary Rita Flaherty revealed that after one year in a Catholic women's college, the girls tested were significantly less feminine than when they entered the college.[63]

Theologically-oriented Protestant and Catholic officials have erected church-related colleges in the belief that the environments at such institutions are conducive to producing heightened religious growth and development in the students. These officials use theological verifiers to buttress their frequent statements that they can "really feel the religious atmosphere in the air at St. Z College." Yet there are some social-science data to suggest that while these theological verifiers might endow the church official with a personal sense of satisfaction and well-being, nevertheless these verifiers are not providing a valid picture of what is really going on. Thus, for example, a longitudinal investigation by Marie Edmund Harvey concluded that in the eastern Catholic women's college studied, there was no significant change in the religious attitude of students from freshman to senior year.[64] Harvey's findings are similar to those of Robert Hassenger who investigated the impact of a midwest Catholic women's college environment on the religious attitudes of its students. Seniors at this college were only minimally different from the freshmen in terms of religious attitudes and values.[65] In one of the most complete reviews of the empirical research on the impact of the Catholic college environment on the student, Hassenger concludes that these environments do not seem to be too significant in altering the religious attitudes and values of the students along the lines intended by the college officials. Rather, the religious attitudes and values of the seniors seem to be quite consistent with those they held as freshmen — although beginning in the late 1960's, there appears to be a trend for the religious attitudes and values of seniors to be moving in a direction away from that desired by the religious officials of the college.[66]

Both the shaping and the assessing of the educational impact of a learning environment upon individuals are tasks for social science rather than for theological science. To be sure, theological science has a key role to play in religious education; however, this role is something other than the structuring of the learning situation.

THE CHRISTIAN LEARNING LABORATORY
AND RELIGIOUS INSTRUCTION

Toward the end of Chapter Three, I observed that the religion class at its most fulsome is a laboratory for Christian living. Such a laboratory represents a learning environment so shaped that the product and process outcomes of the lesson are achieved through the direct experiencing of them. As John Dewey has suggested, the rise of modern science has shown that there is no such thing as genuine knowledge or fruitful understanding — and I might add, mature attitude and value development — except as the offspring of doing, in the broad sense of this term. Individuals have to do something with knowledge or understanding or values; they cannot merely attain these outcomes in their heads.[67] Man is an integer, that is, a being who is called on by his nature to effect an integration in his own lifestyle of being and doing. Commenting on the celebrated Hawthorne experiment conducted by social scientists, Marshall McLuhan observes that this investigation demonstrates behaviorally that when individuals are permitted to join their energies to the process of learning and discovery in a laboratory setting, the resultant increased efficiency is "phenomenal."[68]

Because of their respective natures and thrusts, social science, not theological science, is equipped to shape the learning conditions necessary for the development, implementation, and assessment of a learning laboratory for Christian living. André Godin notes that theologians and theologically-oriented religion teachers are *eo ipso* unacquainted with the effects of socioemotional climate on the teaching-learning process, or in knowing what pedagogical strategy is most appropriate for producing a specific kind of learning.[69] It is only through the understanding of and skill in social science that the religion teacher can so environ the pedagogical conditions that desired learning outcomes are caused in the individual.

CONCLUSION

The purpose of this chapter is to indicate that religious instruction falls within the domain of social science rather than theological science. This is not to imply that religious instruction has little or no relation to theology; rather, it is to point out that religious instruction borrows its fundamental structure and thrust from social science. Each science has its own structure and operational procedures which shape the orientation and direction of those areas or disciplines which it incorporates.

I am further suggesting in this chapter that the traditional view of religious instruction as a branch of practical theology has been responsible for a substantial diminution of the potential effectiveness of religious instruction over the centuries. André Godin has observed in this connection that the theological base for religious instruction has caused religion teachers and curriculum builders to let everything slide along as if experimental techniques, shaping the learning environment, statistical discrimination, and facilitation do not exist or are of very minor concern.[70] Religious instruction, then, has its own ontology distinct from theology, but certainly not removed from theology.

At bottom, what the social-science approach to religious instruction does is to radicate it in the teaching-learning process. By this I mean that the central task of religious instruction becomes the conscious and deliberative facilitation of specified behavioral goals. Incorporating as fully as possible the process and product content of theological science, whether old or new, the prime function of religious instruction is the study into and the implementation of a planned structuring of the learning situation. Quite obviously, then, theology plays a vital and indispensable role in this kind of religious instruction; however, it is theology which is being integrated and plugged into the social science of the teaching-learning situation, not vice versa, as has formerly been the case.

Second, the social-science approach views the environment in which the learning of religion takes place not as constituting a supportive milieu for "getting across" the subject matter of theology, but rather a key factor — and indeed in some ways the controlling force — in the here-and-now dynamic of the learning process. The elements of social time and social space, with all their ramifications, are crucial to the type of teaching-learning which occurs. To be sure, the classroom group is of and in itself a unique psychosocial system, with its own unique psychosocial structure. Again, theology is indispensable here; but the shift in emphasis that I am suggesting is that theology is utilized as only one directional force in the classroom group. This, of course, substantially differs from the typical religion teacher's emphasis in which the classroom milieu is perceived simply as a motivational tool to interest the students in religion, or to "get them going" in carrying out the theological themes of the lesson.

Third, the social-science approach regards religious instruction as a conscious and deliberative joint effort of teacher and students to effect selected behavioral modifications in the learners. The classroom becomes a laboratory for Christian living, a planned and operationalized milieu for facilitating in the students desired changes in behavior. Theology remains as a mode of prime importance; however, theology is used as one, and only one, of the factors involved in the educational structuring of the learning environment to produce these behavioral goals, instead of the *terminus ad quem* of classroom activity.[71]

Placing religious instruction within the domain of social science helps to insure that its future will be brighter than its past. In this connection I believe that Gabriel Moran provides the fundamental structural blueprint for the future of religious instruction when he remarks that the future development of religious instruction cannot consist of either content *or* method, that old dichotomy of what hopefully is a bygone era in religious instruction. To be fruitful, the future development of religious instruction must grow along the lines of the inner relationship of content and method, both in human life and in Christian faith. What religious instruction most needs is to take as its axis sophisticated methodological issues. By methodology here is meant a style of behaving and communicating.[72] This chapter has attempted to show that it is social science, rather than any other kind of science, which is uniquely equipped to most fruitfully address itself to that style of behaving and communicating which Moran terms "sophisticated methodology." Certainly it is the social-science approach which can enable religious instruction to effectively predict, facilitate, and shape religious behaviors in the learner.

FOOTNOTES

1. Morris L. West, *The Devil's Advocate* (New York: Morrow, 1959), p. 274.
2. D. Campbell Wyckoff, "Religious Education as a Discipline: Toward a Definition of Religious Education as a Discipline," in *Religious Education*, LXII, September-October, 1967, p. 393.
3. Philip H. Phenix, "Religious Education in the Secular City: Myth and Mystery in the Secular City," in *Religious Education*, LXI, March-April, 1966. Philip Phenix, it might be noted, is a philosopher of education and sometime theologian.
4. Peter Paul Grande, "Rapport in the School Counseling Interview in Relation to Selected Personality Characteristics of Religious and Layman (Nonreligious) Counselors," unpublished doctoral dissertation, University of Notre Dame, 1964. The instrument which Grande used to measure the degree of rapport experienced by the clients was the Anderson and Anderson Rapport Rating Scale.
5. James Michael Lee, "Counseling versus Discipline: Another View," in *Catholic Counselor*, VII, Spring, 1963, pp. 114-119.
6. Joseph Deharbe, cited in Josef Goldbrunner, "Catechetical Method," in Josef Goldbrunner, editor, *New Catechetical Methods*, translated by M. Veronica Riedl (Notre Dame, Ind.: University of Notre Dame Press, 1965), p. 41.
7. Josef Andreas Jungmann, *Handing on the Faith*, translated and revised by A. N. Fuerst (New York: Herder and Herder, 1959), p. 143.
8. The Publishers, "Introduction: Religious Education for Young Adults," in Patricia Kennedy [Arlin], *Ultimate Concern: Teacher's Manual* (Chicago: Argus, 1968), p. 5.
9. Anna Barbara, "Straining Toward the Future: Eschatological Perspectives in Teaching the Eucharist to Adolescents," in *Lumen Vitae*, XVIII, September, 1963, p. 466.
10. Pierre Ranwez, "The Awakening of a Child's Sense of Sin," in *Lumen Vitae*, XVIII, March, 1963, p. 90.
11. See Elizabeth B. Hurlock, *Child Development*, 4th edition (New York: McGraw-Hill, 1964); Arthur T. Jersild, *Child Psychology*, 6th edition (Englewood Cliffs, N. J.: Prentice-Hall, 1968); Lawrence J. Stone and Joseph Church, *Childhood and Adolescence*, 2nd edition (New York: Random House, 1968); Justin Aronfreed, *Conduct and Conscience* (New York: Academic Press, 1968); Leonard Berkowitz, *The Development of Motives and Values in the Child* (New York: Basic Books, 1964); John Bowlby, *Child Care and Growth of Love*, edited and abridged by Margery Fry (London: Penguin, 1953); Hugh Hartshorne,

Childhood and Character Boston: Pilgrim, 1919).
12. Gerhard Lenski, *The Religious Factor* (Garden City, N.Y.: Doubleday, 1961), p. 270.
13. Randolph Crump Miller, *The Clue to Christian Education* (New York: Scribner's, 1950), p. 112.
14. M. D. Chenu, *Is Theology a Science?* (New York: Hawthorn, 1964), p. 89.
15. Milton Rokeach, "Faith, Hope, and Bigotry," in *Psychology Today*, III, April, 1970, pp. 33-37, 58.
16. T. W. Dean, "The Training of Adolescents to Prayer," in *Lumen Vitae*, LVIII, June, 1963, p. 246.
17. See Josef Goldbrunner, "Catechesis and Encounter," in Josef Goldbrunner, editor, *New Catechetical Methods*, p. 43.
18. Ray Mars Simpson, "Attitudes Toward the Ten Commandments," *Journal of Social Psychology*, IV, May, 1933, pp. 223-230.
19. A closed retreat is that period of prayer and spiritual reflection conducted in an environment devoid of any contact with the outside, temporal, everyday world. Such retreats are typically held in monasteries or so-called "retreat houses" situated in some isolated milieu which promotes withdrawal from the world. An open retreat is that period of prayer and spiritual reflection conducted in an environment in which there is contact with the outside world. Retreatants in such milieux typically return home in the evenings, listen to the radio or watch television, read secular magazines — all in addition to the regular horarium of prayer and spiritual reflection.
20. Thomas C. Hennessey, "A Study of the Changes and the Permanence of Changes in the Religious Ideals of Catholic High School Students after a Closed Retreat," unpublished doctoral dissertation, Fordham University, 1962.
21. Proverbs 23: 13-14.
22. See, for example, Robert R. Sears, et al., "Some Child-Rearing Antecedents of Aggression and Dependency in Young Children," in *Genetic Psychology Monographs*, XLVII, May, 1953, p. 214.
23. John B. Murray, "Training for the Priesthood and Interest Test Manifestations," unpublished doctoral dissertation, Fordham University, 1957. Murray used 400 Catholic college students, major and minor seminarians, and priests in his sample population. His instruments were the Minnesota Multiphasic Personality Inventory and the Guilford-Zimmerman Temperament Survey.
24. Richard P. Vaughan, "Seminary Training and Personality Change," in *Religious Education*, LXV, January-February,

1970, pp. 56-59. For additional empirical data on seminary preparation, see James Michael Lee and Louis J. Putz, editors, *Seminary Education in a Time of Change* (Notre Dame, Ind.: Fides, 1965).

25. Gabriel Moran, *Catechesis of Revelation* (New York: Herder and Herder, 1966), p. 67.

26. Josef Andreas Jungmann, *Handing on the Faith: A Manual of Catechetics*, translated and revised by A. N. Fuerst (New York: Herder and Herder, 1959), p. 362.

27. Angela Dolores Goldbeck, "Another Necessity — Helping Children to Pray," in *Living Light*, III, Fall, 1966, pp. 20-21.

28. Bernard Berelson and Gary A. Steiner, *Human Behavior: An Inventory of Scientific Findings* (New York: Harcourt, Brace and World, 1964), pp. 625-629.

29. See James Michael Lee, *Principles and Methods of Secondary Education* (New York: McGraw-Hill, 1963), pp. 171-172.

30. James S. Coleman, *The Adolescent Society* (New York: The Free Press, 1961).

31. Edwin J. Thomas and Clifton F. Fink, "Effects of Group Size," in *Psychological Bulletin*, LX, July, 1963, pp. 371-384.

32. See Wilford Aiken, *The Story of the Eight-Year Study* (New York: Harper, 1942).

33. J. Wayne Wrightstone, *Appraisal of Experimental High School Practices* (New York: Teachers College, Columbia University, 1936), pp. 186-189.

34. See James Michael Lee, *Principles and Methods of Secondary Education*, pp. 201-208.

35. Gerhard Lenski, *The Religious Factor*, p. 248.

36. Glen M. Vernon, "Measuring Religion: Two Methods Compared," in Richard D. Knudten, editor, *The Sociology of Religion* (New York: Appleton-Century-Crofts, 1967), p. 45.

37. Daniel Brown, "Teaching the Old Testament to American Students," in *The Living Light*, V, Winter, 1968-1969, pp. 65-74.

38. Randolph Crump Miller, *Biblical Theology and Christian Education* (New York: Scribner's, 1956), p. 69.

39. One-third of all the marriages recorded in the parish registers.

40. Karl Rahner and Herbert Vorgrimler, *Theological Dictionary*, edited by Cornelius Ernst and translated by Richard Strachan (New York: Herder and Herder, 1965), pp. 456-457.

41. Theodor Filthaut, "The Concept of Man and Catechetical Method," in Josef Goldbrunner, editor, *New Catechetical Methods*, p. 1.

42. M. D. Chenu, *Is Theology a Science?*, translated by A. H. N. Green-Armytage. New York: Hawthorn, 1959, p. 63.

43. *Ibid.*, pp. 48-49.
44. Paul Tillich, *Systematic Theology*, volume I (Chicago: University of Chicago Press, 1951), pp. 8-9.
45. Bernard Berelson and Gary A. Steiner, *Human Behavior: An Inventory of the Scientific Findings*, p. 574.
46. Robert R. Morocco, "A Study of the Ideals Expressed by a Selected Group of Parochial and Public School Students," unpublished master's thesis, The Catholic University of America, 1957.
47. Johannes Hofinger, *The Art of Teaching Christian Doctrine: The Good News and Its Proclamation*, 2nd edition (Notre Dame, Ind.: University of Notre Dame Press, 1962), pp. 41-42.
48. Josef Goldbrunner, "Catechesis and Encounter", in Josef Goldbrunner, editor, *New Catechetical Methods*, p. 35.
49. For a discussion of this point, see James Michael Lee and Nathaniel J. Pallone, *Guidance and Counseling in Schools: Foundations and Processes* (New York: McGraw-Hill, 1966), pp. 302-304, and *passim*.
50. Stanley J. Segal, "Religious Factors and Values in Counseling: The Role of the Counselor's Religious Values in Counseling," in *Journal of Counseling Psychology*, VI, Winter, 1959, pp. 270-279.
51. See Charles A. Curran, "The Concept of Sin and Guilt in Psychotherapy," in *Journal of Counseling Psychology*, VII, Fall, 1960, pp. 192-197.
52. For a full-length treatment of the relationship of counseling to values, see Charles A. Curran, *Counseling and Psychotherapy: The Pursuit of Values* (New York: Sheed & Ward, 1968).
53. The first of these two sentences is from Gabriel Moran, *Catechesis of Revelation*, p. 116; the second is from Franz Arnold as quoted in *ibid.*, pp. 116-117.
54. Benjamin S. Bloom, "Testing Cognitive Ability and Achievement," in N. L. Gage, editor, *Handbook of Research on Teaching* (Chicago: Rand McNally, 1963), p. 387.
55. Johannes Hofinger, *The Art of Teaching Christian Doctrine: The Good News and Its Proclamation*, 2nd edition, pp. 23-26.
56. Ronald Goldman, *Religious Thinking from Childhood to Adolescence* (New York: Seabury Press, 1968); also David Elkind, "The Child's Conception of His Religious Identity," in *Lumen Vitae*, XIX, December, 1964, pp. 635-646; also Christian Van Bunnen, "The Burning Bush: The Symbolic Implications of the Bible Story among Children from 5-12 Years," in *Lumen Vitae*, XIX, June, 1964, pp. 327-338.
57. William S. Verplanck, "The Control of the Content of Conversation: Reinforcement of Statements of Opinion," in *Journal of*

Abnormal and Social Psychology, LVI, November, 1955, pp. 668-676.

58. Marcel van Caster, "The Subject of Eschatology in Catechesis," in *Lumen Vitae*, XVIII, September, 1963, p. 455.

59. Marie Francis Kenoyer, "The Influence of Religious Life on Three Levels of Perceptual Processes," unpublished doctoral dissertation, Fordham University, 1961.

60. Pius XI, *Christian Education of Youth*, translated by the National Catholic Welfare Conference (Washington, D.C.: NCWC, 1936), pp. 26-27.

61. Sacra Congregatio de Religiosis, "Instructio de juvenum utriusque sexus promiscua institutione," *Acta Apostolicae Sedis*, L, February 24, 1958, pp. 99-103.

62. For various studies on this point, see James Michael Lee and Nathaniel J. Pallone, *Guidance and Counseling in Schools: Foundations and Processes*.

63. Alice Wessell and S. M. Rita Flaherty, "Changes in CPI Scores after One Year in College," in *The Journal of Psychology*, LVII, January, 1964, pp. 235-238.

64. Marie Edmund Harvey, "A Study of Religious Attitudes of a Group of Catholic College Women," unpublished master's thesis, Fordham University, 1964.

65. Robert Hassenger, "Portrait of a Catholic Women's College," in Robert Hassenger, editor, *The Shape of Catholic Higher Education* (Chicago: University of Chicago Press, 1967), pp. 83-100.

66. Robert Hassenger, "Impact of Catholic Colleges," in *ibid.*, pp. 103-161.

67. John Dewey, *Democracy and Education* (New York: Macmillan, 1916), p. 321.

68. Marshall McLuhan, *Understanding Media: The Extensions of Man* (New York: McGraw-Hill, 1964), p. ix.

69. André Godin, "Importance and Difficulty of Scientific Research in Religious Education: The Problem of the Criterion," in *Religious Education*, LVII, July-August, 1962, p. S-169. This article represents a highly sensitive and penetrating analysis of the relationahip of social science and theology in the work of religious instruction. Godin's contribution is especially commendable and courageous in light of the continual misunderstanding and opposition he has encountered from the social press of the theologically-oriented milieu in which this social scientist operates.

70. *Ibid.*, p. S-167.

71. James Michael Lee, "Foreword," in James Michael Lee and Patrick C. Rooney, editors, *Toward a Future for Religious*

Education (Dayton, Ohio: Pflaum, 1970), pp. 1-2.
72. Moran uses the word "thinking" instead of behaving. I trust he will excuse my substitution. This insight into a new structure of religious instruction represents, in my perception at least, one of Gabriel Moran's most profound comments on the nature and structure of religious instruction. It is not altogether clear, however, whether Gabriel Moran (himself a theologian) would agree that it is social science rather than theology which is the vehicle for the sophisticated methodological axis he advocates. See Gabriel Moran, "The Future of Catechetics," in *The Living Light*, V, Spring, 1968, p. 8.

CHAPTER EIGHT

THE PLACE OF THEOLOGY

"Go, go, go, said the bird: human kind
Cannot bear very much reality."

— T. S. Eliot[1]

The work of religious instruction involves activities which are proper both to social science and to theological science. Thus far in this book I have suggested that religious instruction is fundamentally a mode of social science. I have further suggested that much of the ineffectiveness of religious instruction over the centuries has been due to the fact that it has been regarded as a branch of theological science and implemented as such. The immediate task facing religious instruction, then, is to find and specify its own distinct ontology within the framework of social science.

Now all this does not in any way imply an antitheological view, or even a position that theology is unimportant in the work of religious instruction. To be sure, I suspect that a social-science approach places as high a premium on the role of theological science in the work of religious instruction as does the theological approach. There are two basic differences which I perceive between these two major approaches. First, the theological approach would assign to social science the role of "handmaid" or "errand boy" or "technician," whereas the social-science approach would assign to theological science a much higher and inextricably collaborative function. Second, the theological approach views social science as bringing certain aspects of theology into the marketplace while the social-science approach regards theology as being plugged into social science. The social-science approach in no way demeans or disvalues theology; rather it purports to employ theological activity in a broader and in some ways a different manner than simply within the framework of theological science. In this chapter I shall explore the role played by theological science in religious instruction.

A SOPHISTICATED RELATIONSHIP

Religious instruction in both Roman Catholicism and in Protestantism has gone through three somewhat similar phases in the last hundred years or so. In the case of Catholicism, until the early part of the twentieth century, religious instruction was primarily theological in tone. With the advent of the Munich method and other similar pedagogical developments, the first half of the twentieth century witnessed the so-called "methodological phase" of religious instruction. At about mid-century, due to the theological renaissance in the church, the emphasis in religious instruction once again reverted to the theological. This theological period differs from the earlier one in that it is characterized by a greater openness to the personal and ecclesial self, to other Christian persuasions, and to the world. In American Protestantism the three phases in religious instruction can be classified as the missionary phase, the educational phase, and now the theological phase.[2] We can see here a certain similarity between the developmental phases of Catholic and Protestant religious instruction.

In his examination of the relationship of theology and education in the work of religious instruction, Gordon Chamberlin has identified three distinct modes which this relationship can assume. First, theology is indifferent to education. Second, education determines theology — a position which George Coe[3] and Sophia Lyon Fahs[4] seem to have taken during the "education phase" of religious instruction. Finally, theology determines education — the dominant position today in Protestant and especially in Catholic circles. What I am suggesting is that the most imperative need facing contemporary religious instruction is to move into a fourth mode or developmental phase which can be termed the social-science phase.

To avoid any confusion, let me hasten to say that the social-science mode or phase is not to be identified with the former educational phase, with its emphasis simply on teaching techniques or audiovisual aids or recipes for "imparting the Christian message." Rather, the social-science mode is one in which both theological science and social science work in a congenial and mutually supportive capacity. Social science provides the overall framework, to be sure, but in no way does it "dominate" theological science.

Both social science and theological science have their particular functions to accomplish in the enterprise of religious instruction — functions which are unique to their own specific nature and thrust and which therefore cannot be "dominated" by another science. The day and age of any so-called "queen of the sciences" is dead, whether that queen be the theology of the Middle Ages or the physics of the modern era. In other words, while theology in its own special way suffuses those social-science parameters which specify religious instruction, nonetheless it is foolish to assert that theology is "dominated" by social science. Rather, theology accepts reality — this particular reality of religious instruction — as it is, and operates accordingly.

Because of the kind of social science which the instructional process is, a congenial nondominative relationship between theological science and social science is possible. In other words, the parameters and thrust of the instructional process provide an ideal framework and milieu in which theology can operate. The basic point of departure for the instructional process qua social science is to begin with the learner where he is existentially. To be sure, one would be hard put to ferret out a point of departure more congenial to theologizing. Once the point of departure is established, the instructional process is continuously geared toward facilitating behavioral modifications in the learner according to his nature, development, and needs. Again, such an approach provides a natural working environment for theological science. Lastly, an evaluation is made of the degree to which the individual has attained the desired learning outcomes. Final evaluation of one kind or other has always been of paramount interest to theology, with its emphasis on salvation and damnation, grace and deprivation, and so forth. Of course, the particular way in which social science goes about its facilitational and assessment functions differs notably from the procedures of theological science, as I have shown in Chapters Five and Six. What I wish to stress here is that the broad framework and thrust of the instructional process qua social science are such that they are sufficiently congruent to theological science. As a consequence, theology can be quite at ease and natural in its harmonious working relationship with social science. The points of contact between the two are many and complementary.

The nature, structure, and activity of the instructional process veritably teem with ongoing theology. The instructional process is at bottom a lived experience in which the learner grows and develops through personal interaction within a shaped environment. Such personal growth and development through an interactive process is certainly a description of one's becoming a Christian, of growing into Christianhood. The role of theology here is not to give some sort of superfluous baptism to this natural developmental process, but rather to bring this process to even wider significance and meaning. In the process of human growth, Christianity does not destroy nature, nor does it build on nature; rather, Christianity suffuses congruent nature and gives it a special kind of fulsome dimensionality. Here Christianity does not "dominate" nature; rather it works within the parameters of nature, beginning where nature begins, traveling along nature's path throughout the individual's life, at all times suffusing nature with a dimensionality which brings out the latent possibilities inhering in that nature itself. Christianity in the individual grows as he grows and develops. When the individual is a little boy, he has a childish religious life, because he is a child. When as an adult he gets sick or very angry or very much afraid, his religious life becomes shaped and influenced by these activities of his nature. Let me give an illustration. Reception of the sacrament of confirmation does not enable the young adolescent to fly like an airplane; confirmation must operate within the parameters established in human nature.

The relationship between social science and theological science in the work of religious instruction is somewhat analogous to the relationship between Christianity and human nature which I have just sketched. As human nature represents the broad framework, the thrust, the starting point, and the ongoing activity within which Christianity congenially and congruently works, so too social science forms the framework, the thrust, the starting point, and the ongoing activity within which theological science operates within the enterprise of religious instruction. Just as reception of the sacrament of confirmation does not enable the young adolescent to fly like an airplane, so too excellent theology will not of itself transform an ineffective religion class into an effective one. Or to use another example, frequent reception of the sacraments will not raise an individual's I.Q.; the sacraments do indeed bestow spiritual power but these spiritual powers will be given in accordance with the nature and kind of person in whom they inhere. This is not to say that nature (I.Q.) dominates the spiritual power (confirmation), but rather that grace and nature harmonize in a cordial working relationship within the parameters, structure, and thrust established by nature. Unhappily, history is replete with horrible examples of churchmen who have tried to assert spiritual power over temporal power instead of working out a compatible, complementary, and mutually-enhancing relationship. Worse and more harmful, however, has been the historical ignorance of churchmen in their persistent attempt to oversupernaturalize nature — a natural reflection of which is found in the way churchmen have overtheologized religious instruction. The disrespect churchmen have shown toward nature has resulted in countless errors, the end of which — among other things — has been to cause a gulf between science and religion. This selfsame attitude of disrespect is mirrored in the bungled fashion in which religious instruction has been carried on for centuries.

There is good reason to suspect that churchmen and theologians have perceived the pedagogical process of religious instruction as a mere methodological tool for inserting the theological dimension into the lives of the learners. Such a view represents a misconception both of the teaching process and indeed of education itself. The teaching process is not merely instrumental, external to the thing transmitted.[5] Rather, the teaching process comprises the entire unified activity of the facilitation of the complex of product and process contents into the behavioral self-system of the learner. In other words, in the actual existential situation of teaching, the content (whether product or process) is not divorced from the series of actions by which its acquisition by the learner is facilitated. In terms of the more global educational process, the instrumental view held by all too many theologians does not represent a true concept. Education is an intentional social activity involving preplanned structures, environments, support facilities, and processes of implementation. In other words, education is not simply a mere instrumentality for inserting theological content, but rather forms the very life-giving milieu whereby theology, which is of its nature inert in terms of human behavior, combines with human variables to form life-throbbing religion in the self-system of the learner.

What the foregoing suggests is that the instructional process — and indeed the entire educational process itself — implies, in a general way, some sort of theology. The theologizing is shaped and formed by the parameters and thrust of the teaching-learning process. In religious instruction, then, theology is done within the context of the ongoing teaching-learning process. It is in this sense that theology is plugged into social science in the enterprise of religious instruction. It is the theologizing which, operating within the laws of the learner's nature and the inner structure of the teaching process, gives a special significance to the religion class over and above the great value inherent in the educative process.[6] This special significance which theology infuses is not only in the product content sphere of the religion class, but is also in both the process content dimension and indeed in the very structure of the instructional process itself. Thus the religion teacher will select from the vast arsenal of available instructional patterns and behaviors, those which are most conducive to the religious development and learning of the student. It should be noted, however, that this special significance with which theology endows the religion class again falls within the parameters of the instructional process, both in terms of the nature of teaching and learning, and of the so-called natural values emanating from the instructional process itself. It is this last-mentioned factor which seems to be frequently neglected by theologians surveying the field of religious instruction. The very process of growth and development and learning which is at the center of the instructional act provides the student with value and worth over and above the distinctive theologizing which sets off religious instruction from other kinds of instruction. To be sure, theologically-denuded growth and learning and development are not enough; separated from theological process and product content, such growth and learning and development might take place along areligious or antireligious lines. However, the point I am making is that it is the instructional act which per se creates (or shuts off) the conditions whereby an individual can grow or learn or develop. This generalized process of growth and learning and development is then "worked on," as it were, by theologizing, and the end result is religious growth and religious learning and religious development. However, unless theology has the more generalized natural processes to be plugged into, the specifically religious growth and religious learning and religious development would not be possible.[7] Finally, it is the very instructional process into which theology is plugged that of its own nature facilitates the learning of these theologically-unique values and attitudes. Because instruction is the kind of facilitational activity it is, theologically-unique values have a greater probability of being incorporated into the behavioral self-system of the learner than if theology "went it alone."

The new and still evolving concept of revelation makes it more possible for contemporary theologians to accept the social-science approach to religious instruction than it was for the theologians of bygone days. Protestant and Catholic theologians are more and more pointing to revelation as a continuing process, rather than as a corpus of truths left as a deposit by the scriptures or by the historical Jesus.[8] Revelation thus is now considered as the ongoing personal synapse between God and man, either directly by immediate contact such as through grace or primary experience, or indirectly by mediate contact through the church. In the first instance, revelation represents an actualization of man's supernaturally elevated state of transcendence brought about through faith and grace. As such, revelation is always and everywhere operative, present even when refused.[9] In the second instance, revelation is had through the people of God, which is the church. From this viewpoint, the church is a continuation of the people of God of the old testament. The revelational God-man synapse in this case is not that of prayer but "that of the sacraments which transmit the grace of the cross, and particularly of that sacrament which not only transmits grace, but contains Christ himself in his passover to the Father which he accomplished for our sakes: the sacrament of the Last Supper."[10] Revelation in both of the senses I have just described implies that the history of revelation constitutes the ongoing story of God's self-communication which continues in all times and all places in accordance with his supernatural saving providence. In general, contemporary Protestant theology tends to regard revelation primarily as event and experience. Catholic theologians, on the other hand, while incorporating these aspects, appear to be also concerned (perhaps even more concerned) with safeguarding doctrinal and transmissible features, typically those highlighted in the documents of the church.[11]

Revelation is God's self-disclosure now and throughout history in both act and Word for man's salvation.[12] This self-disclosure, this passage from the divine to the human subject is precisely what is meant by revelation in the biblical teaching.[13] In this connection Edward Schillebeeckx observes that the Israelites made no distinction between the word and the event or thing expressed in verbal form. The Hebrew *dābhār*, he notes, meant both (1) a spoken or written word, *and* (2) an event in nature or in history. Thus the phrase "after these words" often meant "after these things" (for example, Genesis 22:1), since words were not only spoken but done as well (for example, Genesis 24:66). This old testament theology of the *dābhār* is deeply significant in that it highlights the personal relationship between God and man. It is not simply the God of creation who discloses himself, but also the God of salvation and of the covenant.[14] This understanding of revelation as personalized and person-filled suggests that when God reveals, he communicates himself, rather than information about himself. Further, he communicates himself with the purpose of entering into a personal relationship with men.[15] A person, Emil Brunner reminds us, is a mystery which can be disclosed only through self-manifestation. Thus it is only in the self-disclosure which is revelation that an individual meets God as person.[16] Hence Paul Tillich could observe that "revelation is the manifestation of what concerns us ultimately. The mystery which is revealed is of ultimate concern to us because it is the ground of our being."[17]

Revelation is what Joseph Ratzinger terms "God's whole speech and action with man."[18] Revelation, then, is not simply words alone or even isolated events accompanied by a word or so of new data. It is God's self and man's self that are in question.[19] Revelation is God himself — or Jesus himself if one prefers — entering into personal communion with the individual.[20] The Christian concept of revelation as the ongoing fulfillment of Jesus as the Christ implies that the saving work of Jesus would continue to be daily renewed and accomplished after he was risen from the dead and exalted through the sending of the Holy Spirit in an abiding and active fashion.[21] The subjective aspect of revelation, then, constitutes an existential introduction of the individual into the blessedness of God's own life, and in so doing effects an inner transformation in the individual. It is the person of Jesus which in the final analysis makes revelation so personal. In Karl Rahner's words, "the unique and final culmination of [God's] history of revelation has already occurred and has revealed the absolute and irrevocable unity of God's transcendental self-communication to mankind and of its historical mediation in the one God-man Jesus Christ, who is at once God himself as communicated, the human acceptance of this communication, and the final historical manifestation of this offer and acceptance."[22]

Religious instruction represents a concerted educational effort to heighten revelation in the life of the learner. Hence it is natural that a theologian's stance toward revelation should exert a significant influence on his view of religious instruction. It was with this in mind that in the preceding paragraphs I provided a short overview of the contours of contemporary theology of revelation. I believe that contemporary theology of revelation contains several features which should enable modern theologians to more readily accept the social-science approach to religious instruction than did their counterparts in bygone days. One such feature is the notion that revelation operates according to the nature of the learner. Revelation represents God's self-disclosure to an individual at the existential point in which that individual is currently situated. In other words, God's self-disclosure operates within the parameters of the kind of individual the person is here and now. This in no way hinders God from disclosing himself; rather it affects and shapes, as it were, the kind and manner of this self-disclosure. So it is with theological science operating within the parameters of the social science which is the instructional process.

A second and related feature of modern theology of revelation is that God's self-disclosure is viewed as operating within the laws of nature. In his revelational activity, God operates within the framework of nature — of time and space, of culture, and so forth. God does not appear to be unduly restricted through this manner of operation; his self-disclosure is sufficiently rich and varied that it seems to work effectively in a wide variety of natural milieux. So it is also with theological science functioning within the boundaries of that sector of nature we call instruction. The ways of theology surely are sufficiently motile and fluid that they can adapt themselves to nature without losing any vitality and relevancy. To be sure, what makes theology relevant is the fact that it is connected to some natural process at the very source and shape of that process, on that process's home turf.

Yet another feature of the contemporary concept of revelation is the deeper appreciation of revelation as a process of communication. Revelation is no longer considered a process by which doctrines were "deposited" or moral norms were laid down. Rather, revelation is regarded as essentially a process of communicating, a process of God in the ongoing act of disclosing himself and thereby interacting in a deeply personal way with the individual. Certainly such a view is congruent with the teaching-learning act, which is not a process of "depositing" doctrines into the heads of individuals or of laying down moral regulations for them to memorize. The teaching-learning process is basically an activity of communication, an interaction of the learner with various features in the shaped learning environment which is the class.

Contemporary theology of revelation has still another feature which should make it easier for modern theologians to accept the

234 THE PLACE OF THEOLOGY

social-science approach to religious instruction: revelation is conceived of as a process fully as much if not more than as a product. In other words, revelation is regarded as God disclosing himself, communicating himself. No longer is revelation thought of primarily or exclusively as a product content which is disclosed or communicated. In Chapters Two and Three I attempted to show how process is at the center of the work of instruction, and how the social-science approach hones and enhances the process dimension to cause the teaching-learning act to become more meaningful and more effective.

I will conclude this section by suggesting that there are two prime elements in current theology which should motivate theologians to accept the social-science view of religious instruction. First, there is the new theology of revelation about which I have spent the last few pages. Second, there is the strong emphasis on process in the work of modern theology. In fact, it would not be too far wrong to suggest that ours is the age of "process theology." It is on this chord of process that I believe theological science and social science will strike a mutual note of regard and working relationship. It is through a deeper exploration of process that I anticipate theologians will come to understand what social science is all about. From there it is only one short step to an appreciation and an acceptance of what the social-science nature and structure of instruction (and religious instruction) are all about. Process should therefore prove to be the bridge.

RELIGIOUS INSTRUCTION AS THEOLOGY:
THE OLD VIEW

Almost all Protestant and Catholic theologians are of the opinion that religious instruction is a branch of theological science and not of social science. I have labelled this the "old view" not because it represents a centuries- or indeed millenia-old position, nor because there has arisen a group of new theologians to challenge this time-honored notion, but essentially because I believe this concept is antiquated in terms of new world developments. Included among such developments are the emergence in this century of a well-developed social science and the resultant deeper understanding of the nature and dynamics of the teaching-learning process. Actually the coming to flower of a mature social science has caused a sharp redirection in much of the world's modes of individual and societal thinking and acting. Theologians apparently have either remained unaware of these highly significant developments, or have failed to incorporate them into a wholly fresh view of religious instruction.

Representative of the old view of religious instruction held by Protestant theologians is Ross Bender's unequivocal statement that religious education must be regarded as a theological discipline. To Bender's way of thinking, religious instruction forms one sector of an overall theological education.[23]   James Smart, one of the staunchest defenders of the old position, stoutly insists that the slight seepage of educational methodology which took place in Protestant religious instruction during the first half of the twentieth century caused the entire religious education movement to be antitheological.[24] Nor are Catholic theologians less vigorous than their Protestant counterparts in upholding the old view. Eugene Mainelli states flatly that religious instruction is a theological discipline.[25] Gerard Sloyan is even more forceful in his insistence that religious instruction is a form of theology and as such must avoid contamination from nontheological sources if it is to flourish and bear fruit.[26]

Of the host of varied factors causing contemporary Protestant and Catholic theologians to still adhere to the old view, I should like to select seven for brief mention and discussion. The first is the age-old tendency of theologians to deny to nature its proper place in the workings of creation. This depreciation of nature possibly is a fallout from the strong Platonic strain which exists at the latent rather than at the manifest level in virtually all of Christian spirituality. Further, the relegating of nature at best to a supportive position and at worst to an impeding role is possibly the result of that kind of oversupernaturalizing of reality which theologians typically engage in. This disvaluing of nature and this oversupernaturalizing of reality lead to such statements about religious instruction as the following: "The life of faith cannot be bought, nor taught, nor learned; it must be begotten by the Holy Spirit and water, by God and the Church."[27] Of course faith must be begotten ultimately by the Holy Spirit — but this is not to say that man cannot structure a learning situation whereby the Holy Spirit will be able to accomplish more easily his work of implanting and quickening faith. To expect the Holy Spirit to do it all is, I suspect, an insult to him. Man must do his part; the Holy Spirit cannot legitimately be expected to go it completely on his own. This kind of oversupernaturalizing quite naturally begets either an outright denial of the validity of the instructional process or a disvaluation of its natural efficacy. The scriptures provide account after account of how Jesus and later his apostles consciously and deliberatively structured the learning situation so that the work of the Spirit could become operable. Social-science research furnishes us with much data and many laws which indicate both how learning takes place and what teaching behaviors are most conducive to facilitating desired learning outcomes. It is the sheerest oversupernaturalization to claim that the acquisition of religious life and behaviors will somehow result apart from the natural laws governing man's existence. If the scriptures show anything, they show how God continuously works within the parameters of that nature which he himself created to teach man what he wished man to learn and what man could learn.

A second factor explaining the prevalence among theologians of the old view of religious instruction is the failure to realize the fact that the world's being God's creation is not tantamount to the word's operating according to theological principles. This erroneous identification of the workings of theology with the operations of nature has led to statements such as: "theology, which is the truth-about-God-in-relation-to-man, is the determining factor in the development of a philosophy of education, of the techniques to be used, of goals to be attained, and of the nature of the learners to be taught."[28] It is common sense, as well as the experience of any parent or religion teacher, that theology has something to say about the supernatural nature of learners, but little if anything to say about how an individual behaves and learns. A theological manual is no substitute for a guide to child care. A person learns according to the laws of human growth and development in their totality, and not according to the laws of supernatural growth and development alone. Further, if a religion class is to be effective, then the decision as to which teaching strategies and techniques shall be used is made by ascertaining which strategies and techniques will most probably cause the desired learning outcomes. This is the work of social science, not of theology.

A third factor which explains the penchant of theologians for maintaining the old view of religious instruction is the assumption that the subject matter determines the instructional process. Theologians do not seem to be able to accept the fact that all learning occurs according to the mode and nature of the learner rather than according to the mode and nature of the theological subject matter. Some theologians baldly assert that religion and theology condition both the core and virtually every phase of the ongoing operation of the process of religious instruction.[29] Other theologians are a bit more sophisticated, as exemplified by statements which declare that religious instruction is that branch of theology which treats of teaching and learning as basically modes and means of response to revelation.[30] Yet any teacher knows it is the learner who is paramount in the instructional process. An effective teaching situation is one which is learner-centered, not subject-centered — a cliché to be sure, but an educational truism nonetheless. Revelation is accomplished through the teaching-learning process itself, just as all revelation on earth is God's disclosing himself to an individual in terms of where the individual is existentially at. This means that teaching-learning is not a mode and means of response to revelation, but that revelation is accomplished, among other spheres, through the instructional process. It is within the shape and parameters of the instructional process that revelation is accomplished, rather than vice-versa.

Still another factor which suggests why theologians maintain the old stance toward religious instruction is their belief that theology possesses more capability than it indeed has. Theologians seem to think that because theological science explains creation in global and ultimate terms, it therefore enjoys competency in all the specific areas within this universal creation. In the arena of natural science and politics, this attitude has caused the church considerable embarrassment, as witness such incidents as the Galileo affair and the political activities of the first estate in prerevolutionary France. In the realm of religious instruction, this same attitude has given rise to statements such as: ". . . any theologian worth anything knows a great deal about insight and communication, how a person comes to believe and how one develops the intelligibility of his faith."[31] Theologians might know a great deal about revelation as communication or about grace as communication, or about faith as communication. But it is foolish to assert that theological science provides data on instructional communication, or on radio communication, or on counseling communication, or on the whole new discipline of communication itself. It is also an unwarranted extension of its capabilities to suggest that theological science contains within itself the methodology and the adequacy so painstakingly developed by social science in its exploration into the psychology of the genesis of attitudes, values, and beliefs. Theology does indeed provide unique explanations of God-and-man communication and of the development of faith. But these explanations are in no way coextensive, nor even objectively more useful than the explanations provided by social science of communication and the development of faith.

A fifth factor explaining why theologians adhere to the old view of religious instruction is an apprehension that theology will be either destroyed or contaminated or at least seriously hampered if it is placed within the parameters — however broad or loose or fluid these parameters may be — of social science. Gerard Sloyan expresses this concern in his usual clear fashion when he writes: "So long as [religious instruction] is dealt with apart from the ways in which God's word is experienced in our midst, so long as it is assumed to be chiefly a matter of social and psychological concern over a message already sufficiently well known, it will not flourish as an activity of the Church."[32] It seems to me, however, that what gives theology its relevance is precisely its intimate involvement with — nay more, its working within — the social and psychological orders of reality. If theology has been so irrelevant over the past centuries, it is because it was conceived and implemented in the hothouse surroundings of seminary and convent. The priceless gift which religious instruction bestows on theology is none other than its placing theology in the human context of social and psychological reality where life is lived. Far from destroying or contaminating or hindering theology, the unleashing of theology to do its work within the broad parameters of the world makes of religious instruction a kind of enabler as far as theology is concerned. It is in this connection that I like to interpret George Coe's notion that religious instruction alters our very concept and living of religion and of theology.[33]

A sixth factor contributing to the prevalence of the old view of religious instruction among theologians is their lack of awareness that the teaching-learning process is a mode of social science. It would appear that theologians regard the instructional process as some sort of formless entity, without structure or substance of its own.[34] Consequently, they seem to perceive the instructional process as simply the grease on the railroad track along which theological goods can be shipped intact and unaffected to the mind and heart of the learner. Pursuing this metaphor, the goods, the railroad car which transports these goods, and the track itself are conceived as theological; only the grease is nontheological. Thus the instructional process is viewed as being simply instrumental, and minimally instrumental at that — the railroad car and the track constitute the real and important instrumentalities. But as I have reiterated many times throughout this book, the instructional process is not merely an instrumentality, or particularly a minor instrumentality. The instructional process constitutes the milieu, the environment, in which the ˙learner acquires the desired learning outcomes. The instructional process, as numerous empirical studies have indicated, is a dynamic substantive in its own right which exercises significant impact on the shape and form and even product content of learning.

One last factor which can be identified as accounting for the advocacy by so many theologians of the old view of religious instruction is their apparent ignorance of the nature, structure, and consequences of social science. Of all the major sciences, social science is the newest. Yet its development has been so rapid and its promise so great that some people are suggesting that the twenty-first century will be the era of the social sciences, much as the twentieth century was the period of the physical sciences. Theologians, with their natural bent toward tradition-directedness — to use David Riesman's term[35] — perhaps have not had to grapple with the impact of social science on the modern world. Small wonder, then, why theologians should regard religious instruction as primarily theological and not basically pedagogical.[36] One of the contributions of social science to the process of religious instruction is the capacity to incorporate both theology and the teaching-learning act into that kind of congenial relationship which I described in the initial pages of this chapter. It is social science which can effect that kind of working relationship between religious instruction and theology which can incarnate the latter into the flesh and blood of real life, and thus flesh out and enliven a theology which has often remained lifeless despite the best attempts of theologians.

Religious Instruction as Practical Theology

Theologians, Catholic and Protestant, typically assign religious instruction to that branch of theology called practical theology (sometimes referred to as pastoral theology, particularly by Catholics). Gerard Sloyan remarks that religious education "is a part of pastoral theology and is allied to the study of preaching and the study of liturgical celebration."[37] In his schematic outline of the branches and divisions of theology, Yves Congar places religious education as a branch of practical theology.[38] On the Protestant side, Campbell Wyckoff writes that religious education "is to be seen as a theological discipline, a branch of practical theology."[39] Virgilius Ferm indicates that catechetics "refers to that branch of theological instruction which concerns the theory and art of religious instruction particularly in preparation for full participation as a member of the church."[40] One of the clearest statements on the rationale for and the place of religious instruction within the framework of practical theology is that of Donald Miller:

> In my view, Christian education is part of the discipline of practical theology. This means that in its fundamental concep- tions it shares the problems of historical and systematic theology — biblical studies included — but it does so within a particular practical situation, i.e., teaching, instruction, and learning. The peculiar characteristic of practical theology is not its message, but its emphasis and its situation. Practical theology is contextual by nature, i.e., it is intimately related to the circumstances within which it occurs . . . . The various areas of practical theology are alike in that their approach is contextual, but they differ primarily with regard to the situation within which they seek to communicate the gospels, to respond in love to the neighbor.[41]

Religious instruction, then, is commonly viewed by theologians as a kind of applied form of practical theology. In other words, religious instruction simply applies to everyday life the theories and insights of grace and revelation which it is the realm of theology to develop. This view has as its logical conclusion the notion that religious instruction is not at all distinct as an area of inquiry; in fact, one might even go so far as to suggest that religious instruction does not have any concrete individuating characteristic in the practical, concrete order. Indeed, there are European theologians who would make catechetics a mode of preaching. Apropos of this, Marcel van Caster writes that there are some persons who would differentiate religious instruction from preaching on the grounds that the former constitutes the "presentation of doctrine in a classroom situation," while the latter transmits this selfsame doctrine "in a more sacred framework." Van Caster takes pains to emphasize that he himself takes the term religious instruction "in its complete and sacred sense." Hence for van Caster, religious instruction "is an activity which 'resounds' the word of God, in short, all activity which makes divine revelation known and which aims at awakening and developing faith."[42] Domenico Grasso states even more clearly this belief that religious instruction is a form of preaching: "What the term 'catechesis' [i.e., religious instruction] fails to express is that religious instruction is simply a communication of ideas, rather than the transmission of facts and actions that are intended to become principles of thought and moral conduct. But this deficiency resides in the nature of preaching itself, of which catechesis is merely one form. For this, too, the term 'preaching' is preferable to any other for describing the phenomenon of the transmission of the message."[43]

If religious instruction in the past has been so often lifeless and so removed from the real world, it is largely because it has been encased exclusively in a framework in which it does not appropriately belong, namely practical theology. And if religious instruction in the past has been so teacher-centered, so transmission-pipeline oriented, so little concerned with integration into the learner's self-system on the learner's own terms, it is largely because religion classes have been operated like pulpits.

It has been a central theme running throughout this book that religious instruction, to echo the words of the theologian, M. D. Chenu, "in its proper function, is not theology."[44] In Chapter Five I defined practical theology as the examination of the relation between God's revelation and man's response to that revelation in terms of the living out of his life as a Christian. The functions of practical theology, therefore, are to discover and explain, first, the conditions of faith and grace present in the dynamic synapse of revelation and of the person's living out his life as a Christian, and second, the relationship of the conditions attendant upon this synapse to the care of souls. In other words, practical theology is the theology of the church's practice; it is not identical to or coextensive with that practice. This is the capital point, and one which I believe many theologians have lost sight of. Practical theologizing constitutes theological reflexion on the self-realizing activity of the church whereby God discloses himself to the world and whereby he communicates salvation. In this capacity practical theology examines and illumines the supernatural base and avenues by means of which the strategy and tactics of Christian practice are carried out. But this examination and illumination are far different from an attempt to existentially identify the theology of the church's practice with that practice itself.

What I am suggesting, therefore, is that although religious instruction is not a branch of practical theology, nonetheless it does represent a rich pasture for theologizing. Earlier in this chapter I mentioned that religious instruction can never be separated from theology. Within the social-science type parameters of the instructional process, theology has free rein to illumine, fructify, and yes, even to expand the nature and practice of the teaching process. This illumination, this fructifying, this expanding, however, are done in a way unique to theology. Theology thus remains true to itself, instead of attempting to do the work proper to other spheres of reality.

Throughout history, there seems to have been a recurrent tendency toward "theological imperialism" on the part of theologians. By "theological imperialism" I mean the proclivity to try to bring totally within its jurisdiction and control all those areas of reality which in one way or another are related to theology. We have seen an illustration of this in the manner in which theologians have tried to wholly absorb religious instruction into the domain of practical theology. Three other examples will further clarify this point. The entire realm of guidance counseling, particularly religious counseling, was until very recently placed within the confines of theology and given the name "spiritual direction." Much of psychology was swallowed up by theology, especially those aspects pertaining to guilt and human development. Finally, ecclesiastical administration and finance were declared to be forms of practical theology. In each of these three instances, it was not until the respective areas had broken free from theological suzerainty and found their rightful places among the broad science to which each properly belongs that significant advances and breakthroughs were made. When religious counseling became a branch of psychology, employing the tools and insights appropriate to that type of social science, the dawn of a great new age in helping relationships was ushered in. When psychology was allowed to pursue its own natural course as dictated by its unique genre, data, and laws, significant new theories began tumbling out about previously jumbled notions of guilt and sin and all sorts of specific personality dysfunctions.

Perhaps a special word or two about church administration and finance might illustrate even more dramatically the whole issue of theological imperialism. Theologians even at this late date are asserting that church administration and finance form a branch of practical theology.[45] Small wonder why church administration and finance are in such wretched shape! All the theology in the world will not help a person prepare a balance sheet or work out a budget for the next five-year period. It is precisely because church officials seriously believe that church administration and finances are forms of practical theology and hence amenable to theological methodology and treatment that so much of ecclesiastical management and finances is a mass of confusion and inefficiency. Neither the Holy Spirit nor a vigorous life of faith, nor a particularly pregnant biblical passage — no, not even an encyclical from the magisterium — will of itself help some ecclesiastical functionary balance a budget or provide the machinery to eradicate his church's fiscal deficit. A 1964 research investigation by Anthony Seidl revealed that seventy-five percent of all American Catholic secondary schools did not even have a budget on which to operate[46] — so great, apparently, was their trust in theology. While I am not aware of any comparable data for 1971, it is reliably estimated that about one-half of all such schools still operate without budgets.[47] A research investigation of the religious education programs sponsored in the major city of a Catholic diocese in the southeastern part of the United States revealed that only seventeen percent of these programs were operating on a budget.[48] Studies conducted by the Office of Educational Research at the University of Notre Dame have discovered considerable administrative and financial inefficiency in the operation of Catholic school systems throughout the United States. That theology has proved to be ineffective in this area can be easily demonstrated by noting the financial plight in which Catholic schools found themselves in the late 1960's and early 1970's.

The point I am trying to make is that theological imperialism erodes both the other reality which theology is attempting to swallow up, and also theology itself. Theology becomes useful to the pastoral life of the church by first of all becoming true to itself as theology. This is to say that theological imperialism, the absorption by theology of sectors of reality inappropriate to it, results in a discrimination and an unfruitfulness not only in that other reality but in theology as well.

A Further Note

Ellis Nelson reminds us that it is patently silly to believe that theology provides clear and ready solutions to the practical problems of religious instruction.[49] The practical problems facing religious instruction are typically those involving pedagogical approaches, strategies, and methods. As such, these problems can be adequately addressed only by that kind of science which has within its capacity the appropriate methodological tools. Throughout the course of this book, I have repeatedly indicated that it is social science rather than theological science, which is equipped by its very nature and methodology to address itself to problems involving the facilitation of desired behavioral modification in learners.

Obvious though this may be, there are still many theologians who seem to adhere to the old position that everything involved in the work of religious instruction, including even the practical aspects, is basically theological. Campbell Wyckoff, for example, flatly states that "questions of [instructional] objective, scope, context, process, personnel, and timing, I am convinced, are theological questions."[50] If by this statement Wyckoff means that theology has a living and fructifying relationship to pedagogical practice in the work of religious instruction, then he is quite in agreement with the social-science approach. If, however, Wyckoff is suggesting that theology determines or gives the practical solution to problems of pedagogical strategy, then I believe he is ascribing to theological science activities beyond its sphere of competency. The question of timing, for example, is a question which is first and foremost within the domain of social science. The developmental stage of the learner and the opportuneness of the utilization of a particular pedagogical method at a specific time — these are matters intimately bound up with the facilitation of learning, and therefore are social-science matters. On a broader framework of timing, such as, for example, overall curricular timing, social science once again comes to the fore. Theological science provides keen insights into and exceptionally profound understandings of the answer to the question of when and under what circumstances a child should make his first communion. But these insights and understandings are translated into practice most fruitfully when they are operationalized within the parameters of social science. By securing hard data on the psychological readiness of the child, his attitudes toward communion, his value and belief structure at a certain age and in a certain culture, the influence of family versus peer group on his personal goals, then by weaving all these data into a pattern which provides us with an adequate picture of where the child really is as a person, the religious educator can ascertain the age and the circumstances which are the most meaningful to the child for gaining from reception of first communion those objectives which theologians and social scientists wish him to acquire.

If theology is not adequate to answer questions pertaining to the practice of religious instruction neither is it adequate to answer theoretical questions concerning it.[51] A useful theory is one which explains the inner relationships and operations of a mass of phenomena and of laws. A theory also has predictive power. In terms of discovering, for example, the optimum time and circumstances for the reception of first communion, personality theory is far more explanatory and predictive than is sacramental theory. However, if sacramental theory is incorporated within the framework of personality theory, and allowed free rein to interact with the various facts and laws inherent in personality theory, then religious instruction has achieved that congenial fruitful working relationship between theology and social science which characterizes the social-science approach to religious instruction.

The Normative Function

Theologians and theologically-oriented specialists in religious instruction commonly regard the normative role as one of theology's principal functions vis-à-vis religious instruction. In other words, theology has the task, among other things, to establish the norms which serve as the bases for religious instruction, and then to verify the extent to which religious instruction has implemented these norms. James Smart, one of the most forceful proponents of this position, has as his central concern the establishment of Christian benchmarks against which every phase of religious instruction can be constantly measured. Smart goes so far as to assert that theology acts as the primary and supreme norm for all areas of religious instruction, including the very learning process itself. From time to time, other sciences and nontheological forms of assistance can be introduced to make the enterprise of religious instruction more effective. However, such sources are allowed to operate only after the theologian has examined them scrupulously to make sure they do not carry with them any assumptions or implementations which might be contrary to the Christian Weltanschauung.[52]

My own position is that although theology does indeed serve as a kind of norm for religious instruction, it is by no means the exclusive or even the primary norm. To hold, as does Smart, that theology is normative over such obvious social-science sectors as the learning process is as theologically nonsensical as it is imperialistic. In terms of the many and appropriate theological product and process contents, theology surely exercises a kind of normative function. But this normative function, vital and indispensable though it is, is not the only major normative function in the work of religious instruction. What I am suggesting, therefore, is that theology does not have *the* normative function in religious instruction. Rather, it plays *a* normative role, a role which it shares with other key variables involved in the total process of religious instruction. These other key variables include such important factors as personality development, for example.

In keeping with the concept which I discussed in the first part of this chapter concerning a new sophisticated fourth stage of maturity in religious instruction, I believe that it is the entire process of religious instruction which by its interactive nature exercises the essential normative function. In other words, because religious instruction is a process and a work distinct from theology or from all other areas of reality, it is an enterprise which to a certain extent builds its own norms. I am not here implying that religious instruction is thereby isolated from or freed from the appropriate norms emanating from theology or from psychology or from education and so forth. Surely theological norms, psychological norms, and educational norms operate at appropriate and relevant points throughout the religious instruction continuum. After all, religious instruction is what its name implies, *religious* instruction, and therefore theological norms permeate the entire framework of the religious instruction enterprise. Notwithstanding, these theological norms exercise their role within the milieu of the ongoing dynamic of religious instruction. If these theological norms are living and not dead, then perforce in such a milieu they take on a color and a shape which are appropriate to and adaptive of the instructional dynamic — without losing their essential theological quality, of course. It is the totality of the process of religious instruction, then, which serves as the guiding norm; the various elements of theology which impinge upon religious instruction serve as a yeast and a wellspring, and yes, as a gyroscope in insuring that the work of religious instruction ever remains faithful to that norm.

Religious Instruction as Messenger Boy

Theologians have for centuries treated religious instruction as a sort of messenger boy by whom the wisdom and understandings acquired by theological science are delivered to the multitude. Johannes Hofinger, for example, describes the methodology used in religious instruction as a "handmaid of the message."[53] Josef Goldbrunner echoes this notion when he affirms that religious instruction must serve as the handmaid of the message inherent in kerygmatic theology. All aspects of religious pedagogy, he maintains, "must become subservient to kerygma."[54] This view of religious instruction as a postal service carrying the message of salvation from theologian to the "listener" is destructive of any kind of viable religious instruction. Certainly such a view will prevent moving into that fourth developmental phase of religious instruction which I sketched toward the beginning of this chapter.

One wonders why Christian theologians and church functionaries are so prone to conceive of religious instruction as a messenger boy for theological science. One possible explanation for this phenomenon is the theological imperialism of which I treated earlier. Another possible explanation lies in a certain ultrametaphysical attitude which seems all too prevalent in Christian circles. This attitude regards the ontological nature of a reality as its highest form; the functional aspect of that reality is concomitantly considered as some sort of material watering down or process degeneration of it. In such a view, theological science, and particularly the speculative or dogmatic type of theology, constitutes the olympian heights, whereas religious instruction represents a marketplace theology necessary as a beneficent concession to the clouded intellects of the masses. Religious instruction therefore has a translation function: to translate the sublime concepts of theological science into the common idiom of the multitude.

Yet another possible explanation for this attitude of theologians is their implicit or explicit denial of an ontology for religious instruction as distinct from theology. Marcel van Caster aptly encapsulates this view when he affirms that the object of religious instruction is a living reality contained in scripture, liturgy, and human experience, all examined in the light of dogmatic and moral theology and anthropology. Theology, according to van Caster, includes all of the following in the process of religious instruction: (1) provides the ordered unity and systematic form required by the human mind for the understanding of revelation; (2) spells out the practical consequences of the message contained in the bible and in the liturgy; and (3) presents revelation in terms which can be understood by men accustomed to modern philosophical thought.[55] According to this view, there is little else remaining for religious instruction to do except to grease the wheels over which the boxcars heavily freighted with theological goods can more easily be transported from the heights to various human waystations.

Throughout this chapter I have attempted to suggest that in its more mature phase, religious instruction is not a handmaid of theology; nor is theology an ancilla of religious instruction. Neither is the other's errand boy. Theological science does indeed work within the parameters of social science in the ongoing enterprise of religious instruction. But this is a far cry from the handmaid notion. Within the broad parameters of such things as the nature of learning, the function of teaching, and the impact of environmental variables on the instructional act, theology operates as it wills, fructifying and in a certain sense guiding from within the shape, the unfolding, and the functioning of the enterprise of religious instruction.

Christians still tend to regard theological science as superior to religious instruction — possibly because they believe that the abstract is superior to the concrete. This is an old Platonic and Aristotelian concept which still affects much of religious thought. But the Incarnation changed all this. If the Incarnation testifies to anything, it bears living witness that the concrete is more valuable than the abstract. Transposed to a hierarchical relation of religious instruction and theology, the Incarnation would seem to suggest that religious instruction is superior to theology, including speculative or dogmatic theology. Jesus himself was first and foremost a person who functioned as a priest and as a religious educator; he did not function as a theologian. To be sure, dogmatic theology and practical theology constituted an essential ingredient in Jesus's pedagogical activities, much as theology forms an indispensable component of the work of any religion teacher. This fact does not detract from — indeed it supports — the fact that Jesus was a religious educator rather than a theologian. It remained for theologians in succeeding eras to extract theological data from the product and process aspects of Christ's instructional activities. Then too, the very Incarnation event itself bears supreme witness that the concrete reigns over the abstract for those of us here on earth. The practical consequence of all this is that no longer should religious instruction be content to linger in the shadow of theology, or serve theology as a messenger boy or a translator or a water boy. Both theological science and religious instruction have their own unique ontologies. Each works closely with the other, but neither is slave or ancilla to the other. It is my firm conviction that once religious instruction is removed from the shadow of theology, once it is emancipated from its position as handmaid to theology, it will grow and thrive and prove to be a wonderfully effective form of Christian activity.

Theology and Religion

There is no generally accepted definition of religion. In fact, there seems to be no agreement even on what constitutes religion. Hundreds of definitions and succinct concepts have been advanced over the centuries as to the nature of religion. Paul Tillich defines religion as "the self-transcendence of life under the dimension of the spirit."[56] William James, speaking of the individual character of religion, describes it as "the feelings, acts, and experiences of individual men in their solitude so far as they apprehend themselves to stand in relation to whatever they may consider the divine."[57] Karl Rahner and Herbert Vorgrimler define it as "man's relations with the holy; subjective religion is veneration and adoration, which becomes objective religion when embodied in creed, words, actions (gestures, dance, ablutions, blessings, sacrifice, sacrificial meal), and law."[58] Adolphe Tanquerey defines religion from the objective standpoint as "that complex of truths and duties toward which one's life is ordained unto God as its ultimate end." He defines religion from the subjective standpoint as "the voluntary disposition nay rather virtue of man whereby he acknowledges his debt of worship and reverence to God through accepting God's truths and fulfilling God's laws in a suitable manner."[59] Norbert Schiffers sums it all up pithily when he calls religion "the quintessence of one's relationship to God."[60] In any event, as I mentioned in Chapter Six, it is easier and more informative to provide an operational definition of religion than a notional one.

Theology is something different from religion. Gerald van Ackeren defines theology as "the methodological elaboration of the truths of divine revelation by means of reason enlightened by divine faith."[61] Virgilius Ferm terms theology the area of inquiry "which concerns the question of God and God's relationship to the world."[62]

The point I am making is that religion tends to be an activity of the whole man, while theology represents principally a work of the intellect, even when the theology is a *theologia orativus*. Religion typically connotes an act which somehow involves the whole person, while theology is understood to mean an activity which is primarily restricted to the domain of inquiry.[63] Josef Jungmann states it quite nicely when he writes that "theology is primarily at the service of knowledge; hence it investigates religious reality to the outermost limits of the knowable (*verum*) and struggles here for the last little piece of truth that can be grasped, without asking in each instance about the significance such effort may have for life."[64]

Although theology belongs chiefly to the area of inquiry, it is not separated wholly from life. As I observed in Chapter Five, theology grows out of, and is done within, the milieu of living faith. M. D. Chenu notes that "the theologian, in his syllogistic deductions, is contantly using his faith as a living filter."[65] The theologian also utilizes his own experience, or perhaps more accurately his interpretation of his own experience, in his work of theologizing. But theology is different from faith.

So also is theology different from religion. In one sense, theologizing can be considered an act of religion because it brings the theologian into converse with God. Similarly, theologizing can be considered an act of religion because, according to the theologians, it must be done in constant obedience to the God of scripture and of faith as he discloses himself to the theologian through these mediums. Still, these represent extensions — and possibly overextensions — of the nature of theologizing. In an organic world, it is difficult if not impossible to place any two realities in watertight compartments. Yet, when all is said and done, there is a significant difference between religion and theology.

The lifestyle of a Christian should be religious, but not necessarily theological. Theology helps a person lead a religious life — sometimes. Experience teaches that at other times theology does not seem to play any part in leading a person toward or away from religion. Sometimes one suspects that the psychophysiological need structure of a person at a particular moment of his development is such that theology can actually turn that person away from religion. Moreover, there are realities and there are circumstances which, at certain moments in a person's life, exercise greater valence than does theology in drawing him closer toward religion or deepening his religious life. There is no *necessary* positive correlation between theology and a person's religious life, although more often than not there will be some sort of positive correlation between the two.

What I have been leading up to in this section on theology and religion is this: just as religion is existentially superior to theology for the individual Christian, so religious instruction is typically superior to theology for this same individual. It is religious instruction, not theology, which has as its aim the modification of the individual's behavior along religious lines. To fulfill its purpose, religious instruction must result in a significant enhancement of a person's religious life. Theology, on the other hand, need not be accompanied by such enhancement to fulfill its own ends. In other words, there should be no grand hauteurism emanating from theology vis-à-vis religious instruction. Each has its own work to accomplish. Each glorifies God best by accomplishing the work proper to it.

Religious Instruction as Pastoral Work

I have indicated that religious instruction has its own unique genre within the broad umbrella of social science, and that it is from the soil of social science that religious instruction will grow and develop to maturity. Religious instruction, then, is not a branch of practical theology. However, I would maintain that it is a form of pastoral work. There is a vast difference between practical or pastoral theology and pastoral work. Practical or pastoral theology is an examination of the relation between God's revelation and man's response to that revelation in terms of the living out of his life as a Christian. Like all sciences, practical theology has as its role discovery and explanation. Pastoral work, on the other hand, is that activity of an individual Christian or of the church by which an attempt is made to develop or enhance the religious life of an individual. There are innumerable types of pastoral work including pastoral care (a term usually reserved for the guidance, counseling, and therapeutic services), pastoral eleemosynaries (a term commonly employed for corporal works of mercy), and so on. Under this broad rubric of pastoral work falls the enterprise of religious instruction. Indeed, religious instruction shares with all the other forms of pastoral work an independence from, but an interrelationship with practical theology.

As a form of pastoral work, religious instruction is closely tied in with the official teaching function of the church. Religious instruction as a mode of pastoral work, represents one kind of the church's teaching ministry. There are other forms of this teaching ministry, to be sure, each with its own special relationship and proper function. Because religious instruction is a form of the church's official teaching ministry, it falls under the general guidance of the church. In this respect, it is quite distinct from the science of theology, particularly as theology is done in university classrooms or in the quiet of a professor's study. To be sure, the work of theologizing always is done within the general *sensus ecclesiae*; however, as an investigative scientist, the theologian has much less restraint put on him by the church than has the religion teacher who is directly entrusted by the church to develop and enhance the religious life of a learner within the general framework of a particular denomination's structure of faith and morals.[66] Yet even here, the religion teacher or other kind of religious instruction worker has a wider freedom than an unduly restrictive conception of pastoral work would indicate. First, to a certain and limited extent, the religion teacher is theologizing in the course of the instructional act. To be sure, this is theologizing in a very secondary and restricted sense, but it is a kind of theologizing nonetheless. In the fourth developmental phase of religious instruction of which I treated earlier, theologizing is not done prior to or subsequent to the religion class; rather, theologizing is done in the religion class in the manner and to the extent that it advances the behavioral goals of the lesson. Religious instruction is not theology, but theology and theologizing form part of each religion lesson. Since theologizing is taking place in the religion class, there must exist a certain freedom for exploration on the part of the learners. Without such exploration, the religion class degenerates into the lowest level of spoon-feeding and the basest form of indoctrination.

A second reason for the wider freedom of religious instruction from the structures customarily placed on many forms of pastoral work by vigilant ecclesiastical officials is the very notion of the church itself. The church is the communion of believers in the broadest relational sense of that term. In most Christian churches, it is heresy to identify the church exclusively with any group of persons less than the whole communion of believers, whether such a group consists of the magisterium, the bishops, the presbyters, the elders, or whomsoever. For a Catholic, the pope is no more the church than the humblest layman. For a Lutheran, the synodical president is no more the church than is the simple but devout believer. When I say that pastoral work (of which religious instruction is a form) is by nature under the guidance of the church, I mean under the guidance of the broad church and not solely under the guidance of the magisterium or the synodical president or the community of presbyters or the ministers. To be sure, the magisterium, the synodical president, the community of presbyters, or the ministers do indeed occupy a privileged place within the church and should be listened to and respected with more than normal attentiveness and reverence. But there have been times in history when the sensus ecclesiae has not been entirely identical or congruent with the sensus magisterii or the sensus episcoporum or the *sensus presbyterorum*. The religion teacher and the religious instruction specialist have a prophetical role to play in the church and in the world. It will be a combination of their deep personal authenticity to themselves together with a profound *sentire in ecclesia* — I do not say *sentire cum ecclesia*[67] — which will enable both teacher and specialist to fruitfully exercise their prophetical role.

FOOTNOTES

1. T. S. Eliot, "Burnt Norton," in T. S. Eliot, *Collected Poems* (New York: Harcourt, Brace and World, 1963), p. 176.
2. D. Campbell Wyckoff, *Theory and Design in Christian Education Curriculum* (Philadelphia: Westminster, 1961), p. 50.
3. George A. Coe, *What Is Christian Education?* (New York: Scribner's, 1929).
4. Sophia Lyon Fahs, *Today's Children and Yesterday's Heritage* (Boston: Beacon, 1952).
5. George A. Coe, *What Is Christian Education?* pp. 54-55.
6. I am not at all sure whether Roger Shinn recognizes that the process of education itself is endowed with value. Shinn seems to imply that it is the theological input which supplies the religion class with all its significance and value. See Roger L. Shinn, *The Educational Mission of Our Church* (Philadelphia: United Church Press, 1962).
7. See John Dewey, *Experience and Education* (New York: Macmillan, 1938), p. 29.
8. Gabriel Moran, *Theology of Revelation* (New York: Herder and Herder, 1966), pp. 46-52.
9. Karl Rahner, "Revelation: Concept of Revelation: Theological Interpretation," in Karl Rahner et al., editors, *Sacramentum Mundi*, volume V (New York: Herder and Herder, 1970), p. 349.
10. Yves Congar, *The Revelation of God*, translated by A. Manson and L. C. Sheppard (New York: Herder and Herder, 1968), p. 186.
11. Avery Dulles, "Theology of Revelation," in *New Catholic Encyclopedia*, volume XII (New York: McGraw-Hill, 1967), p. 442. Karl Rahner implies that Catholic theologians try to achieve a balance between personal and institutionalized revelation, so as not to fall into Modernism. See Karl Rahner, "Revelation: Concept of Revelation: Theological Interpretation," p. 349.
12. W. R. Crockett, "The Theology of Revelation and the Principles

of Union," in *The Ecumenist*, VI, May-June, 1968, p. 153.

13. John Baillie, *The Idea of Revelation in Recent Thought* (New York: Columbia University Press, 1956), pp. 104-108.

14. E. Schillebeeckx, *Revelation and Theology*, volume I, translated by N. D. Smith (New York: Sheed & Ward, 1967), pp. 33-37.

15. W. R. Crockett, "The Theology of Revelation and the Principles of Union," p. 153.

16. Emil Brunner, *Revelation and Reason*, translated by Olive Wyon (Philadelphia: Westminster, 1947), p. 24.

17. Paul Tillich, *Systematic Theology*, volume I (Chicago: University of Chicago Press, 1951), p. 110.

18. Joseph Ratzinger, "Revelation and Tradition," in Karl Rahner and Joseph Ratzinger, editors, *Revelation and Tradition*, translated by W. J. O'Hara (New York: Herder and Herder, 1966), p. 35. Ratzinger adds that revelation "signifies a *reality* which scripture makes known but which is not itself simply identical with scripture."

19. Gabriel Moran, *Theology of Revelation*, p. 46.

20. Werner Bulst, *Revelation*, translated by Bruce Vawter (New York: Sheed & Ward, 1965), p. 140.

21. Heinrich Fries, *Revelation* (New York: Herder and Herder, 1969), p. 87.

22. Karl Rahner, "Revelation: Concept of Revelation: Theological Interpretation," p. 49. Italics deleted.

23. Ross Bender, "Christian Education in Theological Education," in *Religious Education*, LXII, January-February, 1967, p. 19. Like many other Protestants, Bender prefers the term "Christian education" to either "religious education" or "religious instruction."

24. James D. Smart, *The Teaching Ministry of the Church* (Philadelphia: Westminster, 1954), p. 63.

25. Eugene Mainelli, "An Experiment in Religious Education, or We are Trying, Dr. Fahs," in *Religious Education*, LXIII, January-February, 1968, p. 60.

26. Gerard S. Sloyan, "Studies in Religious Education," in Gabriel Moran, *Theology of Revelation*, n.p.

27. Josef Goldbrunner, "Catechetical Method as Handmaid of Kerygma," in Johannes Hofinger, editor, *Teaching All Nations: A Symposium on Modern Catechetics*, revised and partly translated by Clifford Howell (New York: Herder and Herder, 1961), p. 118.

28. Randolph Crump Miller, *Education for Christian Living*, 2d edition (Englewood Cliffs, N.J.: Prentice-Hall, 1963), p. 5.

29. See, for example, Lewis Joseph Sherrill, *The Rise of Christian Education* (New York: Macmillan, 1954); also James D. Smart,

The Teaching Ministry of the Church.
30. D. Campbell Wyckoff, "Religious Education as a Discipline: Toward a Definition of Religious Education as a Discipline," in *Religious Education*, LXII, September-October, 1967, pp. 390-391.
31. Gabriel Moran, "The Future of Catechetics," in *The Living Light*, V, Spring, 1968, pp. 6-7.
32. Gerard S. Sloyan, "Studies in Religious Education," n.p.
33. George A. Coe, *What Is Christian Education?* pp. 23-28.
34. One receives this impression from Randolph Crump Miller, *The Clue to Christian Education* (New York: Scribner's, 1950), p. 15.
35. David Riesman, *The Lonely Crowd* (New Haven, Conn.: Yale University Press, 1950).
36. See, for example, Johannes Hofinger, *The Art of Teaching Christian Doctrine: The Good News and Its Proclamation*, 2d edition (Notre Dame, Ind.: University of Notre Dame Press, 1962), p. 55.
37. Gerard S. Sloyan, "Studies in Religious Education," n.p.
38. M.-J. Congar, "Théologie," in A. Vacant, E. Mangenot, and E. Amann, editors, *Dictionnaire de Théologie Catholique*, tome XV (Paris: Letouzey et Ané, 1946), column 495.
39. D. Campbell Wyckoff, "Religious Education as a Discipline: Toward a Definition of Religious Education as a Discipline," p. 391. Wyckoff uses the phrase "Christian education" in place of "religious education," a practice followed by some Protestants.
40. Virgilius Ferm, *A Protestant Dictionary* (New York: Philosophical Library, 1951), p. 41.
41. Donald E. Miller, "Religious Education as a Discipline: Christian Education as a Contextual Discipline," in *Religious Education*, LXII, September-October, 1967, p. 419.
42. Marcel van Caster, *The Structure of Catechetics*, 2d edition, translated by Edward J. Dirkswager, Jr., Olga Guedetarian and Nicolas Smith (New York: Herder and Herder, 1965), p. 12. As is typical of European Catholic theologians, van Caster uses the term "catechetics" instead of "religious instruction."
43. Domenico Grasso, *Proclaiming God's Message: A Study in the Theology of Preaching* (Notre Dame, Ind.: University of Notre Dame Press, 1965), p. 247.
44. M. D. Chenu, *Is Theology a Science?*, translated by A. H. N. Green-Armytage (New York: Hawthorn, 1959), p. 46.
45. See, for example, Virgilius Ferm, *A Protestant Dictionary*, p. 255; also Donald E. Miller, "Religious Education as a Discipline: Christian Education as a Contextual Discipline," p. 419.
46. Anthony Emanuel Seidl, "A Study of Certain Aspects of

Business Management in selected Catholic Secondary Schools of the United States," unpublished doctoral dissertation, University of Notre Dame, 1964.

47. William B. Friend, Associate Director of the Office for Educational Research, University of Notre Dame, gave me this figure in an interview, June 9, 1970.

48. Office for Educational Research, University of Notre Dame, "Hillsboro County Schools of the Diocese of Tampa, Florida: A Research Study," unpublished research report, 1970.

49. C. Ellis Nelson, "Religious Instruction in Protestant Churches," in James Michael Lee and Patrick C. Rooney, editors, *Toward a Future for Religious Education* (Dayton, Ohio: Pflaum, 1970), p. 155.

50. D. Campbell Wyckoff, "Religious Education as a Discipline: Toward a Definition of Religious Education as a Discipline," p. 393.

51. Curiously, Gabriel Moran makes a similar statement. Gabriel Moran, *Catechesis of Revelation* (New York: Herder and Herder, 1966), pp. 16-17.

52. James D. Smart, *The Teaching Ministry of the Church.*

53. Johannes Hofinger, *The Art of Teaching Christian Doctrine: The Good News and Its Proclamation*, 2d edition, p. 62.

54. Josef Goldbrunner, "Catechetical Method as Handmaid of Kerygma," in Johannes Hofinger, editor, *Teaching All Nations: A Symposium on Modern Catechetics*, revised and partly translated by Clifford Howell, pp. 108 and 112.

55. Marcel van Caster, "Catechetical Renewal and Theological Renewal," abstract of an address compiled by Florence Michels, *Lumen Vitae*, XXIII, March, 1968, p. 151. To anthropology (which he defines in the European rather than in the American sense of the term) van Caster ascribes the role of synthesizing "the essential elements of theology and a modern mentality that would make man the center of both social and cosmic interests." How anthropology is supposed to perform this rather sizable task is not spelled out.

56. Paul Tillich, *Systematic Theology*, volume III (Chicago: University of Chicago Press, 1963), p. 96.

57. William James, *The Varieties of Religious Experience* (New York: Longmans, Green, 1902), p. 31.

58. Karl Rahner and Herbert Vorgrimler, *Theological Dictionary*, edited by Cornelius Ernst and translated by Richard Strachan (New York: Herder and Herder, 1965), p. 399.

59. Ad. Tanquerey, *Synopsis Theologiae Dogmaticae Fundamentalis*, tomus I, editio XXV per J. B. Bord (New York: Benziger, 1937), pp. 67 and 69, translation mine.

60. Norbert Schiffers, "Religion: Concept of Religion: Religion in General," in Karl Rahner et al., *Sacramentum Mundi*, volume V (New York: Herder and Herder, 1970), p. 246.
61. G. van Ackeren, "Theology," in *New Catholic Encyclopedia*, volume XIV, (New York: McGraw-Hill, 1967) p. 39.
62. Virgilius Ferm, *A Protestant Dictionary*, p. 254.
63. These distinctions do, of course, represent a certain degree of oversimplification. A more complex and more thorough analysis would require many additional pages, quite possibly running to a whole new book.
64. Josef Andreas Jungmann, *The Good News Yesterday and Today*, translated, abridged, and edited by William A. Heusman (New York: Sadlier, 1962), p. 33.
65. M. D. Chenu, *Is Theology a Science?* p. 70.
66. Unhappily, ecclesiastical functionaries and officials occasionally fail to realize the freedom which the theologian has within the church by virtue of his function as an investigative scientist. These officials seem sometimes to believe that a theologian is not a theologian but one engaged in pastoral work; hence their censures, denunciations, condemnations, and removal of theologians from university posts.
67. *Sentire in ecclesia* is not only historically more accurate than the commonly phrased expression *sentire cum ecclesia*, but also is more theologically valid.

CHAPTER NINE

THE NATURAL AND THE SUPERNATURAL

"*I wish it wasn't always the wrong people who believed.*" "*Surely the nuns . . .*" "*Oh, they are the professionals.*" *They believe anything. Even the Holy House of Loretto. They ask us to believe too much and then we believe less and less.*"
— Graham Greene[1]

It is possible that some theologians and some theologically-oriented religious educators, particularly those of a conservative cast, might sniff the scent of naturalism, positivism, or secularism in the social-science approach to religious instruction. These persons might think that the social-science approach represents an attempt to minimize the workings of free-flowing divine action in the religion lesson. Or they might imply that placing theology within the broad parameters of social science desacralizes the enterprise of religious instruction, debasing its divine character into the common coin of other kinds of allegedly nonsupernatural educational experiences. Finally, these individuals might indicate that my position that God's action works directly through the natural contours of the teaching-learning dynamic represents a positivistic stance which is inherently inimical to the entire supernatural order.

It is my contention that none of these views is correct. On the contrary, I believe that the social-science approach represents not only a more effective mode of religious instruction, but also is more in keeping with the style of divine action in the world. The social-science approach, then, is authentically supernatural because it works in a harmonizing and suffusing manner with the so-called "natural order," rather than attempting to impose some sort of outside structure upon the exquisitely balanced human-divine living out of the essential withinness of creation. Finally, can an approach which renders religious instruction more effective possibly be naturalistic, positivistic, or secularistic?

A DEMYTHOLOGIZING OF RELIGIOUS INSTRUCTION

Merely removing time-honored (or timeworn) religious labels from specific realities does not imply their secularization. The weather is still the weather and is still suffused with the same degree of divine indwelling and power whether it is referred to as "God's weather" or merely "the weather." Indeed, it might well be that men of the past failed to possess sufficient faith and confidence in God's presence in creation, and for this reason had to affix religious labels to as many things as possible to somehow persuade everybody that the divine was truly present. But the tragedy often was that after a while people mistook the labels for the reality, and in the end identified the reality with the label. In religious instruction, this mentality resulted in all sorts of overpietistic, oversupernaturalistic, and to coin a word, "overchristian" pedagogical practices. When, for example, church officials stated that the religion class should be suffused with the bible, the result often was that biblical passages were brought into the lesson at every conceivable — and indeed at every inconceivable — point. Thus the manifest label "bible" was what was emphasized rather than the possibly more latent but certainly more basic unique God-man relationship which forms the essence and living fabric of the bible. In this regard, Didier Piveteau comments that the religion teacher can be highly biblical without uttering a single word from the bible during the lesson. "There is a way of saying 'Good morning, John' which is a sort of authentic projection of the long-experienced attitude of God towards men and which is very biblical. Yet, a teacher can pour tons of biblical material over the heads of the students in such a way that he negates all the essence of the bible itself."[2]

If secularization has given Christianity a gift, it is this: forcing the Christian religion to purge itself of all traces of an archaic, mythical, and more or less primitive cast of categorization.[3] Christianity is a religion which is full-blooded, vibrant, robust, as much at home in a tavern or in the marketplace as in some shrine or hallowed sanctuary. Christianity is integrally imbedded within the times in which we live; it is also imbedded within the way in which each flesh-and-blood believer works out his everyday existence. Christianity in general, and religious instruction in particular, have for centuries been covered over by layer upon layer of mythical debris.

One of the consequences of this encrustation has been the significant amount of magical elements which have come to be regarded as an indispensable aspect of religious instruction. For example, Protestant religious educators for centuries have attributed a magical quality to the use of the bible in religion class, as if reading and explaining a host of biblical texts during the lesson would itself, in some magical fashion, give rise to faith and love. Catholic religious educators, in their turn, attributed magical properties to the distinctive garb worn by the priest or religious teaching the class. On seeing the special dress of the teacher, it was asserted, the students would see in him a true witness of God and thereby automatically deepen their faith and love for God.

One of the most important contributions which the social-science approach offers to religious instruction is explaining how learning really takes place and how we can most effectively predict ways to make Christian living operational in the lives of the learners. The social-science approach replaces the magical world of myths and pious folklore with objective data about the real world of teaching and learning. In doing so, the social-science approach does not rob religious instruction of its valid element of mystery. The learning process is, in one sense, always a mystery, no matter how much social science learns about it. By analogy it can be said that human gestation and birth remain a mystery no matter how much physiology and psychology one knows. Magic is certainly a cheap prop for mystery. Mystery has no need of tinny myths or superstitious hocus-pocus; it can stand on its own worth. The mysterious in religious instruction is not some sort of foggy, opaque, magical communication of God's life to the learner. We know that under the right conditions, God tends to communicate his life to the learner.[4] What the social-science approach endeavors to accomplish is to create and to structure those conditions which make it possible — but by no means inevitable — for the learner and God to share divine life in a special way. The truly mysterious is the innerness of this divine communication, and indeed why God should want to communicate with such a wretch at all. The redemption has cast light on these mysteries, particularly the latter one; yet it is the very intensity of this light which makes these mysteries even more mysterious. The social-science approach creates the learning conditions which bring about a desired religious behavior. It is no derogation of the validity or worth of this approach that the God-to-man interaction at the deepest levels of the learner's personality remains a mystery. This is as it should be in the instructional dynamic which is at bottom a facilitation of desired behavioral changes emanating from the individual's unique and inviolable personality.

EMPIRICAL PROCEDURE AND GRACE

Some theologians have been ill at ease for decades as they observe one or other of the social sciences investigate the religious experience. To them the realm of grace and indeed of the supernatural is a sector of reality whose ineffableness and spirituality do not lend themselves to the empirical methods typically employed by the social scientist. To be sure, theologians of this persuasion feel that at best social science represents an unwanted intrusion into the domain of the supernatural, and at worst results in false statements purporting to give explanations of religion which can be offered only by a sacred science. The empirical procedures which characterize social science either fail to tell anything about the workings of supernatural grace, or actually interfere with the operation of this grace. In the domain of religious instruction, the use of the social-science approach tampers with the exquisite and deeply personal relationship which God establishes with each soul during the religion lesson. Social science might be able to examine the outer shell of an individual's faith life, but such an examination is superficial and of little value compared to the sensitive interplay of the Spirit with the individual in the deepest recesses of his spirit.

I would suggest that remarks such as these are largely a result of an excessive supernaturalism on the part of those theologians and theologically-oriented religious educators advancing them. Of course the Spirit encounters the individual in the deepest regions of his soul — but not only there. The Spirit's encounter is with the whole person and not just with one of his modes, however deep and private that aspect might be. The Spirit is not a sort of "God on call," that is, a God not in constant contact with the whole person in his myriad facets, but rather a God held in reserve until the person's most profound self is ready and waiting for the divine encounter. Further, if a person is indeed a psychological and behavioral integer, then any modification or deepening of his supernatural life perforce has ramifications in the other and observable aspects of his personality and lifestyle. Action follows being, and where there is an alteration in being there is a subsequent modification in action. Few practices have been so perplexing to non-Christians and Christians alike as the exterior anti-Christian behavior on the part of some who regularly go to church, receive the sacraments, lead an active prayer life, and participate in those religious activities which normally deepen the interior, hidden, and supernatural life of the Christian. The task of social science is to examine and assess the observable behaviors on the ground that from these behaviors valid inferences can be drawn about those inner religious characteristics not amenable to direct measurement. Indeed, this is the meaning of Jesus's statement: "The test of the tree is in the fruit" (Matthew 12:33).

In the religion lesson, the social-science approach enables the teacher to structure the learning situation in such a way that the probability of a meaningful encounter by the individual with the Spirit is enhanced. Working hand-in-hand with theological science in the sophisticated relationship I suggested in the previous chapter, the social-science approach fashions those conditions and variables which are most conducive to the facilitation of the desired learning outcomes. Finally, in the process of assessment and evaluation, social-science tools are employed to ascertain the extent to which the learner's behavior was in fact modified in the desired direction. In no way does this represent an unwanted or unwarranted intrusion of empirical method into the sacrosanct domain of the individual's interior life. On the contrary, this approach constitutes a systematic deliberative manner of augmenting the possibility and also the opportunity that the individual's encounter with God will occur in the only way it can occur, namely according to the dimensions and contours of his own personality structure. God's grace does not work in a vacuum or in an hermetically sealed supernatural tank. This is a capital point typically overlooked by opponents of the important role which social science plays in the study and facilitation of religious behavior. Grace operates within the confines of the individual's personality, however vulgar or disappointing this might seem to the theologically-oriented religious educator.

Perhaps an example will help to illumine the point I am making. Theologically-oriented religious educators have commonly operated on the assumption that their own theological insights into the religious dimension of life enable them to be particularly sensitive and aware of the problems and needs of the youth with whom they work. Moreover, these educators typically believe that theological science as exercised in the instructional or counseling enterprises assists them in ascertaining which major areas of personal concern youth wish the church to help them with. Yet Merton Strommen's 1958-1959 empirical investigation of a national sample of Lutheran congregations in the United States and Canada disclosed that adults, responsible for congregational youth work and religious education programs of one sort or another, entertained substantially inaccurate perceptions of the major personal concerns of the youth with whom they were working. Indeed, there seemed to be significant misperceptions among these religious educators and adult church workers on what the youths expected the church to do for them and to help them with.[5] Strommen has spent the rest of his career in developing and refining a social-science instrument which will assist various denominations in accurately assessing the major developmental concerns of youth, with the ultimate aim of bringing the perceptions of religious educators and church workers into congruence with reality so as to enhance their pedagogical effectiveness.[6]

The work of Merton Strommen and other social scientists has possibly produced beneficial results vis-à-vis religious educators. A 1970 empirical research investigation by Charles Seevers of the psychological problems and needs of selected midwest Lutheran confirmands as perceived by their religion teachers indicated a significant congruence between the expressed problems of the Lutheran youth and these problems as perceived by their religion teachers. The same general finding held true in the case of Catholic confirmands and their religion teachers.[7] While one cannot demonstrate, at least not empirically, that the efforts of men like Strommen and others to introduce the social-science approach into the mentality of religious educators have produced a greater sensitivity to youth needs on the part of these educators, nonetheless this does constitute an interesting research question worth exploring.

There is one interesting finding in the Strommen study which deserves a brief comment. Strommen discovered that in those cases in which the religious educators and Christian youth workers were able to correctly identify youth's most troublesome problems, they were able to do so more because of a projection of their own developmental concerns than because of the acuity of their own perception of youth. An oversupernaturally-oriented religious educator might have concluded that it was possibly an enlightening action of the Spirit on his intellect which enabled him to correctly perceive a few of youth's developmental concerns. But Strommen's social-science approach offers a more parsimonious and indeed a more realistic explanation. In the overall work of religious instruction, I daresay the social-science approach of men like Strommen is far more productive in achieving an effective religion program than are the conjectures of a person seeking an explanation solely in the supernatural sphere.

Oversupernaturalism has characterized the reactions of many Protestant and Catholic religious educators and theologians to significant educational advances made by the social sciences. Until the 1950's most Catholic educators were vehemently opposed to psychological testing — even to intelligence tests — on the ground that these instruments interfered with the workings of divine grace and constituted an invasion of the privacy of the soul.[8] To be sure, the entire spectrum of social science was under attack by church leaders and theologians for allegedly being naturalistic, antisupernatural, and indeed antihuman. Thus, for example, Fulton Sheen, a leading Catholic religious leader and intellectual of the period from 1930-1960, commented that a book on the new psychology written by Edward Murphy, a Catholic essayist and novelist, was a superior treatise on psychology to the books of Sigmund Freud, Carl Jung, Alfred Adler, or Havelock Ellis because Murphy believes in a soul and in salvation.[9] Although attacks on social science by church officials and theologians have abated, still it seems safe to say that there is a residue of bias against what is possibly perceived to be a godless or antisupernatural social science.

Earlier in this book I reviewed a highly significant empirical research investigation by Ronald Goldman which concluded that for learners under the age of ten or twelve, the use of bible stories in religion class results in great confusion and misinterpretation of symbolic material in these stories on the part of the young learners.[10] Now here is one of many instances which can be adduced to indicate that far from hampering or blocking the understanding of the supernatural element in religious instruction, the social-science approach actually provides data whereby we gain a deeper understanding of how religious learning takes place. The Goldman study suggests that it is more supernatural to teach learners that kind of religion which can be meaningfully incorporated into their *natural* lifestyle than to give them so-called purely supernatural material such as the bible is said to be by advocates of the supernaturalist position.

Hard data are in no way estranged from or inimical to the supernatural aspect of religious instruction. On the contrary, the supernatural by its very ontology intimately suffuses the natural and consequently is intimately bound up with the natural. That is to say, any modification in the natural order has a necessary related effect on an appropriate aspect of the supernatural order, and vice-versa. Therefore, the more hard data we acquire on the operation of natural phenomena, the more illumination we will get on the workings of those supernatural realities bound up with these phenomena. If we obtain certain hard data on how children learn, we will thereby gain significant insights on how children learn religion. Further, since the supernatural suffuses the natural, the natural is no longer purely and simply the natural, but is instead an ontological compound of natural-supernatural. Thus when we obtain hard data on the natural, we are also automatically acquiring in a certain way data about a reality which is supernatural as well as natural in character. What I am suggesting in this paragraph is that far from being hostile or irrelevant to the supernatural, the empirical cast of social science is actually necessary for a well-rounded and complete understanding of the supernatural dimension of life and of religious instruction.

Let me illustrate the point I am making. In the mid-1960's Rodney Stark and Charles Glock conducted a careful empirical research investigation of the religious beliefs, religious practices, and religious knowledge of both a regional and a national sample of Protestant and Catholic American adults. Here are a few of the many interesting findings of this study: sixty-five percent of the Protestants and fifty-one percent of the Catholics believe that personal faith in Jesus is necessary for salvation; only twenty-eight percent of the Catholics believe it is absolutely necessary to be a Catholic in order to be saved; sixty-one percent of the Protestants and seventy percent of the Catholics are certain that their prayers are answered; forty-two percent of the Protestants and fifty-seven percent of the Catholics are absolutely certain that their sins are forgiven by God.[11] These are empirical data which reveal important facets of an individual's supernatural dimension. Since a person's belief is ipso facto a religious reality rather than a perception of reality, such empirical data are all the more meaningful. Taking into account social-science data of this kind, the religion teacher or curriculum builder can fashion an adult education program which is relevant to the real lives of the Christians being served.

I might mention an additional finding of the Stark and Glock study to reinforce my point that empirical data are helpful and indeed essential for an adequate understanding of the supernatural dimension of human personality. Stark and Glock set out to examine the shape of religious experience as undergone by a regional sample of Protestant and Catholic adults. The investigators delimited religious experiences as constituting "occasions defined by those undergoing them as an encounter — some sense of contact — between themselves and some supernatural consciousness." Religious experience, then, was conceived by these social scientists for purposes of investigation to be an encounter between God (or supernatural consciousness) and the individual. An important continuum along which these encounters can be appropriately situated is the sense of intimacy between the two "persons" involved. By conceiving of the divinity and the individual undergoing the religious experience as a pair of actors involved in a social or interpersonal encounter, it is possible to delineate certain general configurations of relations between them which can be ordered in terms of social distance. Stark and Glock postulated four general types of religious experience for purposes of their study: (1) the confirming type — the human actor simply notes (that is, feels, senses, et cetera) the existence or presence of the supernatural actor, but the supernatural is not perceived as specifically acknowledging the human actor; (2) the responsive type — mutual presence is acknowledged, and the supernatural actor is believed to specifically note, that is, respond to, the presence of the human actor; (3) the ecstatic type — the awareness of mutual presence is replaced by an affective relationship akin to love or friendship; (4) the revelational type — the human actor perceives himself as becoming a confidant of and/or a fellow participant in concert with the supernatural actor. Within each of these types, several subtypes were specified. Of these, only two subtypes of the responsive type are of concern to us: (a) the salvational — being acknowledged as especially virtuous, "chosen," "elect," or "saved" by the divine actor; (b) the sanctioning — experiencing the displeasure of the supernatural actor, for example, chastised or punished by the divinity. One key advantage of this conceptual schema is that it represents a systematically progressive scale along a line of increased intimacy of the human-divine encounter. For empirical purposes, this system also admits of statistical treatment, and indeed was sustained as an empirically valid methodology. The conclusions of this study showed that forty-five percent of the Protestants and forty-three percent of the Catholics reported that they were certain they had experienced a confirming experience. An additional twenty-eight percent of the Protestants and twenty-three percent of the Catholics believed that they had such a confirming experience, but were not absolutely "sure." As the investigators had hypothesized, confirming experiences are less common than responsive experiences. Of the Protestants, thirty-seven percent were certain that they had responsive-salvational experiences, and an additional twenty-three percent thought they had such experiences but were not certain. On the Catholic side, twenty-six percent were certain they had responsive-salvational experiences, and an additional twenty-two percent thought they had such experiences but were not sure. Sixteen percent of the Protestants were certain they had responsive-sanctioning experiences, and an additional twenty-five percent thought they had such experiences but were not certain. Of the Catholics, twenty-three percent were certain that they had responsive-sanctioning experiences, while an additional thirty percent thought they had such experiences but were not certain.[12]

There are several features of these Stark and Glock conclusions which strongly suggest that empirical methodology is both helpful and necessary to an investigation into the supernatural — not only to clean out the cobwebs of the ancient magical aspects and mythical folklore, but also to throw new light on the intimate operational and suffusional relationship between the natural and supernatural aspects of reality. The importance of this to the work of religious instruction is, of course, obvious. The first feature I should like to comment on is the frequency of religious experiences, notably the confirming experience. Stark and Glock themselves note there are few indications in our culture which would lead an observer to predict so high a rate of supernaturalism in what seems at first blush to be an increasingly scientific, secularized society. For example, few characters in contemporary literature undergo encounters with the divine, and when they do, it is usually clear that they are odd, old-fashioned, or psychologically unbalanced. Theologians might theorize about the death of God, or about galloping secularism, or about the hardening of people's hearts to the divine encounter; however, these contentions are not supported by the empirical data. The second feature is that the Stark and Glock data reveal a significantly higher incidence of religious experience on the part of the respondents than a Gallup survey conducted two years earlier. The investigators suggested that the discrepancy can be explained by the difference of the two populations: Gallup's population was a representative cross-section, whereas the Stark and Glock population was drawn entirely on the basis of membership in Christian churches. In other words, membership in a Christian church does seem to exert a measurable impact on the belief system of this constituency. The final feature is that the Stark and Glock study revealed that the incidence and kind of religious experience was heavily correlated with the denomination to which the respondent belongs. To seek an experience affirming one's personal salvation in Jesus is a much more familiar part of the rhetoric of Protestantism than of Catholicism. This difference of emphasis is reflected in the data, as a significantly higher percentage of Protestants than Catholics indicated they were certain they had experienced a sense of being saved in Jesus. The Stark and Glock findings suggest that as a general rule religious experience increases systematically as one slides along the continuum from the more liberal Protestant denominations to the more conservative Protestant denominations. In short, God does not work in ways so mysterious, so magical, and so opaque that the supernatural remains a riddle wrapped in an enigma. Membership in a certain denomination, while not conditioning how God works, nonetheless does ready the terrain of human personality in such a way that God's operations tend to take on the shape of denominational emphasis. When a religious denomination stresses certain precepts or behaviors or belief systems (all of which can be empirically measured in terms of degree of emphasis), then there is a significant tendency for God to work in the lifestyle of the believer much in accord with these emphases.

Inasmuch as religious instruction has been theologically-oriented rather than social-science oriented, it has been inevitable that ideology should pass for theory in the absence of empirical facts. It has typically been upon ideology and not upon hard data as to how the teaching-learning of religion actually takes place, that religion curricula quite frequently were devised and programs operated. Ideology is no substitute for hard data. Actually, ideology is counterfeit theory which, on account of inadequate foundations, soon tends to become verbal formulae and slogans that render genuine theorizing as well as empirical verification unnecessary and impossible.[13]

RELIGIOUS INSTRUCTION AND INSTRUCTION IN OTHER AREAS

The application and utilization of processes and data from the so-called "secular" sphere of reality does not desacralize religious instruction, or cause it to be "reduced to the natural plane." On the contrary, the application and utilization of these so-called "secular" data and processes make it more possible for the supernatural dimension to blossom and come to fuller flower. Data about the way in which persons learn are not "secular" data, to be ignored because religious instruction deals with the "higher goods" of supernatural faith and revelation. It has never been successfully proven that the basic process by which natural realities are learned is generically different from the way in which Christian truths are acquired by learners. It has never been adequately shown that the basic ways through which desired "natural" learning outcomes are facilitated are substantially different from the fundamental ways in which desired "supernatural" learning outcomes are facilitated. The learner is an integer; he does not possess one complete set of faculties by which he learns natural phenomena, and a second complete set of faculties by which he learns supernatural realities. If the bible indicates any one fundamental pedagogical activity, it is this: God continuously uses every facilitational process to induce desired behavioral modifications in his people, irrespective of whether these facilitational processes can be labelled "natural" or "supernatural."

Social science has shown that children do not and cannot learn certain kinds of symbolic and representational material until they have attained a particular level of psychophysiological maturity. But since theologically-oriented religious educators for centuries have believed that religion is learned in a mysterious, divinely intimate way which perforce is exempt from the "natural" laws of learning, much biblical and sacramental imagery and representations were introduced into childhood religious education. On account of their untested assumption that supernatural learning is somehow substantially distinct from natural learning, religious educators spurned or neglected to extrapolate the advances of "secular" pedagogy to the work of religious instruction. It was only when Ronald Goldman appeared on the scene to directly relate the findings of the psychology of learning to religious instruction in a carefully-controlled experiment, that religious educators began to realize that their assumed dichotomy between the processes of "natural" and "supernatural" learning is a fantasy.[14]

Religious instruction should not take flight to the transcendent or to the mysterious every time a pedagogical problem arises. This kind of pedagogical neognosticism is out of place in any educational endeavor which calls itself realistic and Christian. The social-science approach furnishes religious instruction with the processes, data, and methods requisite for facilitation of religious behaviors in learners — without recourse to the realm of the foggy or the opaque. Josef Jungmann aptly remarks that "we can only deplore the fact that many years had to pass before the experiences gained in secular education could be applied also to the teaching of the Christian faith."[15] Yet even in the so-called "enlightened circles" of Protestant and particularly of Catholic religious education, one sometimes wonders whether the pedagogical advances made in secular education are merely tolerated, or possibly baptized. Indeed, one wonders the extent to which Christian educators have really incorporated these advances which by and large are due to the social-science approach that has characterized secular education since the beginning of the twentieth century. To what extent is Josef Goldbrunner representative of the leading thinkers in religious education when he observes that while a pedagogical method may be correct in secular subjects, it would do violence to the kerygma when blindly carried over to the religion class? Specifically, Goldbrunner states that while a student can discover secular knowledge by himself, he can never discover the message of salvation, that is, divine revelation, on his own. This message, Goldbrunner asserts, "must be announced, proclaimed, transmitted as Word of God, under his mandate."[16] One wonders how this supernatural method of "announcing, proclaiming, transmitting' which Goldbrunner asserts is so distinctive in religious instruction is genuinely different from the secular pedagogical method known as "lecturing — a method, incidentally, which has been shown to be one of the most ineffective of all pedagogical methods.[17]

One implication of the position taken by many religious educators that the process of learning about "supernatural" things is substantially distinct from the learning proecesses involved in acquiring "natural" outcomes is a denial that something of God is present in the specifically-labelled nonreligious ares of study. Such a suggestion that God is not present in all aspects of an individual's learning process, whether "natural" or "supernatural," seems to be shaky theology. To be sure, it smacks of that same kind of religious triumphalism which has described public schools as "godless." Certainly God operates in a different way in the religion lesson than he does in the English lesson or in the woodshop class. But to indicate that God operates in ways which vary according to the nature and structure of different subjects or lessons is not the same as implying that God's activity in the "natural" areas of the curriculum is so distinct as to render the teaching-learning process involved in these areas substantially different from the specifically-labelled "supernatural" areas.

André Godin has perceptively observed that one reason for the absence or even outright rejection of a social-science approach is "the considerable effort which religious educators have exerted to control the value of religious instruction by a faithfulness to its sources (the Christian message) and by its goals theologically enunciated." As a consequence, Godin continues, they are obliged to deduce certain characteristics and outcomes of religious instruction from the essential aspects of its theological content, instead of empirically assessing the process and product results of the religion lesson. For example, these theologically-oriented religious educators declare that when the lesson involves the "transmission" of a religious mystery, then a teacher who does not use specifically labelled "supernatural" pedagogical processes is condemned in advance.[18]

My analysis of the work of theology and the work of social science in Chapters Five and Six indicates that of its very nature theological science lacks the resources and the tools to facilitate behavioral outcomes in learners. Furthermore, theological science by its very ontology lacks the wherewithal to accurately assess the form and the means by which religious experience makes itself felt and acted on by men.[19] Throughout this volume, I have demonstrated that it is directly within the scope of competency of social science to effectively engage in the kind of facilitation and assessment of religious outcomes which I have just mentioned. I hasten to reject the notion that affirmation of the social-science character of religious instruction represents an illicit and invalid intrusion of the natural into the supernatural. On the contrary, all of God's creation is an amalgam of natural-supernatural, and so theologically and realistically, it is ridiculous to posit an "intrusion." If religious instruction is to be rendered effective, we need to focus on the effect which specific and combined teacher behaviors and other situational variables have on the learner, instead of continuing to squander our present efforts on deductively analyzing vague concepts such as "response to God." The phenomenon "response to God" is not an amorphous or enigmatic thing but rather a set of behaviors which are characterized by specific causes and consequences. God engages man where man is at, in his behaviors, in his lifestyle — not in some magical dream world, and not without behavioral consequences in man. This is in no way to deny the supernatural, but instead to demythologize religious instruction.

Josef Goldbrunner emphasizes that in religious instruction the use of any kind of what he calls "progressive" pedagogy (that is, any method other than lecturing) is inappropriate when revelation is the theme of the lesson. "Revelation cannot be discovered," Goldbrunner asserts. "It can only be proclaimed, that is authoritatively proclaimed and listened to."[20] A comparison of this statement with my analysis in Chapter Eight of contemporary theology of revelation suggests that possibly one factor engendering the opposition to the social-science approach in religious instruction on the part of some religious educators is an antiquated theology — specifically, an antiquated theology of the natural and supernatural. Consequently I will devote much of the remainder of this chapter to a brief overview of some of the modern theological conceptions of the natural and supernatural.

THEOLOGY OF THE NATURAL-SUPERNATURAL

Both historically and actually, the distinction between the natural and the supernatural is conceptual rather than ontological. In other words, a separation between the natural and the supernatural is effected only in the realm of thought; in the real, there is no such thing as a purely natural order. In point of fact, man has never existed in a purely natural order. His whole existence is suffused with the supernatural, just as is the existence of every object of creation in proportion to its plenitude of being. All reality is God-soaked. This is not to assert that the natural and the supernatural are identical, for they are indeed distinct. However, they so interpenetrate each other at every sector of created existence as to wipe out the possibility of any reality being natural or secular or nonsacral. This is not pantheism; it is a recognition of the divinized aspect of every form of creation. "Deified man is still man and not God."[21]

Nature, consequently, is never "pure" nature, but as Karl Rahner phrases it "nature in a supernatural order."[22] When an individual encounters any aspect of creation, then, he is encountering both the natural and the supernatural intimately admixed in one reality. Particularly is this true of creation's highest being, man. Man represents the apex of nature superformed by the supernatural saving grace which God continually offers to it.

If there is no real separation between the natural and the supernatural in terrestrial existence, why then do theologians distinguish between them? Two reasons can be given. First, there is a real distinction between them. Grace, for example, is wholly supernatural; it is not natural. Second, this distinction serves a fruitful function in theological science since it enables the theologian to isolate and hence more effectively to investigate the supernatural constituent in terrestrial reality. The unfortunate historical development, however, is that some theologians, religious educators, and layfolk have forgotten that while the supernatural is indeed distinct from the natural, nevertheless here on earth it never exists except as admixed with the natural. Even then the supernatural inheres in the natural only in proportion to what Thomas Aquinas terms the "aptitude" of the natural to be suffused with the supernatural existence. Isolating the supernatural for purposes of theological investigation is scientifically as commendable as it is fruitful; however, we should not forget that such isolation is an investigative device, and should not be mistaken for an integral subsistent reality.

Catholic theologians typically follow Thomas Aquinas in affirming three distinct but interconnected ways in which God inheres in creation. Each of these three ways, as Yves Congar observes, represents a mode "in which God may be with his creation at increasingly deeper and more intimate levels."[23] The first mode and level is God's presence in all beings according to his creative power. For its continued existence, every being requires that God be present within it; in the absence of this constant divine presence, the being would have no existential ground and would immediately cease to exist. Through the suffusion of each created being with his ongoing creative power, God fills the world with his presence. Yet at this first level, God, though present in each being, does not dwell in it in a superabundantly personal way, if I may stretch an analogy possibly beyond its tensile strength. At this stage, the creature cannot have a two-way relational encounter with God — an encounter which by its very nature is reserved only to man. God suffuses the world to so full an extent that the world oozes God, so to speak. Yet the manner of God's suffusion is not at the transactional, mutually sharing, interpersonal level.

The second mode or level of God's inhering in or being with his creatures is through grace proportionate to the creature's union with God as an object: known, loved, and possessed. Through grace, God effects a presence in a creature which is deep and personal. Only in man can God dwell so intimately since of all his terrestrial creatures, man alone is a person. It is in the relationship which is grace that a person can possess God, as it were, in knowledge and especially in love. It is grace that brings about a certain divinization of man. In the first mode or level, God abides in a being through his ongoing power and causality. This divine presence in the creature is pervasive and abundant throughout every aspect of its essence and existence. But in the second mode, God dwells in the being, not just according to his power and causality, but according to his substance. In the first mode, God's presence is involved; at the second level, it is indwelling which comes into play.

The third mode or level of God's inhering in reality is through his being. This permeation of God in man is brought about through the hypostatic union of man and God in Jesus Christ. In the second level, the working of grace results in God's dwelling in man according to His substance; at the third level, the Incarnation results in God's dwelling in man according to His very being. In the person of Jesus, God unites himself inextricably with human nature, which it may be said is the human nature of the Word. Consequently the indwelling of God in man is, in Jesus, the exemplar, total and ontological. Jesus was not Jesus for the first century only; he is Jesus for the present moment too. In the person of Jesus, the natural and supernatural are brought together in an exquisite relationship which serves as a model for the complementary existing and functioning of the natural-supernatural in man. "The union (hypostatic and ontological) of God with humanity in Jesus Christ brings about a corporeal dwelling of God in the midst of our world."[24] "In Christ the whole plenitude of the Deity is embodied, and dwells in him."[25] The person whose existential situation can be described as "being a Christian" thereby shares in the Incarnation. This is preeminently true when he receives the eucharist; it is also true by his personal incorporation in that grand incarnation which is the mystical body of Christ. The mystical body is in one sense an outering or an extension of the hypostatic union.

In summary, nature is a temple of God, a holy place where God's power, grace, and being fill all creation in appropriate proportion to the mode and aptitude of each creature. The first level is that of the cosmic temple, the second level that of the spiritual temple, and the third level that of the theandric temple. Each higher level presupposes and completes the preceding level(s). To encounter any reality, therefore, is to be in communion with a natural-supernatural entity, with a reality abiding in one of the three temples of God.

The classical Protestant tradition is even stronger than the Catholic position in affirming the inseparability of the natural and the supernatural here on earth. Paul Tillich observes that Protestantism denies the ontological dualism between nature and supernature. Consequently, in his pure nature, man is not only the image of God; he also has the power of communion with God and therefore of "righteousness" toward other creatures and himself. With Adam's fall, this power was lost. As a result, man remains separated from God, and of himself does not have the freedom or capacity to return. This is in contrast to the Catholic position which holds that the result of Adam's fall was a weakening, rather than a severance, of communion with God. For Catholicism, man retains some freedom to turn toward God. The point of departure which leads to these divergent Protestant and Catholic positions is the interpretation of grace. Tillich notes that if grace is ontologically a supernatural substance, the Catholic position is tenable and consistent. If, on the other hand, grace constitutes forgiveness received at the center of one's personality, then the Protestant position is valid. Tillich concludes by strongly asserting that it is precisely the Protestant rejection of supernature as a distinct and ontological entity which is at the very bottom of the different Protestant and Catholic conceptions of grace.[26]

For Protestantism, man is a supernatural being by his very nature; supernature is not something added on to him. The consequence of this is that Adam's fall and subsequent sinful deeds by man render a person far more depraved than under the Catholic interpretation. Protestantism has tended to stress the supernatural (whether fallen or redeemed) in all of nature, particularly in that apex of created nature, man. With this emphasis has come a concomitant deemphasis of God's special superadded presence in specified realities, notably in ecclesiastical realities such as sacraments. Catholicism, on the other hand, has tended to accent the supernatural as existing in a special and exalted way in certain realities, particularly in ecclesiastical realities like the sacraments and sacramentals. This stress was accompanied by a downplaying of the inseparableness of the supernatural from any and all reality — even though this inseparableness is orthodox Catholic teaching (for example, Denz. #3891). Tillich believes the Catholic emphasis has resulted in a certain desupernaturalizing and particularly a depersonalizing of all reality, including the interaction of man and God. Tillich observes that in Catholic theology, there is much accentuation on the *infusio Spiritus Sancti* as the ground and source for man's faith in and love for God. Protestantism, he states, regards such a concept, particularly as it is phrased in this way, with suspicion because it reduces the Spirit to a kind of "matter" which is transmitted by the priest in administering the sacraments, in proportion to the recipient's degree of positive disposition:

> This a-personalistic understanding of the Spiritual Presence resulted in an objectification of the religious life which culminated in the practice of selling indulgences. For Protestant thinking, the Spirit is always personal. Faith and love are impacts of the Spiritual Presence on the centered self, and the vehicle of this impact is the "word," even within the administration of the sacraments.[27]

It is against the mythologizing of the supernatural, whether hermeneutically, doctrinally, or sacramentally, that Rudolf Bultmann protests. For Bultmann, myth is that manner of thinking and acting which turns the unworldly into a worldly object Hence Bultmann believes that to be authentic, Christianity must engage in a process of demythologizing. For Bultmann, life and doctrine, natural and supernatural, are woven into a seamless oneness.[28]

I have spent the last few pages discussing the theology of the natural-supernatural to reinforce some of the points I made earlier in this chapter. The social-science approach is not "secular" or "naturalistic," because there is nothing in God's creation which is separated from the supernatural, or which is itself not supernatural (depending on one's theological stance). Further, contemporary theology of the natural-supernatural strongly suggests that the actualization of the natural aspects of man necessarily has a high positive correlation to the actualization of his supernatural dimension. Indeed, to concentrate on the supernatural dimension while ignoring or downplaying the natural milieu in which the supernatural inheres constitutes an almost certain way of impairing and even ravaging the supernatural element. Such a concentration on the supernatural is precisely the focus of the theologically-oriented approach to religious instruction. The old-time missionaries went into Asia and began immediately to teach Christian doctrine in a theologically-centered, transmission approach. Except for certain charismatic teachers, converts were few. Seeing the failure of a direct supernatural approach, these missionaries decided to use the natural as a motivational tool to encourage the Asiatics to learn church doctrine. The natural was a sort of grease on the wheels of the supernatural train. The result was the "rice Christian," a person who ate rice and became a Christian to keep from starving. When the rice gave out, so did the Christianity of the "convert." Finally, the missionaries forged a new approach to religious instruction, one which both prophesized and operationalized the contemporary concept of the natural-supernatural. This approach recognized that ministering to the sick in the village dispensaries, giving rice to hungry families, comforting a bereaved mother — all these are directly religious instruction. The natural is no longer regarded as a time-consuming but necessary means to the teaching of supernatural truths. Instead, the natural is now viewed as the corporeality of the supernatural, a highly significant way in which God and man interact. Doctrinal content is no longer divorced from corporal works of mercy, for each of these activities objectifies, nay is doctrinal content. The task of the missionary in these new circumstances is to assist the individual, at the optimum point in his development, to cognitively clarify, affectively feel and love, and operationally integrate this doctrinal content into his own lifestyle. The corporal work of mercy is not identical to religious instruction; rather the situation in which the corporal work of mercy is done is at once an activity of religious instruction and also the milieu in which other necessary complementary aspects of religious instruction are effected.

The social-science approach to religious instruction has as one of its major foci the creation of those conditions which enhance the possibility of the actualization of the supernatural. Because the teacher or curriculum builder is not God, the instructional conditions which he shapes are perforce natural conditions. Yet, as my analysis of the natural-supernatural indicates, to shape the natural conditions conducive to learning is also to structure — indeed almost directly in a sense — the supernatural conditions attendant upon the effective working of the Spirit in the life of the learner.

Immanence and Transcendence

Throughout the history of Christianity, the prevailing theological opinion has oscillated between the view that God is immanent in the world and that God is transcendent above the world. To be sure, immanence and transcendence are pivotal concepts for explaining the relationship between God and man, between man and the universe, between the natural and the supernatural. Christian orthodoxy, both Protestant and Catholic, has always insisted that God is simultaneously immanent and transcendent vis-à-vis terrestrial reality. However, in various periods of Christianity, more stress has been placed on one over the other, a stress which has fluctuated according to the Zeitgeist.

I am using the term "immanence" to mean the theological doctrine which emphasizes God permeating and suffusing every aspect of terrestrial reality. Immanence thus stands in contrast to "transcendence" which emphasizes God lying beyond and surpassing infinitely the limits of earthly creation. I am employing these terms in a far different and in one sense unrelated way from their use in the philosophical schools of thought known as immanentism and transcendentalism. Some might suggest that the terms "relative immanence" and "relative transcendence," or "Christian immanence" and "Christian transcendence" would dispel any confusion between what I am discussing and the classical philosophical schools of immanentism and transcendentalism. These terms seem unduly cumbersome, so I shall shorten them to "immanence" and "transcendence."

Transcendence is the concept held by those who highlight the relational gulf existing between two realities, one of which is extrinsic and infinitely superior to the other, namely God and the world. The notion of transcendence implies an aspect of discontinuity or break between the realities involved, and suggests that any means of passing from one to the other must be accomplished by a special superabundant activity of the preeminent being.

Immanence is the concept affirmed by those who stress the indwelling of God in all reality in a personal and all-suffusing manner. God's immanence in the world, as I have previously indicated, takes place at three levels: through his power, through his grace, and through his being. Each reality in the universe participates in the life of God at the appropriate level of intimacy.

Christian theology has always maintained that immanence and transcendence are indispensable and complementary viewpoints. The prevalence of one over the other in certain eras has been a matter of emphasis, not an elimination of one or the other. Theology has consistently taught that though God is qualitatively an infinitely higher being than is any created reality, nonetheless he is deeply present within all the world. Raphael's painting entitled "The School of Athens" illustrates this basic difference in stress. Here Raphael depicts all the major thinkers of the ancient world, each engaging in the type of activity which encapsulates his contribution to civilization. Dominating the painting are the figures of Plato and Aristotle who are at the top of a wide staircase, surrounded by all the other principal thinkers of antiquity. Plato and Aristotle are engaged in animated dialogue. Plato's right hand points upward toward the heavens, signifying his stress on the transcendent. Aristotle's right hand is pointing downward, toward earth, expressing his emphasis on the immanent over the transcendent. (Interestingly, the history of philosophy reveals that both Plato and Aristotle took a position somewhere toward the middle of the continuum which has pure immanentism at one pole and total transcendentalism at the other pole.)

Contemporary theology, Catholic and Protestant alike, stresses immanence over transcendence. A number of reasons can be adduced for this. The new theology accords greater importance to the Redemption and the Incarnation than heretofore. Both of these Christological events lend themselves more readily to emphasis on immanence rather than on transcendence. Theologians, too, are coming to real grips for the first time with the evolution of the world and of man. Evolution constitutes a magnificent cosmic affirmation of immanence. There is also a growing concern in theological circles with what can be termed the "social gospel," that is with making religion bridge the gap between theology and the existential needs of the world's poor and underprivileged. When dealing with the poor and downtrodden, or even with affluent people in personal crises, the clergyman soon discovers that the kind of religion these persons need is an incarnational, here-and-now, immanent religion, not a way-out-there transcendent religion. In modern philosophy, personalism and existentialism have exerted great influence. Both of these philosophies are immanence-oriented, veering sharply away from transcendentalism. Interiority, self-realization, freedom, authenticity — all these expressions of immanence are the touchstones for modern personalist and existentialist trains of thought. Contemporary psychology is stressing inner dynamism, self-fulfillment, individual autonomy, and personal actualization. Little wonder, then, that modern psychology can be characterized by a strong immanentist bent. The triumph of political and social democracy in the twentieth century has exerted a strong, though frequently overlooked, influence on bringing about the triumph of immanence. Democracy, whether political, social, or any other sort, has as its core the appreciation of the value inherent in every reality, however common. The man in the street is no longer the "common man," but a unique individual — he has the vote, he has buying power, he has upward mobility socially, economically, and educationally. Finally, the emergence of modern science and technology has dramatically demonstrated that all God's creation, great and small, literally brims over with power and goodness and glory. A few tiny, lowly atoms in the right combination can unleash enormous energy, while some kerosene and oxygen can power a man to the moon and beyond. What further evidence is required of God's intimate indwelling in temporal reality?

The ascendancy of immanence in our age has enabled us to once again appreciate to the extent we are capable, the vivifying and sanctifying aspect of all reality. It is through (but not by) the world that we are brought to flower, and through (but not by) the world that we are saved. This is not to deny or diminish the action of God, but to affirm the way in which God's grace operates. The world, as Pierre Teilhard de Chardin so beautifully expresses it, is the divine milieu. In this vein Teilhard could write: "by virtue of the Creation and, still more, of the Incarnation, nothing here below is profane for those who know how to see."[29]

A charming story in the lives of two elderly twentieth-century Protestant theologians of international renown highlights the point I am making. After an evening of pleasant conversation and companionship, they began, as old men are wont to do, to talk of death. Then one of them said: "I look forward eagerly to heaven. As soon as possible after I get there, God willing, I shall look up Saint Paul. We will have so much to talk about." To which his friend replied: "Yes, but first we must visit with Mozart."

In October, 1958, Pius XII lay dying. In his last moments on earth, he asked that music be played, for this *Stimmung* would draw him closer to the God he had striven to serve so wholeheartedly. To the astonishment of some persons attending the dying pope, Pius did not ask that spiritual motets or Gregorian Chant be played. Instead, he requested Beethoven's First Symphony.[30]

The contemporary emphasis on God's immanence in the world has great significance for the social-science approach to religious instruction. The immanentist position implies that present in every aspect of the religion lesson is God himself. He is present not only in the doctrinal product and process content, but also in the educational materials, in the learning environment, and most especially in the other members of the instructional group. A key task of the religion teacher is to so structure the learning situation that the God dwelling in all the aspects of the instructional environment will be actualized for the student. God is indeed actualized in the instructional environment by virtue of his immanence; the role of the teacher is to enable the student to grasp for himself this divine actualization. God is more immanent in life than in formulations about life. Consequently the religion teacher uses as his pedagogical base the shaping of the learning environment in such a way that the students experience life firsthand. The pedagogical value of doctrinal formulations and other cognitive ex post facto apparatus is to further clarify and heighten the meaning of what the learner experienced and now is experiencing. Religion class is not some formless "happening," but rather a structured pedagogical activity with definite preplanned behavioral outcomes. In such an activity, product and process outcomes in the cognitive, affective, and lifestyle spheres are all indispensable.

Because of God's deep and all-pervasive immanence in the world, the social-science approach to religious instruction cannot legitimately be charged with being "secular" or "naturalistic." These criticisms are as theologically unsophisticated as they are pedagogically silly. Indeed, the social-science approach has as a basic function the focusing of the learner's attention on the means whereby through a felt appreciation and experience of his own immanent activity, he can come into deeper contact with the immanent God who also ineffably transcends the individual's limited mode of being. Reaching the God transcendent through the God immanent is ultimately the most meaningful road which the learner can take in his eternal quest to experience as much of the infinite breadth and depth of the divine as he is capable.

The Temporal

The contemporary theology of the natural-supernatural, combined with the modern ascendancy of divine immanence, has resulted in a new Christian attitude toward the temporal. Three developments within present-day theology have done much to contribute to this changed attitude: a new theology of the Incarnation, a new theology of revelation, and a new theology of evolution.

Theology of the Incarnation. The core of a solid and expansive theology of the temporal is the Incarnation. Because the Word became flesh and dwells among us, all reality has an incarnational structure. The Word's plunge into the terrestrial milieu through the Incarnation has existential ramifications affecting his era and all subsequent ones. So great and so momentous was/is the Incarnation that all temporality is forever more impregnated with the divine. To take the Incarnation seriously is to affirm the sacramentality of all reality. The white-hot fire of the Incarnation bonded and fused for all time the temporal and the spiritual. Consequently there can be no such thing as desacralization, no matter how the labels read. Properly understood, the Incarnation caused the entire world to be a kind of eucharist.

Through the Incarnation, Jesus "entered our human world of things and persons," and so "gave an ultimate meaning to things and to people by his word."[31] Through the Incarnation, Jesus jumped into the temporal and inwardly changed the very structure and basis of all reality. This is a truth of such earth-shattering — yes earth-shattering — import that theologians down through the ages seem to have been afraid to come close to it and explore its richness. Yet, as Pierre Teilhard de Chardin observes, "by definition and in essence Christianity is the religion of the Incarnation: God uniting Himself with the world which He created, to unify it and in some sort incorporate it in Himself. To the worshipper of Christ, this act expresses the history of the universe."[32] For Teilhard, the Incarnation represents the major leap into a drastically new evolutionary period, a leap in which the axis of the noosphere's development for the first time was brought into congruence with the axis of God. It is in the person of Jesus of Nazareth, true God and true man, that Point Omega appears tangibly for the first time.[33]

The Incarnation represents the existential resolution of the antipodal tension between the natural and the supernatural, between immanence and transcendence — if indeed, such a tension were real instead of notional in the minds of theologians. Through the Incarnation, the transcendent God became immanent. Through the Incarnation, the supernatural and the natural were joined in one person, inseparable. The Incarnation effected a permanent transubstantiation of all reality, and the world has never been the same since.

The new theology of the Incarnation clearly implies that any labelling of the social-science approach to religious instruction as "secular" or "naturalistic" is as foolish as it is unchristian. By virtue of the transubstantiation effected through the Incarnation, nothing in the world is "secular." One might in fact say that the secular is the most divine when it reaches the innermost point of secularity — for it is at this point that the secular is being most true to itself and therefore most reflective of that uniqueness which God gave to it. Of all the gospels, it is in John that we find the most sublime passages on the divine and also the most touching of the human events in the life of Jesus. The gospel of John is the most divine because it is the most human. So too with the religion class; it becomes the most religious when it works within temporal structures to affect the most human aspect of the learner, namely his lifestyle. And this is what the social-science approach to religious instruction is all about.

Theology of Revelation. In Chapter Eight I briefly sketched the broad outlines of the contemporary theology of revelation. The new concept of revelation forms a dynamic base for a sound theology of the temporal. Revelation is no longer regarded solely as a corpus of data deposited prior to the death of John the Evangelist. Today revelation is regarded as a continuing process of God's self-disclosure which takes on myriad forms and shapes, from direct Person-to-person revelation to indirect things-to-person revelation. (The theology of the Incarnation shows that because of the transubstantiation of all reality as effected through the Word made flesh, there no longer remains a "thing" in the strict sense of the term, but instead the thing as a kind of corporeality of God. This is not pantheism; it is an affirmation of the reality of God's permeating presence in all entities). Revelation is a process of communicating. It is an operational synapse between God and man.

The new theology of revelation suggests that any branding of the social-science approach to religious instruction as "secular" and "naturalistic" is as theologically unsound as it is pedagogically ridiculous. Revelation is God communicating himself to man in whatever way and form is most suited to the individual at his own unique point of development. Now this is precisely the axis of pedagogy and the base of the social-science approach: to take the learner as he is, and to use whatever realities are effective to bring about a desired learning outcome. Theologically-oriented religious educators often neglect this crucial point, and in so doing ironically fall outside the mainstream of current theologizing about revelation. For example, Theodor Filthaut states that emphasis on instructional methodology in religious education is to run the danger of overlooking the spiritual character of existence. Method is a service-function to doctrinal content, according to Filthaut.[34] Such a view in effect denies the ongoing, communicative, pervasive character of revelation. Method is just as revelatory as is doctrinal content, if one wishes to cling to this pedagogically outmoded distinction. Indeed, in many instances method might be more revelational. I recall the behavior of a European professor of religious education who was once teaching a class of graduate students here in the United States. The theme for his lecture was the charity of Jesus and its relation to the work of religious instruction. In the middle of the lecture two students walked in. The professor put down his notes, turned to the latecomers, reproached them severely, and ordered them out of the classroom — whereupon he continued his lecture on Christian charity and its relation to the work of religious instruction. Students in this class later indicated that this one bit of methodology, unconscious though it was, had more revelational impact on them than did the entire lecture.

Didier Piveteau nicely relates the new theology of revelation to the religion lesson when he writes "perhaps religion teachers have insisted too much on the grammatical form 'God has spoken,' or 'God has saved' as if God's action, which is outside of human temporal categories, is regarded as being in the past. Yet, it is exact to say 'God now speaks' or 'God now saves.' "[35]

Theology of Evolution. The development of a bold new theology of evolution has added a fresh and in some ways a wholly new dimension to a mature theological conception of the temporal. After seventy-five years or so of ignoring or opposing the theory of evolution following the 1859 publication of Charles Darwin's *On the Origin of Species*, theologians began to realize that the entire process of cosmic evolution presents theological science with an incredibly rich mine of new data. Natural science treats of the corporeality of God, as it were. To examine the evolution of this corporeality is to see the ways in which God has operated in the universe over eons of time. To study evolution is to discover in a radically new perspective the breadth and the inextricability in which God has disclosed himself to the cosmos from the dawn of time. More than perhaps any other modern thinker, it is Pierre Teilhard de Chardin who provides the most penetrating and fecund insights into the theological nature of the temporal as objectified in the evolutionary process. For Teilhard, evolution is simply the universe fulfilling itself in a synthesis of centers in perfect conformity with the laws of union — the intrinsically necessary union between natural and supernatural, between nonlife and life, between thinking and loving. It is God, the "center of centers," which through the evolutionary process develops and unfolds the spiritual character of matter until at last Point Omega is reached. At Point Omega, in the final vision, Christianity will have fulfilled itself.[36]

Teilhard, paleontologist and theological thinker, identifies three distinct stages in the evolutionary process: the lithosphere, in which matter was formed and developed; the biosphere, in which life was formed and developed; and the noosphere, in which human thought was formed and developed. Each of these represents a progressively higher level of unfolding on the evolutionary scale. Teilhard believes that the cosmos is still in the process of evolution. However, he maintains that evolution has gone pretty much as far as it can go physically; the next great advances will be social. The end of the world will see a fulfillment of the spiritual. The end of the world, which Teilhard sees as the accomplishment of the inner finality of nature, will be "the wholesale internal introversion upon itself of the noosphere, which has [by then] simultaneously reached the utter-most limit of its complexity and its centrality." The end of the world is the "critical point simultaneously of emergence and emersion, of maturation and evasion."[37]

At the center and at every outering stage of the evolutionary process stands the person of Jesus. Henri de Lubac notes that for Teilhard, Jesus is the cosmic Christ — not only in the moral sense but in the physical sense as well.[38] From the cosmic vantage point, Teilhard wrenches Jesus out of the incredibly narrow historical and spiritual framework into which he has been forced and places him squarely in the center of the universe, where Jesus becomes at once the focal point and true perfector of evolution. "Through him all things came to be, and not one thing had its being but through him" (John 1:3).

> Christ, principle of universal vitality because sprung up as man among men, put himself in the position (maintained ever since) to subdue under himself, to purify, to direct and superanimate the general ascent of consciousness into which he inserted himself. By a perennial act of communion and sublimation, he aggregates to himself the total psychism of the earth. And when he has gathered everything together and transformed everything, he will close in upon himself and his conquests, thereby rejoining, in a final gesture, the divine focus he has never left. Then, as St. Paul tells us, *God shall be all in all*. This is indeed a superior form of "pantheism" without trace of the poison of adulteration or

annihilation: the expectation of perfect unity, steeped in which each element will reach its consummation at the same time as the universe.[39]

Christianity is for Teilhard a phylum of love within the world of nature; it unites man into a mystical body which is deeper, more spiritual, and more fulfilling in an evolutionary way than a social or moral union.

In all so-called "matter" there is an accompanying and usually hidden kind of spirit. Teilhard calls this the "withinness of things." It is this withinness that has the power and drive, so to speak, to advance the being to an increasingly higher level of fulfillment. It is also this withinness which, in inseparable cooperation with the material external, invests each being with its own integrity. All matter contains "a certain quantity of spiritual power of which the progressive sublimation, *in Christo Jesu*, is, for the Creator, the fundamental operation taking place."[40] It is this spiritual power of matter which prevents the Christian from decrying matter or nature as evil, because "there has come one who said, 'You will drink poisonous draughts and they shall not harm you,' and again, 'Life shall spring forth out of death,' and then finally, the words which spell my final liberation, 'This is my body.' "[41] Because of the ongoing maintenance of creation by God, and because of the insertion of Jesus into the evolutionary process with all the existential ramifications attendant upon the incarnational event, Teilhard can exult in "holy matter."[42] All reality for Teilhard is holy: the cosmos and man and the trees and all things in the universe touched by the creation, the incarnation, and the redemption.[43]

The new theology of evolution, whether that advanced by Teilhard or by other contemporary theologians, clearly intimates it is unwarranted to claim that the social-science approach to religious instruction is "secular" or "naturalistic." The duality of matter and spirit, given so much impetus and influence in Western thought by Descartes, is vigorously opposed by Teilhard and the theologians of evolution. The assertion that the social-science approach to religious instruction is "secular" or "not the real thing" is as dualistic in its sphere as Cartesianism is in its. The evolutionary process represents an ontological synthesis of the spiritual and the temporal, a synthesis effected in the developing and evolving entity itself. So too in religion class the synthesis of the divine and the human, of the natural and the supernatural is effected in the developmental process of the student learning and behaving. This developmental process is accomplished within the parameters of the deliberatively shaped learning environment, much as the evolutionary process of beings is accomplished within a natural environment. During the long course of the evolutionary process, God has always seemed to work in the "withinness of things." This withinness was always bounded, in a sense, by its natural parameters. The development of a learner in Christification does not fall outside this evolutionary process. In this connection it might be well to recall that Aquinas teaches that all human souls are equal; it is matter which sets the parameters of the extent to which the soul's powers will be actualized. According to Aquinas, it is the person's body, not his soul, which determines his level of intelligence.[44] For religious instruction, the meaning of the evolutionary process, both in the developing of the cosmos and the operation of the spiritual within the material, is obvious.

An Historical Note

The partitioning of reality into the natural and the supernatural was unknown in the old testament; in fact such a compartmentalization is foreign even to modern Judaism. For ancient and contemporary Judaism, writes Sylvan Schwartzman, every aspect of man's existence focuses on the concept of *Kiddush Ha-Shem*, "the sanctification of God by the way in which one lives." Schwartzman goes on to assert that in any valid interpretation of Judaism, the manner in which one earns his living is as much an aspect of godliness as is his worship — and the quest for truth in the realm of science or philosophy and such is no less a sacred obligation. In short, the notion of the *Kiddush Ha-Shem* implies that man's unifying principle is that of glorifying God through fruitful living.[45]

An excessive emphasis on the part of some early Christians on what they believed to be an impending Parousia led to the development of certain heterodox doctrines, two of which were Manichaeism and Montanism. Both doctrines taught that matter and indeed all of the natural order was evil, and should be shunned in existential pursuit of lofty and higher supernatural goods. It was probably Augustine, himself a Manichaean for nine years prior to his conversion to orthodoxy, who first introduced the dichotomy of natural and supernatural into Christian thought. The influence of the hellenic concept of the autonomy of nature, together with a desire to safeguard the gratuity of grace led the theologians of the Middle Ages to cling to this distinction between the natural and the supernatural. The bifurcation of nature posited by Cartesian dualism further reinforced the notion of the partition of the natural from the supernatural. Despite the admitted obsolescence of the Aristotelian-Thomistic concept of nature, and despite Christianity's rejection of Cartesianism, the compartmentalization of natural and supernatural remains, at least in Catholic thought. Some modern Catholic theologians like Leslie Dewart have suggested that the concept of the supernatural has lost its usefulness for contemporary theism. What modern secular thought teaches Christianity, Dewart maintains, is that the emphasis should be placed on grace, not on the supernatural. A mature theology of grace makes the distinction between the natural and the supernatural "a mere play on words, irrelevant to reality."[46] Which is what Paul Tillich asserts the Protestants have been saying all along.

The "World"

The deprecation or outright condemnation of the "world" by religious educators and other Christians is, of course, a reflection of a basic stance toward the natural-supernatural. What I have tried to indicate in this chapter is that the "world" is permeated and suffused with the divine, else it would cease to be the world.[47] Contemporary theology emphasizes that the "world" constitutes a necessary and congenial condition for the fulfillment of the Christian vocation, rather than a condition of absolute transience and exile. To be sure, without the "world," one could not become a Christian, for it is in and through the "world" and nowhere else that Christianity is accomplished. A Christian who stands with only one leg in the "world" stands also with only one leg in heaven. Thus Friederich von Hügel can write that "the material of the supernatural is not only the heroic, but also, indeed mostly, the homely; just as the material of the natural can, contrariwise, be not homely but heroic."[48] For Pierre Teilhard de Chardin the world was the divine milieu, and even more, a universal Host to be venerated.[49] For Teilhard the "world" is the body of Jesus in its full extension.[50]

To accuse the social-science approach to religious instruction of being too "worldly" makes as bad sense theologically as it does pedagogically. Indeed, it smacks of the mentality of the Judaizers in the days of the Apostles (Acts 15:1). The apostles abandoned the decision to have the Gentiles circumcised because of the vision Peter received prior to his meeting with Cornelius (Acts 10:1-43, especially verse 28). The "world" need not be circumcised, so to speak, to make it supernatural. Like the Christian activity it is, the social-science approach to religious instruction embraces worldness but shuns worldliness. The use of forms and methods of the "world," of social science, is not to denigrate the supernatural; rather, it is to employ those extensions of the body of Jesus (Teilhard's concept) to facilitate appropriate behavioral modification in the learner along Christlike lines.

As recently as the early 1960's, the overwhelming majority of American Catholic prelates, priests, and other professional ecclesiastics held that under ideal circumstances, religion lessons should not be taught by laymen. Laymen, it was believed, were too much "in and of the world" to be able to serve as effective agents for the communication of God's truth to the learner. This mentality is a firstfruit of the entire concept of the "world" as somehow tainted, of the "world" as estranged from the supernatural. The merging of a mature theology of the layman with a developing social-science view of the psychodynamics of the lay vocation has tended to show how supernatural the "world" really is and how the layman is an indispensable kind of religion teacher.[51]

Grace

The old familiar textbook concept of the natural and the supernatural is clearly inadequate, as this chapter indicates. The development of a sophisticated theology of grace is the key to a valid explanation of natural-supernatural reality. It is not really accurate to assert that grace builds on nature, as the standard formulation states. More properly, grace suffuses nature. Karl Rahner phrases it in a highly personalistic vein: "Grace which enfolds man, the sinner and the unbeliever too, as his very sphere of existence which he can never escape from."[52] John of the Cross expresses the interaction of nature and grace in a beautiful style which is typical of this Spanish mystic:

> This garden is the soul; for just as the soul called herself above a vineyard in flower, because the flower of the virtues which are in her gives her a wine of sweet savor, so here she calls herself a garden, because they are planted within her, and are born and grow, the flowers of perfections and virtues whereof we have spoken. And here it is to be noted that the Bride says not "Breathe in my garden," but "Breathe through my garden," for there is a great difference between the breathing of God into the soul and His breathing through the soul. To breathe into the soul

is to infuse into it grace, gifts and virtues; and to breathe through the soul is for God to touch and set in motion the virtues and perfections which have been already given to it, refreshing them and moving them so that they may diffuse into the soul wondrous fragrance and sweetness.[53]

One promising development in contemporary theologizing about grace is the hooking up of grace with charity. On the Catholic side, Leslie Dewart suggests that God's nature as charity or self-gift forms the rationale for that abiding presence of God in all reality which we term grace. It is this charity of God, or his grace, if one prefers this term, which renders inoperable the dualism of the natural and supernatural, since it is God's pervasive charity in all reality "which should normally produce the Christian's appreciation of existence, his enjoyment of life, and the consequent obligation of charity towards our fellow man."[54]   From the Protestant standpoint, Paul Tillich phrases it in a fashion which succinctly synthesizes the basic elements: "Love is unambiguous, not as law, but as grace. Theologically speaking, Spirit, love, and grace are one and the same reality in different aspects. Spirit is the creative power; love is its creation; grace is the effective presence of love in man."[55]

What I perceive contemporary theologians to be saying is that grace is an incarnation of a more suffusive charity, and that grace is realized in those activities, overt or not, which we call charity. Therefore, if we wish to learn more about grace, we should examine the ways and acts of God's love as this love is manifested in the world — indeed as the world itself in a sense constitutes an objectification of God's love. It is as if grace is God's act of loving, and the way this loving is realised in and by men. In other words, a theological examination of grace must begin, work through, and have its end in God's all pervasive love which perforce takes place only in existential lived reality. This dovetails nicely with one of the recurring themes of this book, namely that it is in the entire process of Christian living, and not in speculation about Christian living, or in isolating for special attention the theological dimension of Christian living, that an effective and a whole religious instruction can take place. To enhance the learner's total Christian lifestyle rather than to merely increase his cognitive theological knowledge is one of the axes of the social-science approach. It is in the learning situation which is so structured that the individual's Christian living will be heightened that theological learnings will be acquired most effectively and most fruitfully. After all, what we teach is religion (lifestyle) and not theology (intellectual science).

The Social-Science Approach and the Supernatural

This chapter has indicated that the social-science approach to religious instruction is not naturalistic or secularistic or desacralistic because neither nature nor the world was or can ever become naturalistic or secularistic or desacralistic. God's grace and God's love can never be cooped up within realities labelled "supernatural" or "sacral." The religion teacher has as his central task the enhancing of a Christian lifestyle in the learners by helping to modify their behavior in desired directions. Ultimately this task is a matter of divine grace, but it must employ natural and human resources at every stage along the line. Indeed, God's grace works within and through nature and human resources, and so the more effectively the teacher utilizes nature, the greater likelihood there is that God's grace will become operable.

One gains the impression from reading the works of certain theologically-oriented religious educators that they believe God seems to somehow specially intervene at pivot points during the lesson, and that the ideal class is a sort of waiting for the special action of God. This notion seems to be at variance with both the traditional and the newer theologies. Traditional theology has utilized the principle of metaphysical economy as one of its foundation stones in interpreting the actions of God in the world. According to this principle, God as transcendent cause intervenes in the world very sparingly and with the utmost discretion. God has endowed his creatures with the power of their own fulfillment, a power which he of course sustains. The world is commissioned by God to do what it can in the optimum and noblest possible way. God's glory is developed when the world actualizes the power which he gives it; conversely his glory is in one sense diminished when he has to step into the world to help it out. This traditional theological concept of metaphysical economy is in harmony with such modern theological thinking as exemplified by Pierre Teilhard de Chardin.[56] For Teilhard, a creation which by theological definition is unthinkable without the continuous hand of God in even the minutest phase of its course needs no special intervention. What the principle of metaphysical economy and what the concept of Teilhard both suggest to religious instruction is that God operates within the ways of nature and of men. Consequently the social-science approach is theologically on target because it utilizes deliberatively and scientif- ically shapes those conditions which are definitely known to produce desired religious behaviors in learners. Any approach to religious instruction which represents a mentality of "waiting for God to act in a special supernatural way" reminds one of Eckhart's notion that what man gratuitously takes for God is often an idol. In other words, what some religious educators seem to think is the special intervening work of God in the religion class might indeed be an idol.

There are no specifically labelled "Christian teaching processes." Nor does the bible offer a model for a modern school or the organization of a religious education program. Surely this suggests that what man does most effectively in a particular sphere of activity bears a positive correlation with doing Christianity. It is unchristian to attempt to "baptize" a reality by trying to introject a labelled religious element into a sphere in which religion exists according to the mode of the reality rather than according to the mode of theology or of ecclesiastical activities. Attempts to create "Christian dentistry" or "Christian farming" and the like are no more ridiculous and unchristian than efforts to create "Christian teaching- learning process." At bottom, God is the supreme and ultimate teacher, but this does not mean that he intervenes in the teaching-learning process of arithmetic or history *or* of religion. Teaching glorifies God first and foremost by being as effective as possible. And this is where the social-science approach to the teaching of religion is especially relevant.

Man is a product of nature, of which the supernatural is indispensably and inseparably joined. Since man is a product of nature, his behavior can be ascertained and modified in large part by the methods and uses of social science. The use of a scientific approach is a key to unleashing the tremendous potential of religious instruction.[57] Effective religious instruction first recognizes and then actualizes the intimate inseparable structural relation between the natural and the supernatural.

I would like to underscore the notion that the social-science approach to religious instruction has utmost respect and reverence for the supernatural aspect of nature and of human existence. But it rejects as unsophisticated and not sufficiently religious any concept which would relegate the religious dimension to the purely theologi- cal realm, or to any posited "purely supernatural" order. Religion instruction is, as its name clearly denotes, *religious* instruction.

Theology and the supernatural constantly suffuse the activities of the religion lesson — but in a manner appropriate to the realization of the desired learning outcomes.[58] Any attempt to desupernaturalize all vital experiences, whether eating or playing or sex or studying, is to deprive these experiences of their human dimension — because the supernatural so intimately suffuses the natural as to constitute an indispensable condition for humanification. There must be at every juncture in life an intimate organic connection at every level between the natural and the supernatural. Extrapolated to religious instruction, this means that in every phase there must be an intimate organic relation between theology and social science in working toward the effecting of the desired behavioral modification in learners. This is a natural constituent of the new and fourth stage of development for religious instruction which I discussed earlier.

If religious instruction in the past has yielded to a kind of theological reductionism, it must not now in a new age yield to a social-science reductionism. The social-science viewpoint is, I believe, the most effective general approach for religious instruction. However, throughout the implementation of this approach, the theological mode must be appropriately present and operating. Theology and religious instruction constitute a related, double function of pastoral work in the church. Each has its distinctive point of departure and way of operating within the same divine milieu that is terrestrial existence. Both are at the service of the same charity of God.

FOOTNOTES

1. Graham Greene, *A Burnt-out Case.* (New York: Viking, 1961), p. 214.
2. Didier Piveteau, "Biblical Pedagogics," in James Michael Lee and Patrick C. Rooney, editors, *Toward a Future for Religious Education* (Dayton, Ohio: Pflaum, 1970), p. 111.
3. On this point, see Albert Dondeyne, "Secularization and Faith," in *Lumen Vitae*, XXIII, December, 1968, pp. 597-612.
4. This is not in any way to deny the gratuitous nature of God's grace; it is merely to state that history has shown that when certain conditions are fulfilled, for example, desire for God's life, proper disposition, and God's willingness, God tends to communicate his life.
5. Merton P. Strommen, "A Comparison of Youth and Adult Reactions to Lutheran Youth Problems and Sources of Assistance," unpublished doctoral dissertation, University of

Minnesota, 1960. The Missouri Synod Lutherans were not included in the sample of congregations.

6. Strommen's efforts culminated in 1969 with the publication and initial national testing of his instrument, the *Youth Research Survey*, Books I and II.

7. Charles J. Seevers, "Problems and Psychological Needs of Lutheran Confirmands," unpublished doctoral dissertation, University of Notre Dame, 1970.

8. James Michael Lee and Nathaniel J. Pallone, *Guidance and Counseling in Schools: Foundations and Processes* (New York: McGraw-Hill, 1966), p. 13.

9. Fulton J. Sheen, "Foreword," in Edward F. Murphy, *New Psychology and Old Religion* (New York: Benziger, 1932), p. ix.

10. Ronald Goldman, *Religious Thinking from Childhood to Adolescence* (New York: Humanities Press, 1964).

11. Rodney Stark and Charles Y. Glock, *American Piety: The Nature of Religious Commitment* (Berkeley, Calif.: University of California Press, 1968). There was, of course, significant variation among the denominations lumped under the category "Protestant." The figure I give is the mean for all Protestant denominations.

12. *Ibid.*, pp. 125-140.

13. On this point, see John Dewey, *Democracy and Education* (New York: Macmillan, 1916), p. 169.

14. Ronald Goldman, *Religious Thinking from Childhood to Adolescence.*

15. Josef Andreas Jungmann, *Handing on the Faith: A Manual of Catechetics*, translated and revised by A. N. Fuerst (New York: Herder and Herder, 1959), p. 189. In this ecumenical age, I trust that Jungmann will not object to my substitution of the word "Christian" for "Catholic" in the text.

16. Josef Goldbrunner, "Catechetical Method as Handmaid to Kerygma" in Johannes Hofinger, editor, *Teaching All Nations: A Symposium on Modern Catechetics*, revised and partly translated by Clifford Howell (Freiburg, Deutschland: Herder, 1961), p. 112.

17. James Michael Lee, *Principles and Methods of Secondary Education* (New York: McGraw-Hill, 1963), pp. 297-301.

18. André Godin, "Importance and Difficulty of Scientific Research in Religious Education," in *Religious Education*, LVII, July-August, 1962, p. S-168.

19. On this last point, see Antoine Vergote, "Religious Experience," in *Lumen Vitae*, XIX, June, 1964, p. 211.

20. Josef Goldbrunner, "Catechesis and Encounter," in Josef Goldbrunner, editor, *New Catechetical Methods* (Notre Dame,

Ind.: University of Notre Dame Press, 1965), p. 20.

21. J. P. Kenny, "Supernatural Order," in *New Catholic Encyclopedia*, volume XIII (New York: McGraw-Hill, 1967), p. 817.

22. Karl Rahner, *Nature and Grace*, translated by Dinah Wharton (New York: Sheed & Ward, 1964), p. 135.

23. Yves M. J. Congar, *The Mystery of the Temple: The Manner of God's Presence to His Creatures from Genesis to the Apocalypse*, translated by Reginald F. Trevett (Westminster, Md.: Newman, 1962), p. 238. I am following Congar closely in my discussion of these three ways.

24. *Ibid.*, p. 240.

25. *Colossians* 2:9.

26. Paul Tillich, *Systematic Theology*, volume I (Chicago: University of Chicago Press, 1951), pp. 258-259. Tillich also states that man as a creature has been termed the "image of God," a biblical phrase interpreted as differently as the Christian doctrine of man. Complicating the entire concept is the fact that the bible uses two terms to express this idea, which were translated as *imago* and *similitudo*. These two terms were first distinguished in their meaning by Irenaeus. *Imago* was used to point to the "natural equipment" of man. *Similitudo*, on the other hand, was used to indicate the special divine gift (the *donum superadditum*) which gave Adam the power of adhering to God. In denying the ontological dualism of nature and supernature, Protestantism rejected the concept of the *donum superadditum*, and along with it, the distinction between *imago* and *similitudo*.

27. Paul Tillich, *Systematic Theology*, volume III (Chicago: University of Chicago Press, 1963), p. 116.

28. See, for example, Rudolf Bultmann, "New Testament and Myth," and "Reply to Critics" in Hans Werner Bartsch, *Kerygma and Myth*, translated by Reginald H. Fuller (London: S.P.C.K., 1957), pp. 1-44, and 191-211.

29. Pierre Teilhard de Chardin, *The Divine Milieu* (New York: Harper & Row, 1960), p. 35.

30. Listening to Beethoven's music seems to be a favorite activity of sensitive persons during particularly deep and meaningful moments of their lives. See, for example, D. Pumpinatzi, *Anhören Beethoven: Fünf Jahre vor dem grossen Verrat* (Cannes: Les Rochers, 1963).

31. E. Schillebeeckx, *Revelation and Theology*, translated by N. D. Smith (New York: Sheed & Ward, 1967), p. 55.

32. Pierre Teilhard de Chardin, *The Future of Man*, translated by Norman Denny (New York: Harper & Row, 1964), p. 33.

33. On this point, see Joseph V. Kopp, *Teilhard de Chardin: A New*

Synthesis of Evolution (Glen Rock, N.J.: Paulist Press, 1964), p. 57.

34. Theodor Filthaut, "The Concept of Man and Catechetical Method," in Josef Goldbrunner, editor, *New Catechetical Methods*, translated by M. Veronica Riedl (Notre Dame, Ind.: University of Notre Dame Press, 1965), pp. 6-10.

35. Didier Piveteau, "Biblical Pedagogics," in James Michael Lee and Patrick C. Rooney, editors, *Toward a Future for Religious Education*, p. 109.

36. Pierre Teilhard de Chardin, *The Phenomenon of Man*, translated by Bernard Wall (New York: Harper & Row, 1959), pp. 292-294.

37. *Ibid.*, p. 287.

38. Henri de Lubac, *The Faith of Teilhard de Chardin*, translated by René Hague (London: Burns & Oates, 1965), pp. 35-36.

39. Pierre Teilhard de Chardin, *The Phenomenon of Man*, p. 294.

40. Pierre Teilhard de Chardin, *The Divine Milieu*, p. 85. Some italics deleted.

41. Pierre Teilhard de Chardin, *Hymn of the Universe* (New York: Harper & Row, 1965), p. 64.

42. Pierre Teilhard de Chardin, *The Divine Milieu*, p. 81.

43. Teilhard died as he had hoped he would, on the feast of the Resurrection.

44. Thomas Aquinas, *Summa Theologica*, Ia, q. 76, a. 5.

45. Sylvan D. Schwartzman, "Religious Education in the Secular City: Religious Rout or Resistance?" in *Religious Education*, LXI, March-April, 1966, p. 92.

46. Leslie Dewart, *The Future of Belief* (New York: Herder and Herder, 1966), p. 210.

47. See James Michael Lee, "Notes Toward Lay Spirituality," in *Review for Religious*, XXI, January, 1962, pp. 42-47.

48. Friederich von Hügel, *Essays and Addresses on the Philosophy of Religion* (New York: Dutton, 1921), p. 284. Upper cases deleted.

49. See Pierre Teilhard de Chardin, *Hymn of the Universe*.

50. *Ibid.*, p. 37.

51. For a further development of this point, see James Michael Lee, "Layhood as Vocation," in Willis E. Bartlett, editor, *Evolving Religious Careers* (Washington, D.C.: Center for Applied Research in the Apostolate, 1970).

52. Karl Rahner, *Nature and Grace*, p. 134.

53. John of the Cross, *Complete Works*, edited and translated by C. Allison Peers, revised edition (Westminster, Md.: Newman, 1953), p. 270 (of volume II).

54. Leslie Dewart, *The Future of Belief*, p. 207.

55. Paul Tillich, *Systematic Theology*, volume III, p. 274.
56. Some theologians would deny that Teilhard is a theologian. While Teilhard was indeed not a professional theologian in the formal sense of the term, certainly he did much theologizing, which — according to one school of modern theology — makes him a theologian in a way.
57. Ernest Ligon, *Dimensions of Character* (New York: Macmillan, 1956), p. 29.
58. Some persons, in their zeal to emphasize the educational aspect of religious instruction, seem to have unduly downplayed or denigrated on a broad scale the role of the supernatural and the theological in the work of religious instruction. See, for example, Sophia L. Fahs, *Today's Children and Yesterday's Heritage* (Boston: Beacon, 1952).

CHAPTER TEN

TOWARD A REDIRECTION

"Take a sad song
And make it better."

     - The Beatles[1]

The vast amount of empirical research done on the teaching-learning process indicates that instruction is a complex activity. Teaching is no simple task in which an individual stands in front of a class and "teaches." Rather, teaching is a variegated and multiform process of structuring many instructional variables to interact in such a way that the desired learning outcome is produced. Knowledge of how learning occurs, awareness of which variables will cause a particular learning outcome to ensue, and skill in fashioning these variables into a situation which will facilitate the desired learning outcome — these are the pedagogical armamentaria of the teacher. Therefore, if religious instruction is to move forward and to become optimally effective, the teacher will have to be steeped in a knowledge of the teaching-learning process based on relevant empirical data, to be able to synthesize theological and educational objectives into desired behavioral outcomes, and to possess the skill necessary to structure the learning situation so as to bring about the realization of these desired outcomes.

    This kind of teacher competency can come only from a social-science approach. By its very nature, theological science cannot form the basic framework out of which the ongoing instructional dynamic is able to operate. What is urgently needed in religious instruction, then, is a basic redirection which neither excludes nor minimizes theological content, product as well as process. The social-science approach represents the answer to this need; in fact this new approach goes even further, for it heightens theological content precisely because *eo ipso* it is directed toward transforming theological content into religious behavior and facilitating the acquisition of desired learning outcomes.

Certainly we are long overdue for a basic change and a fundamental overhaul of the religious instruction enterprise. Religion teachers openly testify, and religious education leaders privately admit that the old theological approach is not working. Religious instruction is an enterprise encrusted with untested assumptions about how persons learn religion and how Christianity is optimally taught. Operational criteria for ascertaining the effectiveness of religious instruction are virtually nonexistent, except for some scattered instruments designed to assess cognitive outcomes. There is no Catholic religion curriculum which has been validated in terms of the degree to which it accomplishes what the curriculum builders claim it will accomplish. One gets the impression that all one needs to do to be a curriculum builder in religious instruction is to have some teaching experience and a typewriter. Certain Protestant denominations spent millions of dollars and thousands of man-hours in devising religion curricula before realizing that empirical validation is indispensable. Consequently these Protestant confessions have begun to move slowly toward incorporating validation procedures into their curriculum-building. In the areas of affective learning outcomes, and in the all-important zone of Christian lifestyle outcomes, very little validation has been undertaken by religious educators.[2]

The social-science approach to religious instruction is so obvious that one wonders why it is regarded by some religious educators as new or innovational. Perhaps the theological crust covering religious instruction for so many centuries has been so thick as to prevent religious educators from beholding what is obvious. It is not unknown in the history of mankind that theologians have only grasped certain obvious concepts long after these were operationalized by the "secular" world. One has only to think of civil rights or war as cases in point. But it is my own conviction, one supported by a religious educator as seasoned as Carl Pfeifer, that those religion reachers who are in fact doing an effective instructional job are employing a social-science approach. Probably in most cases these teachers are not aware that they are operating within social-science rather than theological parameters, but the fact remains that they have learned it is the social-science approach which indeed works in producing the desired learning outcomes.

There is nothing inherently difficult about the social-science approach to religious instruction. What does prove difficult for some religious educators is that this approach does call for a basic reorganization of the way in which they greet reality in general and teaching in particular. This point will be a recurring theme throughout this chapter. The social-science approach does not entail some minor realignments in methodology or in theory. On the contrary, it represents a fundamental and basic redirection in the theory, the strategies, and the tactics of the entire religious instruction enterprise. The social-science approach is an essentially different way of encountering reality and of structuring the religion class. It is this basic difference between the social-science approach and the old theological approach which is bewildering to some and threatening to others.

Fads come and go in religious instruction. For example, in the late 1950's and early 1960's, salvation history was the rage in Catholic religious instruction. Today salvation history still makes an input into the religious instruction enterprise, but in a way quite different and much less emphatic than in its heyday. I am firmly convinced the social-science approach is not a fad and that it will not fade from the scene after a few fleeting years of ascendancy. I say this with utmost confidence based on historical evidence from other instructional enterprises highly analogous to the teaching of religion. In the first half of the twentieth century, virtually all cognitive, affective, and skill areas of teaching went from a product-content approach to a social-science approach. Most of the instructional advances which have ensued in those areas have been due to the adoption of a social-science approach. In short, the social-science approach has proven highly effective in every teaching domain in which it has been used. Furthermore, the social-science approach has remained the primary axis around which the teaching of cognitive, affective, and skill subjects has developed and improved — so much so, in fact, that with each passing year the social-science approach becomes more entrenched as the framework within which the instructional activity takes place. Throughout this book I have indicated the host of ways in which the teaching of religion is analogous to the teaching of other cognitive, affective, and skill subjects. Consequently we can legitimately extrapolate the degree of proven success of the social-science approach in other subjects to a high probability coefficient that the same approach will likewise be eminently successful in religious instruction. Indeed, religious instruction seems to be the only area within the entire teaching enterprise which has remained impervious to and aloof from the systematic and comprehensive adoption of a social-science approach.

The adoption of this approach will place religious instruction within the broad parameters of social science and in so doing will give to religious instruction that autonomy which it so desperately needs to become optimally effective. It is the lack of autonomy which has severely crippled the development and maturation of religious instruction. Heretofore, religious instruction was always a subsidiary of theology, a notion which has been responsible for transforming religious instruction into messenger boy or handmaid for theology. The low status of religious instruction today constitutes perhaps the principal consequence of the messenger-boy idea. Doubtless this explains the dearth of outstanding scholars and researchers in religious instruction to the extent that such individuals are present and working in other areas of endeavor. Out of the ranks of theology, budding scholars and researchers do appear from time to time. But all too frequently these men forsake the field of religious instruction and go full-scale into theological scholarship because the messenger-boy notion causes it to be less substantial and less deep than theology or other areas of scholarship. Theologians who do remain in religious instruction for a protracted period of time are often regarded by their theological colleagues as persons who "couldn't make it" in theology, and therefore had to be content with a lower-level kind of activity more suited to their mediocre abilities. The most academically talented theology students at the universities are encouraged to pursue careers in theology; the less scholastically gifted are left to drift into religious instruction as either a consolation prize or as a milieu appropriate to their competencies. Once in a while there emerges from the ranks of social science a scholar or researcher of outstanding promise, interested in pursuing a career in religious instruction. Such individuals, notably in Europe but also in the new world, are either deliberately ignored or clubbed down by the ruling theologically-oriented religious educators. Or again, these persons grow weary of having to explain and reexplain concepts and data which are regarded as elemental and completely proven in social science — concepts and data which the religious educators regard as radical, unfounded, or at the upper levels of sophistication.

If religious instruction is to grow and develop, it will have to gain that autonomy which is a prerequisite for the maturation of any field of endeavor. Religious counseling began to truly flourish when it was liberated from theology and developed an autonomy within the broad parameters of social science. So it is too with religious instruction which historically has represented an effort by the various denominations to indoctrinate their members or future members. Inherent in this kind of endeavor is the wholehearted emphasis on theological transmission. The more nearly intact the theological doctrines of a particular denomination could be transmitted to the learner, the better was the quality of religious instruction judged to be. Consequently the more nearly religious instruction mirrored theology, the more closely it was tied to theology's apron strings, the more superior it was perceived to be. With the new emphasis on individual liberty within the churches, with contemporary theological insights on revelation, incarnation, and nature, the time seems favorable for theology to emancipate religious instruction from its colonial status and grant it independence. Free to actualize its own ontology, religious instruction will quite naturally find its home within the framework of social science. With the ensuing development of religious instruction under the social-science umbrella, theologians will discover that religious instruction will bestow myriad gifts upon theological science, not the least of which is the effective incarnation of theology within the lifestyle of learners. Thus transformed into religion, theology will assume new vibrancy and relevance, in any event in the educational sector of life.

RELIGIOUS INSTRUCTION AS A PROFESSION

With this new autonomy for religious instruction, there will subsequently blossom forth a full-blown profession. Because it has historically been a messenger boy for theology, religious instruction was always kept in a servant capacity instead of being allowed and encouraged to develop as a profession. Without autonomy there can be no profession; without professionalism there cannot be effective religious instruction. As a profession, religious instruction will generate many developments, all of which are indispensable for its maturation. Models for activity, scholarship, and research will be developed according to the distinct ontology of religious instruction. The development and implementation of models are essential for the fruitfulness of all major enterprises for they provide a systematic, unified, and integral framework within which the enterprise can grow in a cohesive and effective manner. Models put into structural relationship the set of basic paradigms which lead to the development of new strategies and the resolution of old problems within religious instruction.

Religious instruction as a profession will also promote both a sense and a structure of unity. A sense of identity will come at last to religious instruction. Religious education specialists and religion teachers alike will perceive themselves as belonging to a single profession rather than as workers in some sort of amorphous activity called religious instruction. More than any other single factor, structure and sense of unity have been responsible for the rapid strides during this century in the whole field of guidance and counseling. And this structure and sense of unity resulted only after the guidance and counseling field became autonomous and made itself a profession. Religious instruction can profit from this lesson.

The development of a profession of religious instruction will tend to attract high-level scholars and researchers to the enterprise. The insights of scholars and the conclusions of researchers represent one of the most important ingredients requisite for the continuous growth and deepening of an enterprise. It is a maxim in the business world that the more successful the corporation, the more advanced has been its research division prior to its commercial success. One only has to think of IBM or Xerox or DuPont in this connection. The amount of first-rate scholarship and research which has been done in the field of religious instruction is rather small. With the emergence of an autonomous profession of religious instruction, this condition should change drastically. When medicine came out of the barber shop and into the laboratory, when it became a profession rather than a sideline occupation, research began to flower in that enterprise.

Finally, the development of a profession of religious instruction will bring about a more sophisticated and ongoing process of training and renewal for religion teachers, curriculum workers, and others. One of the greatest weaknesses of religious instruction has historically been that any religionist was regarded as capable of teaching religion. The only qualification a religion teacher had to have was corporeal existence and denominational commitment. Sunday schools and CCD programs have traditionally employed volunteer workers from among their church membership. Since priests, ministers, and women religious had more denominational commitment, more background in theology, and were "closer to God," they were regarded as religion teachers and curriculum builders *par excellence*. Systematic training programs of any depth in which the cognitive and affective domains were meshed with the theory and practice of facilitation skills have been virtually unknown. Curricula in Protestant seminaries have traditionally included a smattering of course work in religious instruction, typically as part of an overall sequence in practical theology. Until the late 1960's very few Catholic colleges or universities had graduate programs in religious instruction. Data are unavailable on the number of these institutions which currently offer systematic programs at the undergraduate level for the professional preparation of religion teachers. Just as the professionalization of medicine led to a systematic training program for physicians, just as the professionalization of guidance and counseling resulted in a comprehensive training program for guidance workers, so too the professionalization of religious instruction will bring forth a high-level kind of training program for religion teachers, administrators, and curriculum workers. In addition, such professionalization will result in that kind of ongoing, top-quality systematic program of inservice renewal courses which are so vital to the maintenance and development of professional competencies.

THE AGE OF SOCIAL SCIENCE

To a certain extent, the period between 1750 and 1850 can be characterized as the era of the humanities, the period between 1850 and 1950 as the era of the natural sciences, and the period beginning in 1950 as the era of the social sciences. Man has produced beautiful works of poetry and masterpieces of philosophy. He has subdued the earth in a breathtaking array of technological and scientific accomplishments. Now he is engaged in the quest of educating himself more fully, coping with his psychological dimensions more competently, and working in group situations more fruitfully. With the aid of theoretical explanations and data-based conclusions, social science is providing the basic framework and thrust by which man in the modern age is achieving self-fulfillment.

Andrew Greeley and others lament the fact that priests, ministers, and women religious tend to have a woeful ignorance of the nature and dimensions of social science. Due to this ignorance, theological science in general has not sufficiently capitalized on or integrated the basic thrust and conclusions of social science. As the self-proclaimed handmaid and messenger boy of theological science, the bulk of present-day religious instruction (which is theologically-oriented) is even further removed than is theology from an awareness of social science. What I am suggesting is that the theological approach to religious instruction represents withdrawal from the world, a world which increasingly is becoming a social-science world. Any kind of religious instruction which is not social-science oriented is ostrich-like, burying its head in the sand as the advances and the needs of the times pass it by.

It is a well-known social phenomenon that active defense follows the stage of withdrawal. It is not surprising, therefore, that the social-science approach, though quite new,[3] is already beginning to encounter some stiff opposition from the theologically-oriented religious educators who by and large control the field. Thus, for example, one of the more recognized figures among this group criticizes the social-science approach as being "restrictive."[4] One can only speculate as to the degree of awareness of world events and openness to reality which characterizes a mentality that labels the advances of the past half-century as "restrictive."

It is certainly true that the prevailing current of religious instruction is theologically-oriented. This is evidenced by most of what is being written in the literature, discussed at conventions, and concretized in graduate training programs. The theological orientation suggests that once again religious instruction has fallen behind the times. The theology is more sophisticated, to be sure, but the approach is basically the same. Apropos of this, I am reminded of a cartoon I once saw. It depicted a white traveling salesman talking to some natives in a remote jungle thicket in Africa. The salesman was attempting to sell trinkets to them — trinkets which were spruced-up versions of age-old trinkets. After listening to the salesman's pitch, one of the natives responded: "This is the *new* Africa. You're still on the beads-and-trinkets kick, when what we need are stereo parts."

If religious instruction is to be optimally effective, it will have to meet the needs of the times by utilizing the most sophisticated approaches which the times have to offer. Religious instruction has suffered for too many centuries from a "look homeward angel" mentality. The Middle Ages are gone; let the dead bury their dead. The cumulative experience of the twentieth century has shown that the role of theology in religious instruction can be heightened and vivified by placing it within the broad framework of social science. Marshall McLuhan observes that "general staffs are always magnificently prepared to fight the previous war."[5] In this regard, the history of religious instruction might not be too dissimilar from the history of general staffs.

SOME BLOCKS TO CHANGE

A reorganization of the enterprise of religious instruction so that learning is produced in the most effective manner is a slow work. There are many factors which individually or in concert conspire against bringing to pass that fundamental kind of redirection which is urgently needed in religious instruction. In this section I shall briefly discuss a few of these factors.

The fact that the theological approach to religious instruction is the traditional one tends to militate heavily against the adoption of a significantly different kind of approach. On account of the tradition-directed character of most Christian churches, fundamental changes in the ways of thinking and behaving typically come about only after an incredibly long struggle, if at all. Christianity tends to equate the old with the true. Saints are persons who lived in bygone days, and revelation more often than not is identified with a book written millenia ago. It is difficult to persuade the mass of Christians, and especially the ecclesiastical leadership, that there is a basic distinction between a tradition and the debris of the ages. We all know that it is not a great mark of wisdom or character to put one's feet in cement and then to stand there. But it is precisely this kind of behavior which all too frequently has been championed in the name of sharing in the permanence and abidingness of God. Christians, like most religionists, are prone to identify every activity carried out under church auspices as somehow sacred and therefore not to be tampered with. This tradition-directedness has more often than not prevented Christian churches from being incarnational within the times, and has had a fossilizing effect on both doctrine and practice. To adopt a social-science approach is not to give religious instruction an heretical character or to lessen its enhancement of Christian outcomes. Rather, it is to make it a living thing, to augment its effectiveness, and to serve both Jesus and the church more successfully.

A second factor militating against a basic change in approach is that in many ways the American religious instructional enterprise still suckles at Europe's breast. This is much more applicable to Catholic religious instruction than to that of the Protestants. Most of the so-called deeper, serious Catholic writers on religious instruction have been and still are Europeans. One only has to think of names like Nebreda, Goldbrunner, van Caster, Schreibmayr, Hofinger, Babin, Piveteau, Audinet, Jungmann, and Drinkwater to see my point. Yet anyone who has travelled extensively throughout Europe and the new world, or studied Continental and American thinkers knows that Europeans and Americans approach reality in a fundamentally different way. For example, Europeans conceive of Christian contemplation as an activity done in a quiet, interior-directed, meditative-reflective fashion. It is incomprehensible to a European that contemplation can be carried on à l'américain, namely as an integral part of some ongoing overt activity. For an American, the classic dichotomy of being and doing does not make sense. Because of the European a priori hellenic mentality, the social sciences have made relatively slow progress on the Continent. This is reflected in the writings of European specialists in religious instruction. By and large, these individuals are ignorant of the social-science approach, or even the possibility of a social-science approach to religious instruction. Indeed, if they were to become aware of its existence, doubtless they would reject it immediately on a priori hellenic grounds. Again, it is this European mentality and orientation which have played such a great part in shaping the fundamental attitude of Catholic religious educators and which will not make it easy for the social-science approach to gain ready acceptance on this side of the Atlantic. When at last American religious educators wean themselves away from Europe's breast and fashion for themselves a religious instruction dynamic which incorporates the American genius, then the time will be ripe for the social-science approach to come to the fore.

Another barrier to a fundamental change in the approach to religious instruction is the demonstrated fact that education is an enterprise not conducive to reform. Education is in one sense a matter of politics and we are all familiar with the obstinacy of politicians in power to set their face toward basic reform. Further-more, religious instruction, whether conducted in church-related schools, in Sunday school or CCD milieux, or in informal settings, still is part of an overall social institution and therefore resistant to change. It is as if the religious education enterprise is a kind of baptized civil defense system against pedagogical fallout. Innovation is threatening, and major innovation is extremely threatening. To conquer this block to progress, religious educators will have to come to the realization that the social-science approach does not attack, threaten, or minimize basic Christian values. They need to discrimi-nate between basic doctrinal change and basic pedagogical change. To be sure, the social-science approach deepens the fundamental Christian value-system by enhancing the effectiveness of religious instruction and opening it even more to the incarnational modern world.

A fourth obstacle to a rapid wholesale adoption of the social-science approach to religious instruction is that its implementation involves more work and greater imagination than does the theological approach. It is much easier to operate the religious instruction enterprise on *a priori* principles than to do empirical research on instructional effectiveness. It is far simpler to transmit the good news of salvation by imparting, or straight lecturing, or lecturing-in-the-guise-of-discussion than it is to structure the learning environment so as to produce desired outcomes. It requires less effort to devote pedagogical energies to cognitive learning outcomes than to the complex of cognitive-affective-lifestyle behaviors. Less time and less money are needed to train religious educators in theological content than to train them in theological and social-science content, in affective awareness, and in pedagogical skills. Only when religious instruction assumes top priority in the church's galaxy of educational activities will ecclesiastical officials make the necessary investment in time, money, personnel, facilities, and training programs to surmount this obstacle to the wholesale adoption of the social-science approach.

Yet another block is that the persons occupying leadership positions in religious education programs typically are not professionally trained to the equivalent degree as are their counterparts in secular educational enterprises. In the Catholic sector, very few administrators of religious education programs at the national or diocesan level hold a doctorate in religious education — or even in theology or in "straight" education.[6] Yet by virtue of their position these individuals are regarded as "experts in religious education" by the bishops, clergy, and laity, and are entrusted with the development of the field. To be sure, the appropriate level of professional preparation for power functionaries in Catholic religious education is rising, but only slowly.[7] Ross Synder contends that within Protestantism the situation is no better. He asserts that virtually anyone can call himself an expert in religious education. National denominational and church council staffs are composed almost exclusively of people who have no advanced training in any area of study, yet speak as wise men.[8] Because of their lack of the doctorate in religious education the leading Protestant and Catholic functionaries in this area typically do not possess that level of professional competence which would equip them to understand or implement a major pedagogical overhaul.

A final block to the adoption of a social-science approach is related to the one just mentioned. The ultimate and penultimate authority figures in Catholic religious education tend to be bishops, priests, or religious, with a sprinkling of pious layfolk. These persons are typically trained in theology at one level or another, and so are inclined to encounter all reality out of a philosophical-theological framework. Consequently a social-science mentality is quite foreign to them. I find it takes from six to nine months of continuous, steady, and intensive immersion in a social-science approach before my Catholic clerical and religious graduate students in religious instruction are able to shift gears, as it were, from a purely philosophical-theological way of greeting reality to a social-science mode. Seminary, novitiate, and church-school training tends to produce a person whose outlook on life is non social-science or even implicitly anti-social-science. Consequently the introduction of the social-science approach to religious instruction on a wide scale is unrelated or opposed to the way in which leading Catholic religious functionaries greet reality. Since there is a natural tendency to perpetuate one's own stance toward life and to extinguish what appears to be unrelated or in conflict with that stance, the power people in religious education quite understandably will be cool and unreceptive to a social-science approach. A salutary resolution of this problem lies in vigorous preservice and inservice professional training. Eventual replacements for those men and women currently in leadership positions should be sought from among those who earned their doctorate in religious education at a university whose program is either based on a social-science approach or at least introduces them to that approach at an appropriate level of depth. Persons now occupying positions of authority in religious education might seek intensive inservice experiences in the social-science dimension by workshops, short courses, modified internships, and the like.

During my discussion of the factors which tend to hamper the widespread adoption of the social-science approach to religious instruction, I briefly indicated some steps which might be taken to overcome their restraining influence. I should like at this point to mention four other things which can be done to help unblock any congealed opposition to the acceptance and implementation of the social-science approach.

Religious instruction has a distinctively prophetical role to play vis-à-vis the church, the world, and theology. By prophetical in this context I mean hastening and advancing the future by introjecting what will be into what now is. In other words, I am using the term prophetical in the sense of the attempt to make tomorrow's Incarnation occur today. Religious instruction has as one of its main tasks the extension of the frontiers of church, world, and theology. The social-science approach represents a fruitful way for religious instruction to exercise its inherently prophetical role. It can introduce into the church's structure, worship, and pastoral ministry fundamentally new ways by which conditions can be environed whereby grace can become more operative in the lives of men. By ending isolation of religious instruction from the mainstream of American pedagogy, it can exert a yeasting influence on the entire American educational enterprise. It can help theology expand its own parameters and at the same time make it more relevant to the modern world by infusing the social-science dimension into its very bloodstream. In any event, its prophetical role suggests that religious instruction ought not always wait for developments first to happen in the church, in the world, or in theology, and then set about to implement these developments. Rather, its prophetical role implies that to be true to itself, religious instruction must blaze new paths and open up new frontiers.

To be effective and worthwhile, basic pedagogical decisions must be based on hard research data. Little by little ecclesiastical authorities and religious educators are beginning to appreciate this. Expansion of the research function, either by means of research bureaus at the national or diocesan level, or by sponsored research studies conducted by outside agencies will tend to emphasize the crucial value of the social-science approach in the work of religious instruction. From this point the road can be paved without too much difficulty for the wide-scale introduction of the social-science approach in every phase of religious instruction.

Imagination implies the power to break out of the prevailing and traditional modes and devise new and more effective ways of accomplishing things. In this sense the social-science approach constitutes the imaginative in the area of religious instruction, even though it is tried-and-true in "secular" education. To introduce an approach which is imaginative vis-à-vis religious instruction necessitates that there be men of imagination within its ranks. This requires the recruitment of leaders, high-echelon functionaries, and teachers who possess personality characteristics quite different from the traits of many of the individuals currently in these positions. The relevant empirical research data reveal the following profile of creative individuals vis-à-vis their less creative counterparts: they have less authoritarian attitudes; they are more autonomous, more dynamic, and more integrative; they place higher value on practical matters and utility, more emphasis on harmony and form, and give less importance to mystical values and acceptance of the church as an institution.[9] The use of creative imagination — which perforce implies the presence of imaginative individuals — will do much to place the religious instruction enterprise on a social-science axis.

Few worthwhile things have ever been accomplished in the absence of courageous individuals. So too it is with religious instruction. Until very recently courage was not always a particularly visible or distinguishing characteristic of religious educators. But with the introduction into their curricula of materials on racial brotherhood and sexual understanding, religious educators inched forward into what hopefully will prove to be an era of courage. This newfound courage can be applied not only to new and controversial areas in the curriculum but also to the very structure of the entire religious instruction enterprise. Indeed, because of the mass of hard research data on the effectiveness of the social-science approach in every area of educational endeavor in which it has been tried, it really does not demand too much courage to introduce this approach into religious instruction. What courage will be needed in such a venture is that involved in struggling with the forces of tradition and conservatism. In the 1960's, with some of the new religious curricula, steps were taken along the path of courage. I do not think it is too much to hope for that this same courage will give strength and impetus in the 1970's and 1980's to men and women who attempt to put religious instruction on a social-science axis.

TOWARD A NEW ERA

The work of religious instruction is constructive, not critical. Religious instruction is not basically aimed at eliminating heretical misconceptions of students or correcting their errors on doctrinal or moral matters. Rather, religious instruction is thrusted toward the building up of new experiences in cognitive, affective, and lifestyle behaviors which are as correct and as fruitful as possible. It is my firm conviction, one supported by the relevant empirical research, that the social-science approach, and not the old theological approach, is eminently suited to accomplish this important task.

Riding in the social-science rocket, religious instruction can break out of the gravitational pull of past failures and enter the fourth sophisticated realm which I briefly sketched toward the end of Chapter Eight. Gone will be the old duality of content and method, a duality which failed to produce optimum results for religious instruction precisely because it attempted to fragment a unitary reality. Gone too will be the resultant hybrid status of religious instruction as a field of study and inquiry, since this hybrid character constitutes a direct extension of the content-method duality.[10] What fuses content and method into one reality is the totality of the learning experience which is being facilitated. The duality of content and method is a natural outcome of the position that the goal of religious instruction is cognitive. But when the goal of religious instruction becomes the amalgam of knowledge, love, and action fused into a behavioral lifestyle, then such a dichotomy of content and method crumbles.[11] Concerning teaching-learning, it is its unitary life activity of facilitating and of being facilitated which renders any dichotomy of content and method existentially impossible. In the fourth and highest level of religious instruction, theology, operating freely within the broad parameters of social science, is thereby brought to an inner relationship with social science which is fluid and mutually nutritive — a relationship which becomes an inseparable association in the teaching-learning act.

This fourth and most sophisticated stage of religious instruction necessarily implies a fundamental passover into social-science territory. Such a passover cannot be accomplished by pouring new wine into old wineskins, or by rearranging a few pedagogical or theological aspects here and there. Rather, this passover implies moving on from the present third stage through the break boundary into the fourth level. This break boundary is the point at which religious instruction suddenly changes its fundamental approach or passes some point of no return in its dynamic existential processes. It is only with great effort, sustained by high-level scholarship and research, much love, hard work, and God's grace that religious instruction will be rocketed through the break boundary. With the piercing of the break boundary and the subsequent entrance into the fourth world, the fundamental values inherent in religious instruction will remain the same. However, some old gravitational pulls and certain familiar points of reference will drift away. This is quite natural since religious instruction will have passed into a new world, a new era. When this occurs, it should not be a period of panic or fear, but rather a time of openness and suppleness. It will be during the years immediately following the passage through the break boundary into the social-science milieu that some of the most exciting and exhilarating developments in religious instruction will take place. What we do now will determine whether we will be there when the passover is accomplished.

I sincerely hope that theologically-oriented educators will not attempt to stall or worse yet, to reverse the tide of history, preventing a penetration through the break boundary which I have just described. Hopefully these persons will come to accept the nature and ways of the teaching-learning dynamic which is the *métier* of social science. Let them not lament that religious instruction is perforce intimately tied in with learning and facilitating — else they naively expect religious instruction to achieve on earth what can only be accomplished in the kingdom.

There is today an atmosphere of pessimism and gloom about the present state of religious instruction. I believe this attitude is the result of looking backward at past flops rather than looking forward to future possibilities. Religious instruction has not failed because it has never *really* been tried. The social-science approach represents the hope of the future for religious instruction. It is not a single methodology or a bundle of tactics; it is, as its name implies, a whole approach, a different land. I believe the point at which religious instruction will enter this new land is near at hand.

FOOTNOTES

1. John Lennon and Paul McCartney, *Hey Jude*.
2. A notable exception to this is the instrument developed by Merton Strommen and his associates to assess attitudinal and value outcomes in adolescents. Strommen's instrument was validated on nearly ten different Protestant denominations. In June, 1970, William Friend of the University of Notre Dame sought to involve the Roman Catholic Church in this crucial Strommen project. An episcopal committee representing the bishops met that month in Washington with Friend and Strommen. The bishops "endorsed" Catholic participation in the project but declined to back up their endorsement with the funds necessary to participate in the project. A clerical spokesman for the bishops described the action of the episcopal committee as " a major victory" for Friend and Strommen.
3. It would seem that the first time a systematized concept and

training program in the social-science approach to religious instruction made its appearance was in the spring of 1967 when the department of education at the University of Notre Dame formally announced the establishment of an M.A. and a Ph.D. program in religious instruction based on the social-science approach. Subsequent to the distribution of the details of these graduate training programs, the next public elaboration of the social-science approach came with the publication of my three articles in the September, October, and November, 1969, issues of *Today's Catholic Teacher*. The following spring my chapter on "The Teaching of Religion" was published in the book *Toward a Future for Religious Education* (Pflaum Press). Also in the spring of 1970 there appeared the final revised copy of the M.A. program in religious instruction at St. Louis University. This detailed program brochure, written by Robert O'Gorman, further elaborates on the social-science approach to religious instruction.

4. Florence Michels, "America: United States: Currents in Religious Education," in *Lumen Vitae*, XXIII, December, 1968, p. 711.

5. Marshall McLuhan, *Understanding Media: The Extension of Man* (New York: McGraw-Hill, 1964), p. 243.

6. Data collected by the Office of Educational Research at the University of Notre Dame support this statement.

7. James Michael Lee and John T. Hiltz, "Diocesan Religion Programs: A National Survey," in *Catholic Educational Review*, LXVI, December, 1968, pp. 553-565.

8. Ross Snyder, "Religious Education as a Discipline: Toward the Foundations of a Discipline of Religious Education," in *Religious Education*, LXII, September-October, 1967, p. 395.

9. Bernard Berelson and Gary A. Steiner, *Human Behavior: An Inventory of Scientific Findings* (New York: Harcourt, Brace and World, 1964), p. 227.

,10. From a theological standpoint, Gabriel Moran has given an admirable critique of the futility of the content-method duality. John Dewey did much the same thing a half-century before from the educational perspective. See Gabriel Moran, "The Adult in Religious Education," in *Continuum*, VII, Autumn, 1969, pp. 7-9; and John Dewey, *Democracy and Education* (New York: Macmillan, 1916).

11. See James Michael Lee, *The Purpose of Catholic Schooling* (Dayton, Ohio: NCEA and Pflaum, 1968).